P9-CQW-622

Management gurus

Management gurus

What makes them and how to become one

Andrzej A. Huczynski

London and New York

First published 1993
by Routledge
11 New Fetter Lane, London EC4P 4EE

Simultaneously published in the USA and Canada
by Routledge
a division of Routledge, Chapman and Hall, Inc.
29 West 35th Street, New York, NY 10001

© 1993 Andrezj A. Huczynski

Typeset by Witwell Ltd, Southport
Printed and bound in Great Britain by
Mackays of Chatham PLC, Chatham, Kent

All rights reserved. No part of this book may be reprinted or
reproduced or utilized in any form or by any electronic,
mechanical or other means, now known or hereafter invented,
including photocopying and recording, or in any information
storage or retrieval system, without permission in writing from
the publishers.

British Library Cataloguing in Publication Data
A catalogue reference for this book is available from the
British Library

ISBN 0-415-02244-4

Library of Congress Cataloging in Publication Data
has been applied for

ISBN 0-415-02244-4

For Janet, Sophie and Gregory

Contents

Figures

Tables

Exhibits

Acknowledgements

I should like to express my appreciation and gratitude to all those who provided valuable advice and assistance during the various stages of the preparation of this book. In particular, I should like to acknowledge the help of my friends and colleagues, Phil Beaumont and David Buchanan. I am grateful to Mrs Sylvia Kerrigan, who typed the manuscript.

Management Ideas Poem

Paul Holland

With Herzberg, Mintzberg and Mr Argyle
I'm desperately trying to develop a style
But will I ever get the chance to Schein
Often I feel I'm in de Klein

I'm looking for a Handy solution I shout
But as soon as I'm interested it just Peters out
I've looked everywhere (at Fielder on the roof and Maslower down)
Till I'm Reddin the face and begin to frown

I'm not as Jung as I used to be (keep it quiet)
But Freud egg and Drucker l'Orange are not my diet
Even in Tescos during Shopenhausers
They Kant stop talking about the brain's mystical powers

I've looked at TA and got my fingers Berned
My cross-transactions have Vroom for improvement – so I learned
Without Fayol when I'm counselled I just get a Block
I get de Board feeling so easily I never take stock

Learning styles may have helped me (but I lied)
However, I discovered, 'Honey, it's Kolb outside'
My search has been rewarded (partial I'd admit)
When asked for my opinion I say it's all Tannenbaum and Schmidt

I'm sorry if the above doesn't scan
But I'm afraid I missed the meter man

(Holland 1989: 96)

Chapter 1

Introduction

Why do certain management ideas achieve widespread popularity and bring fame and fortune to their writers, while others do not? Those authors who have achieved celebrity have had their ideas taught in business schools and on in-company seminars. They are discussed in the books and journal articles of other writers; sections of their writings appear in books of readings. Such a degree of continuing exposure is not limited just to when the authors are alive: their ideas continue to flourish after their deaths. Hence, these management writers achieve fame during their lives, and immortality after it!

Fortune refers to the income that these writers can expect to earn from the sale of their ideas. The income flows come in the form of royalties from their books, from sales of audio and video cassettes, workbooks and associated training materials. Most spectacularly, it can come from personal appearance fees at conferences and company seminars. In 1987, Tom Peters was rumoured to be charging $25,000 per presentation, and Rosabeth Moss Kanter's consultancy fee was $17,000 per hour. Is it luck, or do their ideas have something in common? The author argues that for a management idea to secure fame, fortune and immortality for its writer, it has to meet five prerequisites. Specifically, the idea has:

1 to be timely – that is, it should address itself to the problems of the age.
2 to be brought to the attention of its potential audience. Ideas do not promote themselves. Business school academics, management consultancies and training and publishing companies play an important role in the dissemination of the ideas.
3 to address organizational requirements in a way that meets the individual needs and concerns of the managers at whom it is addressed.
4 to possess the essential ingredients which allow potential users to perceive it as relevant to meeting their needs.
5 to be verbally presentable in an engaging way. Not because the majority of managers will learn about it at a public presentation session, but because video and audio-based materials will be developed from the author's presentation of the idea itself.

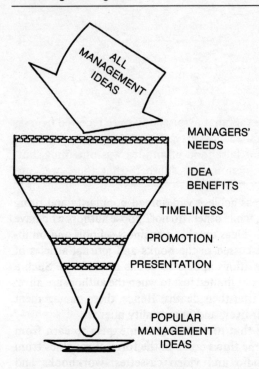

Figure 1.1 Distilling the popular management ideas

The analogy of the filter funnel can help to explain why only a very small fraction of all the available management ideas ever achieve popular status. As the ideas are tipped in at the top, they flow down through ever finer filters. These filters have labels such as managers' needs, idea benefits, timeliness, promotion and presentation. Because the majority of the management ideas fail to meet requirements, they get filtered out, only a very small number of them re-emerge at the other end as popular management ideas (see Figure 1.1). This explains why there have only been six truly popular management idea families in the last hundred years.

The 1980s generated a great interest in management ideas and gurus. During that time, a small number of management commentators attained guru status. Their books sold in their thousands and even millions, royalties flowed in, and their ideas were merchandised through diaries and newsletters, as well as through traditional means such as audio and video cassettes. The appearance money that they charged to make presentations at conferences and on in-company programmes matched that of film, television and pop stars. How can certain management ideas be so attractive and bring such high rewards to those who develop and present them? The purpose of this book is to answer these questions.

Certain ideas, such as those of Herzberg *et al.* (1959), continue to be popular even after other writers have demonstrated flaws in the research methods and have challenged them. The fact that newer and methodologically sounder ideas have became available, has not reduced the popularity or discussion of older ones like those of Abraham Maslow (1943), Douglas McGregor (1960) or Rensis Likert (1961). These continue to have a profound effect on management teaching.

Many years ago, John Dryden said that a 'falsehood once received from a famed writer becomes traditional to posterity'. Since then, other authors have commented that the truth or falsehood of an idea was one thing, but that its acceptance and dissemination was another; that there was no apparent correlation between the significance of an idea and its popularity; that *what* was said was less important than *how* it was said; and that ideas received acclaim not because they were true, but because they were *interesting*.

Since nomenclature represents a potential problem, this will be dealt with immediately. What is collectively referred to as *management thought* in historical accounts of the subject by authors such as Wren (1973) consists of theories, research findings, frameworks, propositions, beliefs, views, saws and suggestions. It is an untidy hotchpotch of diverse offerings. Linguistically therefore, it is convenient to adopt a set of standardized labels for use throughout this book. The term *management idea* is applied to all abstract thought units or systems of such units. Kramer defined a management idea as a fairly stable body of knowledge about what managers ought to do. He said that it:

> derived from inductive and deductive reasoning. It is systematically organized knowledge applicable to a relatively wide area of circumstances. As a system of assumptions, accepted principles and rules of procedures . . . [it] assists managers to analyze and explain the underlying causes of a given business situation and predict the outcome of alternate courses of action.
>
> (Kramer 1975: 47)

Where there can be said to be sufficient similarity between these ideas or systems of ideas, then the term *family of management ideas* will be used. Finally, where the idea or idea system spawns a clearly defined set of actions which go beyond mere thought, but actually seek to alter the behaviour of individuals, groups or organizations in some way, then the *label idea technique* will be applied.

Which then are the most popular management ideas of the twentieth century? The results of a survey of academics and practitioners in the field and a content analysis of professional journals, popular texts of selected readings and a reprint series was used to establish this. Matheson (1974) reported the findings of a survey carried out among the 2,123 members of the American Academy of Management which sought to identify contributions that 'had greatly influenced management thought and research'. In the late 1970s Pollard (1974; 1978) summarized the work of forty-two writers on management ideas which gave students 'a fair cross-section of the writings on management'. Books by Pugh, Hickson and Hinings (1983) and Pugh (1984) summarized the contributions of selected management writers and contained extracts from their original books. Authors were chosen because:

> All have attempted to draw together information and distill theories of how organizations function and how they should be managed. Their writings have been theoretical in the sense that they have tried to discover generalizations applicable to all organizations.
>
> (Pugh *et al.* 1983: 9).

Another source with which to identify the popular management ideas comes from Miner (1980; 1982). The management ideas in his book were nominated by 'recognized scholars in the field of organizational study. More than thirty-five individuals suggested theories for consideration. All theories on which most of the scholars were agreed are discussed here' (Miner 1982: 453).

Finally, some more recent texts were consulted (Tosi 1984; Koontz 1961 and 1980; Clutterbuck and Crainer 1988 and 1990; Pierce and Newstrom 1988 and 1990). The last of these considered the popular texts of the 1980s based on the dimensions of their *market acceptance* (volume of sales achieved); *provocativeness* (presenting viewpoints which run counter to traditional management thought); *distinctiveness* (presenting a variety of interesting topical themes to managers); *author reputation* (those having a strong reputation and the quality of their thinking and the insights they have historically generated). Using these references, each management idea mentioned was held to be 'voted for'. A total of 129 names were identified. More recent writers did not appear often in the voting. The length of the final list indicated that beyond a hard core of writers, there is little consensus as to who the really influential contributors are. The top-ranked management writers are shown in Table 1.1.

A total of 129 management writers and their votes were grouped into 'families' of management ideas. Table 1.2 lists these families in chronological order. To these five families a sixth is added. This is labelled guru theory. This school acquired prominence in the 1980s. While not yet featuring extensively in management textbooks it has received widespread attention in the financial and business press (Lorenz 1986a; Byrne 1986; Clutterbuck and Crainer 1988; Pierce and Newstrom 1988 and 1990).

These diverse writings which together constitute guru theory include the thoughts of well-known chief executives such as Lee Iacocca, Harold Geneen, John Harvey-Jones and John Scully; of management consultants like Tom Peters and Philip Crosby; and of modern business school academics like Michael Porter, Rosabeth Moss Kanter, Henry Mintzberg

Table 1.1 Most popular management writers

Position	Name
1	Henri Fayol
	Douglas McGregor
3	Peter Drucker
	Frederick Herzberg
	Tom Peters
6	Frederick Winslow Taylor
	Rensis Likert
	Chris Argyris

and Kenneth Blanchard. Since they are so diverse and since they draw so much of their authority from the idea developers themselves, it was felt that guru theory was an appropriate label. The focus of this book will not be upon the validity or accuracy of these management ideas, but on the reasons for their appeal to practising managers and management students.

Reflecting on the history of management thought, one can discern bodies of organizational practice which draw upon a tradition of research and theorizing (of sorts) which goes back to the work of Taylor at the beginning of the century. Despite the efforts to dignify this body of writing as 'theory', a distinguishing feature of it has been its fierce pragmatism. Such pragmatism reflects both the concern to be applied knowledge and, in the view of many critical observers, the result of a conscious or form-ulated refusal to ask any fundamental questions about the nature of organ-ization.

A consideration of popular management ideas involves an examination not only of the world of applied theory at the level of subject matter, but also of the enormously lucrative world of management consultancy and training which requires 'touchstone ideas' for its own legitimation and development. This imposes two types of constraint on the nature and form of the evolving management ideas. First, the ideas and their associated techniques must be acceptable to the organizations which pay the fees. Key aspects of orga-nizational life, such as its political nature, thus tend to be excluded. Issues of conflicting attitudes are also frequently displaced into various semi-ther-apeutic and psychological treatments.

A second limitation on what can be said and written, if it is to achieve popularity, arises from the connection between management thinking and the paying organization. This affects how the management idea is packaged and sold by a consultant as a training service. The popular management ideas which will be considered in this book are likely to be presented in the form of logos or pseudo-theoretical models which form the basis of a two or three day training programmes. Thus, pragmatic ideas in the form of McGregor's 'Theory X and Theory Y', Maslow's 'Hierarchy of Needs', Herzberg's

Table 1.2 Grouping of the most popular writers into management idea families

Idea family	Writers
Bureaucracy	Blau
	Scott
	Brown
	Crozier
	Jacques
	Michels
	Selznick
	Thompson
	Weber
Scientific management	Taylor
	Gantt
	Gilbreth
Administrative management	Barnard
	Fayol
	Follett
	Mooney
	Sloan
Human relations	Mayo
	Brown
	Roethlisberger and Dickson
Neo-human relations	Argyris
	Bennis
	Blake and Mouton
	Herzberg
	Likert
	McGregor
	Maslow
	Schein
Guru theory	Drucker
	Peters
	Porter
	Kanter
	Iacocca
	Blanchard

'Motivators and Hygiene Factors' and Peters and Waterman's '7-S' model will be included. All of these can be summarized on one page of a course handout in the form of a logo or on an overhead projector transparency.

Critics of the managerialist school (Salaman 1978; Clegg 1975; Clegg and Dunkerley 1980) have argued that an important function of management ideas has been to legitimize the existing structures of power and authority in organizations which would have contested had they been presented directly. For this reason, management ideas have needed to be communicable and comprehensible to a wider group of people other than just top managers.

They have had to be understood by both middle and junior managerial ranks as well as by those being managed. Although the families of management ideas to be investigated appear superficially to differ greatly, they can all be said to represent a broad consensus on the nature of organizational management in a capitalist society that goes back for a hundred years. While there is no formulated agreement on particular areas in the field of management ideas, there is a broadly accepted model and a set of assumptions about organizational structure and technique. This represents a sort of common-sense understanding of what management is or should be in an organization.

Such a high degree of consensus is not surprising. The common underlying agreement referred to might be called the 'capitalist imperative'. The ideas to be discussed all emerged from Europe and the United States. The capitalist form of organization therefore specified objectives such as profit maximization, and the role and power relations between those involved in the production process. It set limits on which goals could be pursued and which forms of work organization were acceptable if the fundamental system was not to break down. Mimicking the communist system of organization, the capitalist system rejected any questioning of either the basic terms on which the management of the organization was conducted, or of the political disposition in which it existed. These potentially troublesome questions were simply bracketed, acknowledged in asides, or obliquely referred to in externally determined matters such as the contracts of employment and their regulation by law. The political nature of organization is rarely referred to directly in any of the popular management literature.

A distinction needs to be drawn between the task of critiquing the management ideas themselves and that of conducting an analysis to explain their popularity. Each of the management idea families has been subjected to a great deal of censure. Some of this has come from critical writers who have challenged the implicit values and perspectives of the management ideas. A second body of criticism has emanated from those who have claimed that the management writers' assumptions were invalid, that there were major methodological flaws, and that the proposed techniques which were implemented did not produce the results claimed. This particular body of criticism will not be explicitly addressed in this book since its primary objective is to explain the popularity of the management ideas themselves. The critical literature will be selectively used since these writers have challenged those aspects of the management ideas which, it is argued, give them their appeal to managers. It has been found that it is often the critical perspectives on these management ideas which provide the initial indication of the likely reasons for the popularity.

A major difficulty in seeking to explain the popularity of certain sets of ideas in the history of management thought is the uncertainty of what is being considered. Given a theoretical framework such as scientific management, there are a number of different perceptions of it. For example, one can describe, analyse and evaluate:

1 what the originator of the idea actually said (based on original sources)
2 what the teacher, tutor or consultant has interpreted the originator to have said (based on an analysis of textbooks and teacher's lecture notes)
3 what the manager or management student understands the originator to have said, based on a presentation or reading (identified from an interview with the manager, or a review of the student's exam script or lecture notes).

Such differences are not uncommon. Economists have long distinguished Marx from the Marxists, and Friedman from the Friedmanites. It is often the case that what the originator of an idea said, and what his interpreters (e.g. business school academics or consultants) and idea consumers (managers and management students) have understood him to say, have differed.

Since the early 1950s business school academics have played an important (but decreasing) gatekeeping role of bringing selected ideas to the attention of managers. In the absence of such academics, for example, in the period 1900–40, management ideas such as scientific management and administrative management were promoted and interpreted by consultants and managers.

A comparison between the original writings of the management idea developers of the six management idea families and their popular interpretations all reveal differences of interpretation. In some cases the original idea was reformulated to such a degree that management lecturers could be charged with misrepresentation. To illustrate this point a sub-set of two management idea families are selected at random. These are scientific management and human relations.

Patzig and Zimmerman (1985) reported inaccuracies in the reporting of management ideas and the creation of 'pseudo-history'. The authors considered Taylor's four principles of scientific management (Taylor 1911: 36–7) in relation to their presentation in eleven randomly selected textbooks. They found that nine of these books presented the four principles inaccurately, while three reported Taylor's work in a way that could easily lead to misunderstanding. In addition, they found that some writers had left out some of the principles while others had added new ones. In a similar vein, Peter Drucker (1976) argued that the 'well known facts' about Taylor were a myth.

Turning to human relations, in his original account, Roethlisberger (1941: 156) argued that the Hawthorne experiments had shown that 'the factors that make for efficiency in a business organization are not necessarily the same as those factors that make for happiness, teamwork, morale, or any other word which might be used to refer to co-operative situations'. Yet Patzig and Zimmerman (1985) found a textbook claiming that the

Hawthorne studies have discovered that 'management has at long last discovered that there is greater production, and hence greater profit when workers are satisfied with their jobs. Improve the morale of a company and you improve production' (Parker and Kleemeir 1951: 10). Vroom (1964: 181) claimed that 'human relations might be described as an attempt to increase productivity by satisfying the needs of employees'.

Patzig and Zimmerman (1985) attributed such inaccurate reporting of management ideas by lecturers to basic laziness. That is, their reluctance to take the time and trouble to return to the original sources. They were concerned about two consequences of these inaccuracies. First, they feared that managers would come to perceive such texts as untrustworthy and would avoid implementing the ideas presented. Alternatively, the teaching of inaccurate theory would result in managers coming away with a mistaken grasp of the idea and, when they applied it, would find that it did not work. Patzig and Zimmerman asked how management academics could maintain credibility in their academic institutions with their colleagues and other corporate clients when they seemed unable to report their own ideas accurately.

Not all business school academics have been so stringent. Lee in fact argued for the reformulation of management ideas in order to produce what he called 'appropriate theories' for consumption by managers. His argument was that there was an 'experiential learning gap' between what a theory could do to explain the practitioner's reality, and what the manager needed to know. Thus, management ideas had to be taught in an 'appropriate' as opposed to an 'inappropriate' form. The latter was one which might confuse the manager by over-emphasizing the complexity of life. It might cause 'paralysis-of-analysis' and might place the need for full understanding ahead of the need to act effectively. In contrast, 'appropriate' versions of popular management theories were:

> created by taking the core idea of the parent theory and turning them in some simple way without too much jargon. . . . Important caveats may be dropped and attempts to increase impact and teach-ability may result in the loss or distortion of meaning of the underlying theory . . . when the educator is a skilled professional, the underlying ideas have been converted into something which is in effect a new, more appropriate theory.
>
> (Lee 1987: 25)

For Lee, the best support for this reformulated management idea was not its explanatory power but its widespread acceptance by practitioners because of its high usefulness to them. His ultimate test of a management idea was that it was a 'reasonable reflection of reality as perceived by the practitioner', that it could 'assist in the development of personal conceptual frameworks which will be of value in support of practical goals' (Lee 1987: 250). The aim of appropriate theory was not to be right but to be useful.

What Lee in effect offered was an argument to legitimize the reformulation of original management ideas into a form which would give them wide ranging popular appeal along the lines being identified in this book. Indeed, he identified *theories of useful error* which were management ideas which, despite their scientific inadequacy, were useful for the development of insights among practitioners who were not themselves scientists. He contrasted these with *theories of necessary simplification* which, although accurate by scientific criteria, were so complex that they had to be introduced to practitioners in an appropriate (simplified) form by conscious reformulation on the part of the consultant or business academic. Alongside these one might add Patzig and Zimmerman's (1985) *theories of unconscious reformulation* where scientifically adequate or inadequate ideas were incorrectly communicated by lecturers or consultants. Lee argued that the management ideas used in post-experience management education, even though they may be of limited validity were:

> essential for the proper education of managers [but] ... it is the widespread use of such theories which is responsible for many of the attacks directed at those who teach management in the academic world. Our discipline is not seen as academically respectable by our colleagues who work in more traditional areas.
>
> (Lee 1987: 247)

Critics of this view have argued that if engineers or doctors were taught such 'appropriate' theories they could kill either themselves or others. Discussing the techniques based upon the vast range of what have been collectively referred here to as management ideas, Anthony noted that the basic idea from which such techniques were distantly derived could not have been appropriate, 'but the image in which it is presented must be acceptable and be deemed appropriate' (Anthony 1987: 258). Given this difference between the original and the reformulated management idea, the author will examine the latter which might be termed 'popularly received wisdom'.

Chapter 2

Popular management ideas

INTRODUCTION

Chapter 1 showed that throughout this century, only six management idea families had achieved widespread popularity and managed to establish themselves in the history of management thought. This chapter briefly considers each of these families in turn. It begins with bureaucracy, and goes on to examine scientific management, administrative theory and human relations. The post Second World War idea families – neo-human relations and guru theory – are considered in proportionately greater depth, since past management books have tended to neglect them.

BUREAUCRACY

Weber's theory of bureaucracy is often presented alongside the work of administrative management writers such as Fayol, Gulick and Urwick, who will be considered later. Weber's own work was set in a historical-philosophical context. However, its specific conclusions established the basis for the work of these other writers. Weber was a German sociologist-philosopher (1864–1920) and not a manager, engineer or a management consultant. His interest was in the process of social change, and in particular, in the effect of *rationality* on religious thought and capitalism. By rationality he meant the kind of action or mode of organizing in which goals are clearly conceived and all conduct, except that designed to achieve the particular goal, is eliminated.

From this historical perspective he examined different types of authority. Charismatic authority, he said, was based upon a belief in the sacred or extraordinary characteristics of the person giving the order (e.g. Christ). In the traditional form of authority, orders were obeyed because people believed that the person giving them had traditionally done so (e.g. king or lord). In the legal-rational form of authority, the orders were obeyed because people believed that the person giving them was acting in accordance with legal rules and regulations. The term that Weber applied to the organizational form built upon pure legal-rational authority was *bureaucracy*.

Fully developed and in its most rational form, bureaucracy necessarily presupposed the concepts of legitimacy and authority. The Weberian model of bureaucracy offers a stable and predictable world which provides the blueprint for 'rationally designed' structures in which 'rational' individuals carry out their prescribed roles and actions. For Weber, 'rationality of action' had to be judged against some objective standard and this formal rationality was reflected in the management thought and literature that succeeded it. For Weber, the bureaucratic form of organization possessed the features of specialization, hierarchy, rules, impersonality, full-time officials, career focus and a split between public and private activity.

Weber (1948) wrote that bureaucracy existed in ever purer forms in the modern European states and, increasingly, in all public organizations since the time of princely absolution. The larger a modern capitalist enterprise was, the more complicated it became. Every organization exhibited a more or less stable pattern based upon a structure of roles and specialized tasks. The interest here is not directly upon the validity of Weber's ideas but upon the appeal that bureaucracy, as a management idea, has had for managers over the years through to the present day.

SCIENTIFIC MANAGEMENT

A second popular idea family to be considered is scientific management. This focused upon the shopfloor and upon the techniques that could be used to maximize the productivity of manual workers. While it is not likely to be applied in its pure form, scientific management does represent a template for a great deal of job design work that has been done during the twentieth century. Scientific management principles continue to be widely applied today. In a typical manufacturing organization one will see scientific management ideas and techniques being applied to the shopfloor, and bureaucratic principles of organization being used in the office areas. Watson reminded his readers that:

> Books which relate the history of management thought frequently give the impression that scientific management is a thing of the past but, in the realm of practical realities, its doctrines and techniques still dominate contemporary work design . . . the psychologistic assumptions underlying the approach still hold great sway among practical men.
>
> (Watson 1980: 36)

Developed originally by Frederick Winslow Taylor during the early years of this century, scientific management has exerted a continuing influence on organizational design and management practice. Taylor was a American engineer who established the foundations of the process of work measurement. Time-and-motion study techniques gave Taylor's ideas the claim to be a science. He based his work upon the accurate and scientific study of unit times (Taylor 1903: 58). His aim was to increase productivity by improving the performance of the workers by selecting manual tasks and fragmenting them into their simplest and smallest componants.

Taylor is best known for his book, *The Principles of Scientific Management*, which was published in 1911. In it, he explained that in order to increase the productivity of labour, it was necessary to highlight the national loss being incurred through inefficiency; that such inefficiency could be remedied by systematic management; and that the best management was a true science, and rested upon a foundation of clearly defined laws, rules and principles.

Even before his rise to eminence, Taylor had developed and espoused his ideas on management. He argued for an empirical approach to the management of industry that was based upon the application of some specific techniques. These had the capability of being applied to any industrial setting since, he argued, organizations were subject to certain laws in their operation. There were certain constant and regular features in organizations. Observation and experimentation could discover what these were.

Taylor was appalled by the inefficiency of industrial practices that he witnessed and set out to demonstrate how managers and workers could both benefit by adopting his scientific approach. The history of scientific management is well known and documented. Taylor drew attention to 'systematic soldiering' (deliberate underworking by employees). This he attributed to weak management control which allowed individuals discretion about the work methods they used. They wasted time and effort, in his view, by using inefficent rules-of-thumb work methods.

At the turn of the century in the United States, managers expected their employees either to possess the appropriate skills for the work they were given, or to learn them from those around them. Notions of systematic job specifications, clearly established responsibilities and training needs analyses, were all unknown. Taylor sought to change this. He argued that mental and manual work should be separated. Management, he claimed, should specialize in planning and organizing the work, and the workers should specialize in actually doing it. Taylor regarded this as a way of ensuring industrial harmony as everyone would know clearly what was expected of them, and what their responsibilities were. He also saw clear advantages in making individuals specialize in activities so that they would become expert and highly proficient in them.

Scientific management was based upon four key principles which Taylor (1911: 36-7) said involved new and heavy burdens for managers. These were, first, the development of a science for each element of a person's work which would replace the old rule-of-thumb methods. Second, the scientific selection, training and development of workers to replace the previous practice of their choosing their own work methods, and training themselves as best they could. Third, co-operating 'heartily' with the workers so as to ensure that all the work was done in accordance with the scientific principles developed. Finally, an almost equal division of work and responsibility between management and workers. Management would take over the work for which it was best fitted. Previously, almost all the work, and the greater part of the responsibility, had been placed upon the workers.

Taylor's ideas came to be incorporated in organizational design through the twentieth century. The principles were instituted regularly and extensively for over seventy years, and continue to be applied. No longer are they called Taylorism or 'scientific management'. At the start, these ideas were so novel that Henry Ford's application of them received media attention. Many decades later, it was the *non-application* of scientific management techniques, in places such as the Volvo car plant in Kalmar, that stimulated media interest. Taylor's work was developed and extended by Gilberth, Gantt and the scientific management writers who followed him.

ADMINISTRATIVE THEORY

The primary focus of this management idea family was the determination of what types of specialization and hierarchy would optimize the efficiency of organizations. The application of these two concepts produced a very mechanistic form of organizational design which paid little attention to people and which saw them as cogs in a wheel. Administrative management is built around four key pillars. These are the division of labour, the scalar and functional processes, organizational structure and the span of control. Additional concepts include discipline, unity of command, unity of direction, remuneration, subordination of the individual interest to the general interest, centralization and *esprit de corps*.

The writer who is most closely, although not exclusively, associated with this management idea system was Henri Fayol. Fayol spent his career in a French mining company and rose to the post of managing director. He believed that the techniques of successful management could be described and taught, and that *managerial organization* was as valid an area of study as *worker organization*. Fayol sought to discover a body of principles which would enable a manager to build up the formal structure of the organization and to administer it in a rational way. To quote Mouzalis:

> The solution to this problem, according to the theory lies in the discovery of a set of principles which, when correctly applied to the particular situation, will prove invaluable guides to the construction of a rational-efficient framework for management.

(Mouzalis 1967: 89)

The original diffusers of administrative management ideas were not social science or business school faculty but consultants and other managers. Once administrative management had established itself in this way, it passed into management history, began to feature extensively in textbooks and was taught by management teachers and students.

Those who followed Fayol refined these concepts and added to them, often stressing some particular point or theme. Mooney and Riley (1931), for example, emphasized the 'co-ordinative principle' seeing it as the central one. They laid particular stress upon the scalar principle – the process within an organization whereby authority was co-ordinated from the top. Other classical writers such as Gulick and Urwick developed the notion of rationalizing the work process by bringing it together in as centralized an area as possible.

The assumptions of the administrative management have received extensive critical analysis. They have been subjected to intensive research. Nevertheless, the majority of practices recommended by this idea system continue to be central to the way in which modern organizations are organized. While some of the principles advocated by the administrative management writers may have been defective, their overall scheme for building machine-like bureaucracies, with managers and officials strongly in control, have continued to be applied over time. Administrative management is not a historical fossil but continues to represent a major model for the design of large highly-integrated organizations of today.

The criticism that the proponents of administrative management have received has centred around the status of the *principles* which they expounded. Some of these describe management activities, while others indicate what managers should be doing and exhort them to do things in a certain way. Occasionally, among the writings, one finds an expression of a relationship between organizational variables ('The narrower the span of control, the more levels of hierarchy there will be').

Criticism of the principles came thick and fast. 'Contradictory proverbs' said March and Simon (1958: Chapter 2); 'simple minded deductions' wrote Perrow (1973). 'They form neither a coherent conceptualization pattern of determination nor an accurate description of concrete reality' said Clegg and Dunkerley (1980: 102). Despite failing all the tests set for them by academics, the principles of administrative management, like those of scientific management, have had a major and continuing effect on management thought and practice. Even their most hardened critics have had to admit that the ideas have been enormously influential in shaping and structuring organizations to the present day. Administrative management may have been scorned by social scientists. Nevertheless, there is a highly successful, durable and expanding business of management consulting as well as an endless series of successful management books, which rest upon the principles of administrative management.

Fayol began the task of listing the principles of adminstrative management and others went on to continue his work. Administrative management is a label which refers to a body of writing which has received
contributions from many different authors at different times. These include
Urwick, Brech, Allan and many others. This idea system lacks much of the
logical consistency of some of the others. Nevertheless, despite its contradictions, it does share a core number of common characteristics with
other popular idea families.

HUMAN RELATIONS

Human relations arose from the American wish to humanize their society
without interfering with the free operation of market forces (Butler 1986:
104). Human relations promised a land in which everybody accepted that
it was socially and economically desirable that there should be the greatest
degree of competition outside of the firm, but that any competitive or
contentious elements within it were both socially and economically
undesirable.

It would be incorrect to see human relations as a reaction to scientific management or to describe it as rediscovering the social aspects of
work which scientific management ignored. This is indeed the popular
description contained in many introductory management and industrial
sociology textbooks. There is, however, an alternative and equally convincing explanation. Taylor may well have known about the potential
dangers for management of work groups. In place of his attempt to
destroy work group solidarity, the human relations writers prescribed
an alternative tactic, but one which nevertheless sought to achieve the
same goal. That goal was to control the work group and the means was to
integrate it into the organization. In this respect, the human relations
idea of personnel counselling (as a way of countering trade unionism
in the United States) had a particularly significant effect. This focus
on people also meant that fundamental *structural* redesigns were avoided.
The critical writers would argue that human relations represented a
change of management tactics rather than any fundamental shift in
objectives.

The human relations movement drew heavily for its academic suste-
nance on a series of famous experiments called the Hawthorne studies. The
Hawthorne studies refer to a series of research projects which began in
1924 at the Hawthorne plant of the Western Electric company located in
Cicero, just outside of Chicago. They are linked with the name of a
Harvard Business School professor, Elton Mayo, whose involvement in
the work has been the subject of much controversy. The initial aim of the
research was to examine the relationship between working conditions and
output.

At the beginning, the investigators adopted a physiological approach. Early results, however, suggested that variables such as illumination could not be treated independently of the meanings that workers gave to them. The researchers concluded that economic motives were relatively unimportant in motivating workers and in raising productivity. Rather, they argued, solidarity was the key. Subsequent research was carried out using interviewing and non-participative data collection methods. Conclusions were drawn about supervisory styles and the existence of an *informal organization*. Names such as the Relay Assembly Test Room, the Bank Wiring Room and the Mica Splitting Group passed into social science research folklore and history. Nevertheless, the Hawthorne studies remain among the most diverse and most controversial pieces of social science research ever conducted.

Human relations never derailed the original ideological thrust of Taylorism. In fact, Mayo wrote two articles, one in 1924 and a second in 1925, for the Taylor Society Bulletin. The way in which the human relations writers reported and interpreted the Hawthorne studies persuaded many managers that friendly and relaxed supervision in the factory would *result in* higher productivity. Even though the causal link may have been in reverse (high productivity causing a relaxed supervisory atmosphere), managers tended to see things as they wished to see them. In popular management mythology, human relations came down to, 'being nice to workers'. Reduced to its essentials, the human relations message was carried by six propositions:

1 A focus on people, rather than upon mechanics or economics.
2 People exist in an organizational environment rather than an unorganized social context.
3 A key activity in human relations is motivating people.
4 Motivation should be directed towards teamwork which requires both the co-ordination and the co-operation of the individuals involved.
5 Human relations, through teamwork, seeks to fulfil both individual and organizational objectives simultaneously.
6 Both individuals and organizations share a desire for efficiency, that is, they try to achieve maximum results with minimum inputs.

The growth of human relations was fostered by the problem of motivating employees, that is of persuading them to share the goals of the organization. When in the 1920s and 1930s Mayo addressed himself to the problem of workers not behaving in the way managements would like, he convinced managers of the idea that the way to deal with this difficulty was to retain both hierarchy and spcialization while forming the equivalent of the 'family' in the workplace. Authoritarianism would remain but would take the guise of a paternalistic interest in the worker who would respond in a filial manner. The *family concept* gave further justification to treating as taboo competition between departments in the same company.

Instead of conveying the depressing message that informal groups worked against management wishes, Mayo became the hero of the age by providing a new gospel. Managers could smile once more and could hope to manipulate the informal group. The solution that he offered was simple. Because the workers' need to belong was so obsessive, their emotions would lead them to espouse the cause of any group which had exhibited social concern for them. Worker were therefore psychologically vunerable to capture. The informal group captured the individual, but the firm could capture the informal group. Mayo had the formula with which to do this. All the previously bad references to groups were wiped clean and, as far as management was concerned, group theory began (again) with Mayo.

The reception given to Mayo's message by managers showed that they, as much as workers, were ready to welcome the psychological safety of a comforting myth. Watson (1986) argued that the 'so-called evidence' of human relations ideas was regularly and heavily interpreted to fit the beliefs and hunches which derived from Mayo's political preferences and social beliefs. The Hawthorne studies, wrote Watson, could best be viewed as an instructive test of half-true stories. Like any myth, it mixed fiction, exaggeration and one-sidedness with an element of truth.

The appeal of human relations to managers was considerable. It offered an edifice of scientifically acquired evidence in support of the most satisfactory (managerial) conclusion that 'the requisite skills could release the enthusiasm for co-operation with management which work groups possessed as the result of their deep-felt need for belonging' (Child 1969a).

The 'human relations fad', as Argyris (1957) termed it, was prompted by a number of factors, only one of which were the research studies themselves. The authors of the studies, Mayo, Roethlisberger and Dickson, presented evidence to managers to show that productivity and human relations were closely related. If workers could be helped 'to belong', human relations would be improved, and the workers made more productive.

A second potent factor was the growth of unionism. This revealed to management the extent of worker discontent. Much of this was blamed on poor management. The third factor, according to Argyris, was the development among managers of a sense of responsibility. Additional factors cited included an increase in the size of organizations which caused a lack of communication between top and bottom levels. There was the greater specialization in work organization and the technical developments. Both created human problems. Increased labour costs encouraged management to make full use of labour while the higher standard of living permitted an emphasis on human factors. As will be argued in greater detail in Chapter 4, the time was right for human relations ideas to take off.

Human relations represented just the first of many attempts to bring

social science into the service of management. Despite endless disappointments the applications continue to this day because of the hope that is
offered. First, the hope of increased *efficiency*: that social science can
produce unparalleled co-operation in the workplace which will transcend or
utilize conflict, and potentially displace the necessity and rationale for trade
unions. Second, there is the hope of *satisfaction*: the belief that efficiency
will bring about the possibility of achieving the satisfaction of deep human
needs at work at no cost to the employer. Third, there is the hope of
management contribution: that the achievement of efficiency and satisfaction will be attained by a newly enlightened and expert management in
command of the total technical, social and human environment. Through its
control of work, management controls human happiness, fulfilment and
even perhaps sanity.

NEO-HUMAN RELATIONS

The survey of popular management ideas which was reported at the
beginning of this book placed the neo-human relations (NHR) management
idea family in top position. The influence of these US writers on management thought began in the late 1950s and has continued ever since. The
ideas have passed into American and British management practice in the
form of staff appraisal and counselling, supervisory training and job design.
All the writers to be discussed in this section:

1 viewed 'conventional' formal organization as a set of techniques embody-
   ing specific psychological assumptions
2 asserted that the conventional formal type of organization generated
   individual psychological distress and suggested that managers replaced
   these with more organic structures
3 offered technical organizational prescriptions to improve matters
4 held that managers should trust their subordinates to be more responsible
   for the performance of their jobs
5 suggested that managers should permit their subordinates to participate
   in making up the content of their own jobs

The basic thesis of neo-human relations (NHR) was that, above all, the
worker wanted the opportunity to grow and develop on the job. The writers
visualized that it would be this which would bring an end to industrial
conflict. They assumed that if employees were allowed to do responsible and
meaningful work, their attitude to the company would become entirely
positive, and they would come to share the goals of management.

During the 1950s and the 1960s the implicit authoritarianism of human
relations had become socially unacceptable. This hastened the adoption of
the neo-human relations. In their view, competition between individuals and
departments in the company continued to be an anathema. However, NHR

writers did offer a vision of a firm in which, because of the elimination of hierarchy and specialization, people not only were given room to grow but also became involved in a co-operative process.

Butler (1986) wrote that by the 1950s, management had reacted against the crudeness of Taylor's formulations and had found that Mayo's informal group was not as malleable, emotive and non-rational as they had been given to believe. He speculated on what the next motivational fad should be and suggested that it would contain the following features:

1 It should allow a return to dealing with the individual rather than the group.
2 It should be an amalgam, retaining the best aspects of Taylorism and Mayoism while limiting their disadvantages.
3 The new idea should call upon employees to return to self-reliance and the Protestant work ethic, but not be so independent that the firm loses control.
4 Employees should be able to develop their new-found self-reliance only through work in the organization.

While it would have been absurd to expect any theory (or more accurately, any social philosophy) to satisfy such unrealistically demanding specifications, NHR did meet nearly all of these criteria. A new initiative was required and was supplied by those who made up the NHR family of ideas.

While building upon Mayo's views and the Hawthorne studies, NHR emphasized the contribution of Abraham Maslow (in the view of some critics, too selectively and too zealously). All the neo-human relationists recognized people's needs for acceptance, status and recognition. However, they went further and argued that employees wanted to develop and apply their full range of abilities and obtained satisfaction through achieving demanding but worthwhile objectives.

NHR ideas were put into practice through the techniques of organizational development (OD). A major aspect of OD, indeed a defining characteristic of it according to Beckhard (1969), was the involvement of senior managers in the change programmes. The literature advised OD change agents always to 'start at the top'. Blake and Mouton (1969), for example, asserted that to change a company it was necessary for those who headed it to lead the change of it. Argyris (1970) in his description of his consultancy approach wrote that he always began with a discussion with the chief executive of the company.

The way in which OD was introduced into companies (top-down by OD consultants selected and paid for by management) ensured that the process was constantly under management control. This acted to reassure management and added to the appeal of the NHR ideas which underpinned the OD interventions. The consultant entered into a relationship with management with an implied agreement about areas of activity and areas of reservation. Kahn (1974) noted that senior management assumed that, in most cases, the OD process would neither alter nor infringe their traditional prerogatives in matters of staff selection, resource allocation and decision-making freedom. The contract implied an agreement to induce satisfaction, motivation and productivity. However, consultants were precluded from becoming involved in issues relating to resource allocation, availability of equipment, choice of supervisor or the allocation of rewards.

The tendency has been for OD consultants to leave the role structure (and hence the power structure) of the organization intact. Instead, their focus was upon those activities and stylistic characteristics that were left to the discretion of the individual. This gave OD interventions a heavily individualist focus which was only partly abated by its concern with teams.

Few organizational development (OD) efforts actually bring about the type of structural changes that goal congruence and bureaucratic demise theories would hypothesize. Under appropriate conditions, the Argyris approach could influence people directly, change organizational climates and processes and yield performance effects. However, it achieved this while leaving organizational structures surprisingly unaffected. Perhaps this was the very feature that appealed to managers. NHR offered specific techniques such as laboratory (or T-group) training. This was used in the belief that if managers could become more authentic, increased their interpersonal competence, changed their values and ultimately their behaviour, then their organizations would develop more appropriate structures than the traditional pyramidal ones.

Organizational development, as originally conceived, involved data collection, organizational decision-making and the development of a commitment to that decision. Thus, interpersonal change was viewed as a prelude to organizational change. The theories of leadership presented tended to be offered in value-laden terms. Legge (1978) argued that the values, processes and techniques that clustered under the umbrella-like label of OD which the neo-human relations movement gave birth to, were a response to the problem of organizational adaption to rapid rates of technological and social change. The values were particularly important and Margulies and Raia (1973) summarized the six main ones:

1 Providing opportunities for people to function as human beings rather than as resources in the productive process.
2 Providing opportunities for each organizational member, as well as for the organization itself, to develop their full potential.
3 Seeking to increase the effectiveness of the organization in terms of *all* its goals.
4 Attempting to create an environment in which it is possible to find exacting and challenging work.

5 Providing opportunities for people in organizations to influence the way in which they relate to work, the organization and to the environment.
6 Treat individual human beings as people with a complex set of needs, *all* of which are important to them in their work and life.

It is important to distinguish here between public support and private action. What managers claimed publicly to support, and what they actually did in their organizations, will reveal the gap between espousing certain management ideas for public effect and actually translating them into fundamental structural changes and implementing these within organizations. Fincham and Rhodes made this point:

> the efforts to humanize work are seen to serve an *ideological* purpose, rather than necessarily being part of management practice. They represent a body of ideas that may be called upon if management is being held open to public criticism, and that is favoured by certain sections of management (like personnel and public relations) concerned with the firm's outward image, yet with little real impact on work process.
>
> (Fincham and Rhodes 1988: 169)

The ideas of some of neo-human relations writers who received a high rating in the survey described in the previous chapter will now be briefly examined.

Abraham Maslow, 'Needs Hierarchy of Motivation Theory', 1943

Maslow (1943) presented his theory of human motivation based on a hierarchy of seven sets of needs. The theory itself was never conceived with management or organizations in mind. In his original writings, he addressed social issues in terms of the effect of societal factors upon the mental health of individuals. He wrote that his book expounding his ideas was in the realm of science or pre-science, rather than exhortation, or of a personal philosophy, or literary expression.

He hypothesized that, on average, the physiological needs of human beings were generally 85 per cent satisfied, the safety needs 70 per cent satisfied, the social needs 50 per cent satisfied, ego needs 40 per cent satisfied, and the self-actualization needs 10 per cent satisfied. Only unsatisfied needs in the individual acted as motivators. He proposed that while the needs could be considered in a loose, step-wise progression, it was possible for higher level needs to emerge at some point *prior* to the total satisfaction of the lower level needs.

Maslow is one of several theorists whose original ideas have been misrepresented to such a degree that what people *think* he said is actually more important than what he *actually* said. The popular interpretations have transformed Maslow's 'suggestion' into an 'estimate'; changed his societal average into an individual needs score; implied that his theory was based on empirical research; and reduced the number of his need categories from seven to five.

What managers and management students are taught is that Maslow differentiated between higher and lower level needs; placed them in a hierarchy of ascending order of importance to the individual; stated that a satisfied need no longer monopolized an individual's behaviour which became focused upon satisfying the next level up; and that only unsatisfied needs acted as motivators (except the self-actualization need). Such popular interpretations led managers to believe a number of things. First, that for motivation purposes, they should focus only on higher level needs and could ignore the first two levels of needs which included employee demands for job security and wages. Second, that this needs hierarchy applied to all people in all cultures and in all situations. Third, that all people looked for the satisfaction of their higher level needs at work, rather than outside of it.

After reviewing a range of motivation studies, Wahba and Bridwell (1975) concluded that Maslow's theory received 'little clear or consistent support from the available research findings' (1975: 9). Miner's (1980) judgement was that the available research did not support Maslow's theory to any significant degree. However, this did not imply that the theory was wrong but merely that it was not supported. What then accounts for the popularity of this theory? Blackler and Shimmin wrote that although Maslow's theory was difficult, if not impossible, to test empirically:

> it has an inherent appeal and face validity in explaining why different needs and motives may be expected to operate in different situations. . . . For this reason and because it has often been presented as a prescription for 'good' management practice (i.e. design your organization and managerial strategies to encourage self-actualization and the people will voluntarily integrate their own goals with those of the organization), it permeates much of the advice offered to managers and others concerning motivation at work. Indeed, 'self-actualization' is becoming a term in common parlance.
>
> (Blackler and Shimmin 1984: 79)

Brown (1980: 157) commented upon the attraction of the human potential movement to management consultants, management educators and to managers. She felt that its assumptions and beliefs fitted in well with the post-1945 social climate in which control of the employee, based on greed and fear, became unfashionable. Maslow's ideas came to be adopted by social scientists and researchers who came to form the NHR school of management thought (e.g. McGregor 1960: Likert 1967; Argyris 1962). All of these writers saw a clash between an individual's psychological aspirations and needs on the one hand, and the contemporary organizational structures and management styles on the other. To reduce this incongruity and secure worker commitment, they advocated remedies such as group decision-making and participatory management styles.

Maslow's needs hierarchy theory has been widely taught to managers, and has been used by them to guide their decisions about employees (Matheson 1974) and about how organizations should be managed (Clark 1960–1: 202). It is attractive to managers because it is an *on-the-average* theory. The generalization which can be universally applied is that 'employees may be expected to always want more'. Except for the case of the need for self-actualization, the theory, as understood by managers, neither stresses individual differences nor requires the measurement of individual motivational patterns before action is taken. Instead, it considers groups of individuals as being defined partly by external circumstances. In this form, the theory is well suited to the needs of broad managerial policies on human relations matters. This is because these operate in 'on-the-average' terms.

The theory implies that, to the extent that management could control conditions in the workgroup's environment, it could induce certain motivational patterns and obtain the benefits of increased production output and reduced turnover and absenteeism. The theory also includes 'when–then' propositions. For example, *when* job conditions are poor in terms of pay and security, *then* employees will focus attention on the work itself, *so then*, if management wishes to obtain significant motivational consequences, it has to change these work conditions. Similarly *when* job conditions improve, *then* the behaviour of the supervisors become important, so *then* management needs to train them. *When* the job conditions improve still further, *then* the role of the supervisor becomes less important and the work itself re-establishes its importance as a motivator. Finally, *when* people move up the needs hierarchy, *then* they will become motivated only by the higher level needs.

Many managers have used the theory to understand changing employee motivations. It applying it, they have tended to telescope the needs hierarchy into a dichotomy with physical and safety needs on one side and higher level needs on the other. In this formulation, the watershed mark is quite low on the hierarchy, whereas in Maslow's original formulation it was placed much higher. The theory has not contributed to the development of scientifically based managerial practice but has instead been added to the stock of working ideas used by managers to understand, predict and influence employee motivation and performance. In Etzioni-Halevy's (1985) terms, it has provided a general orientation towards human or social reality.

Douglas McGregor, 'Theory X and Theory Y', 1960

McGregor shares with Maslow the distinction of having an incorrect interpretation of his theory gain wider circulation than his original idea. McGregor (1960: 33–4) presented a set of assumptions about human motivation and behaviour which he said were implicit in management literature, theory and practice. He labelled these Theory X assumptions. These were that average human beings had an inherent dislike of work and would avoid it if they could. That because of this, people had to be coerced, controlled, directed and threatened with punishment in order to get them to put in the necessary effort to achieve organizational goals. Finally, the average individual wished to avoid responsibility, had little ambition, wanted security above all else and preferred to be directed. The consequences of holding such assumptions, according to McGregor, led managers to rely on 'rewards, promises, incentives, or threats and other coercive devices' (1960: 42). The first three words of the preceding quotation are most important. They are the ones most often omitted in accounts of what McGregor wrote. McGregor then went on to outline the assumptions related to Theory Y.

In an earlier article McGregor described the range of management styles which were *all* based on Theory X assumptions. These behavioural patterns ranged from coercion, threat, close supervision and control at one extreme, to 'soft' methods involving being persuasive and achieving harmony at the other. However, popular accounts of McGregor focus only on one aspect of behaviour that Theory X managers employed ('hard' techniques) and ignore the others. Finally one can note that most books incorrectly report McGregor as saying either that Theory X and Theory Y are the only two sets of assumptions that managers make about people or that they are at the extreme ends of a continuum.

McGregor's work has been discussed in terms of management style. Worker's hostility to management and its directions was the result not of personality characteristics of the employees, but as a reaction to their lack of job satisfaction. Following Maslow, the McGregor argument held that worker needs were related to the intrinsic rather than extrinsic aspects of work, and thus could not be directly met by management. The manager's job from this perspective was to create the conditions which would allow workers to meet these needs themselves by the way they led and managed their employees (McGregor 1967).

Taking these ideas as their points of departure, consultants and business academics reinterpreted and sought to convince managers of the one-best-way of Theory Y management. Management control was retained in this formulation since managers continued to be responsible for organizing the elements of the production process. The two were held to be complementary. Discussing the relationship between Maslow and McGregor, Butler (1986) argued that 'Without McGregor the management world would never have heard of Maslow. But Maslow gave McGregor intellectual credibility, and in management circles, McGregor gave Maslow fame'.

Frederick Herzberg, 'Motivation Hygiene Theory', 1959

Herzberg's impact on management thinking (Herzberg *et al.* 1959) has been described as spectacular (Brown, 1980: 159). There were two major aspects of Herzberg's contribution. First there was the theory itself, and second there was the technique that it spawned – job enrichment. Writers have made the distinction between what Herzberg originally wrote and what academics and managers believe that he said. What he actually said was that two sets of variables (called hygiene factors and motivators) together influenced worker motivation. What he did *not* say was that hygiene factors were less important than motivators. The cost-conscious manager was attracted to the proposition that investments in salary, fringe benefits and working conditions could yield only limited results.

The message that has been passed down in seminars and short management texts is that the *only* way to motivate people is to offer them psychological growth. This is an incorrect concept which is hugely appealing to many managers. His attractive technique can be applied within an existing organizational framework. The job enrichment approach, which was initially developed from Herzberg's work, came to be promoted by many representatives of the neo-human relations school. It even became institutionalized in the 'Quality of Working Life' programmes in many countries. Lupton described Herzberg's ideas in the following way:

> If you wish (as employer or manager) to have an efficient organization, you must set to work to improve the performance of the individuals who presently work for it. It does not matter who the individuals are, what they can do, what they are doing, what the organization does, how it does it, or what it is, there will always be scope for re-dividing and re-designing its tasks so as to enrich them, and for so arranging the context of administrative procedure, supervision and interpersonal relationships, that they will not inhibit motivation and satisfaction.
>
> (Lupton 1976: 123)

In the reinterpreted version of Herzberg's theory one can discover virtually all the elements which will be shown to give an idea of manager-appeal (see Chapter 3). The Lupton quotation clearly signals the *universality* of the idea's application. It was held to be relevant to all organizations. Herzberg's idea stressed only two types of motivation variables and thus was easily *communicable* to managers. It specified a set of precise *steps* through which the technique of job enrichment could be applied. Blackler and Shimmin mentioned the fascination which the theory possessed for managers who did not seek rich conceptual insights into analytical theory but who wanted guiding principles for action:

> Herzberg's theory . . . while poorly regarded by psychologists nowadays, is accepted readily enough by hard-pressed managers who want no more

than a general rule of thumb to help guide their approach.
(Blackler and Shimmin 1984: 133)

The exact form of job enrichment could be customized to each company thereby offering a *contribution or ownership* dimension. Herzberg, like Taylor, believed that the 'tyranny of the group' suppressed the satisfaction of individual needs. The focus of his theory and the target of his technique was upon the *individual* in the workplace. In contrast to some of the 'participative management' writers, Herzberg argued that the workers should not be involved in deciding the types of enrichment to which they were to be subjected. His explanation was that they were not always competent to contribute to the discussion and decision. The effect of this point was that the answer to the very critical question of who controlled the production process was management. Thus the requirement for *management control* was met. Buchanan commented that the technique of job enrichment was easy to understand, and suggested ways of improving employee motivation and performance which did not involve higher wages (a hygiene factor) and which left organizational structures, management roles and authority intact.

The role of management was *legitimized* since it was management which had the knowledge and expertise to decide upon the form of enrichment. Moreover, from Herzberg's perspective, everyone in the organization was potentially a motivator-seeker or a hygiene-seeker. Hygiene-seekers were held to be mentally unhealthy individuals who had been blocked at the hygiene level by some unfortunate past experience. It was management's job to help them through this problem. The coincidence with Mayo's views about the non-rationality (reverie) of workers is significant here.

It has been argued that the appeal of Herzberg's idea lay partly in the motivational concepts used. These focused on power–authority relationships from the standpoint of how management used them to create a productive work climate. The theory identified sound and unsound alignments of motivations towards productivity in the industrial situation. It was based upon the idea of *human nature* as being of the 'animal–Adam' type. This view held that humankind was concerned with avoiding pain from the environment. Hence, companies had to deal constructively with hygiene and maintenance issues at work, paying particular attention to work layout, physical job demands, personal status and so on.

A further basic need of humankind stemmed from their 'human-Abraham' nature which sought growth from tasks (Herzberg 1966: 76). Some writers, particularly those from the critical Marxist tradition, have seen job enrichment as a cosmetic attempt to increase the skill and discretion of workers without interfering with management authority in any significant way. Miner (1980) acknowledged that the idea lacked the research to confirm it but noted the tremendous appeal it possessed for managers since its publication.

It may be that the popularity of the motivation-hygiene theory, and particularly the idea-technique of job enrichment, stemmed from the fact that it provided managers with the pay-off that they wanted. That pay-off may not have been, as it is often assumed, in the area of increased productivity and product quality, although this was always a possibility. Empirical research studies showed two things. First, that a great deal more was written and talked about job enrichment than was actually put into practice. Fincham and Rhodes (1988) reported that there was widespread acceptance of work humanization at the level of public policy. Several European governments (including Britain's) and international bodies supported initiatives in this area. However, the true impact on the shopfloor was far less significant (see Wall 1982).

Many schemes never progressed beyond the experimental stage while others were discontinued after a short time. According to Fincham and Rhodes a number of experiments which claimed far-reaching job enrichment results involved only cosmetic changes. Child (1984: 43) put the number of European job enrichment schemes at 100 or so. Guest *et al.* (1980) reported that job enrichment scheme managers judged half the schemes to have been 'very beneficial'. Only half of the workers interviewed at the plants concerned were aware that any change had taken place, and only a small proportion of these identified the changes as either positive or significant.

Second, there are examples of highly successful job enrichment programmes being abruptly terminated by management (Marglin 1979). This fragmentary evidence leads one to the conclusion that, in the climate of the time, job enrichment could have provided a banner to which managers and organizations might flock and thereby espouse publicly an idea which had become fashionable in the way that companies being 'green' is fashionable in the early 1990s.

Management could say these things without actually having to implement them in practice. If they were forced to or wished to embark on job enrichment programmes, Herzberg had written the rules in such a way as to give management a continued control over the labour process. In some cases, it appeared that the programmes did go beyond the limits set by managers. Workers' enthusiasm resulted not only in increased productivity but also in demands for increased worker control. It was at this point that such programmes were terminated. Parallels can be drawn with the quality circle movement of the 1980s.

Rensis Likert, 'System 4 Theory', 1967

Likert (1967) developed a psychologically focused, universally applicable theory. His message was that democracy paid in management. He advocated the integration of individuals into the organization through groups which in turn were integrated into the organization's official structure of decision-making by being made to overlap by means of their continuing 'linking-pin' members who belonged to more than one group.

Likert sought to establish a single cause linking people's attitudes and their performance. His theory strongly emphasized the connecting of workgroups, their interactions, and the practical considerations of profit and loss. The measures he used for scoring the dimensions of human organization were motivation, communication, interaction, decision-making, goal-setting, control and performance. They were all held to relate (except for the last), either directly or indirectly, to people's states of mind.

Likert's theory focused upon leadership and expanded to encompass lateral and vertical inter-group relationships, organizational climate and social systems. He went on to prescribe what should be done for improvement, saying that organizational performance would be raised if all organizations resembled his System 4 model (one of four models which he described). Likert clearly stated his normative leadership preferences for the universal application of his 'one-best-System 4-way':

> System 4 harnesses human motivation in ways that yield positive co-operation rather than fearful antagonisms on the part of the people in the organization; by contrast, Systems 1 and 2 tend to develop less favourable attitudes, more hostile attitudes, or more submissive attitudes.
>
> (Likert in conversation with Dowling 1973: 34)

Likert did present a great deal of empirical supporting data when arguing for the replacement of Systems 1 and 2 with System 4. However, this is in itself insufficient to explain the popularity of his idea among managers. He did claim a *universal* relevance for his prescription which added to its appeal. He believed that there were general principles applicable to all managerial situations even though the actual applications would vary with the particular company climate involved. His belief in universal and transferable properties was founded on his view of *human nature* which held that inherited essence was the same everywhere and that culture, while it may influence the application of management principles, was not itself a principle.

Leadership, in his view, affected productivity through its effects on subordinates. The pattern might be complex, but the chain of causation was single and uni-directional. The task of leadership was to ensure that all the interactions and all the relationships were experienced by organizational members as supportive. That is, they were ones which built and maintained employees' sense of personal worth and importance (Likert 1961: 103). This basic principle ascribed an extremely influential role to the leader. Leadership was reflected in the managerial and supervisory practices which underpinned the System 4 scheme.

Likert's approach to organizational development involved strengthening the use of managerial power and authority in order to exercise *control*. His approach assisted the organization-as-client to assess the character of its human organization. He concluded that differences in managerial leadership produced four different types of organization – exploitative-authoritative, consultative, participative and benevolent autocratic.

The focus on leadership was only one aspect of the theory that gave it its appeal. The four different styles of management matched the four systems of organization (1, 2, 3 and 4) and related to the 'linking pin model' of organization. The key aspects of Likert's theory were easily *communicable* to managers.

The work possessed a *common-sense* appeal through the use of a survey instrument which was used to help managers 'picture' their own organization. These data were summarized, fed back to the managers, and evaluated against this theory so as to assist in the identification of the human organization currently existing. Furthermore, since the theory and the scales described what would be required to move to a participative group style (claimed to be the most suitable for facilitating productivity and satisfaction), it was possible to plot the *series of steps* which would be essential for achieving such a change.

Robert Blake and Jane Mouton, 'Managerial Grid', 1964

Robert Blake and Jane Mouton's model drew heavily upon Likert's (1961) work. Grid theory owed a strong intellectual debt to the early Ohio State University studies on leadership which examined the dimensions of 'consideration' and 'initiating structure'. This work was also developed at the Survey Research Centre at the University of Michigan where Likert was a faculty member. It was the Michigan researchers who first conceptualized two leadership dimensions which they labelled 'employee orientation' and 'production orientation'. These were held to be independent and a leader could be high or low on both (Katz *et al.* 1950).

Bryman (1986) analysed these two research studies and concluded that there was a clear resemblence between the two Grid dimensions and the Ohio studies' preoccupation with consideration and initiating structure. He stated that, 'there is often an implicit view among many writers that the former arose out of the latter' (Bryman 1986: 71). The marketing expertise of Blake and Mouton rather than the originality of their thought is what they are perhaps most noted for. Some observers have felt that Blake and Mouton's outstanding contribution to the investigation of leadership has been in their ability to package their concept. They have provided a method for explaining and developing training programmes which focus sensitivity training and organizational development on the leadership concept. Their Grid made the slippery concept of leadership much easier to handle for many managers.

To emphasize the similarities between Likert's work and Blake and Mouton's Managerial Grid, it is instructive to identify aspects of Likert's 1961 book which contain ideas related to leadership, behaviour and performance. For example, Likert considered whether a supervisor should be employee-centred or job-centred. His review of the literature led him to conclude that neither extreme was appropriate but that:

> If a high level of performance is to be achieved, it appears necessary for the supervisor to be employee-centred and at the same time to have high performance goals, and a contiguous enthusiasm as to the importance of achieving these goals.

> (Likert 1961: 8)

There is evidence to suggest that Blake and Mouton's starting-point for the production of their Managerial Grid was either Likert's conclusion in his 1961 book or the research by Katz *et al.* (1950) cited earlier. Although the Managerial Grid is likely to be familiar to readers, it is possible to describe it in such a way as to highlight some of the variables which account for its popularity among managers.

The Grid is presented to managers as a straightforward procedure for organizational improvement based on apparently self-evident, *common-sense* propositions. The Grid is a classification of styles of management based upon two variables – 'concern for people' and 'concern for production'. There are nine degrees of concern for each of the two dimensions, and this gives a matrix consisting of 81 cells, each representing a possible management style. Of these, only five positions are focused upon and named – that in the middle and those at each of the four corners of the matrix. These are shown in Figure 2.1.

The use of two dimensions and the discussion of only five styles of management added considerably to the *communicability* of the theory to its intended management audience. So too did the uni-causal explanation which claimed that:

management style → attitudes → behaviour → organizational
performance

The focus of the Grid was upon *leadership* or the style of management. By this, Blake and Mouton meant managers' beliefs about their society, subordinates, colleagues and job, and the way in which they expressed these in their behaviour at work. Each of the five styles was labelled. The 1/1 manager (see Figure 2.1) would be a person who showed concern neither for the well-being of his subordinates, nor for the efficient use of the non-human resources given to his charge. A 1/9 manager would be a tough, no-nonsense individual, who expected people to get the production out on schedule and would use any stick or carrot to push or pull them in that direction. The 9/1 manager was the softie who let production slide in case he

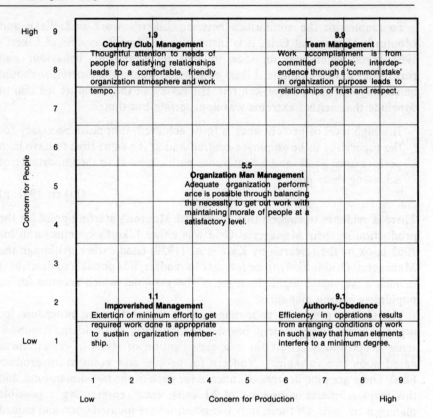

Figure 2.1 The Managerial Grid
Source: Blake et al. 1964: 136
Copyright © by the President and Fellows of Harvard College, all rights reserved

offended anyone. The 9/9 manager was one who commanded the confidence of her subordinates, was solicitious as to their welfare and personal development, but who, at the same time, could deploy both human and non-human resources in ways that led to high operating efficiency. The 5/5 manager was on the right lines but had a long way to go. She was the honest trier.

The *step-by step* approach was a major feature of Grid approach. The programme consisted of seven phases. These started with the individual and worked through the group up to the level of the organization. Thus the Grid method had an individual, a team and a company focus. Further 'stepping' or staging was provided within each of the phases by the use of self-administered questionnaires. Such tight structuring has been a major feature of the Grid Development packaged approach. These instruments were used as part of the training room materials in an educational programme which sought to create and develop 'more productive problem-solving relationships' (Blake *et al.* 1964).

The Grid programme has been widely used throughout the world since the 1960s. Part of its appeal can be attributed to the fact that it offers a *single solution perspective* or preferred single management style (labelled 9/9), which is claimed to be *universally* applicable. Moreover, that style is held to be positively associated with career success, productivity and profitability, as compared to any other style (Blake and Mouton 1978: 128). At the same time, however, the Grid approach has received criticism from many writers. Quinn and McGrath (1982) suggested that there was little empirical evidence to demonstrate the validity of Blake and Mouton's claims. Moreover, the Grid's values and prescriptions have been challenged (Strauss 1973; Bernardin and Alvares 1976). However, it is not within the remit of this book to deal with these criticisms. One should merely note Anthony's (1977) assessment that the pronouncements of Blake and Mouton 'probably represent one of the strongest influences on current management thinking, it is solemnly (and uncritically) taught in many management centres and universities and it has influenced the policies and structure of companies such as BP and ICI.'

Chris Argyris, 'Goal Congruence Theory', 1964

Goal congruence theory was developed by Chris Argyris. It has been outlined in three of his publications (Argyris 1957; 1964; 1973). The basic idea that Argyris put forward was the necessity for organizations to create circumstances in which adults could develop healthy personalities. Organizational design should ensure that the personal growth needs of individual development and organizational needs for productivity were matched. This view gave the name to his theory. Argyris therefore contributed to the self-actualization theme which was at the heart of the neo-human relations movement.

He argued that individuals developed or progressed to different degrees along six dimensions. Forces within society (including organizations) and within people could inhibit this process of development. A second building block in Argyris's theory was the concept of organization as epitomized in administrative management theory. Here he was concerned with principles such as task specialization, chain of command, unity of direction and span of control. In his view, such a formal organization was incompatible with the development of a healthy, mature state in the individual. The effect of this contradiction was, over time, to make healthy employees passive, dependent and submissive.

Argyris argued that most workers existed in companies that oppressed them to some degree. Close supervision, minute instruction and job specialization were considered as burdensome. Workers were likely to react by developing some defence mechanism such as apathy, aggression, vacillation or ambivalence. All of these reactions imposed some strain upon individuals and, through them, upon the organization. Argyris's very tentative answer was job enlargement and reduced supervision. Work design and supervision by management were the control tools of administrative management. They impeded adaptation to change, had a deadening effect on individual motivation and broke the link between individual input and organizational performance. Argyris argued that they also prevented an individual achieving self-actualization.

Argyris did not have a one-way view of causation, from management style to performance. He acknowledged the need to amend the structures to support a modified management style. His prescriptions were underpinned by a view of human beings who looked for challenges, worked in adaptive groups and sought common goals. He claimed a universal application for his theory. However, the theory had difficulty in explaining violent conflict, opposing constituencies and power fights.

Paul Hersey and Kenneth Blanchard, 'Situational Leadership Theory', 1969

Originally called the Life Cycle Theory of Leadership, the renamed Situational Leadership Theory used a contingency approach which stated that the effective leadership style was the one that fitted the particular situation. As with the Ohio studies mentioned earlier, managerial behaviour was classified into two categories. The first was *task behaviour*, which was concerned with a manager engaging in one-way communication with a subordinate to explain what has to be done. The second was *relationship behaviour*, which involved the manager in engaging in two-way communication with a junior so as to provide him with socio-emotional support, psychological stroking and facilitating behaviour.

The key feature of Hersey and Blanchard's leadership theory which distinguished it from its predecessors was its emphasis on *subordinate maturity*. This was defined as a person's willingess to direct their own behaviour. Such maturity, it was argued, should be considered only in relation to each specific task. In Hersey and Blanchard's formulation, employees were not considered to be mature or immature in a general way, but instead, they were held to possess different degrees of maturity in relation to specific tasks.

From this brief description of Situational Leadership Theory, one can see that, although the words may be different, the echoes of the Ohio studies, the Tannenbaum and Schmidt's (1973) leadership style progression model and the Blake and Mouton Grid Development model are all strong. Explaining its major commitment to Situational Leadership, the Xerox

Corporation cited 'the model's intuitive appeal and quick acceptance by our managers' (Gumpert and Hambleton 1979).

It may be that intuitive appeal did play a major part in this particular idea's popularity amongst personnel and training managers. Bryman (1986) noted that this leadership theory had not generated a great deal of research. He concluded 'that there is virtually no evidence to substantiate its fundamental tenets' (1986: 147). Did such a lack of evidence matter to the manager? Bryman thought not:

> its . . . [Situational Leadership Theory's] . . . concentration on just one situational variable, and the absence of a research tradition deriving from it, render it of little utility for leadership researchers. Ironically, it may be the very simplicity of the model and the absence of negative evidence that has made it so popular within management circles.
>
> (Bryman 1986: 149)

The recurring features of some of the main neo-human relations ideas are presented in Table 2.1.

GURU THEORY

In order to bring popular management thinking up to date, it is necessary to consider developments in management thought that have occurred since 1980. This period has seen a great number of diverse management ideas being offered. One commentator observed that business writing had become big business. *Publishers Weekly* noted that, 'Dieting, sex, whimsey, food and gossip are no longer first in the heart of bibliophiles. With no near competitors, business was the strongest selling subject in the United States in 1983' (Maryles 1984, cited in Freeman 1985: 345–50).

At first sight, it appears that guru writings represent a random collection of diverse contributors with no linking theme, brought to prominence by a renewed interest in business and management. However, closer inspection does give credence to Heller's (1990) suggestion that the central contention of this management idea family is that 'the only object of business is to compete with others for the favours of the customer as King'. Indeed, Ohmae (1987) had earlier stated that the central fact of business today was the emergence of consumer sovereignty.

Underpinning this guiding notion are at least five beliefs. First, that the innovation which leads to improved products and services cannot be planned, but is dependent on many 'tries' by many employees. Second, that you are more likely to 'act yourself into a feeling' than 'feel yourself into action'. Third, that an organization can be effectively co-ordinated through its value system and culture, rather than through rules and commands. Fourth, that customers are the main source of innovation. Fifth, that a strong customer orientation is important and has implications

Table 2.1 Recurring features found in the main neo-human relations ideas

Date of origin	Author	Label/ 'Magic Words'	Topic	Level of analysis	No. of dimensions	Dimensions or 'Magic Word' vocabulary	Preferred
1940s	Fleishman/ Ohio studies	consideration initiating structure	leadership style	individual	2	democratic and autocratic leadership	democratic
1954	Maslow	hierarchy of needs	motivation	individual	4	physiological safety, love, esteem and self-actualization needs	high level
1957	Argyris	self-actualization	individual	individual		congruency	self-actualization
1959	Herzberg	Hygiene-motivation theory	motivation	individual	2	motivators satisficers	motivators
1960	McGregor	assumptions of human nature	leadership style	individual	2	Theory X and Theory Y	Theory Y
1961	Likert	participative management	leadership style	individual	4	leadership style - autocracy - benefit autocracy - consultative leadership - participative - approach	System 4

1964	Blake and Mouton	grid management	individual	2	1/1, 1/9, 9/1, 9/9, 5/5	9/9 manager
1964	Berne	transactional analysis	individual behaviour	3	parent, adult, child	adult
1964	Tannenbaum and Schmidt	choosing leadership patterns	leadership style	7	leader control shared control shared control group control	as appropriate
1977	Hersey and Blanchard	situational leadership	leadership style	2	task behaviour relationship behaviour	as appropriate
1978	Adair	action centred leadership	leadership	3	group needs individual needs task needs	awareness of all
1970	Reddin	3-D theory of managerial effectiveness	leadership	3	concern for people, task effectiveness	as appropriate
1973	Vroom and Yetton	decision quality decision acceptance	leadership	5	leader decides, consults, shares, delegates	as appropriate

for management attitudes and behaviour towards staff. These themes, to different degrees, and with different emphases can be found in the writings of the various gurus.

Guru theory seeks to help managers build strong business systems which can successfully compete in their chosen market segment. Since each guru idea relies for its authorization upon the individual who developed and popularized it, the term 'guru theory' is used as a convenient label to refer to these different contributions that have been so influential during the last ten years. The label encompasses a rag-bag of prescriptions which include the importance of innovation, more teamwork, more empowerment of the individual, more employee participation, fewer levels of hierarchy, and less bureaucratization.

One can distinguish between *academic or formal* types of management education and the *non-academic or popular* forms of management knowledge. Although the latter have been viewed with suspicion by the business schools, they have begun to penetrate the formal curricula. Thomas (1989) noted that it would be naive to equate the widespread purchase of any popular management text such as *In Search of Excellence* or *The One Minute Manager* with either widespread reading, common interpretation, or indeed any influence on the reader's beliefs or behaviour. One does not even know if the readership of these popular texts consists of managers. Such problems are typically encountered by those who have attempted to investigate the social significance of cultural products. Even if 'the student of popular culture teeters between cliché and gibberish', as Goodlad (1976: 225) wrote, the risks seem worth taking. Formal and popular forms of management knowledge each have their own distinctive forms of transmission. Thomas observed that:

> These forms of knowledge are seen as elements of broader, antagonistically related cultures which have co-existed with growing unease as management education has developed in the higher education system.
>
> (A. B. Thomas 1989: 1)

He went on to argue that the Thatcher government's promotion of the notion of 'popular capitalism' and the 'enterprise culture' with its critique of the traditional education system had given legitimacy to popular management assumptions. It had revitalized them, and had led to their extension to all forms of management education. Thus the growth in, and success of, popular management texts was a *reflection* of this underlying cultural shift. At the same time it constituted an expression of what he called the 'domain assumptions' of popular management.

Thomas argued that popular concepts of management (its tasks, knowledge-base, mode of acquisition) were as old as management itself. They emphasized the practical, rejected theoretically informed knowledge and devalued any form of formal instruction. Dismissing texts which might embody a codification of such conceptions, the popular culture of management has been sustained by the face-to-face transmission at the workplace or by experience.

The world of management texts, an essential part of the transmission of bodies of knowledge and of certification, has traditionally been the province of the academic system. It was only in the 1980s that the non-academic management book re-established itself. Freeman (1985), Menkes (1987) and Knowlton (1989) independently concluded that publishers, authors, booksellers, agents and even the general public recognized the commercial value of the guru books. Detractors, however, continued to complain that best-seller lists represented common and even vulgar popular taste. They felt that the once staid world of business book publishing had been transformed. Sales ran into hundreds of thousands, sometimes millions, royalties came in six figures, business titles were best-sellers, and authors commanded huge sums as speakers at conferences.

The US sales of the top business books are shown in Table 2.2. History may reveal the interest in business to have been either a temporary phenomenon, or the beginning of a continuing trend. The author can only offer an analysis of the current writings as they are seen now. Many business magazines and newspapers regularly carry articles about the best-selling business books and the management gurus (referring to them as the 'prophets of profit'). They address the business book publishing explosion as a generalized phenomenon and fail to make any distinction between the contents of these different books or the backgrounds of their authors.

An investigation of the management publications revealed that four different types of business books could be distinguished. The largest category consists of books aimed directly at minor business executives. They promise to teach them (as a quasi-academic exercise) how to do certain things better than before. For example, how to communicate, market, sell or manage. In the United States, these are known as 'how-to' books and they sell exceptionally well.

The second category consists of the 'what-can-we-learn-from' business books. These examine the inner workings of large, often multinational corporations. They seek to learn from the evidence of success, to draw conclusions that would be of use to tycoons-in-waiting that allegedly form their readership. A popular form of this book genre are the practical reminiscences of successful corporate executives. These detail their managerial style or the financial coups that made them both rich and famous. Behind this type of book is the implication that the reader need only duplicate this style of behaviour in order to reach a similar eminence. However, there inevitably lurks a sub-text that actually implies that you must also be a genius (like the writer) to make it all work.

The third category of business book, more straightforwardly, seeks to explain the increasingly complicated world of finance, the stock market, exporting or whatever. A fourth category is represented by books which are survival guides seeking to help readers cope with difficult times. John Kenneth Galbraith described this sector of the publishing business as the 'cottage industry in predicting disaster'. Titles include *Surviving the Great Depression of 1990* (Batra 1988); *How to Prosper during the Coming Bad Years* (Ruff 1979); *Crisis in Investing* (Casey 1983); and *Megatrends* (Naisbitt 1982). The focus here will be upon the first two categories of books mentioned. Some others will also be referred to due to their high volume sales. These do not fit exactly into the categories just presented. Having distinguished between the different contents of the books, one can classify them more usefully according to the background of their authors. Heller wrote:

> More pervasive, and more profitable than the computers of IBM, were the acolytes of American management technology. They came from all sides – highly motivated professors of motivation, consultants command-ing the world's highest fees, expatriate managers whose salaries (and tax positions) would embarrass an Italian boardroom, visiting lecturers of every posture, sellers of packaged management development aids, witch-doctors.
>
> (Heller 1986: 40)

The authorization of a management idea stems from its author's position, which can be based upon academic research, experience of consultancy or experience of management. Table 2.2 indicates the book sales of these different authors. A useful way of considering guru theory authors is to differentiate between academic gurus, consultant gurus and hero-managers.

As the label suggests, academic gurus are business school professors and others who have an educational institution affiliation. Consultant gurus are independent writers and advisers. Hero-managers are current or past chief executive officers (usually of major American or British multinational companies) who are acknowledged to have been successful. Each speaks from a different base of authority. The different writers in each class are shown in Table 2.3.

Contrasting these three classes of guru one can argue that, having been prominent during the 1950s and 1960s, academic management gurus are now experiencing more competition. Among the best known academic ones are Michael Porter (competitive advantage), Kenneth Blanchard (One Minute Manager), William Ouchi (Theory Z), Henry Mintzberg (roles of managers) and Rosabeth Moss Kanter (innovation and organizational change).

The consultant-guru school was probably founded by Frederick Winslow Taylor. Its most popular current representatives are Tom Peters, John

Table 2.2 Best-selling business books in the United States 1979–88

Author	Book	Year of publication	Copies sold	Rating in the year
Ruff	*How to Prosper During the Coming Bad Years*	1979	450,000	No. 3 among all best-sellers
Casey	*Crisis in Investing*	1980	438,640	No. 1 among all best-sellers
Cohen	*You Can Negotiate Anything*	1981	205,000	No. 9 among all best-sellers
Naisbitt	*Megatrends*	1982	210,000	No. 15 among all best-sellers
Peters and Waterman	*In Search of Excellence*	1982	1,160,491	No. 1 among all best-sellers
Iacocca	*Iacocca: An Autobiography*	1984	1,055,000	No. 1 among all best-sellers
Iacocca	*Iacocca: An Autobiobraphy*	1985	1,510,000	No. 1 among all best-sellers
Halberstam	*The Reckoning*	1986	208,000	No. 22 among all best-sellers
Batra	*Surviving the Great Depression of 1990*	1987	549,000	No. 6 among all best-sellers
Trump	*Trump: The Art of the Deal*	1988	900,000	Ranking unavailable

Source: Fortune, 13 February 1989, pp. 61–3

Naisbitt and Gifford Pinchot. These people are the inheritors of the traditional re-established by Peter F. Drucker after the end of the Second World War.

Finally, there is the hero-management school currently represented by the tycoon texts of people like Lee Iacocca, Harold Geneen, Mark McCormack, Victor Kiam, John Sculley and John Harvey-Jones. The modern contributions in this tradition are practising (or recently retired) successful managers who write down the 'secrets' of success and also take the opportunity to expound their philosophy of life. Henri Fayol and Alfred P. Sloan were

Table 2.3 Academic gurus, consultant gurus and hero-managers of the 1980s

Academics	Consultants	Hero-managers
Mintzberg	de Bono	Geneen
Kotler	Naisbitt	McCormack
Porter	Ohmae	Kay
Bennis	Pinchot	Kiam
Blanchard	Peters	Avis
Ouchi	Waterman	Calzon
Levitt	Goldratt	Harvey-Jones
Kanter	Crosby	Morita
		Trump
		Iacocca
		Sculley

probably the founders of this approach, but they did not engage in personal promotion to the extent of their more recent successors.

In discussing these writings the business press rarely if ever makes any distinction between these three types of contributors. They are referred to collectively as management or business gurus. One dictionary definition of 'guru' is a Hindu or Sikh spiritualist teacher. The personal nature of his guidance is stressed. Gurus appear in all walks of life and in all aspects of business. They may therefore meet some basic human need. One finds production management gurus (Goldratt), quality gurus (Deming) and financial gurus. This is an issue which will be considered in Chapter 5 where such a functionalist explanation is presented.

The use of the word 'guru' in business journals emphasizes three features. First, in the British press (but not in the American) the word seems to be used with a slightly pejorative tone. The Americans tend to use it more positively to indicate a far-sighted and visionary individual. The British business press (perhaps reflecting British management's preoccupation with practical and immediate issues, and with a suspicion of anything theoretical or abstract), generally give the term a negative connotation. Second, the term guru stresses the active search by business people for hidden knowledge or secrets. Third, it indicates the preparedness of individuals to carry out, sometimes uncritically, the recommendations or directions of the guru whom they follow.

Guru theory took off at a time when managers appeared to need extra guidance and ideas. The rise of modern management guru theory can be dated to the early 1980s. The movement is still strong. At one level, guru theory represents a break with the academically dominated neo-human relations movement represented by people like Argyris, McGregor, Maslow, Herzberg and Likert. At another level, however, it represents a continuation of those ideas, albeit adapted to the circumstances of the 1980s and 1990s. An analysis of the message themes being put forward shows that employee commitment, responsibility, creativity and putting people ahead of the bureaucracy are still very much in vogue. Peters and Waterman (1982) argued against the rational, the quantitative and the logical. They stressed the importance of leadership vision, culture and people and concluded that 'soft was hard'.

The difference between the NHR and the guru schools has much to do with the underlying needs of managers. In the 1960s when NHR rose to prominence, its people-oriented message was set in the context of the American boom. In the United States, the 1946–65 period saw its industry at full stretch as it tried to meet unfulfilled domestic demand which had been pent up during the Great Depression. Such demand remained largely unsatisfied during the period of the Second World War. Hence, from the mid-1960s, after its internal demand had been satisfied, American industry turned its attention to the needs of European markets. The profits and industrial problems of this period led to a management concern to make work more interesting for employees. In this way, it was felt, industrial action, absenteeism and high labour turnover could be reduced in a period of prosperity.

The Quality of Work Life (QWL) projects were instituted to achieve the aforementioned aims and to increase productivity and employee commitment. Their purpose was to meet the inner needs of workers so that they would not go elsewhere. During the later years of this period, consultants reinterpreted the ideas of academics like Argyris, McGregor and Likert. The turning-point for the United States and Europe came in the 1970s with the combined effects of the OPEC oil price rises, the Japanese challenge and the increasing political and social unrest.

The change was documented by many writers, none of whom became management gurus. The bringers of bad news are rarely rewarded. In this context one might mention Pascale and Athos (1982) who, while well known in academic circles, never achieved the popular acclaim or visibility of Peters and Waterman. Pascale and Athos might be termed 'pessimistic writers' in that they berated American industry and its managers for their failures and shortcomings. They pointed to Japan and suggested that US companies should adopt their practices. While such comments might have been valid, they were generally resented by those at whom they were directed. Few people enjoy having their faults pointed out. Pascale and Athos's book sold in respectable although not astronomical numbers.

William Ouchi's book, *Theory Z*, represented a middle-ground book. Published in 1981, he was an early-wave guru of the modern era. Ouchi was not at all pessimistic about America's ability to fight back economically. He referred to Japanese industry, and identified aspects of it which were easily exportable to the United States. He offered his Theory Z as a hybrid which contained the best elements of both Japanese and American practice. He pointed out that some US companies, such as Hewlett-Packard and IBM, were already performing excellently, and could provide models that other American corporations could emulate. Thus Ouchi was among the first to write about excellent companies and excellent performance.

Three books of the time sounded warning bells about threats to American economic dominance: William Ouchi's (1981) *Theory Z*, Robert Reich's (1984) *The Next American Frontier*, and Ken Auletta's (1984) *The Art of Corporate Success*. The landmark article on the theme was written by Robert Hayes and the late William Abernathy (1980). It appeared in the *Harvard Business Review* under the title 'Managing Our Way to Economic Decline'. These authors may have been perceived by many business management readers as prophets of doom. Americans do not generally like to come second in competition and are rarely satisfied with equal first. For this reason, these critical books were acknowledged, but were not huge sellers. It was Peters and Waterman who first provided the optimistic, up-beat message. They stressed that one did not have to look abroad to learn how to manage. Some of the greatest successes were American born and bred.

Before discussing each of the three sub-schools of guru theory in more detail, it is appropriate to make a few general points. First, modern (post-war) management ideas in general, and guru theory in particular, are American inventions. In terms of management textbooks, teaching materials and empirical research on management topics, the United States holds an unassailable position. Thus, the phenomenon which is being described in this section is American in origin. By comparison, the non-American contributions to guru theory have been negligible. This does not imply that the value and worth of European contributions is any less. It is rather that they have failed to achieve a widespread visibility throughout the world. Guru theory as a phenomenon is made-in-America, for consumption in America, but is also available for export to Europe and any other parts of the world which might buy it.

Second, as a result of this, all the top-ranking management gurus, academic, consultant and hero-managers are Americans, No British business school can claim to have a faculty member to match the international status or financial rewards of its North American counterparts. The only European consultant who has achieved any sort of international reputation is Edward de Bono, who is best known for his books and seminars on lateral thinking.

Some observers attribute the absence of any major British academic gurus to British managers' preferences to learn from practical experience, either their own or that of other managers. Reg Revans, the British writer most closely associated with the learning-from-experience approach called Action Learning, has established a reputation among British management development experts, if not among managers themselves. Revans and de Bono differ from their American counterparts in at least one important way.

Whereas the American gurus offer a *content message* ('use this leadership style, motivate people this way'), the British gurus focus on how managers can learn from their experience or use their brains more creatively. Thus they offer a *learning process message*.

In Britain there are comparatively fewer opportunities for guru exposure. The United States has countless business seminars and conventions. Prominent celebrities can go on this 'mashed-potato' circuit. There are of course management seminars in Britain, run by organizations such as *The Economist*, the Confederation of British Industry (CBI) and the British Institute of Management (BIM). However, with a few exceptions, these tend to feature fellow managers as presenters. It is rare for a British management academic to be the keynote speaker at a management conference, whereas American management academics appear regularly at their equivalent events. Some management seminars have only practising managers as speakers (with no academics in sight). For example, one of the largest annual meetings of personnel and training personnel in Britain takes place in Harrogate and is organized by the Institute of Personnel Management (IPM). The contribution of such business academics rarely exceeds 10 per cent. *Management Today* commented that British managers believed that:

> lessons are best learned from practical experience, your own, and that of other people. The view that managers learn more from each other than from teachers is perhaps one reason for the extraordinary dearth of leading lights in the academic teaching world. No business school [in Britain] can point to any one 'guru' whose ideas are particularly influential; the ideas themselves seem to be old ones reformulated, the difference from previous years being in the methods by which they are taught.
>
> (*Management Today* 1985: 73)

It appears that the production of gurus, whether academic, consultant or hero-managers, requires a collaboration between two parties. First, there needs to be a supply of people who are willing to put themselves up for stardom. For example, some management academics such as Blanchard and Herzberg have promoted their ideas through public seminars and training films, while Iacocca and Kiam have advertised their own companies and products in television commercials. Second, the book-buying public and the conference-going management community must be willing to support such activities. The Americans do seem to be willing to support such a process while the British do not. On the business seminar and conference circuit the top management speakers can command the top appearance fees $25,000 and over. A British pop star working in the United States commented on television that US audiences conspired to make anyone successful, while in Britain the opposite was true. Perhaps there is also a cultural aspect to this point.

Finally, one can add the point made by Rein *et al.* (1987) about the existence of a supporting media machine. While film stars, television 'personalities' and sports stars feed their stories to a hungry media (and thereby attain continuing self-publicity and self-promotion), academics and business leaders do not have that same support. Such business guru support as there is, is stronger in the United States than in Britain.

All gurus offer some form of reassurance to their readers. In an uncertain world, managers seek such reassurance. They want to know that if they only imitate these marvellous men and adopt their management recipes, they can overcome the most difficult management challenge. All the gurus gain their currency from their relevance to the changing times. Despite the fact that deep down, most managers may know that there are no universal rules of success (otherwise they would have been found by now), they nevertheless continue to seek out, and perhaps overvalue, examples of perceived success.

The inspirational value of the guru texts should also not be underestimated either. The books extol the virtues of the managers deemed to be responsible for corporate success. America's business champions are presented and accorded heroic qualities. They are elevated, even if temporarily, to the position of role models. Successful entrepreneurs such as Mark McCormack give readers tips on how to stay one step ahead of the competition. The message of the guru texts is that everyone can be a winner, if they only try.

The three sub-schools of guru theory distinguished are labelled academic, consultant and hero-manager. Anthropologists have traditionally distinguished between *medicine men* (whose power and wisdom was claimed to be based upon a specific body of knowledge that they possessed) and *sorcerers* (who were held to have superhuman qualities). Following this classification, one would place academics and most management consultants in the medicine man category, and locate the hero-managers in the other.

ACADEMIC GURU SCHOOL

The definition of an academic guru is someone who, while occupying a position at an educational institution, has developed and popularized his or her ideas on some aspect of management. Thus Kenneth Blanchard, who has been a professor of leadership and organizational behaviour at the University of Amherst in Massachusetts, and who is joint author of *The One Minute Manager* (Blanchard and Johnson 1983), is among the best known and one of the highest earning academic gurus in the United States. His topic is management leadership which is very general and therefore has a wide appeal.

Most academic gurus specialize in particular fields. During the strategic planning vogue of the 1970s, Igor Ansoff was considered to be the leading

Table 2.4 Academic gurus

Academic	Book	Year of publication
Kotler, Philip (Northwestern University)	Marketing Management	1967
Porter, Michael (Harvard Business School)	Competitive Advantage	1985
Kanter, Rosabeth (Harvard Business School)	The Change Masters	1985
Mintzberg, Henry (McGill University)	Nature of Managerial Work	1973
Blanchard, Kenneth (University of Amherst)	The One Minute Manager	1983

academic guru on the subject. During the 1960s and 1970s a small elite of academics working in the field of organizational development were the leaders in this field, for example, Warren Bennis, Gordon Lippitt and Richard Walton.

The contemporary scene reflects this continued specialization. Henry Mintzberg (McGill University) wrote about strategy formulation and business planning; Philip Kotler (Northwestern University) is an expert on market strategy; Michael Porter (Harvard Business School) is an expert on competitive advantage. A brief summary of some of these academic gurus is contained in Table 2.4.

Although many of these people act as consultants, and may run their own consultancy firms, what distinguishes academic gurus from the other two guru groups is their decision to remain in academic life. Despite this point, the academic guru category is the most difficult to conceptualize. As categories, the consultant gurus and the hero-managers are more self-contained. The classificatory difficulty stems from the fact that it is possible to divide academics who are 'academics' gurus' and those who are 'managers' gurus'. The categories tend to be mutually exclusive. Business management academics who might receive popular acclaim from management practitioners may be held in relatively low esteem by their academic peers. Conversely, those academics who were highly rated by their colleagues for the intellectual calibre of their researches and ideas, are often rejected by managers as too theoretical or abstract.

In recent years there has been a blurring of such boundaries. Academics such as Mintzberg, Kanter, Kotler and particularly Porter, all of whom are rated as first-class researchers by fellow academics, have also found a popular appeal among managers. In addition to publishing highly technical books, these writers have also been invited to present their ideas to meetings of managers. Are we therefore witnessing the development of a new type of academic guru? If so, what has changed to blur the division referred to earlier?

If this is indeed happening, it may be that as more managers complete MBA-type programmes, they become more sophisticated, and are able to understand and apply more complicated management ideas. Whether such an explanation is correct is difficult to test. One can probably make more progress by assuming that the American academics themselves have done something different from their predecessors to make their message appeal to two different audiences. Approached from this angle, one can test some of the ideas presented by Davis (1971).

Davis argued that in order to be interesting to the widest range of listeners, researchers needed to design the propositions to be communicated (based on their research findings) in a way that took account of the assumptions of their different audiences. Knowing that an audience would find interesting any proposition that attacked the assumptions it held about a topic, the guru needed first to identify and then publicly specify the assumptions about their topic (new technology, employee motivation, competitive advantage). The guru then needed to come up with a proposition that refuted them. There were, however, some complications.

While it was relatively easy to come up with a proposition that refuted an audience assumption, it was usually difficult to specify precisely what this potentially deniable audience assumption was. The reason for this was that the assumption was not necessarily a unitary thing. The audience frequently divided itself into segments. The most important of these were those who held a *common-sense assumption* about a topic (usually managers), and those whose assumptions were *conditioned by the intellectual speciality* of their discipline (usually fellow academics). Berger and Luckman (1967) made this distinction between laymen possessing conventional wisdom on the one hand and experts possessing esoteric knowledge on the other. Further sub-divisions were likely to exist but the guru's task was to produce propositions which refuted assumptions on as wide a scale as possible. It may be possible to explain the across-the-board success of the new-wave academic gurus in terms of their ability to identify and differently refute the different assumptions of their two main audiences – managers and fellow academics. Their predecessors were either unable or unwilling to do this.

CONSULTANT GURU SCHOOL

The second category of gurus are the consultants. Perhaps the best known consultant guru is the Austrian-born Peter Drucker. Descriptions of his

Table 2.5 Consultant gurus

Consultant	Book	Year of publication
Drucker, Peter	The Practice of Management	1954
Blake, Robert, and Mouton, Jane	The Managerial Grid	1964
Kepner, Charles, and Tregoe, Benjamin	The Rational Manager	1965
de Bono, Edward	Lateral Thinking for Management	1971
Crosby, Philip	Quality is Free	1979
Peters, Tom, and Waterman, Robert	In Search of Excellence	1982
Naisbitt, John	Megatrends	1982
Deal, Terrence and Kennedy, Allan	Corporate Cultures	1982
McKenna, Regis	The Regis Touch	1985
Goldratt, Eli, and Cox, John	The Goal	1989
Pinchot, Gifford	Intrapreneuring	1985
Deming, W. Edwards	Out of the Crisis	1986

influence on western management thought (that is, American management thought) dwell on the breadth and depth of his knowledge and upon his ability to draw on and reconstruct the relevant parts of his knowledge store into a form that can help managers. This is an excellent description of a medicine man in the traditional anthropological context.

In a unique article entitled 'Why Read Peter Drucker?', Kantrow (1980) referred to Drucker's rigour of formulation and his encyclopedic knowledge of management and related fields. In the eyes of his supporters, Drucker has the ability to offer in-depth analysis of situations and to relate different ideas and facts to each other. While modern consultant gurus like Tom Peters may acknowledge their debt to him, Drucker may be said to be the leading Old Testament prophet, even though his influence is far from being on the wane. His books continue to be reprinted and they sell steadily. His progress has been steady and regular. He therefore contrasts sharply with the meteoric rise (and fall) of some of the modern gurus. Despite his more recent contributions which have dealt with Japan and entrepreneurship, in many managers' eyes, Drucker is still primarily associated with the rationalist view of management and organizations.

Despite espousing the Theory Y management style, Drucker advocated that managers *made* (rather than encouraged) people to become productive. He is traditionally identified with the notion of the large industrial corporation occupying the centre of society. This gives him a top-down image which is less fashionable in the world of the 1990s which is seeking to stimulate entrepreneurial innovation and trying to manage joint ventures and strategic alliances. If Drucker is an Old Testament consultant guru, who are the New Testament ones? Table 2.5 offers some suggestions.

HERO-MANAGER GURU SCHOOL

Hero-managers constitute the third type of management guru. They are the successful chief executive officers (CEOs) who have committed their thoughts to print. In the analogy being used, they are the sorcerers rather than the medicine men. The rise in the popularity of the hero-managers might be explained by the need of the reading managers for gossip or their optimistic belief that they too could do well if they learned the tricks. Chapter 5 examines the evidence for the proposition that managers constantly seek unorthodox sources of power and knowledge and that they are eager to listen to those who have developed their own approach to ensure their own salvation through profit.

The hero-manager's approach is not based on research, study or consultancy experience. It is developed from learning-from-experience. Its authority comes directly from success. By distilling the essence of what successful managers do (irrespective of context) it is believed that the secrets of success can be revealed. Thus, it is the hero-manager (there are few women) who is held to possess this supernatural force. Their guidance is on offer. That same guidance, if offered by a lower being, would not carry the same force. As will be shown, most of the 'spells' contained in the books of hero-managers can be found in any popular management guide. They tend to be of the 'treat people well and they will work hard' variety. The difference comes from the person who writes down or utters the words. Because that person has been the chief executive of a major multinational corporation, those words are held to possess magical qualities.

There are two types of hero-manager books. These are the multi-biographical ones shown in Table 2.6 and the quasi-autobiographical shown in Table 2.7. The prevalence of the former in Britain may reflect the lack of British managers capable of being elevated to hero status or their reluctance to commit their thoughts to paper. In the past, some potential British hero-managers such as Sir Ernest Saunders, Gerald Ronson and Asil Nadir have embarrassingly fallen from grace.

The problem of having managers as heroes is that hero-status depends not on one-off achievement, but upon the ongoing health and prosperity of the company. This may be outside of the control of that manager. Whereas consultants and academics can move in and out of companies, hero-managers have their future linked with one organization. In Britain, the majority of CEOs in well-performing companies have had a lower visibility than their US counterparts. In Germany too, chief executives are entreated to 'be outstanding but not to stand out'. In the introduction to their multi-biographical book on hero-managers, Ritchie and Goldsmith wrote that:

> the fate of British industry, the jobs of millions of people and the standard of living of the whole country rests in the hands of a few exceptional businessmen. . . . There have been some heroic struggles to overcome the problem pressing British companies towards bankruptcy. In every case, these desperate endeavours have been led and inspired by individuals. These are the men we call the New Elite.
>
> (Ritchie and Goldsmith 1987: 1)

The second type of hero-manager contribution is quasi-autobiographical. 'Quasi' because the successful businessman or manager, with the help of a named or unnamed ghost-writer (usually a journalist), recounts the secrets of his success and frequently uses the opportunity to include some of his own personal philosophy about life. This genre of managerial literature has a long tradition. The earliest form of it was produced by the Frenchman, Henri Fayol in 1916. In that year, the *Bulletin de la Société de l'Industrie Minérale* printed Fayol's *Administration Industrielle et Generale*. Indeed, as Pugh (1984) has pointed out, despite producing a range of writings, Fayol's reputation rests on a single monograph which is frequently printed as a book.

Having retired after thirty years from the job of Managing Director of the metallurgical combine Commentary – Fourchambault – Decazeville, Fayol wrote down his definition of management, and the principles of how to manage. He thus occupies the first place in a line of authors who have done exactly these two things. Each has expressed their view or vision of management. They have emphasized their particular understanding of what is important. Having done so, they frequently itemize the steps to be taken or principles to be adhered to, in order to fulfil that vision. At one end of this time continuum is Henri Fayol, while at the other are Jan Carlzon, John Harvey-Jones and Lee Iacocca.

One should perhaps just notice a trend in this literature. As one progresses through to the present day, the general emphasis of these types of books is towards stressing the individual and his own qualities and contributions. By contrast, Fayol focused on the nature of the managerial task as he saw it. Alfred Sloan in his book, *My Years with General Motors*, did not write about himself but about the history of the corporation of which he was an architect. Some recent quasi-autobiographical texts are shown in Table 2.7.

Table 2.6 Hero-managers: multi-biographical texts

Author	Book	Year of publication	Hero-managers discussed
de Bono, E.	*Tactics: The Art and Science of Success*	1986	David Bailey Chris Bonnington Mike Brearly Terence Conran Harold Evans Hans Eysenck Lord Forte Heather Jenner Verity Lambert Mark McCormack Robert Maxwell Peter Parker Clive Sinclair Jackie Stewart Virginia Wade
Robinson, J.	*The Risk Takers: Portraits of Money, Ego and Power*	1985	Richard Branson Terence Conran James Hanson Ashraf Marwan Robert Maxwell Asil Nadir Ian Postgate Paul Raymond Tiny Roland Gerald Ronson Jacob Rothschild The Roux Brothers Clive Sinclair David Thieme Gordon White
Carlisle, E.	*Mac – Managers Talk About Managing People*	1985	MacCallum MacCormack MacDuff MacGuffy MacIntosh
Kay, W.	*Tycoons: Where They Come From and How They Made it*	1985	Nigel Brockes Terence Conran Michael Golder Harry Goodman James Gulliver John Gunn Noel Lister Robert Maxwell Gerald Ronson Clive Sinclair David Thompson Mark Weinburg

Table 2.6 Continued

Author	Book	Year of publication	Hero-managers discussed
Ritchie, B. and Goldsmith, W.	*The New Elite*	1987	Michael Edwardes John Egan Stanley Grinstead John Harvey-Jones Christopher Hogg Trevor Holdsworth Colin Marshall David Paistow Peter Walters
Peters, T. J. and Austin, N.	*Passion for Excellence*	1982	Don Burr Jan Carlzon Bill Creech Max DePree Bill Gore Stew Leonard Tom Melohn Tom Monaghan William Schaffer Len Stepanelli Bob Swiggett Les Wexner

The primary attraction of the hero-manager literature, whether multi-biographical or quasi-autobiographical, is as an exemplar. The management readers of these books appreciate that their authors have 'been there and seen it'. They have been through the swamp and come out, perhaps a little scathed, on the other side. Analysing John Harvey-Jones' BBC series *Troubleshooter*, *The Economist* (1990) attributed its success to the fact that it ignored numbers, filtered work and the challenge of management through one eccentric personality, and depicted companies through the people who worked for them (and not just their bosses or balance sheets). All this displayed ideas and problems with which viewers felt familiar. Best-selling management books have done something similar.

Second, the publishing houses have realized that they can sell business books by the hundreds of thousands if they create a market for them. They have therefore been developing ever more effective ways of marketing the CEOs and their books. Why do people buy these books in such numbers? Writing about the great and the good is a time-honoured tradition which is not restricted to managers or businesspeople. The managers who wrote their books had in most cases reached celebrity status before their publication. Thus they merely took their place alongside the TV and film stars,

Table 2.7 Hero-managers: quasi-autobiographical texts

Author	Book	Year of publication	Organization described
Townsend, P.	*Up the Organization*	1971	Avis
Edwardes, M.	*Back from the Brink*	1984	British Leyland
Geneen, H.	*Managing*	1985	ITT
Ash, M. K.	*Mary Kay on People Management*	1984	Mary Kay Cosmetics
McCormack, M.	*What They Don't Teach You at the Harvard Business School*	1984	International Management Group
Kiam, V.	*Going for it: How to Succeed as an Entrepreneur*	1987	Remington
Morita, A.	*Made in Japan*	1987	Sony
Harvey-Jones, John	*Making it Happen*	1988	ICI
Trump, D.	*Trump: The Art of the Deal*	1987	
Iacocca, L.	*Iacocca: An Autobiography*	1985	Ford and Chrysler

politicians, pop stars and members of royal families, whose biographies and autobiographies have always sold well.

Lee Iacocca's autobiography has now outsold even Peters and Waterman's book, *In Search of Excellence*. This can be partly explained by the fact that few of the most senior executives of America's largest corporations have appeared 63 times on television advertising their company's products or have been seen in 93 per cent of households in the United States. Moreover, few people have lived through the boardroom battles that Iacocca did. Thus, his high book sales are at least partly due to the high level of public visibility that he has achieved during his career.

If guru theory was the staple diet of the 1980s, what will be the theme of the 1990s? Storm (1990) reported that organizations like the Bank of England, British Gas, Ernst & Whinney, Mars, and Legal & General were sending their executives to be taught how to do the Whirling Dervish Dance, so as to allow these top managers to find their 'core of inner peace, and so increase their business potential'. This holistic approach to business seeks to blend the inner directed focus of the 1970s neo-human relations ideas, with the hard-nosed, profit-focused theme of the 1980s. The aim it

"My problem was I kept reading books on leadership and excellence and management when I should have been working."

Source: Harvard Business Review, May–June, no. 3, 1987, p. 91

seems is to produce *spiritual warriors*, and the label given to this activity is *new age training* (NAT).

Writing from the American perspective, Rose (1990) observed that the new age paradigm presents a new way of looking at the world, and stimulates new behaviours. The old world view, built upon Newtonian physics, is seen as mechanistic and overly analytical. The new paradigm draws upon quantum physics, cybernetics, chaos theory, cognitive science, and eastern and western spiritual traditions which view everything as interconnected. Reality is not seen as absolute, as a by-product of human consciousness. In the United States, a new age think-tank, Global Business Network, is underwritten by companies such as AT&T, Volvo, Nissan and Inland Steel. In addition, Proctor & Gambol and Du Pont are offering their employees personal growth experiences to spur them on to creativity, encourage learning, and promote 'ownership' of company results.

The Esalen Institute, located at Big Sur in California, and out of fashion since the self-aware 1970s, is planning to play a major role in new age training (Rose 1990). Following the precepts of *aikido*, the emphasis is on harmony rather than dominance. Esalen is back in business offering a new menu of techniques from stress reduction to creativity enhancement. The personal growth thinkers who, in the 1960s, would have avoided all organizations for fear of contamination, now view them as living laboratories in which to try out their ideas.

Some of the NAT recommendations do not differ greatly from the management guru ideas of the 1980s. Flexible, less hierarchical organizations, empowered workers taking their own decisions, and global thinking replacing national horizons in a borderless world. NAT is underpinned by the notion that reorganization and automation has its limits, and that productivity leaps are achieved only through winning the hearts and minds of employees.

So, is new age thinking new? Tichy (Rose 1990) wrote of NAT that no one element of it was new, but that attention to the soft issues of management was new to American multinationals. Given the attention paid by guru writers like Peters and Waterman (1982) and Deal and Kennedy (1982) to the soft (human) issues from the early 1960s, one can challenge Tichy's assessment. The antecedents of NAT lie elsewhere and concern the exploration of the inner self rather than the social role.

In the mid-1960s, research by Agor (1986) revealed the part played by intuition in management decision-making. The theme was developed in *Financial Times* articles (Dixon 1988), and perhaps achieved academic respectability when studies by the International Management Development Institute (IMD) confirmed the extent of the use of intuition (Dixon 1989). What Agor called *intuition*, the IMD researchers labelled *vision*. It is partly this mental ability to piece together the various notions which have not previously been combined, that new age training seeks to develop through dancing, medicine wheels, and the use of the *I Ching*. The IMD is now running courses to help managers use their intuition to better effect. Thus, what is new about NAT is its focus on human consciousness, and its link to organizational performance. Jack Welch, CEO of General Electric, said that he wanted people rewarded 'in both the pocket and the soul'.

The new elements come by adding creativity and intuition to numerical analysis in order to aid decision-making; recognizing love and caring as a workplace motivator; and placing the mental and spiritual enrichment of employees alongside the pursuit of profit as a valid enterprise goal. In Britain, one company which offers new age training is called Decision Development. In the words of one of its partners, 'We are not dealing merely with minds and techniques, but with the spiritual, emotional and creative aspects of clients' (Storm 1990: 28). The company also uses the American Indian Medicine Wheel (*International Management* 1991) to take managers on a journey to discover their spiritual, emotional and creative self. The wheel allegedly enables trainees to access their inner selves by examining their dreams and fantasies. In addition to dancing and medicine wheels, new age training uses an inward focused version of outdoor activities which involve mythical quests of the 'Dungeons and Dragons'

Source: *Financial Times*, 28 March 1989, p. 28

variety (*International Management* 1991) where managers dress as druids and witches to find a magic elixir to revive a dying dragon child.

Thynne (1991) reported that TV-am, a British breakfast television station, had adopted a new age strategy in its effort to regain its franchise when these were to be auctioned. Mr Bruce Gyngell, the company's Australian chairman, was reported to be a supporter of American personal growth therapies. At a personal growth seminar and development workshop, the staff of the station were invited to focus their spiritual energy and inner peace. This collective consciousness-raising event sought to achieve a renewal, not only of the participants themselves, but also of the television franchise. Unfortunately for TV-am, this process of renewal did not extend to the company's franchise. In late 1991, it was announced that its bid had failed and Sunrise TV had won the breakfast television franchise.

New age training is also run internally by companies. IBM's 'Fit for the Future' seminars introduce employees to the *I Ching*, a Chinese divinatory oracle and fortune-telling exercise. It is claimed that it links internal intuition with external events. IBM's manager of employee development was quoted as saying that, 'It helps employees understand themselves better' (*International Management*, 1991: 44).

Some versions of new age training are controversial. The Scottish Office sent thousands of its employees on a 'New Age Thinking' course run by Louis Tice of the Pacific Institute, which aimed to train the minds of workers to make them 'high performance people' in their work and private lives. Some US workers objected to being exposed to this sort of training and sued their employers. The US Federal Equal Employment Opportunity Commission decreed that under the Civil Rights Act, employees were free not to participate in motivational training if it conflicted with their religious beliefs.

As examples of a progression in management ideas, NAT ideas collectively represent a new, challenging and potentially threatening paradigm for managers and organizations. The proposed approach replaces numerically based, top-down, hierarchically based control by professional managers, with a model that puts customers and employees at the centre of a network structure which emphasizes interconnectedness. The research data from this study would predict that, given the elements of new age thinking, at best it will be paid lip-service to (much discussion and espousement to camouflage a lack of fundamental change), while at worst it will be quickly discarded for the next fad. However, Francis Kinsman, founder of Business Networks and hence someone with an investment in its continued success, was quoted as saying that 'Before long, the spiritual and mystical will penetrate the business world. Business will discover that it's profitable to love your neighbour' (Storm 1990).

© Pettie & Taylor, 1990. Alex appears in *The Daily Telegraph*.

Chapter 3

Recurring themes

INTRODUCTION

In the previous chapter, the six most popular families of management ideas were introduced, and each was described briefly. An analysis of each of these reveals certain recurring features which can partly account for their popularity among managers. Three major themes were identified, each with its own set of characteristics.

Main theme	Constituent characteristics
Understanding of work world	• communicability • individual focus • malleable human nature
Status enhancement	• legitimation or self-affirmation • unitary perspective • contribution-ownership potential • leadership focus
Practical application	• control • steps or principles • universal application • authorization • applicability

While only three of the six management idea families possessed all twelve features described, each had the majority of them. These attributes are interdependent, complementary and overlapping. Let us consider them in more detail.

UNDERSTANDING OF WORK WORLD

The first recurring theme to be found in popular management ideas is that they help managers understand better the world of work. *Understanding* refers to elements of the idea which make it easy for managers to get to grips with it. It has three components. *Communicability* refers to the management idea being easily understood initially by the managers, and then by those to whom managers have to explain it. *Individual focus* means that the idea both explains employee conduct and recommends action in terms of individual behaviour. Finally, *malleable human nature* denotes that the idea contains a clear statement about the nature of human beings as people who are both basically good, and capable of being changed. These three aspects of understanding will be examined in turn.

Communicability

Communicability refers to the idea's ease of understanding. Managers have to deal with an increasing complex world. They have difficulty understanding excessively technical language; have a short span of attention; a limited span of memory and judgement; and tend to be more convinced by certain modes of communication than others. Popular management ideas take these limitations into account.

Popular management ideas possess clarity of communication and minimize technical jargon while, at the same time, avoiding obviousness. Watson (1980) argued that many managers looked to social scientists for simple prescriptions, panaceas and formulae. But for scientists to offer these in simple straightforward terms would raise suspicion. For this reason 'magic words' had to be used which required managers to use a little (although not a great deal) of effort to 'unwrap' the idea-parcel. This process of unpacking encouraged managers to feel that they had achieved something of significance. It gave them a feeling of participation and ownership.

Hence, a degree of mystification is in order, and is achieved by the use of either acronyms or relabelling. Acronyms are popular in management (MBO, SWOT, JIT, TQM, LBO, SPC, MBWA). They give a pseudo-scientific precision to commonplace observations and make them appear at once sociologically profound and wittily dismissive. In a similar way, the renaming of complex processes and concepts makes them more widely available for general consumption. Berne's (1964) Transactional Analysis (TA) offered its users the opportunity to play around with a new and fanciful vocabulary.

Since many managers have relatively short spans of attention, due partly to the nature of their work, the popular ideas are short and sharp and can be easily grasped. Network researchers at MTV, the US satellite television music station, suggest that the current optimum US attention span is sixteen minutes (Lyttle 1991). Other writers have put the figure lower for non-music television. Garner (1989) wrote about the 'Three-Minute Culture' which was the average amount of time that the average American viewer watched a TV programme before switching channels. It is also the length of a pop single; longer than a British commercial break for adverts; and much longer than most news items. Garner speculated that as the volume of information available to us increases, only a mind that works in three-minute bleeps will be able to deal with it. Perhaps popular management ideas will come in three-minute explanational bleeps.

Turning to span of memory and judgement, Miller (1956) identified a number of constraints on human information processing. He referred to the *span of immediate memory* which, for many different test materials, appeared to be about seven items. He also discussed the *span of absolute judgement* that could distinguish up to seven categories. These imposed severe limitations on the amount of information that humans were able to receive, process and remember.

Many well-known psychologists argue that the ability to think and process information is influenced by the way in which the human brain works. The key characteristics of information processing is the brain's serial mode of operation (processing only a few symbols at a time); its finite nature; and the fact that the symbols being processed are changed in limited memory structures whose content itself can rapidly be modified (Simon 1969: 52–3).

In order to deal with a complex environment, managers simplified things. They did this by allowing only some information to penetrate (*specialization*), by blocking access to information (*isolation*) and by using mottoes, rules-of-thumb, heuristics, concepts and hierarchies of concepts (*simplification*). The information received was organized simultaneously into several dimensions, sequences of units or chunks. It was recoded by taking different input events, grouping them, applying a new name to the group, and then remembering the new name rather than the original input events. The number of variables and relationships proposed must be adequate to comprehend the complexity of the problem. The popular management ideas manage not to go beyond the manager's information-processing capacity.

What about preferred communication modes? How do different communication formats influence managers? People do not live by pie-charts alone, or indeed by bar-graphs or three-inch statistical appendices to 300-page reports. People live, reason and are moved by symbols and stories. Much has been written about ex-President Reagan's talent as a story-teller. Even his most stalwart supporters often blushed at the gap between statistical reality and this chosen story. Researchers attest to the power of stories.

In the beginning was the word, and it was spoken, not written. Ever since then, people have been telling stories. For thousands of years, it was through the medium of stories that knowledge was passed on. It was the story-teller who was the chief teacher and entertainer. Not surprisingly, 'story-telling' is deeply ingrained in the human subconscious. As a way of grasping reality, it predates written and rational thought by many millennia. No wonder therefore that managers respond so positively to the presence of a story-teller like Tom Peters.

Yorks and Whitsett (1985) commented on the attractiveness to managers of the case study or case history. This generated a vicarious experience in managers enabling them to internalize the results of the research project. It gave them a concrete demonstration of the feasibility of the proposed principles. The transfer of knowledge to the real world application was seemingly established in a setting with which managers could identify. The field report study invited oversimplification, both by the nature of its data and by the 'believability' of its tone.

Tversky and Kahneman (1974) referred to the concept of 'representativeness' (being influenced by vignettes that were whole and made sense in themselves). The consequences of representativeness were that managers did not pay attention to prior outcomes (history did not move us as much as a good current anecdote); they were hopeless about sample size, finding small samples as convincing as large samples (sometimes more!); if two events vaguely coexisted, they leapt to conclusions about causality; and managers reasoned with simple decision rules (in a complex world they placed emphasis on gut-feeling).

Popular management ideas are not greatly concerned with establishing causality, since this is not important for managers. They limit the number of variables or dimensions they present, and offer seemingly simple solutions. Their authors wrap them up in acronyms or relabel them, to give them a spurious legitimacy and the opportunity for managers to 'unwrap' them. They 'chunk' information by pre-coding it, and communicate through stories, cases and anecdotes rather than statistical analyses or reports. Let us now relate this to the popular management ideas.

Managers could easily understand the principles of bureaucracy. They comprehended the notion of rules, regulations and the idea of categorizing employees. The big message was the importance of the division of tasks in order to increase predictability of behaviour, speed up skill development, and facilitate the surveillance and evaluation of staff. Managers appreciated that, in attempting to control outside influences, the bureaucratic organization sought to stabilize and routinize its own processes in the interests of internal efficiency.

Taylor's scientific management principles were also easily understood by the practising manager and the management student alike. Grounded in work-analysis and time-and-motion study, the fundamentals of scientific management are both easily communicated and have a face-validity. While the more sophisticated and elaborate elements may be more obscure, the basic core ideas are easily grasped.

Being developed and promoted by managers and management consultants, the principles of administrative management were clearly understood by the managers at whom they were directed. Few appeared either to notice their contradictary nature or, if they did, seemed capable of explaining it away to themselves. Each principle was specific and unequivocal. Their appeal lay in their having been developed out of management practice.

Human relations ideas too were easily grasped by managers. This was due both to the limited number of key ideas offered, and to the fact that the teachings of Mary Parker Follett and Mayo were interpreted by managers as saying that the 'human side of management' involved, in essence, a process of personal persuasive leadership. British management writers of the 1930s were already coming to interpret Follett in terms similar to the recommendations of the Mayo scheme. Indeed, according to Child (1969b), the whole continuity of human relations in British management thought was expressed far more in terms of recommended managerial methods, than in the finer points of conceptual analysis. It was this continuity at the level of technique which helps to explain how management thought was so readily able to absorb the ideas expressed in such diverse values as those of the Quaker employers, Mary Parker Follett and Elton Mayo.

The high level of communicability of neo-human relations ideas accounts for a large element of their popularity among past and present managers, and indeed by business school academics. In discussing Maslow's idea as it applied to organizations, Watson wrote that:

> It undoubtedly has some basic credibility with those who read it – or read brief accounts of it in textbooks – as the hierarchy turned into a simple triangular diagram must have been drawn up on the blackboards of tens of thousands of management lectures and seminars over the years, not to mention possibly hundreds of thousands of essays and examination scripts submitted by students of business and management.
>
> (Watson 1986: 107)

McGregor's ideas have been presented as a stereotyped scheme of how managers tend to think about employee motivation, offered in a simplistic formulation. The issue is often presented as making a simple choice between a Theory X and a Theory Y style of management. The universality of the scheme is related to its application irrespective of the specific work being done by the particular group of employees involved. This greatly assisted in its communicability. In discussing Herzberg, Hackman and Oldham stated that:

> In sum, what the Herzberg theory does, and does well, is point attention directly to the considerable significance of the *work itself* as a factor in the ultimate motivation and satisfaction of employees. And because the message of the theory is simple, persuasive and directly relevant to the design and evaluation of actual organizational changes, the theory continues to be widely known and generally used by managers.
>
> (Hackman and Oldham 1980: 58)

Guru theory, in contrast, has relied as much on *how* something was said, as on *what* was said. The book, the conference presentation, the audio-cassette, the video and the in-company seminar, have all been part of the message, and have supported each other. Despite his depth of thought, Drucker said that he always tried to express himself simply in order to be effective. His ideas had 'one moving part'. There is a contradiction here, however. He offered his audiences 'mind packages' (such as his five rules for effective acquisition) and at the same time criticized modern management gurus who make things too simple and easy (Kantrow 1980).

Drucker's reputation, and that of consultants like him, has rested heavily on their ability to communicate. This was a point which has not been missed by the modern gurus such as Blanchard and Johnson. Blanchard discovered that managers generally read only the first chapter of any book, and so wrote a one-chapter book – *The One Minute Manager* (Blanchard and Johnson 1983). Thomas (1989) analysed it and explained that it was written in the form of a short story modelled upon the style of the parable. It used generous dialogue and concepts from behaviour modification theory which had been ruthlesssly boiled down and renamed. Positive reinforcement became 'catching people doing things right'. The book contained no arguments to support the prescriptions offered and was designed to be skimmed.

Managers reject flavourless textbook prose, preferring the stylistic and intellectual simplicity of *The One Minute Manager*. The book scored highly on ease-of-readability. It was simply written, high in human interest, full of short sentences, words with few syllables, many personal pronouns, and contained a great deal of simulated dialogue. While guru books like *In Search of Excellence*, *Megatrends* and *Theory Z* are not in the same category, they do share many similarities with *The One Minute Manager*. De Bono communicates through the use of lateral thinking examples and exercises. Ohmae's message in his *The Mind of the Strategist* is graspable in a single sentence – to survive companies must become insiders in the so-called triad community of Europe, Japan and the USA.

The text of *The One Minute Manager* was particularly interesting, said Thomas. It was both a story and pseudo-allegorical. It was a story because the technical information which it communicated to the reader was presented in short story form. The fictional narrative occupied just over 100 loosely packed pages, while its layout and form conveyed to the reader the impression of a short story. The continuity was broken by the periodical insertion of checklists and plaques. The latter consisting of brief aphorisms displayed on an otherwise blank page ('Share it with others').

The book was only *pseudo*-allegorical since, while it might have carried a second meaning as well as that of the surface story. Thomas claimed that there was no evidence of any second meaning, and the text was in fact intended to be read at no more than surface level. The literary form, while unusual, is not unique. Ritti and Funkhouser (1987) wrote an organizational behaviour text which at first glance appeared to be a book of short stories. One can speculate that the adoption of this literary form made the text easy to read for the manager. This is what the endorsements said. The style serves to differentiate it from the other popular management books.

The communication style of many of these gurus is propagandist, designed to have an effect, to persuade. They do not so much explore ideas as sell them. Witt and Ireland (1987) claimed that Peters and Waterman's work was one of advocacy rather than of science. Like their predecessors, the neo-human relations school, Peters and Waterman's ideas have left science a long way behind, and have rapidly acquired the status of a social philosophy or quasi-religion.

The quasi-religious messages that the gurus hope to promote offer great potential for charismatic delivery. Of course, not all such presenters take advantage of this opportunity, and some even succeed despite (rather than because) of their presentations. The great orators have all been salesmen, believing in their product and selling it hard. The presenters are overcome by a belief in themselves. It is this belief which speaks so persuasively, so miracle-like, to the audience. In contrast, scientific presentations are by their nature low key. Propositions are stated, with the evidence for and against them. These are weighed and a conclusion is drawn. For this reason, the content of a guru message will have a greater impact on an audience than a scientifically focused one. This is the result of the different presentation potentials offered. The issue of presentation is so important that Chapter 7 will be devoted to a consideration of it.

The hugely successful book, *In Search of Excellence* (Peters and Waterman 1982), contains examples of the communication devices that have been described. At the outset, the reader learns of the distillation of the seven important variables of excellence. These are too numerous to achieve a maximum impact, but nevertheless are just within the capacity of short-term memory. The seven variables are re-labelled so that they all begin with the letter 'S', and thus represent the McKinsey 7-S framework which conveniently doubles as a logo (see Figure 3.1).

Peters and Waterman wrote:

> Anthony Athos at the Harvard Business School gave us the courage to do it that way, urging that without the memory hooks provided by alliteration, our stuff was just too hard to explain, too easily forgetable.
> (Peters and Waterman 1982: 9)

In an audio-tape on the subject of excellence, Peters informed the audience that, after practice, he could label and explain all seven concepts in sixty seconds. He does in fact do this, hardly pausing for breath. Modern guru theory may thus be nearer show business (edutainment?) or to some form of religious experience. Tom Peters is regularly referred to as a 'management evangelist'.

The more effective the marketing of an idea is, the better the logo, the more memorable the saws, then the less likely it is that the idea itself will be

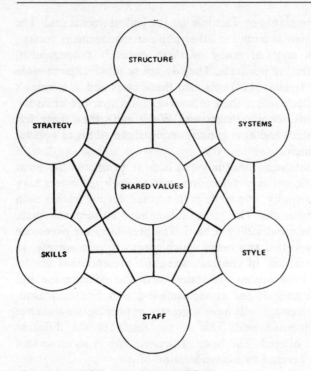

Figure 3.1 7-S framework (modified)
Source: McKinsey, 7-S Framework © in Peters and Waterman 1982: 10

deeply scrutinized by its readers or listeners (Anthony 1986). The 'excellence' literature continues a well-established tradition of not encouraging its readers to think for themselves. In *In Search of Excellence* (*ISOE*) Peters and Waterman demonstrated that they believed that the acronyms, logos and memory hooks were all necessary to the marketing of ideas to a managerial leadership who had serious intellectual difficulties to overcome. Whether any popular management writer has ever failed by underestimating the intellectual ability of his audience is not known. However, the *ISOE* formula of reducing ideas to easily remembered steps to success may have been a decisive factor in enticing such a large number of managers to read and discuss ideas which previously they had not considered to be particularly interesting. Carroll (1983) felt that it was the informal writing style of the authors which gave it appeal. Peters and Austin's (1985) sequel, *A Passion for Excellence*, carried the uncomplicated approach to 'practicality' a step further. This time the authors suggested that only four and not seven attributes of excellence had to be mastered in order for a firm to achieve great things. This number is much nearer the magic three figure and well within the capability of short-term memory. While this book may not have broken new ground, it did sell many copies.

When the sales of business books slow, they can be repackaged into audio-tapes or turned into executive training seminars. Bennis and Nanus's (1985) *Leaders: The Strategies for Taking Charge* sold 300,000 copies in hardback and paperback yet still failed to make the best-seller list for that year (Knowlton 1989). It was then recycled as a popular series of seminars that helped Harper & Row sell more copies of the book as well as audio-tape versions. Bernie Brillstein, the chairman of the Brillstein Group, has paid between $20,000 and $50,000 to option the film rights of Bruck's (1989) *The Predator's Ball* which chronicled the saga of Mike Milken and Drexel Burnham Lambert's junk bonds scandal.

Individual focus

Individual focus refers to the management idea addressing individual behaviour issues such as motivation, communication, personality and delegation. This is in contrast to focusing on abstract or macro-level issues such as organizational structure or technology. Salaman (1978) argued that among the morally sustaining ideas of organizations was that of *structuralism*. This held that the way in which organizations were structured was beyond choice and was instead the outcome of modern, scientific and rational principles and outside forces which were beyond everyone's control.

Since the structure of the organization was held to be given, any desired change had necessarily to take place in the behaviour of its members. The fondness of managers for individualistic folk psychology, which helps them to understand 'how people tick' is emphasized over the need to 'set up the right organization' (Watson 1977). When managers seek social science inputs from external management consultants, they prefer psychological rather than sociological models and solutions. Klein (1976) noted that the managers at Esso, whom she studied, tended to explain their problems in structural (sociological) terms but looked for solutions only in terms of personality (psychological) characteristics.

It appears that managers' 'natural' mode of explaining human behaviour is in psychological rather than sociological terms. It may have been this single fact that made organizational development (OD) so popular in the United States during the 1960s and 1970s. This preference is reflected in individually focused OD interventions, and a reluctance to change structures or alter organizational power relationships. Much OD activity involves fitting individual behaviour into an organizational plan.

Knowing the popularity of this individualistic orientation, aspiring gurus should present their ideas so as to suggest that changes in organizations are ultimately determined by modifications to employee behaviour through the application of different patented and packaged human relations cures. Huczynski and Buchanan (1982) commented on how managers looked for tools and techniques with which to 'repair' individual employees who manifested human relations problems. The majority of popular management ideas stress individual behaviour.

One popular idea that does not stress the individual is bureaucracy. Along with the other grand theories of organizational structure, bureaucracy ignores factors associated with individual behaviour. It thus distinguishes itself from the other ideas. Bureaucracy sees personnel as system-givens rather than as variables. They are viewed as inert instruments performing the tasks assigned to them. This feature of bureaucracy acts to differentiate it from other popular management idea families.

Scientific management, on the other hand, is a psychological-individual theory that focuses on individual behaviour and explains it in physiological and psychological terms. It is primarily a theory of line management, task organization, and supervision for greater efficiency, work measurement and incentives. Although matters concerning the choice of tools and the properties of materials figured prominently in Taylor's analyses, it was his work on shopfloor worker movements for which he is perhaps best remembered. This has now been labelled time-and-motion study. The control of individual performance was of prime importance to him. He defined management as knowing what one wanted people to do, and then seeing that they did it in the most efficient way.

Taylor's view of the individual workers was a low one. His observation of their 'systematic soldiering' indicated to him their 'natural instinct to take things easy'. This innate tendency of workers together with management's failure to design, allocate and plan scientifically, conspired to hold down production. Taylor did not see soldiering as a consequence of people's sociability. He felt that management should relate to each worker as an individual and satisfy his personal self-interest. Hence, his explanation of work behaviour was a psychologistic one (Watson 1980). Given the one-to-one relationship he envisaged, Taylor (1911) stressed the importance of interpersonal skills:

> No system of management, however good, should be applied in a wooden way. The proper personal relationships should always be maintained between the employers and men; and even the prejudices of the workmen should be considered in dealing with them.

Administrative management (along with bureaucracy) viewed organizational members as 'inert instruments performing the tasks assigned to them' (March and Simon 1958). It ignored individual motivation and people were viewed as a given, rather than as a variable in the system. The implication of this was that existing personnel could be easily removed. The capacities of people and machines depended on which machines were used and how the people were trained.

Human relations aimed to restore individuals with their needs and drives, to a central place from which Weberian bureaucracy and administrative management had removed them. Human relations tended to atomize the human relations in work groups by treating them as if they were attributes of individual group members. Consequently, it ignored the organized network of social relations that characterized group structures (Miller and Form 1964).

In some of Mayo's writings (Mayo 1949) there was a holistic perspective which sought to explain behaviour in terms of *society* rather than by reference to *human nature* or people's instincts. However, Mayo and his followers did encourage a psychologistic orientation and this is the one that has secured the greatest popularity and which continues to be written about and taught today. Mayo achieved this by emphasizing the importance of supervisory skills at the lower levels of the organization. The effect of this was to distract attention away from the issues of structural, technological or economic conflicts, and direct it towards the question of how to establish worker commitment.

In the end, the question of how individuals related to each other was held to be more important than the way in which their economic, social and task relationships were structured. Roethlisberger and Dickson (1964a) explained worker attitudes in terms of a complex systems model in which facts and sentiments were distinguished. This suggests that 'distorted' complaints by employees were signs of their social disequilibrium. The writers identified the spontaneous, unplanned, informal system, and argued that it was a maintenance or interference factor in both the personal and the organizational balance. This perpective emphasized the analysis of meaning at the level of the individual actor.

Since the grievances of workers were irrational and based on sentiments, management's job was to deal with the emotional and social needs of workers. If it was successful, it could hope to achieve increased output and harmonious working relationships. The key to understanding individual behaviour was held to lie in the way in which the informal group socialized its members into a particular set of norms and values. The human relations movement tried to find ways of increasing productivity by manipulating social factors.

Crudely summarized, if the group manipulated the individual in demonstrating certain group-supported behaviour (e.g. restriction of output), then it was legitimate for management to fight back. Mayo's research offered managers guidelines on how to influence individual behaviour so as to achieve management goals. The strategies included widening the individual's loyalty from the group so as to encompass the company as a whole. It involved replacing irrational and negative sentiments with positive ones.

Turning to neo-human relations (NHR) ideas, these all shared a psychological perspective in that they analysed occupational behaviour predominantly in terms of individual needs, satisfactions and motivations.

Research on employee motivation focused upon individuals in the here-and-now, as if it was meaningful to study them in isolation from the society within which their attitudes were formed. Nord (1974) commented on how organizational development (OD) strategies for planned change were 'strongly psychological; sociological perspectives on human nature seem to have been neglected'. Friedlander (1965) said that:

> the use of psychological theory to explain and understand employee motivations and values has generally been limited to the analysis of individual differences. . . . There has been limited concern with the influence of social location and social class upon the worker's value system.
>
> (Friedlander 1965)

The importance placed upon the individual perspective in NHR meant that it avoided the need for changes in structural arrangements and hence in power relationships within the organization. Yet, despite its focus on individual needs, NHR did imply the need for structural modifications. Herzberg's job enrichment for example suggested task expansion and increased employee discretion. Likert advocated the integration of the individual through groups which were to be integrated into the organization's official structure of decision-making by being made to overlap by means of their 'linking pin' members. Does this contradiction challenge the argument?

The answer seems to be that once again the proposed changes turned out to be more cosmetic than real. Watson (1987) argued that job design efforts did not represent any fundamental departure from the basic traditional principles. Kelly (1982) suggested that it was the exaggeration of the centrality of job specialization to Taylorism which led to the belief that NHR job redesign represented a rejection of Taylorian principles. Kelly's view was that job specialization was of less importance to Taylor than was the general intensification of effort through *increasing managerial control over labour*. At times, this could involve making tasks less specialized rather than more.

Turning finally to guru theory, a substantial amount of advice that is offered by these writers refers to person-to-person issues. There are exceptions as one would expect with such a diverse literature whose only common feature is temporal proximity. For example, Michael Porter's (1985) topic is competitive advantage, Eli Goldratt's is Just-in-Time (Goldratt and Cox 1989) and Oliver Wight (1981) focuses on material requirements planning. Even here, however, if one digs deeper beyond the surface, one can find references to people and their needs and motivations with respect to making the system work.

The majority of the gurus tend to focus on people issues. The essence of what the Harvard Business School does not teach you, according to

McCormack (1984), is how to read people and how to use that knowledge in order to get what you want. McCormack's message on the topic is carried in two and a half pages of his book, and the wisdom is contained in twenty-four words – listen aggressively, take a second look at first impressions, take time to use what you have learned, be discreet, be detached, observe aggressively, talk less.

Lee Iacocca's book of 341 pages contains 16 pages which are devoted to the 'Key to Management'. Once again the key is applied to the individual. Iacocca insists on having quarterly reviews of subordinates' performance, makes suggestions about decision-making, motivation, delegation, and the importance of having a strong ego and the vital role of team spirit. Jan Carlzon (1987) informed his readers that it all comes down to treating people decently and asking them to shine. He stressed a market orientation and people involvement. Even Carlzon's closing maxim had an individualistic focus. He wrote, 'A man who does not have information cannot take responsibility. A person who has the information cannot avoid taking responsibility.'

The latest nascent popular management idea – new age training – also focuses on the individual. It addresses their spiritual, emotional and creative aspects. Managers develop 'respect for and contact with the divine in all things and explicitly in his or her self' (*International Management* 1991). It is claimed that new age training is a 'study of the whole self, rather than simply the mind'.

Malleable human nature

A malleable view of human nature holds that people's behaviour is a consequence of law-like, cause-and-effect processes which are capable of being manipulated. The opposite of this view is the belief that humans are anarchic, meaning-creating or self-choosers. The popular management ideas stress that people are bound by the laws of nature and social science, and are purposeful creatures who act to satisfy their needs. They also reinforce the optimistic, common-sense belief that people are basically good, altruistic, intelligent and so on. While researchers like Milgram (1974) and Zimbardo *et al.* (1974) have demonstrated that people can be cruel, uninsightful, self-centred and anti-social, the chance of these authors ever becoming management gurus is small (Furnam 1990).

By establishing the baseline assertions that people are basically good and are triggered by external influences, popular ideas then go on to explain how the manager can manipulate worker behaviour by exploiting these externals. Such views of human nature have the quality of self-fulfilling prophecies and derive from value-based assumptions rather than from scientific facts. Their very advocacy can bring about which was first claimed or pretended to be inevitable. By basing themselves upon such a view of human nature, popular ideas also place themselves beyond the realm of scientific investigation, and become more like social philosophies. This in turn makes them more easily defensible in the face of hostile, empirically based challenges.

A modern management idea which promotes this malleable view of humankind is Adair's Action Centred Leadership (ACL). It is premised on an image of what it is to be a person at work. Readers and listeners recognize and identify with this image to a large degree. Individuals are seen as belonging to a group, as needing recognition and competition, craving meaning, and liking to be informed and asked for views. ACL tells managers that employees can be handled if they are approached in the right way from the outset. They can motivate and discipline themselves, and do not always put money first.

By ignoring people, bureaucracy says little about their motivations. However, it does possess an over-arching, legal–rational value-system that embodies rules which are held to be internalized, and which orient the behaviour of its members. Bureaucracy created a different form of employment relationship, one which was based upon employee commitment to the organization (Littler 1982). It attempted to ensure employee integration and involvement, partly by structural means such as the provision of careers and long-term contracts, but also by the internalization of organizational rules which were felt to be rational and fair. In principle, bureaucracy provided a solution to some of the employee problems which taxed managers, and led them to develop various management ideologies because it seemed to make managerial authority legitimate, and provided norms of effective work performance.

What was Taylor's basic assumption about workers? His views about human nature can be gleaned from his writings. Apart from a kind of Calvinistic work ethic and a trust in monetary incentives, Taylor did not include any motivational terms in his model. Motivation was largely assumed to be an intrinsic morale matter. The essential ability to work was taken as given by him. He wrote that first-class people were not only willing but also glad to work at their maximum speed provided that they were paid between 30 and 100 per cent more than the average for their trade. His guiding motivational principle was that money and personal ambition were more powerful incentives than exhortation. The Taylorian model of human nature was a machine model. He approached the organization from a mechanistic frame of reference, and its employees were considered to be tools of production.

Administrative management's view of people was that they would, within respectable tolerances, behave rationally. That is, they would act as the formal plan required them to do. The most basic property of formal organization was its essential rationality. The task of the organizer was to create a logically ordered world in which there was proper order and in which there was a place for everything and everything was in its place. Fayol considered that motivation depended on money, job design, discipline and supervision. Administrative management organizational designs generally conformed to what McGregor later labelled Theory X assumptions. The planner did have to take into account the human element, and motivation was considered more of a question of organizational design than supervisory skill. Any adjustments required to deal with people, represented temporary deviations required to deal with the idiosyncrasies of personalities. People should be loyal to the formal structure if it was to work effectively. *Esprit de corps* was stressed. Employees were viewed as inert instruments performing the tasks assigned to them. Personnel were considered as a given rather than as a variable in the system.

At the heart of human relations was a view of workers as social animals. Their needs and drives were affected as much by the other people around them as by their own innate motives. To understand workers, said Mayo, one needed to see them as individuals acting within a group. It is from this basic view that sprang the emphasis on the management of the informal group, the meeting of social needs and the training of supervisors in human relations skills.

Mayo's ideas for better human relations related to management's dominant assumption that employees were lazy and apathetic. It therefore followed that they needed rejuvenating, motivating, inspiring and generally 'firing with enthusiasm'. This approach was based on the notion that a selling approach was effective with people. The messages that managers communicated to employees acted to inspire them.

The non-rationality argument is at the centre of Mayo's ideas and relates to his view of human nature. He acknowledged that mechanization produced montonous work that induced in many workers what he called 'a low-grade reverie' through which problems which were molehills came to be perceived as mountains as a result of obsessive thinking. Mayo's argument was that the work situation contained no elements to dismay the worker once its true reality was understood. Since there was no disparity between reality and the reverie of the 'normal person', it followed that those who were dissatisfied with their situations must be victims of their own obsession, that is, *a priori* evidence that the complainant was abnormal.

This version of Catch 22 is what, in the view of some writers, made Mayo a management saint. The view of workers as non-rational creatures of sentiment appealed to those managers who were already practising *corporate fascism* (Rose 1978). It reinforced their prejudices. By stressing the rationality of management and the irrationality of workers, human relations' view of human nature gave it a distinct appeal to managers.

Before NHR content theories of motivation were popularized, there were two 'models of man' on which management theory and practice were based. These were the Rational Man and the Social Man models. The former saw people expending effort to secure their economic interest while the latter saw them as seeking affiliation and supportive interests in the workplace. The NHR theorists introduced a new model, that of Complex Man. This individual possessed a bundle of social and self-actualizing needs. Given the appropriate conditions in the workplace, he could show high levels of self-direction. Complex Man did not avoid responsibility but, because of the routinization of work and close supervision, he had little opportunity to exercise or develop such responsibility. The role of management was to create the conditions to tap this human resource. The NHR theorists are often also referred to as the *human resource management school*.

NHR's dynamic Complex Man model fitted in well with the humanitarian attitude which was attractive to the business community which, at that time, was growing in size and influence. Industry and commerce were having to deal with rising social and industrial unrest. Maslow's model of people was a central component in the NHR paradigm. Although he held that cultural factors could overwhelm 'instinctoid' need, he generally treated human nature as fixed, and sought to discover the nature of constancy of the organism.

The disillusionment with macho-management in recent years is reflected in more humanistic approaches espoused by the guru writers. However, unlike their neo-human relations colleagues of the 1950s and 1960s who saw humanism in terms of rights, today's guru writers see it as a question of necessity. The heavy and direct forms of control have failed to elicit the employee commitment and creativity necessary for today's ever more competitive world. By offering courses that force people to realize their full potential, *new age training* also seeks to help them become confident, creative and adventurous.

In the face of these challenges, future approaches are required which can unlock and build upon the unique human ability to innovate and tailor products and services to the needs of customers. The increase of women in senior management positions in the United States has acted to stimulate androgynous management styles. However, such innovative activity continues to take place within a boundary of managerial control which, if not looser, is less visible and obtrusive. The gurus encourage executives to think that if they get the essentials right, they can trust their subordinates to act in line with organizational goals. This saves managers the task of having continually to rack their brains as to how to combat lower-level employee obstructive behaviour.

STATUS ENHANCEMENT

Status enhancement is the second major recurring theme in the popular management literature. It refers to managers' need to maintain and enhance their own self-esteem and gain the esteem of others. Management ideas which assist in achieving this objective will be espoused. Four elements are included. First, *legitimation or self-affirmation*. At the start of the twentieth century, the popular ideas were those which legitimized the role of management. Now that management is accepted, what is more important is that the idea confirms a view held by the manager. Second, the *unitary perspective* refers to the idea emphasizing that managers and workers have common interests even though these are not always apparent to them. Third, *contribution–ownership potential* means that while prescribing the steps to be followed to implement it, the idea is not so inflexible that it cannot be adapted by its users, and customized to their own needs. They thus gain a feeling of personal ownership of the idea. Finally, *leadership* means that the idea stresses the leadership aspect of management.

Legitimation or self-affirmation

The managers of organizations, although not necessarily acting as an organized group in society at large, did have certain objective interests in common by virtue of the common problems and experiences to which they were exposed. Whenever enterprises were set up, a few commanded and many obeyed. The few, however, were seldom satisfied to command without higher justification even when they abjured all interest in ideas. Even where knowledge was developed with an ostensibly purely technical purpose, as with much of the writing about organizations, it tended nevertheless to be framed in such a way so as to meet a particular management group's need (Watson 1980).

Such views about management were thus 'partial' in that they strove to be consistent with the way in which managers preferred to see (and preferred others to see) the enterprise. Much organizational theory, therefore, paralleled a great deal of published managerial thinking to which it was closely related. Child (1969b) pointed out that management thought had both a *legitimatory* and a *technical* function. The former was primarily linked to the securing of social integration and approval for managerial authority and the way in which it was used. The latter was primarily linked to the search for practical means of rendering that authority maximally effective. There is then a difference between the Hawthorne studies and what Mayo subsequently wrote. It was Mayo's flamboyant writing which gained the acceptance of managers and which formed the basis of later American management theory.

Bureaucratic forms of organization acted to legitimize the role of managers in the organization. Baker (1972: 38), commenting on Burnham (1962), claimed that he had vulgarized Weber's ideas, and 'added enormously to the managers' myth – the belief in social, political and economic necessity of oligarchic, rational authoritarian directions in particular, and of society in general'.

The legitimizing aspect of scientific management emerged in Taylor's claim that his system was more than just a way of running an organization. Braverman (1974) argued that the separation of the worker's task from the knowledge that the worker might possess, acted to make the labour process dependent on managerial practices, rather than on worker ability. Hence, one could argue that such a separation was as important in creating and maintaining a role for managers, as it was in achieving increased productivity. Managerial functions 'exist only at the expense of the de-skilled shopfloor jobs, or are directly concerned with devising new forms of regulations and integration' (Salaman 1981).

The references cited here are clearly those of critical commentators. However, as will be shown later, many organizational change strategies of the late 1980s in the United States and Britain have sought to rekindle workforce commitment. The strategies used all involve some degree of worker empowerment. In the past such experiments have been resisted and terminated by managements. The current attempts at restructuring and job redesign have often coincided with major reductions (of up to 50 per cent) in middle management levels (*Business Week* 1988; *The Economist* 1988a). Buchanan argued that giving office and shopfloor workers discretion over managerial sections of an organization's operations was a greater threat to managerial legitimacy than having individual workers who have little or no idea of how their fragmented tasks contribute to the work of the organization as a whole.

In Taylor's view, the role of managers was essentially that of controllers, and that was the basis of their power. Their obligation was to the needs of the system, and people were viewed as necessary components of that system. The manager was therefore responsible for directing and controlling their behaviour in line with the system's needs. As a controller, the manager was expected to take corrective action if such compliance was not forthcoming. Buchanan wrote that:

> Taylor's approach to work design perpetuates the higher status and authority of managers, who work in clean offices, do no manual work, take all the responsibility for decisions, and take home higher financial rewards.
>
> (Buchanan 1989: 81)

One of the reasons for the popularity of Taylorist techniques was their perceived effectiveness in ensuring a continued high status role for the manager in the production process (Marglin 1976). Scientific management legitimized management by securing approval for its exercise of authority by demonstrating that it possessed an expertise (Child 1969a).

Taylorism did originally have a number of radical elements: for example, the proposal to reform managerial authority and that both workers *and* managers should be bound by the same logic of scientifically determined rules. In one of Taylor's visions, the manager was to become the worker's servant or assistant. The manager's function was to ensure that the worker had all the assistance of efficient organization, training and unimpeded material supply (Marglin 1976; Rose 1978). Many of these ideas share similarities with the writings of the mid-1980s, such as those of Tom Peters (1989), W. Edwards Deming (1986) and Jan Carlzon (1987).

These equalitarian elements became less evident by about 1911, when Taylor's book was published. While managers accepted the technical components, and used them to enhance their own status, the unpalatable aspects of his philosophy were conveniently forgotten. Indeed, the scientific management systems of some of Taylor's successors, such as Bedeaux, were preferred because they limited the restrictions placed upon them. Managers were not prepared to abandon their status or their formal authority to any joint submission to a new democracy.

Anthony (1977) argued that management required not merely compliance, but open and acknowledged compliance. In fact, management required fealty. Management's need for its authority to be acknowledged, in his view, meant that the political aspects of scientific management (Taylor's unprecedented democracy) were something that management could not acknowledge, just as it could never abandon control in order to regain it. Thus, management set out to find a basis for its authority which could be used as an alternative to the one supplied by scientific management.

Using a distorted version of political theory, the image created by management for itself out of scientific management ideas, was that of a balancer or arbiter of pluralistic coalitions. Management sat in objective and impartial judgement, deciding what was in the best interests of all. Such a position gave it a formidable claim to the exercise of legitimate authority in industry based on a modified version of scientific management which had had all the unhelpful bits taken out.

Considering administrative management, among its main concepts was *authority* – the right to get things done. These writers were keen to legitimize their position of influence, and held that authority originated entirely from ownership. They saw authority as being given by the owners to the board of directors, who in turn delegated it to the managing director, and from thereon it went down the management chain. The possession of formal authority in the chain of command was considered by the proponents of this school to be sufficient to enable a manager to get people to work effectively.

In his book, *Administration Industrielle et General*, Fayol (1949) identified six functions in the operation of any enterprise. One of these six was *administration* or management. He wrote about the importance of it as a distinct function to be studied and practised in its own right. While Fayol did not explain how organizations actually worked, he did offer a vision of how some managers would like them to work. The continued existence of success of all organizations depended on decisions being made and tasks being completed. This overriding purpose placed the organizational structure in a control process perspective. The manager was regarded as a problem-solver or the controller of a system who engaged in planning, execution, motivation, adjustment, and in making choices.

The human relations movement produced a theoretical approach to understanding work behaviour which provided a managerial ideology more fitted to an American inter-war period when trade union representation was increasing and when management was on the defensive (Bendix 1963). The change from small to large-sized enterprises was accompanied by a corresponding shift in the ideological justification advanced for managerial authority.

Hard work and superior ability had been the authority base. However, growth in size meant that promotion within a factory (rather than establishing one's own) began to be an avenue to success. The importance of technical skills declined, as that of interpersonal ones rose. Management ideology therefore became justified not upon the Puritan values of hard work or even enterprise, but on the ability to handle human relations effectively. Industrial problems came to be seen as human relations ones offering career advancement to those who possessed the new techniques which allowed them to co-ordinate a growing and increasingly specialized workforce.

Junior managers and supervisors were expected to absorb the shocks in exchange for the right of entry to the illusionary brotherhood of management (Mant 1979). Human relations, in Mayo's view, offered a unified vision of management with no internal divisions. Mayo had had an unshakable conviction that managers in the United States comprised an elite who had the ability, and therefore the right, to rule the rest of the nation. He pointed out, for instance, that many of America's managers were 'remarkable men without prejudice' (Mayo 1933). This was an irresistible message for managers.

Human relations' approach to motivation emphasized the importance of management incentives and controls, peer group social forces, social satisfactions and output norms. This acted to dramatically increase the centrality of the role of the supervisor. The onus for securing worker performance was placed largely on his shoulders. Human relations therefore greatly enhanced the role and status of supervisory and general management. It offered supervisors and managers membership of an elite of paternally benevolent administrators who were effective and scientifically informed.

Mayo's argument in his book, *The Human Problems of an Industrial Civilization* (1933), was that human collaboration at work had always required a 'non-logical social code' which, unfortunately, had been destroyed by social and technological change. Thus Mayo gave to management the key role of manipulating social harmony through the application of counselling and leadership skills so as to re-establish equilibrium in individuals and society. The model recognized that human beings may not be wholly satisfied by fair treatment and equitable pay alone. Hence, the manager's role was not only that of controller. He was also expected to take preventive steps to ensure that employees were co-operative and compliant.

NHR ideas considered managers to be independent actors. There was nothing, for example, in McGregor's theory about employees trusting their managers or trade unions trusting their corporate managements to be fair and honest (Lee 1971). McGregor's Theory X – Theory Y followers saw managers as responsible for getting workers to co-operate with management and to identify with organizational goals. Management remained responsible for organizing the elements of the productive process.

From the NHR view, the manager's role was not that of a controller, but as a developer and facilitator of the performance of the technical and social systems. The manager was presumed to be working with bosses and colleagues in the process of goal-setting, and with juniors in defining objectives and procedures. The manager carried the obligation to deal with any new and recurring barriers to performance. While self-control and self-direction among employees was assumed, this did not remove the maintenance aspects of the controller's role. It legitimized the manager's responsibilities to remove restrictions and to create and develop new investment opportunities in order that the employee's full potential could be utilized.

NHR supporters accepted the existing distribution of power within organizations as legitimate. McGregor's Theory Y assumptions and Management-by-Objectives were ideas that were introduced as ones which would *not* alter management's authority in any way (Nord 1974). Herzberg and Maslow tempted managers to believe that the conditions of optimum worker productivity were exactly those from which they could obtain psychological gratification. Herzberg's theory was held to state this explicitly and a similar conclusion was drawn from both Maslow's model and Argyris's work. The ideological implication was an apparent rationale for the acceptability of the status quo and for management's part in it (Blackler and Brown 1980).

Many of the gurus, including Mintzberg, have focused on the unique aspects of the manager's job. They stressed its complexity and difficulty. In so doing, they reinforced the general view that managers were very special people who were doing a unique job. In the past, they may have felt inadequate because they believed that they were expected to make perfectly logical decisions with inadequate knowledge. The Rational Man model stressed such managerial behaviour.

Guru theory challenged this. The emphasis of Peters and Waterman was on the 'soft Ss'. It had the effect of legitimizing the anti-logical, pro-intuitive aspects of managerial work. Much of this was reflected in the right brain/ left brain debate. Edward de Bono's work is particularly relevant to this area. He told his readers and audiences about the anti-logical aspects of lateral thinking ('the mind must wobble before it can leap'). The overall effect of such guru pronouncements has been to improve the manager's self-image and self-confidence. The intuitive, gut-feel approach that the manager used to be ashamed of was now applauded.

Mintzberg focused on managerial activities which he considered to be the components of a set of roles. While delineating those roles, he located their origin in the structure of formal authority. He promoted the ideal of the managerial role being rationalized through the careful specification and programming of its activity content. The image that emerged from the guru literature was that of a 'professional' who carried out impartially the universally and technically defined functions of management. In this vision, organizations were assumed to fulfil societal and communal needs and, by the application of their professional expertise to companies, the work of individual managers was seen to be socially responsible as well as personally rewarding.

Now that management's role in society is both accepted and esteemed, the self-affirmation potential of a management idea rather than its legitimizing function has become more important. Self-affirmation refers to the idea's ability to confirm some aspect of the manager's own beliefs or attitude. It includes the notion that the management idea could have been the manager's own. This is to say, so close to managers' own experience or belief that they could have thought of it themselves! Popular management ideas thus confirm a manager's views and thereby legitimize them. In such circumstances, the manager has a sort of vicarious ownership of the idea. This is related to the attribute of common sense which will be described later. Sharpe reported his impressions of attending a John Fenton Sales Seminar. Mr Fenton, somewhat like Billy Graham, is able to fill large auditoria with salespeople and motivate and inspire them to future successes. After watching one such performance in order to analyse the elements of its success, Sharpe concluded:

> I got the impression that the response to the roadshow was something like – 'there but for a bit of thought go I'. All the anecdotes and ripostes were close enough to reality for us to believe that we might have thought of *that* trick, *that* response or *that* line ourselves – at least on a good day.
> (Sharpe 1984: 15)

Other evidence supports this argument. Peters and Waterman made the observation that 'seasoned audiences are heartened that the "magic" of P & G and IBM is simply getting the basics right, not possessing more IQ points per man or woman' (Peters and Waterman 1982: 17). This quotation stresses two points. 'Getting the basics right' refers to doing the common-sense things that all of us should do (and normally do) but occasionally forget. Peters and Waterman comment that 'The answer is surprisingly simple, albeit ignored by most managers' (Peters and Waterman 1982: 56). The second part of the quotation, which refers to IQ, suggests that all the managers reading the book are capable of doing these things. They do not require any special abilities to do it. Interestingly, A. A. Milne, the author of *Winnie the Pooh* and himself a detective novelist, described what he felt were the characteristics of a good detective story:

> the detective must have no more special knowledge than the average reader. The reader must be made to feel that, if he too had used the light of cool deductive reasoning and the stern logic of remorseless facts (as, Heaven bless us, we are quite capable of doing) then he too would have fixed the guilt.
>
> (Milne 1926: 202)

Perhaps there is some aspect of human involvement that transcends management idea appeal, and is in some way universal.

Unitary perspective

The unitary perspective holds that managers and workers share the same fundamental interests. Any conflicts are the result of misunderstandings or bad communications. Did bureaucracy convey this idea? No explicit evidence was found in the literature to support this proposition. Weber (1947) did propose the first structural-functional theory of organization. The organization was to be treated as a largely stable phenomenon having unitary goals, predictive rules and regulations and a hierarchy of rational legal authority. An essential characteristic of the ideal type bureaucracy was a coherent set of goals which gave a clear direction and which formally translated into the various sub-tasks to be achieved. Thus there was an implicit reference to the notion of commonality of goals.

Fayol's formulation of administrative management was fundamentally one of consensus. Employees were seen as coming to work primarily to maximize their wages and the job of management was to design jobs, the organization and the payment system, in such a way that if people worked hard then they would be rewarded. If management had done its job properly then the increased efforts of workers would mean greater productivity and this would lead to higher profits. Everybody benefited. The workers received higher wages, the owners secured higher dividends, and the managers would be pleased to know that they had done a job well. Fayol emphasized the necessity for harmonious co-ordination between the parts of the company in the interests of what he called the 'organic whole'. Writing about the administrative management school, Woodward (1965) said that this management idea took for granted 'that people who join an employing organization either accept it and its purposes, or can be educated to do so, with the result that they will behave in a way that advances organizational goals.'

Human relations was a unitary philosophy which promoted the view that there were no fundamental conflicts of interest between employers and workers. A basic tenet of it was that there were no 'win–lose' situations. Everyone could win. This was because the application of the ideas improved both efficiency and productivity which created a larger pie to be shared. The strategies of human relations (continually refined after the Hawthorne experiments) were simply an attempt to establish community relationships in the context of subdivided labour, unquestioned management authority over job design and planning, management evaluation of performance and wage payment, and unchanged hierarchies of power. The Mayoite studies showed 'no recognition of the existence of realistic conflict or its functions. Behaviour which is the outcome of a conflict situation is almost exclusively dealt with as non-realistic behaviour' (Coser 1956).

The effect of this was to see conflict as a failure which management could sort out, usually by 'improving communications', by recognizing informal groups and infiltrating them with lower level management (supervisors). Then, all the causes of conflict would disappear. Trade unions and industrial relations were removed from any position of importance thereby allowing management to achieve a representative role in its relationship with its workers.

The central role attributed to conflict, and to non-realistic or non-rational behaviour in Mayo's vision, parallels in the eyes of some writers the view held by communist regimes. That is the conviction that protest against the system was, by itself, an indication of the poor mental state of protestors, meriting a stay in a psychiatric hospital. Is this an exaggeration? Farber (1982) reviewed the human relations principles and the material and moral incentives used in the communist world. He demonstrated that both assumed a basic harmony of interests between their employees and managers; and both ignored the fact that work incentives were used in combination with coercion, and that the workplace itself was run in an undemocratic manner.

Mayo promulgated the view about the harmony of interests even more vigorously than Taylor. He did not allow for Taylor's limited awareness that some differences might exist. Since Mayo saw no conflict, he rejected both unions and the need for any form of collective bargaining. Mayo, no more than Taylor, questioned the fundamental organization of capitalism, especially in regard to those who sold their labour power. Mayo's recommendations were intended to create cohesive social groups, and thereby to integrate managerial with worker goals. His teachings emphasized the *doctrine of human co-operation*. Conflict came to be seen as an evil to be removed and to be replaced by harmony. All conflict was treated as being of the same type and was held to occur as a result of the lack of social skills. Conflict was considered to be the cause of poor performance. The way to increase productivity therefore was for the manager to smooth out all the conflicts and to re-establish harmonious working relationships.

Critics have argued that the emphasis on harmony and the neglect of conflict was the result of Mayo's pro-capitalist management bias. The co-operation envisaged was to be on management terms and in management's image. In Mant's view, human relations':

> essential lure was the implicit fantasy that industrial administration might be conflict free (everybody has a share) *if only* people would co-operate and pull together, *if only* the 'whole person' could be engaged wholeheartedly in work, if only the foreman had leadership. It was an agreeable, fantastic, 'if only' sort of world view, in which the unions were necessarily cast as obdure, destructive and reactionary; and so, in time, they became.
>
> (Mant 1979: 55)

NHR ideas too were based upon the belief that the needs of the individual and of the organization were one and the same. The most satisfying organization in which to work would also be the most efficient. NHR taught the importance of relating work and organizational structure to the needs of employees. In this way employees would become happy, the organization would obtain their full co-operation and effort, and efficiency would be increased. Employees should be given the feeling that the company goal was worth the effort, they should be made to feel part of the company, taking pride in their contribution to the goal. This meant that the company's objectives had to inspire confidence in the intentions of management, and convey the belief that each employee would get rewards and satisfactions from working towards those objectives. In short, NHR writers pointed to a perfect balance between organizational goals and employee needs.

NHR suggested that since super-ordinate or meta-goals existed, most conflict was not of the zero-sum variety. It could therefore be resolved by consensus. The differences were held to be about the most appropriate way to achieve the agreed goals. There would be no conflict provided management conferred adequately with the workers. The approach contained four implicit assumptions. First, that management's position was that which any 'reasonable' people would adopt provided that it had been properly explained to them. Second, that all people of goodwill thought alike. Third, that virtually all basic conflict was avoidable. Fourth, that since there would be conflict about means, this should be managed creatively to produce the best solutions.

McGregor saw employees as neither passive nor resistant, but as anxious to assume responsibility, co-operate with management and identify with organizational (that is managerial) goals. The task of management in this idea was to create the organizational conditions and methods of operation, which would allow individuals to achieve their goals by directing their efforts towards the achievement of organizational objectives.

NHR implied that a failure of workers to achieve higher level needs bred in them an obsession with cash rewards. As a doctrine, this was attractive to managers (despite its fragile scientific foundation), because it suggested that workers could be satisfied with rewards other than money (Rose 1978). Herzberg, for example, listed hygiene and motivational factors. Managers interpreted his theory to mean that the demand for greater intrinsic rewards would be accompanied by a decline in demand for increased extrinsic rewards. A theory was offered which was concerned with efficiency and profitability, and which showed a fortuitous concurrence between individual and organizational needs. This allowed managers to accept the programmes of these researcher-consultants with confidence.

The NHR writers therefore helped managers to cope with the problem of conflict which they had viewed as damaging. They likened organizations to coalitions of interests in which conflict was held to be legitimate and unavoidable. The 'point-of-production' resistance of workers was interpreted by the NHR advocates to be a problem of poor communication. That is, managers and workers were unable to understand each other's point of view.

From Mayo's time, right up to and including modern guru theory, many popular management ideas have cast the organization in the role of the family. Hence the most popular management ideas have generally been as preoccupied with internal co-operation as with external competitiveness. Nevertheless, argued Butler (1986), the unconvincing myth continues to persist that competition outside the company boundary is commendable but that competition inside of it is reprehensible. Inside 'togetherness' is the theme.

Citing the OD techniques based upon neo-human relations ideas, Stephenson (1985: 253) argued that 'Underlying the OD position there is an acceptance of a unitary view of organizations and a rejection of a pluralist view.' It was specifically aimed at engineering consensus, though in the guise of what Schein had called 'an adaptive coping cycle', and what Beckhard (1969) termed the 'healthy organization'. The corollary of this perspective was that any disruption of this smoothly operating unitary system was deemed to be unhealthy and undesirable (Honour and Mainwaring 1982).

Guru theory implicitly assumed a unitary perspective on organizations. In some ways it resembled human relations ideas in that it took as its starting-point the belief that organizational employees wanted to contribute to organizational goals and that the job of management was to identify and remove the bureaucratic barriers that prevented them from doing so. The gurus berated managers for failing to provide the leadership vision that would help to put all that organizational commitment into practice. Guru theory also echoed aspects of scientific management in its assumed belief that increased performance would benefit management and employees in equal amounts. Finally, one can note that new age training also holds that the company benefits to the fullest only when the employee is involved as a whole person, 'integrated in body, mind, emotions and spirit' (Storm 1990).

Contribution-ownership potential

Contribution potential refers to the ability of management ideas to be partly created by managers themselves. The appeal of popular management ideas is based partly on their potential for being modified or adjusted in some way by their adopters. How does this aspect relate to the notion of universality of application to be discussed later? While managers prefer non-contingency ideas, they also value an idea that can be adapted and modified within prescribed, narrow limits. There is no incompatibility between the two notions of universality and contribution since the modification or customization will tend to be marginal, that is, sufficient to create a sense of ownership for its user, but not large enough to destroy the 'big idea'.

The concept of *consumer manufacture* holds that in the economy of the future, the end of the manufacturing chain for goods and services will be occupied by consumers in their own physical space. For example, the Polaroid photograph, electronic home banking (where customers access their own accounts, pay bills and withdraw cash) and the adding of carbonated water to soft drink concentrates.

Shifting the determination of the product's final configuration down-stream into the consumer's space has a number of consequences. When it is consumers who create and control manufacture, then they may consume more. Manufacturers should seek out ways to push end-of-production downstream, into the space of the consumers since this may result in renewed product growth. The same principles can apply to management ideas and techniques. If the final version of the idea can be 'manufactured' in the manager's head, then it will be mentally retained and applied. In addition, if the idea's associated technique (be it a quality circle or corporate culture programme) can be assembled on the premises, then it too will be used more widely.

How does the trainee guru create an idea that can be finally manufactured in a person's head? There are two ways. First, the guru can make that idea a little opaque so as to necessitate the individual to 'unpack' it. This relates to the point made earlier about neither communicating in too simple language (rejected as obvious) nor in too obscure language (rejected as academic). The solution is to relabel or 'acronymize' the idea contents allowing the manager to unpack its contents.

Popular management ideas wrap simple propositions up in a package form and attach impressive sounding labels such as 'hygiene factors', 'system

4 management' or 'managerial grid'. Watson (1980) argued that the small amount of effort that managers had to expend on 'unwrapping' the idea-parcel gave them a feeling of achievement and satisfaction. Such packing and unpacking was based upon the simple proposition that people in work organizations would work more effectively if they were allowed to participate in the management of their own work.

A second way in which managers can achieve idea-ownership is to have an idea presented to them in the form of generalizations that are amenable to manipulation. Argyris (1972) wrote that customers would tend to select a product which needed their own involvement and effort to implement successfully. Managers were thus offered the possibility of both psychological success and a feeling of competence. Management ideas which gave their users a great deal of freedom of application, and therefore a feeling of ownership, were likely to be preferred. Thus popular ideas are those which are able to create ways in which the managers can gain a sense of ownership of them. Content-wise, they are flexible enough to permit the reinterpretation that their users require. In this sense, a social philosophy is preferable to definitive, unambiguous research findings.

Contribution-ownership potential, however, is not a major feature of bureaucracy. As with any other popular management idea, there is scope for modification by the implementer. For example, different principles of bureaucracy can be given different weights and so on. Thus, while the model does not explicitly encourage modification, neither does it preclude it. The same is true for administrative management. With so many principles on offer, managers could select those which suited both their organizational circumstances and their own personal ends. Every application of scientific management had to be customized to meet the prevailing circumstances of the company implementing it. Thus, each implementing manager could claim to have made a unique and personal contribution to the application of Taylor's scientific management principles.

Human relations gave even greater scope for freedom of contribution. It rested on the belief that management had only to develop the necessary skills for creating the right conditions in which workers could demonstrate their commitment. Management was thus given direction by human relations, and told that it should attempt to 'integrate workers into the organization'. However, it received little guidance on exactly how to do this. Managers were told only that individuals should be socially integrated into the primary worker group which in turn would be managed so as to operate in a way which was consistent with management's desires.

Colleague groups would be established and fostered by management and recruits introduced into these. Individuals would be guided away from group loyalties which did not fit in with management's aims, and informal leaders would be used as communication channels. The scope provided by the implementation of the techniques gave the opportunity for managers to personalize and customize their implementation of the human relations approach and thus achieve a feeling of ownership for its implementation.

Virtually all NHR ideas offered the potential for simplification for a mass management market. Their popularity rested heavily upon the communicability of their core notion. NHR idea packages were frequently constructed so as to be capable of being easily 'unwrapped' by managers. In this process of unwrapping (that is coming to grips with the fundamentals of the idea), the manager achieved a sense of idea ownership. Maslow's 'message', for example, was taken to be that it was easy enough to motivate people with simple rewards when they were hungry and insecure but once they were better off in these respects, then they looked for something more. The short struggle with the key concepts of physiological, safety, ego, social and self-actualization needs and its hierarchical display (in triangular form) could give managers the feeling of such idea ownership. Interestingly, guru theory offers relatively little scope for such an individual contribution, and one would predict its long-term influence to be limited.

Leadership focus

Leadership focus refers to a popular management idea strongly alluding to the notion of leadership. Ideally, the word *leadership* should be incorporated in its title. In 1988 *The Economist* reported that leadership was on many a business school curriculum, inspired arcane articles on the subject, and filled 'conference seats with would-be leaders' bottoms.'

The concept of leadership is one of the distinguishing features of a popular management idea. The 1980s saw a continuing interest in leadership in the context of managing major corporate transformations. Anderson *et al.* (1985) studied seventeen companies that had been revitalized, and they identified 'a championing leader' as a major success factor. Other top-selling authors also put the idea of leadership at the centre of their writings (Peters and Waterman 1982; Bennis and Nanus 1985; Clifford and Cavanagh 1986). The success of General Norman Schwarzkopf during the 1991 Gulf War reignited and intensified the interest in leadership.

What accounts for such an interest in the topic of leadership? Two explanations are offered. The first relates to the raising of the self-esteem of the individual manager. The 'myth of leadership' provoked an aura of romance and mythology that was deeply ingrained in our culture (Blackler and Shimmin 1984). Such myths might be considered as ideological preferences. Two of these myths were that leaders were invariabaly important, and that effective leaders possessed particular personality characteristics.

The myth of leader importance developed because those who occupied leadership roles often felt frustrated and ineffectual. Hence they tended to be attracted to those management ideas which reinforced their own views as to how they would *like* to see themselves. Some writers had identified the leader as the linchpin in the organization claiming that the survival of the organization was dependent on leader behaviour (McGregor 1960; Likert 1961). The second myth concerned the possession of traits. No single trait has been found to be associated with effective leadership. Nevertheless, the strength of popular imagery in the field has made the approach appealing to managers. It has recently been reinforced by the writings of the 'hero-managers'. Since every desirable human characteristic has, at one time or another, been associated with effective leadership, all managers are likely to possess at least some of what have been claimed to be characteristics of an effective leader. Thus, the trait approach allows managers to draw comfort from the belief that they have achieved their success by virtue of their superior individual qualities. Hence, management comes to be seen as an exclusive club with selection criteria that all managers can meet in their own way. All are thus special and acceptable in different ways.

Another explanation for the popularity of leadership relates to its ability to explain the inexplicable. Leadership has been treated as one of the ways in which people come to understand the causes of important organizational events and outcomes. Leadership appears to have been sanctified and been given a key role in our phenomenal constructs of organized activities and their outcomes. As an explanatory concept, leadership possessed a heroic, larger-than-life value. Lacking the necessary information with which to explain the causes of a decline or an improvement in a company's fortunes, change comes to be attributed to defective or inspired leadership. Leadership thus becomes a residual, 'catch-all' explanatory category (Meindl *et al.* 1985; Meindl and Erlich 1987).

Does bureaucracy stress leadership in some way? While the model can be implemented in different ways, its 'structural individualism' supports the Great Man Theory of Leadership. This holds that organizational structure is largely determined by the attributes of the person at the top. Other than this, bureaucracy does not stress leadership issues in any significant or explicit way.

Scientific management advocates of work specialization had little to say about leadership *per se*. They had no clear idea of the problems of reintegrating fragmented job roles (Littler 1982). However, to manage the fragmented work, managers needed to ensure that all the planning and allocation of work was done by them, that all the work was monitored and allocated, and that a payment-by-results system was introduced to motivate the workers to apply themselves to maximum effort. Leadership under Taylor's formulation was a matter of applying science, while motivation was a question of offering a financial return commensurate with the effort expended towards the tasks designed by managers. Thus, Taylor's version of leadership was not concerned with personal power or vision-creation that we have come to associate it with today.

Administrative management considered leadership in terms of the *qualities* of leaders. Employees could become dependent, passive and subordinate to the leader. Recognizing this problem, administrative management recommended having technically competent, objective, rational and loyal leaders. Being so technically competent, these leaders would not have the 'wool pulled over their eyes'. Their objectivity and rationality would reflect their interest in the formal structure and would prevent them becoming emotionally involved. Leaders had to be impartial and loyal when evaluating others so that they could inculcate that same loyalty into their subordinates.

Mayo tied his findings to the conservative sentiments of business leaders by advocating the non-intervention of governments. His ideas therefore struck a chord with the leaders of industry. Mayo stressed the primary role of managers, believing that deliberate planning of co-operation was not to be achieved by government institutions, but rather through the development of administrative elites within the private, and more particularly the industrial organizations of our society. The popular version of what human relations said was that good leadership led to increased productivity. It improved morale which led to increased effort.

Thus for the early human relations writers, the key to higher performance was through enhanced leadership skills of managers, rather than through incentive schemes. To Mayo, the 'human side of management' involved a process of personal persuasive leadership. This participative style of leadership could translate the 'vision of a true industrial democracy into a dynamic living reality' as the writers of the time put it. Mayo's notion of democratic leadership meant, not so much that workers should be consulted, as that they should be advised of the change that management had already decided upon. Little wonder, therefore, that human relations appealed to managers since it matched their need for achievement, success and career advancement. It was the younger managers who were most attracted to this 'new management'. They saw it as a way of increasing their influence and effectiveness in the bureaucractic organization. Human relations thus became a tool for internal politics and career advancement for managers in organizations.

A common theme of NHR was its emphasis on the involvement of workers. The promotion of these ideas also reinforced the leadership aspects of managers' roles. Participation was held to be a 'good thing' productivity-wise because it stressed adaptation and the development of the individual's own learning capabilities. Moreover, it was considered ethically right to involve employees in the decisions that affected them. The romance of leadership, mentioned earlier, included the myth that a particular leadership style was invariably more effective than others. NHR theories of leadership such as those of the managerial grid during the 1960s reflected this perspective.

Turning finally to guru theory, a distinguishing feature of many of the popular British and American business magazines was the way that they emphasized the role and importance of the manager in general, and of the chief executive in particular. An issue of *Business Week* is typical of the style. It contained numerous photographs of leading international businessmen. The associated captions read:

Italian Renaissance: Romano Prodi brings new life to IRI.

Rose: At 32, he may be on his way to building a billion dollar corporation.

CSX Chairman Watkins: Assembling a Transportation Carrier of the Future.

How Bob Price is reprogramming Control Data.

Roger Smith: Revolutionary of the American Factory.

Research by Langer (1983) revealed that managers expressed an expectancy of personal success which was much higher than objective probability would warrant. They tended to overestimate the impact that they had upon an organization. This illusion of control represented the overconfidence by individuals of their ability to produce positive outcomes. However, it did confirm a personal belief that they controlled events and that events did not control them.

As managers are constantly seeking ways to control outcomes in their environment, they form hypotheses about the contributions that their actions can make to such outcomes. Hence they will seek out information that supports their hypotheses, while innocently ignoring disconfirming evidence. The popular business magazines, because of their orientation and style of articles, act to confirm the hypotheses that managers and businesspeople have when regarding their ability to control their environment.

The business press with its general uncritical veneration of business leaders is hungry for heroes who can act as models. Conflicts in boardrooms, whether at ICI or at General Motors, have the flavour of, and are reported as, television soap opera. The message that the media reports and the message that readers seem to want to hear is that at whatever level in the organization, the individual manager *has* control and *can* turn things around. This runs counter to the alienating belief that managers and chief executives are powerless, incapable of having much impact on the organization, and generally react to external forces over which they have no control.

Guru theory is strong on leadership and the message that leaders can make a difference. Peters emphasized the leadership contribution. Pfeffer (1981) wrote that managers preferred explanations which provided them with the feeling of having control over events. In situations where such control was lacking, they used 'symbolic control'. For example, statements which asserted causal links between management actions and positive environmental outcomes. In their letters, consulting firms acclaim their contributions to a firm's good fortunes. All this acts to create the illusion of a management in control (Salancik and Meindl 1984).

PRACTICAL APPLICATION

A third recurring theme to be found in popular management ideas is their focus upon implementation. This is achieved by the idea possessing five key elements. *Control* refers to the idea's perceived potential to increase managers' control over their areas of responsibility. *Steps or principles* involves the idea possessing a set of clear steps or guiding principles which assist in the process of its adoption and implementation. *Universal application* concerns the idea's claim to a universal application in all organizations. *Authorization* relates to the credibility base of the idea – science, common sense or company use. The more bases of authority that an idea can appeal to, the greater its credibility. *Applicability* pertains to the confidence that the idea will produce a pay-off for its users in a short time.

Control

A recurring feature in most popular management ideas is their claim to offer managers increased control over their work environment and over the labour process in particular. Managers' feelings of powerlessness and impotence stem from having their decisions overturned by senior management without explanation, having to participate in discussions when the other people's minds were already made up, being passed over for promotion or a salary increase because of quotas, or working for a boss who did not defend the department from senior management's attacks. Such concerns were additional to having one's performance judged on the work of other people who were often uncooperative and unpredictable. The search for and adoption of particular management ideas and techniques could, in this context, be seen as an attempt to reassert control over the world of work.

It is perhaps not accidental that the majority of management ideas and their techniques are focused upon controlling the most unpredictable element in the organizational world – people. The three grand strategies of labour control are mechanization, labour differentiation and education. The first prescribes tasks, routines, times and specifications. Differentiation relates the organization that follows from that logic to an order of different jobs with different grades, levels of authority and pay, while education teaches the principles upon which the first two are based (Anthony 1986).

The more that a management idea is perceived by managers to increase their control, the more attractive it will be to them.

There are at least two explanations of managers' need for control. The first is social-psychological and states that the majority of organizations are bureaucratic and are run by people with an authoritarian approach. They attract like-minded persons. Since their personalities fit, these people are themselves promoted. The authoritarian personality has a preference for power and control. This orientation emphasized the importance of charisma and the 'Man of the Moment' notion (Dixon 1976).

The second explanation for the manager's need for control is a sociological one put forward by Braverman (1974). Using military terms himself, he argued that organizations were one theatre of war in the class struggle between the proletariat and the bourgeoisie. Managers, acting on behalf of shareholders, were caught in the middle and constituted the first line of battle in dealing with a recalcitrant workforce which was ready to subvert their aims and schemes. Managers sought to control and cajole the workers and make their behaviour predictable. The problem was that managers were human as well, and had feelings about and a need to subjugate and control others. Thus, argued Braverman, managers questioned their self-image and legitimacy.

One of Weber's axioms was that if management did not gain control of an industry then the 'management' of that industry rested with labour. Management control was seen as something that had to be wrested from the workers. Bureaucracy could be seen as part of the power relationships between the controllers and the controlled (Gouldner 1954). It was a method of control through which senior organization members attempted to impose their wills upon subordinates when they found that the other control mechanisms were inadequate (Merton 1957; Blau 1955; Crozier 1964). Salaman noted:

> Bureaucracy is necessary to control and monitor the labour of alienated and recalcitrant employees. The development of bureaucracy entails the centralization of control, the de-humanization of rationality or instrumentality, and the differentiation of the workforce.
>
> (Salaman 1981: 135)

Rationality reflects the application of a formal structure of administration as a means of managing complex tasks. Bureaucracy thus permits the calculation and predictability of future outcomes, together with accountability, and more control of activities. For Weber, the ideal type of bureaucracy contained formal control specified in rules and regulations created by management which devised stable procedures and limited authority.

Perrow (1977) was concerned that bureaucracy both mobilized social resources for desirable ends and inevitably concentrated them in a few hands of those who might use them for ends which others may not approve of, be unaware of, but which they might have to accept because they could not conceive of any alternative. The whole process of rationalization had its parallel in the centralization of the other organizational resources into the hands of the managers who were able to exercise discretionary power. The rationality of bureaucracy had its own appeal. It increased the control exercised by managers, while at the same time projecting a neutrality. Weber stressed the rationalistic view of organizations with its emphasis on means–end relationships, the maximization of efficiency, decision-making as a logical process, and the design of structural arrangements to achieve these outcomes.

Scientific management also offered managers greater control. Industrial organization was conducted so as to minimize the worker's independence and maximize the manager's control over the labour process. Three principles were basic to this. These were first, the *separation of planning from performance principle* leading to management taking over from the workers, the responsibility for planning. Second, the *scientific methods of work principle* which held that management should take over from the workers, the decisions about which methods of work to be used. Finally there was the *managerial rules principle* which not only recommended the use of rules, but also specified the sort of rules to be implemented and hence assisted with the implementation of the theory at an operational level. Scientific management offered the answers to three major managerial problems. How to organize work most effectively? How to keep employees working hard? How to exercise control over the process?

Taylor articulated a rationale for the expansion of managerial work. The ideal was for managers to appropriate the traditional expertise of workers and then translate it into standardized rules and even mathematical formulae that would replace custom and practice (Willmott 1984). This proposed rationalization process allowed the managerial element in the labour process to become virtually detached from the act of production, thereby massively expanding the controlling role, and hence the power, of managers.

What was special about scientific management was that although it aimed primarily at achieving managerial control by the detailed description of performance, it also aimed at securing employee commitment. Uniquely, it sought to overcome the contradiction in these two objectives. The synthesis was achieved in the way that it demanded allegiance to the scientific laws that were revealed in the process of job analysis. In Taylor's view, there could be no argument about what was to be done and what was the right way to do it. Neither could there be any argument about interests. As production increased considerably, there was not much room for disagreement about the division of the spoils. Taylor (1911) claimed that his system 'substitutes joint obedience to fact and laws, for obedience to personal authority. No such democracy has ever existed in industry before'. Henry Ford (1922) was able to say that 'the work and the work alone controls us'. Of course this was not the case in practice. However, it did give managers a convenient retort to the complaints of workers and unions.

Administrative management writers attempted to synthesize their experiences into an easily learned set of principles, prescriptions and rules. They hoped that these would allow managers to control and improve organizational performance. In this model the organization was seen as an instrument for producing a profit for its owners, while the purpose of management was to convert inputs (capital, labour, materials) into profit by the exercise of managerial control.

Barnard (1938), one of the major figures in administrative management, argued that a major role of the executive was to ensure 'the willingness of persons to contribute efforts to the co-operative system'. In his view, material inducements were insufficient to achieve the optimum level of co-operation. Thus managers needed to preserve what he called 'the fiction of superior authority' which ensured 'a presumption among individuals in favour of the acceptability of orders from superiors'.

In terms of organizational control, even human relations ideas which advocated participation and alluded to 'power equalization' did not seriously challenge the essentially hierarchical character of control in organizations (Dickson 1981). It has been argued that human relations offered a more subtle form of persuasion to replace the somewhat crude devices offered by the scientific management writers. It was human relations' contribution to management control and ideology which was one of its main appealing features. Clegg and Dunkerley (1980) felt that it had significance 'as part of the apparatus whereby organizations attempt to impose and maintain control of production.' Miles (1975) claimed it allowed 'the manager to retain his role as controller of the system while minimizing conflict and gaining the compliance of a loyal, perhaps devoted, group of subordinates.'

Mayo's solution to the problem of managerial control was persuasion in the guise of new forms of solidarity to replace those destroyed by individual processes of de-skilling and isolation introduced by the combined effects of Taylorism and Fordism (Clegg 1979). Managers drew the conclusion that production workers needed to feel that they were involved in the enterprise and respected as individuals. Since actual participation and personal respect were impractical, the job of the manager was seen as being to manufacture the *appearance* of involvement and respect.

The NHR writers offered to teach managers a form of control that was not imposed from outside of employees but which operated from *within* them. Superficially, much of the activity of OD (information sharing, authority and decision delegation) appears to suggest a reduction of management control. However, in nearly all cases, the limits about what decisions could be made were tightly set and required management go-ahead. Critics have argued that these OD techniques (now relabelled employee commitment programmes), far from lessening management control, may have actually *increased* it (Dickson 1981). Because a great effort was placed upon the communication of management objectives, employees may have come to better understand and more readily accept these objectives. In consequence, control through the management hierarchy came to be supported by peer group pressure.

NHR did not reject the explicit notion of control. The principle of hierarchy espoused and Likert (1967) always represented his ideas on a hierarchical organizational chart. Argyris (1970) envisaged a weakening but not an elimination of hierarchy, by a strengthening of 'matrix' groups. He did not conceive of a flat hierarchy.

In the way they tackled their chosen subjects, the guru authors acknowledged and legitimized the idea that the manipulation of power to one's advantage was at the heart of the management role. Managing and politics were seen as inseparable and the power to persuade was perhaps the most important of all. It is not that this idea was new, rather that these authors made it explicit. The guru writers argued that if managers listened and talked to their employees, they could grasp control of the signalling system which pointed out the direction of excellence in the company. Managers could manage the agenda, nudge the day-to-day decision-making system, and thereby impart new preferences and test new initiatives.

Steps or principles

Steps or principles refer to checklists, roadmaps, guides and associated idea-implementation technology which accompany the management idea itself. Their purpose is to reduce managers' anxieties about travelling safely from where they are to where would like to be. It shows them how the management ideas can be put into practice.

Discussing how a book of such length as Peters and Waterman's *In Search of Excellence* (*ISOE*) achieved managerial appeal and came to be widely quoted in company circles, Godfrey (1985: 25) suggested that 'The *ISOE* formula of reducing ideas to easily remembered steps to success may have been the only thing that could have enticed such a large number of managers.' Those management ideas which have achieved popularity have tended to give users either a clear set of detailed principles (e.g. Fayol's span-of-control) or else have offered them a detailed step-by-step guide to what should be done and how ('Deming's 14 Step Roadmap'). The idea of Total Quality Management, for example, is supported by a plethora of principles and implementation technology. Kanter (1985: 249) complained about the 'imposition of mindless formulae for action – giving people a set of role motions to go through that have worked somewhere else or have been specified in minute detail.' She reluctantly acknowledged, however, that the 'formulaic nature of guidance' did appeal to managers, and noted that many American corporations were fond of the 'appliance model of organizational change'. This involved buying a complete programme, such as a quality improvement package from a dealer, plugging it in, and hoping that it would run itelf.

Gellner (1985) studied the ideas of the philosopher, Nietzsche. He asked why it was that his ideas did not gain as wide an appeal as those of Freud (which were based on Nietzsche's). He concluded that while Nietzsche sketched his ideas out in a loose, general and unspecific way, Freud's presentation was full of laws, and offered a concrete and identifiable position, and a technique through which individuals could achieve their goals in the face of real problems.

Eric Berne (1964) took the process one step further. His transactional analysis (TA) model owes much to the fact that he made Freud's ideas even more specific and step-guided. He took the notion of ego, superego and id, and relabelled them Parent, Child and Adult. Berne showed clearly what principles should guide behaviour modes; how to understand the behaviour of others (in terms of 'games'); and demonstrated the steps required to respond effectively to the behaviour of others (counter-games). Transactional analysis has been one of the most popular ideas in the neo-human relations family.

Theoretical ideas are more appealing to managers if they can be translated into action. If a theory or model offers a clear set of steps to be followed or a set of principles to be instituted, then the chances of a positive response among managers and the subsequent implementation of the idea technique is significantly increased. Bureaucracy offered ten such principles which were detailed earlier. In terms of their prescriptive character, they were similar in form, if not in content, to those offered by Peters and Waterman (1982). The principles offered guidelines for senior managers designing their organizations.

As an idea-system, scientific management offered both techniques and principles. The techniques – standard minute values, critical path analysis, optimum batch size, and so on – were a direct inheritance of Taylor's system. For managers, they were not just the tools of their trade, but an expression of their professionalism, a three-step technique for designing manual jobs that was easily understandable by managers. It involved *task fragmentation*, the discovery of the *one best way*, and the *selection and training of employees*. A carefully calculated monetary payment which rewarded above average performance underpinned the operation of Taylor's approach.

The advocates of scientific management were concerned with producing *principles of scientific management*. They saw these as the features of any scientific approach. The advocates claimed that the principles did provide a collection of guidelines as to how managers ought to organize in order to be effective (Horn 1983). Scientific management therefore was both a philosophy and a logically consistent package of idea-techniques for the efficiency-minded production engineer. Clegg and Dunkerley (1980) called them a set of principles, a checklist of ideas, and inventory of guidelines. March and Simon (1958) described Taylor's work as consisting of a set of operating procedures.

The rules, principles or precepts of administrative management were all phrased in a very concrete and practical way. Written by managers for managers, they were manifestly capable of being applied. To use Kelly's (1980) term, administrative management 'offered a step by step guide . . . for getting things done in management'. Human relations, in its turn, offered a series of suggestions which were specific enough to permit implementation. For example, it recommended the application of a participative style of leadership in which the supervisor would exercise authority in an 'approved' (i.e. paternalistic) manner. It recommended the training of managers in the acquisition of such techniques. Other recommendations included the building up of communication, making allowances for the influence of informal groups, and offering a quasi-clinical counselling service to allow employees to let off steam (Wilensky and Wilensky 1952).

NHR sought to make the exercise of authority by managers less autocratic and more acceptable to employees but none the less real. They did this by fostering the conditions under which the individual and the workgroup could identify with the objectives of the organization. To this end NHR ideas offered specific prescriptions and guides (see Table 3.1). These may not have been what their authors had intended to say.

Blanchard and Johnson (1983) managed to distil the essence of management into three points in *The One Minute Manager*. Ohmae (1987) reduced company survival to the '3 Cs' – commitment, creativity and competition. De Bono transformed his ideas into a set of thinking exercises. However, it is not enough to communicate a simple message. What is also needed is an explanation of the mechanics of implementation to the audience. Mintzberg has generally failed on this dimension. Dixon (1986b) reported how a participant at one of Mintzberg's seminars, who had been told by him to encourage innovation, complained that he needed to be told *how* to do this. How was he to get his executive colleagues (especially those at middle management level where the worst inertia lay) to take the point and act on it. Mintzberg did not know what companies should do in the future to make themselves more innovative. In the eyes of this participant, he knew only how it had been done in the past among a handful of companies that he had studied. Finally, new age training courses provide 'structured opportunities for people to access, in a coherent way, their potential for creating the life they want' (*International Management* 1991).

Table 3.1 Summary of some neo-human relations principles

Maslow (1954)	Hierarchy of needs going from physiological at the bottom to self-actualization at the top. Needs that have been satisfied no longer motivate.
Herzberg *et al.* (1959)	There are two types of needs – hygiene and motivators. Only the latter lead people to action.
McGregor (1960)	Use Theory Y principles as the basis for your organization and management style.
Likert (1961)	Use System 4 participative group management style to maximize performance. Integrate group decision-making into structure through the use of linking-pin individuals.
Blake and Mouton (1964)	Most effective style is the 9/9 Team Management approach which is both highly task and person focused.

Universal application

Universal application is the management idea's claim that it can be used in all organizations. There are two ways in which universal application can be claimed. The first of these is *content* universality (as in the case of bureaucracy, administrative management or human relations ideas). The content universalists claim that all organizations share fundamentally the same features. Thus, the specific idea prescriptions offered (e.g. span-of-control, human relations training for supervisors) can be applied to all of them. A second approach is to claim *process* universality, as in the case of scientific management ideas. The process universalists do not claim to have a single best solution, but a single best process to arrive at the best solution.

The management idea and its technique should be capable of being applied in a wide range of different organizations and contexts. In contrast, situational specificity contributes to an idea's demise and may partly explain the faddish nature of management ideas which suddenly appear and then equally suddenly disappear.

The problem remains of how our guru achieves such universality of appeal. When consultants prescribe certain interventions, their arguments are frequently supported by anecdotal evidence and analogical reasoning. The former consists simply of illustrative examples that suggest one possible outcome that might result from a given organizational practice. This is based on the premise that an intervention which is successful in one instance will also be successful in similar circumstances. Moreover, if the package is adopted by well-known and successful companies, the mere fact of its adoption (irrespective of the success achieved) represents an endorsement of the idea or technique. This will motivate (and perhaps pressurize) other companies to adopt it just in case it is successful. Levy-Leboyer commented on the widespread use of social science:

New ideas which are easy to grasp and which answer the important problems of the day are quickly understood and applied, in fact, the simpler they are the more attractive they look. New techniques are no less tempting. In both cases, the attraction of novelty is rarely moderated by checking proof or scrutinizing available evidence. . . . Users of new theories and new techniques do not bother about generalizability, inter-cultural differences or statistical significance. They usually take a theory for granted as soon as it is available in print. And new techniques are accepted as being efficient because they are used elsewhere. Even worse, psychological tools, once adopted, resist evidence from well founded refutation.

(Levy-Leboyer 1986: 26)

Could the principles of bureaucracy be applied to any organization? The proponents of bureaucracy claimed that they could. The principles themselves have undergone a considerable revision since their original presentation by Weber in the early years of the twentieth century. Part of the appeal of bureaucracy lay in its ability to structure virtually any large organizational system. Given our current state of knowledge, bureaucracy has become the structural template for the large organization across the world. Bureaucracies have arisen in western industrialized capitalist countries, in developing Third World countries, and in communist systems. The underlying belief is that the greater the rationality, formalization, standardization and centralization of the enterprise or institution, the more effective it will be.

The choice of bureaucracy as an organizational form is made easy for large-system designers because of the lack of any available alternative form. Non-bureaucratic forms of organization do not appear to be appropriate to the needs of professional, task and group systems. As organizations grow, bureaucracy is often superimposed upon the existing system in order to deal with its expanded size.

While there was a clear intention in Weber's writings to signal the technical superiority of the bureaucratic form of organization, his comments were set in the historic context of the organizational forms that had preceded it, and which were based on charismatic and traditional forms of authority. He himself was not seeking to 'sell' bureaucracy. Indeed, he was critical of its effects on both modern society and on the administrators who inhabited it. Nevertheless, Weber's message was capable of being vulgarized by succeeding writers to give the impression that there was 'one-best-way' to organize which was applicable in all situations.

Proponents of scientific management argued that it could be applied in all organizations. Thus, it claimed a universal application. Indeed, it is difficult to envisage any organization in which at least some of the techniques such as time-and-motion study could not be used. The underlying rationale of scientific management was that its techniques could be applied to any industrial situation since all enterprises were subject to certain basic laws in their operation.

Administrative management authors claimed universal applicability for their principles as well. They were descriptions of what should happen rather than of reality. Lupton (1976) referred to the assumptions of structural universalism which held that if the injunctions are followed, they will lead to efficiency, 'whatever or wherever the organization'. Urwick stated that:

> there are principles which can be arrived at by induction, which should govern arrangements for human associations of any kind. These principles can be studied as a technical question, irrespective of the purpose of the enterprise, the personnel comprising it or any constitutional, political or social theory underlying its creation.
>
> (Urwick 1937: 49)

Underlying much of administrative management was the assumption that basic similarities in the structure and processes of organizations could be identified, conceptually analysed, and made explicit. The universally applicable principles of management, thereby distilled, would replace the traditional, intuitive, rules-of-thumb which were currently in use. Honour and Mainwaring observed that administrative management writers:

> were concerned to draw lessons from their experience which would be of universal applicability to work organizations. They were concerned predominantly to promote the efficient use of all resources in pursuit of what they perceived to be clearly defined goals'
>
> (Honour and Mainwaring 1982: 69)

Mayo believed that harmony and co-operation was the natural state of organizations in which workers gave freely of their commitment. Where this was not happening, barriers must exist to the giving of that wholehearted support. It was the job of management everywhere to identify and remove those barriers which were held to exist in all organizations. Hence the principles of human relations must be applicable to all organizations. In that sense, human relations considered all organizations to be alike (Likert 1967: 241) and any differences, for example in terms of markets or technology, were viewed as irrelevant.

All the NHR writers were perceived to be offering a 'one-best-way' prescription. Their ideas were universalistic in that they suggested that certain needs were shared by all workers, at all levels, and their response to the work situation could be explained in terms of the extent to which these needs were satisfied (Daniel 1973). Turning to the gurus, they recognized all organizations to be imperfect. However, because imperfections and employee recalcitrance were regarded as endemic features of all human organizations, the ideal was to minimize the inevitable organizational dysfunctions by doing what was objectively necessary to maintain and improve the functioning of the institutional structure. The solutions offered by the gurus claimed a universal applicability.

All manufacturing companies could improve asset utilization by the use of MRP and Just-in-Time concepts. There was no service or production operation in either the private or the public sector which would not benefit from a dose of excellence. No organization would reject the opportunity to gain a competitive advantage over its opponents. Every enterprise would want its employees to be creative problem-solvers and entrepreneurs. What firm did not wish to improve the quality of the product or service it provided to its customers? The list could be extended and the names of the relevant gurus inserted. However, it is sufficient to demonstrate that modern guru approaches are intended for the very widest consumption. New age training, similarly, sees 'everything in the world as connected'.

Authorization

Authorization refers to the basis of the belief in the management idea and its associated techniques. It answers the question for the manager, 'How do I know that it is true and will work?' It also provides the basis for the manager's defence should the adopted technique fail or be shown to be suspect. Historically, the popular management ideas have been authorized upon one or more of three bases. These are common sense, scientific research and adoption by others. The power of these is cumulative in that the more bases the guru can appeal to, the more attractive the guru's idea will become to managers.

The *common-sense* appeal of an idea to managers can be considered at a personal (or psychological) level, and at a control (or sociological) level. The first of these involves managers accepting and acting on the idea. Those ideas which appealed to the intuitive common sense of the manager had the greatest chance of becoming popular. Lupton (1976) wrote that job enrichment had a 'plausible ring' among managers. Peters and Waterman (1982) commented that the 'basics of management excellence don't just "work because they work". They work because they make excellent sense'. Peters' subsequent book 'disgorged no magic. The absence of magic – practical commonsense – turned out to be its biggest selling point' (Peters and Austin 1985).

Blackler and Shimmin (1984) commented on the difficulty of getting managers to base their decisions on knowledge that ran counter to 'common sense', 'natural' assumptions or short-term expediency. Common sense is neither common, nor is much of it sense. It has to be constructed by the individual, and is something which one might invent to avoid having to examine one's own practices or beliefs too deeply or at all. The poverty of common sense is evident after a moment's reflection. Yesterday's common sense, for example, asserted the superiority of men over women. No social, political, economic or political progress can be made if all knowledge comes from common sense.

This point not withstanding, the field of management treats words like 'theoretical' and 'academic' with disfavour, if not contempt. The stress on managerial common sense encouraged 'practical people to celebrate their own supposed being-in-touch-with-reality by scorning the theorists whom they see as being afraid to "dirty-their-hands" or to "get-their-feet-wet" (Watson 1980). This celebration of hard-headed, atheoretical practicality reflected the abstraction, opaqueness and even silliness of much of the theory that was on offer. However, it also acted as a defence mechanism which functioned as a two-finger salute to those who stayed away from the coal face.

Managers' preferred processes of knowledge acquisition support this view. These stress learning from the experience of doing a job in preference to formal courses of instruction; working within the team; the view that learning could not be transferred easily to the workplace; and that programmes should develop the natural, intuitive, entrepreneurial feel which the orderly scientific approach inhibited (Hall 1985).

Common sense is therefore an important basis of appeal. The figure-ground switch of currently perceived elements in the manager's work environment seems to result in a positive (and non-threatening) assessment by the manager of the idea as commonsensical. A management idea which can take this form is also perceived to challenge the manager's way of seeing and doing things. Objectively, what one has here is contradiction. The idea is perceived to be simultaneously commonsensical *and* challenging. Yet the research reveals that such contradiction is neither acknowledged nor experienced as problematic by managers. Indeed, such a unique contradictory position may hold the key to understanding what makes a popular management idea such a rarity.

Popular management ideas succeed in not offering their audience anything too outlandish for them to accept (Davis 1971). It appears that the mind had no room for the new and different unless it is related to the old. There were three possible responses when people checked a new piece of information against their existing knowledge or bank of common sense. If it was already known, it was considered redundant, and no learning took place. If it was too radical, some reason would be found for discrediting the information, in order to defend an existing 'world view' from attack. Finally, if the idea was new but involved only a limited rearrangement of existing views, then learning took place (Butler 1986).

Levy-Leboyer (1986) suggested that scientific refutation did not determine the popularity of a management idea. Instead it was its acceptability which was the determining factor. With so many different ideas around, managers were attracted, first by those which were new, and second, by those which possessed an intuitive, commonsensical appeal or face validity. Other studies have shown that management ideas and the techniques based upon them would be resisted by managers if they appeared to be critical of what managers had done, or did not agree with their expectations, values or experiences (Carter 1971; Caplan 1977); or worst of all, if they actively threatened managers' 'stability of cherished beliefs and world views' (Zusman 1976).

From the sociological-control perspective, it is useful to consider common sense using the Marxist Antoni Gramsci's concept of *hegemony*. Hegemony involves the constant winning and re-winning of the consent of the majority to the system that subordinates them. The construction of 'common sense' is a key hegemonic strategy. Gramsci would argue that if managers' ideas can be accepted as *common* (i.e. not class or manager-based) sense, then their ideological objective would be achieved and their ideological work disguised. For example, Taylor's 'laws' of scientific management, the techniques of organizational development and the procedures of quality circles, all offer a common-sense appeal. The shopfloor employees as 'consumers' will find it difficult to object to the imposition of these idea-techniques. After all, they're 'only common sense'!

A second basis of idea authority is *scientific research*. In Britain, managers prefer common sense and practical ideas to more sophisticated and complex techniques, especially those based on scientific social science research. Indeed, many of the latter are regarded with suspicion and scepticism. Managers and the media appear to be reluctant to take research findings seriously and instead tend to give prominence to 'pseudo research' and to the opinions of individual managers. The appeal of the commonsensical-intuitive approach has been greater than the strength of research validity. Guion (1975) observed that managers lacked the time and resources to develop and evaluate a theory of their own, and did not have the patience to master the intricacies of a fully elaborated theory developed by others. Managers therefore fell back on simple theories obtained from 'consultants, hucksters or colleagues'. Guion noted that managers rarely assessed the validity of a management idea on the basis of statistical or even empirical evidence.

Thomas (1989) considered how common sense and science linked up. He illustrated this with the case of *The One Minute Manager* (Blanchard and Johnson 1983). Here, the authorization of the proposed techniques was achieved within the story itself by the 'convincing' explanations given by the 'One Minute Manager' to the acolyte's questions. Rather like Watson to Holmes, the young man simply 'saw' that it was true and made sense.

Outside of the story, noted Thomas, authorization took the form of the prominent display of the authors' qualifications (PhD and MD), consumer endorsements, two pages of description of the authors' backgrounds, and a list of acknowledgements listing thirteen names, ten of which were prefixed with the title 'Dr'.

The absence of a list of references was consistent with the story mode which presented the content as 'a compilation of what many wise people have taught us and what we have learned ourselves'. Thomas felt that the story mode relieved the authors from any obligation to provide a rigorous justification of the procedures that they advocated. It is significant that the books of Edward de Bono, the propounder of Lateral Thinking, similarly do not contain any references.

According to Gellner (1985), truth was not, in fact, an advantage in producing a burning faith. He argued that although popular belief systems needed to be anchored in the 'obvious' intellectual climate, they could not consist entirely of obvious, uncontentious elements. An idea or a concept without an element of conflict was not an idea at all but rather what the Americans refer to as 'a motherhood, apple and the flag revised'. Thus, he felt, ideas which had a cogency, obviousness and acceptability could not be used as marks which distinguished a school of thought. Truths which were demonstrable or obvious did not fulfil the task of distinguishing the 'believers' from the rest. Only a difficult belief could do that. Gellner wrote that the belief or idea must contain an element of *both* menace and risk:

> The belief [idea] must present itself in such a way that the person encountering, weighing the claim that is being made on him, can neither ignore it nor hedge his bets. His situation is such that encountering the claim, he cannot but make a decision, and it will be weighty one, whichever way he decides.
>
> (Gellner 1985: 41)

The third and final way in which a management idea can gain authority is by virtue of being *adopted by a well-known company*. When management ideas are transformed into products such as consumable management techniques, training materials or system-wide interventions, their purveyors' catalogues all regularly include lists of users. The presence of names such as IBM, ICI and BP does four things. It confirms that managers are in good company if they adopt the technique; it allows them to identify their organization with these successful ones; it reassures them that the technique has been examined by people in those companies who have committed themselves to it; and it provides a defence in the case of failure showing that their decision, in the circumstances, was reasonable, even if it was ultimately proved to be wrong.

As far as authorization for an idea is concerned, the guidance for the guru is clear. If possible, the idea should be founded upon a scientific base, at least to the extent of being able to claim that 'research shows . . .'. The idea itself should not be incompatible with the manager's broad belief system, but neither should it be so exactly in tune with it that it is rejected as being obvious or irrelevant. Instead, it should involve a re-arrangement of the elements in the manager's world while leaving it broadly familiar. If possible, it should involve an element of risk, opportunity or menace. Again, this difficult balancing act may be responsible for the very small number of truly popular management ideas.

Weber's ideas were based on his historical research. Bureaucracy appealed to managers' common sense. It possessed a face-validity, because it was grounded in a rational approach that attracted adopters. The bureaucratic model made it clear to managers that the organizational discipline in the factory was founded upon a completely rational basis.

Scientific management's title implied that scientific laws could be derived from management practice and that these were related to ways of doing work and paying wages. Establishing such laws involved managers using scientific methods. In Taylor's view, the methods that were used in engineering could be applied to management. Reich commented on this idea:

> The very name of the new discipline suggested benign progressiveness. *Management* implied guidance and restraint necessary for social harmony. *Science* bespoke disinterestedness and rigour. Together, the words 'scientific management' provided the perfect banner for a new wave of reformers who sought to control and regulate society rather than uproot it.
>
> (Reich 1984: 63)

The common sense logic of the administrative management principles was also appealing. The usefulness of the principles as guides to actions appeared self-evident. They represented helpful approximations of what went on in organizations and they possessed face validity. Its writers attempted to elaborate principles of sound management 'in a common-sense manner' (Mouzalis 1967). Since the principles themselves were based on the observations of actual organizations by different writers, it is not surprising that there was such a close correspondence between the evolved trial-and-error practices in organizations and the principles propounded by those who studied and who wrote about them.

On what basis of authority did the human relations writers promulgate their ideas? Mayo was responsible for the growth in the use of training techniques intended to improve human relations skills and the literature on subjects such as leadership and planning change in organizations. The face validity of human relations and its common-sense appeal should not be ignored. Mayo promised the manager greater output, the workers' devotion and social prestige. 'Somehow', said Rose (1978: 124), 'his proposals for securing them rang true.' His ideas also had the backing of the research and the publications of the Hawthorne studies themselves. Although observers may now question the degree of empirical support for human relations, at the time it was the biggest piece of industrial social science research ever conducted.

A core belief of NHR ideas was that employees would be most motivated when they achieved 'psychological growth'. This possessed a considerable common-sense and intuitive appeal to managers. One only had to watch babies delight in their new achievements to confirm this gut feeling. This goes some way to explaining why NHR should receive such widespread acceptance among managers. NHR provided a range of idea-techniques or interventions which sought to improve employee effectiveness and relations. These included job enrichment, participative leadership styles, improvements in working conditions, improved communication and consultation strategies, as well as team-building training. The majority of organizational development (OD) approaches tended to rely on their common-sense appeal rather than upon any scientific validation. Kahn (1974) noted the relative dearth of evaluative studies of OD packages and in particular, of empirical studies which compared different approaches with one another. There were a few exceptions (Bowers 1973; Friedlander and Brown 1974; Greiner 1977).

Watson (1986) too attributed the popularity of NHR to its run-of-the-mill, common-sense assumptions. That is, what he described as a woefully simplistic generalization such as 'people only go to work for money' which elicited from managers the response 'it's common sense, isn't it?'. It was a form of common-sense knowledge which was based upon easy, unthought-out, taken-for-granted assumptions. Anthony critically commented upon behavioural science management teaching. He felt that:

> One of the most noticeable characteristics of many of these writers on management is that their style is propangandist, designed to have an effect, to persuade. To be sure, in that the approach is supposed to be grounded in the behavioural sciences, there is often a great paraphernalia of proof, validation and experimentation. Blake, for example, has a whole chapter headed, 'Career Accomplishment and Managerial Style' in which he sets out to prove his position. The assembly of pseudo-science includes the 'Managerial Achievement Quotient' (MAQ) which is the measure of individual performance. Blake presents the following example,
>
> $$MAQ = \frac{5(9-L)}{Age\ to\ 50-20}$$
>
> in which L is the actual managerial level subtracted from a constant 9, which is based on 8 levels in a hierarchy. 5 is a 'constant progression

factor' showing intervals of time in moving an individual from the bottom to the top in 40 years (Blake and Mouton 1964: 229).

(Anthony 1977: 236–7)

Anthony was less then convinced about the validity of this approach as he went on to say that:

The reader might well have concluded by now that managers would be better (and more cheaply) employed studying the entrails of chickens and he might also have entertained the passing thought that we were all wasting our time on such ponderous nonsense. The truth is that it probably represents one of the strongest influences on current management thinking, it is solemnly (and uncritically) taught in many management centres and universities and it has influenced the policies and structure of companies such as BP and ICI. It would take a considerable programme of research to validate the hypothesis that all behavioural science management teaching is rubbish, so we shall have to content ourselves with the unproved assertion that most of it seems to be so.

(Anthony 1977: 236–7)

Turning to the management gurus, the basis of authorization differed considerably between the different types of gurus. The academic guru work was embedded in academic research which could stand up to academic testing. In contrast, consultant guru theory has showed itself to be sceptical of scientific theories, and parts of it have returned to one of the less respectable philosophical positions – that of crude empiricism.

The search is on for *what works* (in terms of economic performance), in order to describe the characteristic features that seem to accompany success, so that these can be imitated. The search takes two forms. It either examines what the world's leading economic countries do (e.g. Japan, South Korea, Taiwan), or focuses on the leading companies about which books were written (IBM in the USA; Marks & Spencer in Britain). Other parts of consultant guru theory, like *The One Minute Manager*, achieve authorization by provision of 'convincing explanations inside of the text, and a prominent display of authors' qualifications (degrees, consulting experience, previous publications, consumer endorsements, and lists of acknowledgements), outside of the text' (Thomas 1989).

Part of the appeal of ideas such as Blanchard's *The One Minute Manager* is that they are modelled on the technique of Management-by-Objectives (MbO), which has the distinction of being among the most widely used and most influential management techniques in the post-war period. Moreover, MbO ideas and principles have now been generally accepted. They have become incorporated into staff apprasial systems and have entered the subconscious of most managers. Thus, when faced with Blanchard's 'new idea', One Minute Managers ring a bell of recognition deep inside their heads. It is therefore not rejected as new and alien but as something that fits into their existing stock of knowledge of experience. Mikes (1984: 9) wrote that people will always choose the philosophy whose seeds they have been carrying around in their souls or brains.

A recurring aspect of the different guru messages is their common-sense nature. If a new idea can be shown to be a version of common sense, its threat to the potential adopter is reduced. The main test of common sense used by their management readers is that of face-validity – does it feel right? Mikes (1984) suggested that a great many brilliant and inspiring things have been said which remain brilliant and inspiring regardless of whether they are right or wrong. Throughout the history of philosophy, he argued, *what* was said has always been less important than *how* it was said. Dazzling arguments leading to false conclusions have always carried more weight and have been more celebrated than sound thinking served up on sauce of dullness.

Many new management terms achieved overnight popularity, and then subsided into disuse. The managers using them did not really know what they were talking about. The gurus who brought the terms into prominence used them in such a vague way that their true meaning could not be discerned. This was not accidental: the gurus were being protective. In any discipline, the person who came up with a new idea first surrounded it with a defensive network of jargon. This made it difficult for rivals to steal the idea, while also making it difficult for anyone to grasp the idea too readily. If the idea were transmitted in plain English, there would be the danger that the acolyte would quickly see the whole thing, and claim that it was obvious!

New age training, lacking an immediate common sense appeal or research base, depends heavily on the authorization of users. In a short, 1,700 word article (*International Management* 1991), the names of twenty-three different organizations are mentioned to give credibility to the approach. In fact, this is an underestimate as three organizations (IBM, Shell and the International Stock Exchanage) are each mentioned three times in the article, and four others (American Express, Olivetti, Cabinet Office and Rowntree Mackintosh) are each mentioned twice.

However, there is some evidence that Davis's proposition does not fit entirely as far as management theory and ideas are concerned. Davis (1971) considered his audiences to be essentially apathetic or hostile in their attitude to the ideas presented. The audience for management guru products is neither. To judge by the book sales figures it is both highly committed and positive, at least in the United States. Given this fact, the top management gurus can serve up the obvious while glorying in the fact. Thus the first chapter of Peters and Austin's *A Passion for Excellence* (1985) is entitled 'A Flash of the Obvious'. In it, the authors explain that there is nothing new under the sun and that what they will be telling the reader in the book is common sense anyway.

"They changed all the buzzwords and no one told me."

© Leo Cullum, 1986

The question that is raised therefore is why should common sense be so attractive to managers? Why are they prepared to pay to buy books, videos and audio-tapes, and attend seminars, to be told what they already know? The answer to this must lie somewhere in individual psychology. The question will be explored in greater depth in Chapter 5. Here, however, it is perhaps enough to say that for managers to be told the 'real answers' to their questions (although not in exactly the terms they would have used) does two things. First, it confirms the managers' view of things, and second, it raises their self-esteem by the discovery that the guru agrees with them!

Applicability

Applicability refers to the dual notion that the proposed management idea possesses a practical application that will produce a benefit or *pay-off*. That pay-off should be attainable within a *short period of time*. Pay-off pertains to management's perception that the idea or its technique will actually provide the benefits or gains claimed for it. Such benefits might be explicit (e.g. reduced costs) or hidden (e.g. adopting job enrichment, ostensibly to give workers more discretion over their work, but mainly perhaps to allow management to keep its control over the work process intact). Thus, it is not always clear what management may see as the major pay-off of any particular idea. Oliver (1990) discussed the highly visible pay-off offered by J-I-T.

Let us now consider the time scale of that pay-off. A feature of popular management ideas is their ability to produce results quickly for their users. The application of the bureaucratic model involves the analysis of jobs and their delineation into highly specialized tasks. When this happens, the jobs and the people in them, become highly amenable to prescription, and the bureaucratic process begins to dominate. Such specialization and routinization are held to increase the efficiency of task performance.

Whatever the benefit, it is frequently difficult for aspiring gurus to demonstrate objectively the effectiveness of a particular management technique. More often, they rely on indirect methods. By listing their past customers, they imply that these have found the product or service offered to be beneficial. From this perspective, our gurus need to build a client list and display it prominently in their advertising literature.

A second dimension of applicability is speed of pay-off. Any management idea that offers the possibility of results quickly gives its promoter a competitive edge. Reich (1984: 164) wrote that 'Managers who anticipate a short tenure with their firm unsurprisingly have little interest in the long-term solutions to basic problems. Their goal is to make the firm (and themselves) look as good as possible in the immediate future.'

To be popular, therefore, management gurus have to ensure that their idea and its technique are perceived as offering swift and tangible results. Note the word 'offer'. It might not actually deliver these, but that is a different matter. In its promotion, including explanation, the buyer must feel that practical benefits can be secured in the short term (whether or not they actually are).

As a form of organization did bureaucracy actually work? It was the technical superiority of bureaucracy over its historical predecessors which, in Weber's opinion, accounted for its increasing adoption. In a section of his book, he made a statement which would not have been out of place in a product description of an advertising leaflet selling the concept of bureaucracy to managers:

> Business management throughout rests on increasing precision, steadiness and above all, the speed of operations. . . . Bureaucratization offers above all the optimum possibility for carrying through the principle of specializing administrative functions according to purely objective considerations.

> (Weber 1948: 215)

The implementation of scientific management did reduce costs and increase profits. In some cases, the benefits were dramatic. It therefore fulfilled one of the basic criteria of a popular management idea – it had a pay-off. Horn

(1983) estimated that by 1915 only about 1.3 per cent of American wage-earners worked under scientific management. However, he admitted that a larger proportion were affected by some part of it. Applications of the approach grew between the First and Second World Wars and after 1945, and the technique continues in existence today.

Exceptional performance improvement results were often obtained by Taylor and his followers in a very short time. They redesigned individual tasks and the relationships between the production tasks. As early as 1911, the cost savings obtained at the Bethleham steelworks confirmed the effectiveness of scientific management. The number of employees was reduced from 500 to 140, and output per man rose from 16 tons to 59 tons per day. This resulted in a reduction in cost handling from $0.072 to $0.033 per ton. The savings achieved by the application of Taylor's ideas were between $75,000 and $80,000 at 1911 prices. In the years that followed, the appeal of scientific management rested on the quick pay-off that the application of time-and-motion studies produced.

However, for the first time, doubts are being raised about its appropriateness in a situation where information technology is radically changing the nature of work. The continued use and expansion of Taylorism did not lie in its power to reduce conflict between management and workers. Instead, and despite its shortcomings, it was seen by managers as a way of enhancing the firm's chances of survival. Taylor himself was unhappy that so few firms had adopted his scientific management ideas in their entirety. Most managers adopted only those parts that enhanced their status and the short-term profitability of their company.

The major variable in the design of jobs, said the administrative management writers, was the minimalization of immediate production costs. This was achieved by specializing skills in order to reduce skill requirements. This is turn reduced learning times. Underlying the principles of the idea was the basic economic assumption that the concentration of effort on a limited field of endeavour increased the quantity and the quality of the output. The greatest pay-off obtained was in the specialization of work which was greatly increased. Time-wise, administrative management offered a clear and direct improvement in the way that organizations were run. In some ways they were the only ones on offer. They drew heavily upon the largest and most successful organizations of their time – the armed forces and the church. By applying the principles, managers would immediately and significantly improve the performance of their own organization.

Perhaps the most important aspect of human relations thinking was in the field of supervisory and junior management training schemes. These schemes, which became very popular across a range of organizations, tended to emphasize the importance of *communication* and the *careful handling of people*. Instead of altering work organization, existing structures were maintained intact, and marginally humanized through more sensitive people management. The pay-off was the ability of management to claim it had made major changes when in fact it had not.

Discussing the outcomes of NHR applications, especially OD interventions, Kahn (1974) concluded that 'significant increases in performance, attendance and satisfaction have been accomplished by organizational changes'. He gave examples of OD interventions which included the division of labour, the definition of individual jobs, job redesign, job enlargement, job enrichment and so on. He emphasized that management's primary concern in most cases was with productivity and profitability, and only secondly with job satisfaction and the meaningfulness of work. However, OD packages promised an explicit linkage between satisfaction and productivity. Likert (1961) himself felt that 'democracy pays in management'.

NHR writers said virtually nothing about the basic economic and political structures of organizations. While expounding employee-oriented principles, the school was impotent as a force for humanistically oriented change (Nord 1974). Ironically, it was its very impotence to change contemporary management practices that gave it such an appeal in the eyes of managers. The pay-off for managers may not have been in terms of productivity gains, but more in terms of social prestige, as they were able to talk about their concern for people with reference to job enrichment programmes which on the shopfloor had a limited application and produced minimal results. In order to be able to shape the behaviour of workers, managers had to acquire the necessary skills. What was the pay-off to them of doing so? Rose (1978) suggested that:

> The Lewinians were beginning to realise the Mayoite aim: leaders (managers) they showed, through communication (social skills), could manipulate participation (informal organization) to produce a superior group climate (morale), thus enhancing satisfaction (integration) with the group life (social system) and improving performance (output).
>
> (M. Rose 1978: 163)

Human relations held that because the problem of performance was seen to be located within the employees, there was no need to engage in the time-consuming task of changing the form of management control. Human relations suggested easily implementable solutions which claimed to offer fast results to managers who were uninterested in human issues. Anthony (1986) argued that all the people-centred activities could be seen as aspects of management which were considered by many line managers as irritating, tiresome or embarrassing. Personnel departments, in his view, were monuments to the refusal of managers to recognize their responsibility for labour. Human relations techniques which were spawned by Mayo's writings offered managers a way to opt out of their responsibilities.

All the guru texts have an explicit or implicit message of 'how-you-can-do-it-too'. For example, *In Search of Excellence* (Peters and Waterman 1982), offered a guide on how all managers can make their companies excellent. Ouchi's book, *Theory Z* (1981), contained a set of case histories of Theory Z companies. In *Megatrends*, Naisbitt's (1982) 'how to' recommendations related to the importance of tuning into trends, since they will take you to better times (Freeman 1985). Others show how to become rich quickly or to avoid personal economic disaster. Testimonials are available from companies such as Cunard Ellerman to support new age training (NAT). This division of Trafalgar House sent half of its UK staff on a NAT course and claimed to have saved £1.5 million, 50 per cent more than it had planned (*International Management* 1991).

Early in the twentieth century a consultancy tradition, based on the application of psychology to organizational problems, established itself in the United States. This tradition often favoured a short cut to rapid results in a highly competitive market (Rose 1978). The clear idea-techniques or interventions which were based upon NHR ideas all had the potential of being quickly implemented. The majority involved off-site training sessions (e.g. T-groups, team-building) while others could be incorporated into company working processes (e.g. attitude surveys, confrontation meetings). As the chapter on promotion will show, the brochures of consultants who sold their OD services frequently promised results in eighteen months or less. The general thrust of guru theories is that it gives its readers two assurances. First, if the advice is followed business results will be improved. Second, and in consequence, the world will be a better place.

CONCLUSION

An analysis of the six most popular management idea families has revealed three recurring themes, each with its own set of features. These are summarized in Table 3.2, which highlights the point that not all of the six families possess all of the twelve features discussed. This finding suggests two things. First, that a management idea can achieve popularity without having all the twelve characteristics, provided that it has the majority of them. Second, it appears that factors other than just content of the management idea itself play a part in securing popular status for it.

Since popular management ideas have not been studied from this perspective before, it is impossible to compare this analysis with others. However, an investigation was carried out by Gellner (1985) who sought to explain the popularity, not of management ideas, but of psychoanalytical theory. Since Gellner's work has been quoted throughout this chapter, it is appropriate to end by considering some of his conclusions and lay these alongside those made in this chapter. Gellner studied Freud and the psychoanalytic movement (Gellner 1985: 26 and 42) in order to account for its appeal among practitioners and clients. He concluded that the appeal of psychoanalysis could be attributed to the fact that it offered its users and practitioners a number of crucial advantages. Comparing Gellner's suggestions with the features identified in popular management ideas in this and other chapters, one can immediately discern similarities. To stress the similarities, the terms used in this chapter and elsewhere in the book are placed alongside those of Gellner.

1 *Specificity*
  (Steps or principles)

If offered specificity whereas previously there had been only general outlines.

2 *Recipe*
  (Steps or principles)

It promised succour in a plague. It contained a recipe for the personal desired salvation, whereas before there had been only ambiguous indications.

3 *Organization*
  (Promotion, Chapter 6)

It possessed an organization to support and promote its ideas.

4 *Terminology*
  (Communicability)
  (Authorization)

It possessed a scientific terminology whereas before there had been only a literature.

5 *Insider status*
  (Authorization)

It achieved the inclusion of its ideas into the prestigious context of medicine whereas previously they had existed in the not greatly eminent ambience of philosophy.

6 *Time*
  (Historical context Chapter 4)

It possessed links to the background convictions of the age.

7 *Common sense*
  (Communicability)
  (Authorization)
  (Legitimacy)

It stunned its potential proselytes with what they more than half knew (but never knew how to put into words). It provided good reasons for believing its claims.

8 *Unverifiable*
  (Contribution potential)

A quick and conclusive test of the truth of the ideas was unavailable.

9 *Tension*
  (Requirements of managers,
  Chapter 7

It engendered a tension in potential converts with its promise *and* its threat. It invoked in them an inner anxiety as evidence of its own authenticity. It provided some good reasons for doubting or fearing its truth.

Table 3.2 Summary of characteristics possessed by the six management idea families

	Understanding of work world			Status enhancement				Practical application				
	Communicability	Individual focus	Malleable human nature	Legitimation	Unitary perspective	Contribution-ownership potential	Leadership focus	Control	Steps or principles	Universal application	Authorization	Applicability
Bureaucracy	●			●				●	●	●	●	●
Scientific management	●	●	●	●	●	●		●	●	●	●	●
Administrative management	●			●	●			●	●	●	●	●
Human relations	●	●	●	●	●	●	●	●	●	●	●	●
Neo-human relations	●	●	●	●	●	●	●	●	●	●	●	●
Guru theory	●	●	●	●	●	●	●	●	●	●	●	●

Chapter 4

Historical context

INTRODUCTION

Managers running organizations in capitalist economies face recurring problems such as maintaining control, increasing productivity and motivating staff. The particular management idea favoured as a solution to these problems, at a given point in time, will be greatly influenced by the social, economic and political factors of the period. Victor Hugo wrote that 'Nothing, not all the armies of the world can stop an idea whose time has come'. Business writers have noted the same thing:

> new themes in the thinking of managers become more popular as the economic trends which prompted those thoughts touch the lives of more people. An intellectual fad is a reliable, if slightly lagging, indicator of underlying economic activity. So the first place to look for signs of a new fad is in the economy itself.
>
> (Stuart 1986: 119)

> from the debris of these notions, the emerging view has been of less certainty and more variability in prescriptions for management practice. The conclusion should not be that Argyris, McGregor and Herzberg were wrong (nor were Fayol, Taylor, Mayo *et al.*) but that their ideas were bound by place and time.
>
> (Wren 1973: 490)

Why do some ideas appear, receive emphasis and win emotional support, while others are neglected and remain suppressed? A management idea is a product of its past as well as the harbinger of the future. It is a product of its cultural environment and finds its roots in the evolving economic and social milieu. An explanation of how the environmental background of each period facilitated the growth of certain management ideas can benefit from the use of Sutton *et al.*'s (1956) threefold classification. This discussed the period's *cultural heritage*, that is the dominant value orientations of society as well as the broader cultural movements; its *institutional framework*, its historical antecedents such as unions, size of organization and research ideas around; and the *motivational context*, that is the needs and roles of members of the organizations, specifically of managers.

Littler (1982) argued that all processes of idea institutionalization and diffusion took time. Historical lags would always exist between the ideas of intellectuals and those of active practitioners. In the United States, human relations did not 'happen' in the 1930s when Mayo conducted his studies. It established itself and became institutionally significant only in the 1940s in the United States, and in the 1950s in Britain. To ignore such a cultural lag was to fail to locate an idea within social space.

Since each environment is culture-specific, one needed to avoid committing what Littler (1982) called the 'Ambrit fallacy'. This was the tendency to fuse the history and culture of two very different societies, the United States and Britain, and to seek to draw sociological conclusions on the basis of this unrecognized conflation. To avoid this, it will be shown how historical elements in the United States facilitated the development of management ideas there, and how different factors helped their transfer to Britain.

The history of management ideas can be considered as a series of waves washing up upon and altering the foreshore before being swept back and replaced by other waves (Anthony 1986). The beach represents the body of ideas and techniques which guide managers' thoughts and actions and constitutes an amalgam of wave action over a period of time. Other writers have referred to the 'historical legacy of ideas' (Bendix 1963) and to the 'fund of available ideas' (Child 1968a). This wave–beach metaphor is a powerful one in helping us to understand the history of management ideas. It distinguishes points in time at which management ideas were initially born, and describes the conditions under which they had their greatest impact.

A review of the historical literature on management distinguishes four major historical periods. These are the Rational-economic, Social, Psychological and Entrepreneurial (see Table 4.1). Each period provided the fertile ground in which the original seeds of particular management idea were able to grow and subsequently to flourish in both the United States and in Britain.

Table 4.1 Summary of historical periods

Period	Representatives (examples)	Period of original development
Rational-economic	Taylor, Fayol, Weber	1890–1930s
Social	Mayo	1920s–1950s
Psychological	Maslow, McGregor	1940s–1950s
	Bennis, Walton	1960s–1970s
Entrepreneurial	Peters, Kanter, Iacocca	1980–1990

RATIONAL-ECONOMIC PERIOD

Cultural heritage

Derived from the philosophy of hedonism, the convictions of this period in the United States held that humans' actions were aimed at maximizing their self-interest. It was this which guided human behaviour. The American management philosophies up to and including the present have been dominated by a ruthless quest for the monopolization and exploitation of raw materials and renewable resources (cattle, people).

Humankind was held to be primarily motivated by economic factors, doing what would secure for them the greatest economic gain. The economic incentives were controlled by the organization, so employees were passive agents who, since they responded to economic laws, could be manipulated, motivated and controlled by the organization. Their feelings were considered irrational and should be prevented from interfering with the rational calculation of self-interest. Organizations had to be designed in a way which neutralized people's irrational feelings and unpredictable traits. McGregor (1960) later called these Theory X assumptions.

The closing decades of the nineteenth century witnessed unprecedented changes in the social and economic realms of the United States. Between 1865 and 1900 the country was transformed from a rural and handicraft economy to an America which, by 1890, led the world in industrial output. Articulated most forcefully by the efficiency proponents, the new perception of labour was a radical departure from older, populist notions.

The managerial perception was voiced in a crude and unsophisticated form. It came to be subsumed under four distinct but interrelated headings. These were an acceptance of the inherited laziness of humans; a perception of labour as bestial or machine-like; the endorsement of the economic nature of the needs and aspirations of working people; and a rejection of unionization and collective bargaining.

In the United States, several factors facilitated the shift to centralized managerial control in the 1880–1920 period. This represented the favourable backcloth to the development and popularity of Taylorism and his scientific management ideas and techniques. The process of industrialization in American industry was distinguished by the speed with which the economy threw off its familial frameworks and shifted instead to an economy of large corporations. By 1900, there were 1,500 companies with more than 500 employees. Nearly one-third of these employed more than 1,000 people. This was not a situation which was paralleled in Britain.

One aspect of this, the creation in the United States of a high wage economy, created a large potential market for mass-produced goods. This, together with the size of the population, set the economic context for the early development of the large corporation. This dominated the mass production and mass distribution industries. The existence of mass produc-

tion provided the basic rationale for the application of systematic management systems such as Taylorism and later, Bedeauxism and Fordism.

A second cultural feature was the character of the workforce. The
industrial labour force consisted largely of immigrants. In the 1907–8 period
these represented between 35 and 85 per cent of the workers, even though
the foreign-born population in the United States never rose above 15 per
cent of the gross population figure (Littler 1982). The effect of this was to
create a wide social gulf between employer and employee. Noble (1977)
argued that American employees of the time were more likely to be
dehumanized and treated as commodities. The high percentage also caused
ethnic turnover in some groups who filled the worst paid jobs. These people
moved to better paid jobs as circumstances permitted. This created a culture
of casualism, of rapid job mobility, and of transient links with employing
organizations. In the period 1900–20, employee turnover of 100 per cent per
year was not uncommon in many factories. In such circumstances, Taylorist
ideas were invaluable in helping to manage factories (Montgomery 1979).

Workers could move between companies because of expanding job
opportunities and recurring labour shortages of skilled craftsmen. Such
shortages, together with an influx of immigrants, meant that because skilled
craftsmen were rare and expensive, they were assigned only to important
work. All the surrounding tasks were assigned to cheaper semi-skilled or
unskilled workers. Simplification of tasks was achieved by task fragmentation and specialization. For this process to be successful, it required that
some new means be found to co-ordinate and integrate the sub-divided
work. The significance of Taylorism, at least in the United States, came
partly from the need to reduce and keep down labour costs in the context of
a high wage economy.

At the time, Taylor's ideas were considered as liberal and progressive by
many employers and were not initially welcomed. Nelson provided a
detailed account of the extent to which Taylorism was utilized and resisted
by American industrialists and managers (Nelson 1975). The ideas promised
to create within the factory context what a young Princeton professor and
future American President, Woodrow Wilson, had recommended should be
introduced within the government service, that is an end to arbitrary,
corrupt and inefficient rule. Both Taylor and Wilson were confident that
efficient management would drive politics out of the workplace and out of
government administration. The idea that conflict could be eliminated by
improved management had an enormous appeal to business leaders.

The spread of Taylorism coincided with the early and dramatic growth of
concentrated large-scale production at a point when the American capitalist
system exuded a high degree of confidence. As an ideology and philosophy
of labour relations, Taylorism's utilitarian view of motivation was compatible with this bold and self-assured period of American capitalism even
though both owners and managers resisted Taylor's ambitions for total

control of the factory by engineers. Scientific management was seen as superior to the systematic 'industrial betterment' approaches of the time (such as those of the National Cash Register company) because it addressed itself to the issue of the control of the work process.

The managerial ideas and institutions which arose during this period appeared to be applicable to society as a whole. Taylor argued that the principles which had been applied to factories were capable of being used in homes, farms, commerce, churches, philanthropic establishments and universities. The managed organization replicated itself in these areas and gave them stability, order and prosperity. Taylorism acquired an immense amount of ideological and political influence through a cult of efficiency which came to dominate practically every aspect of American life by the early twentieth century. By 1914, the USA had embraced scientific management with unabashed enthusiasm. In that year, 69,000 people attended an efficiency exposition at Grand Central Palace in New York to hear Taylor speak (Reich 1984).

Institutional framework

The large corporations engaged in mass production had their own problems. Factories experienced bottle-necks, inefficiencies, poor co-ordination and inadequate controls. The managerial ideas that arose during this period were grasped by managers to solve their problems. They gave the USA the fruits of high-volume, standardized production.

Businesses that standardized and co-ordinated their work achieved spectacular efficiencies. The management hierarchies which employed sophisticated techniques to supervise and monitor subordinates gained significant cost advantages. Successful firms invested in machine production and developed managerial systems. Throughout this era, the real benefit lay in the relative efficiency with which these inventions and resources were managed. The successes of the companies which adopted these ideas and the competitive advantage they gained, stimulated others to emulate them in order to compete.

Managerial ideas were also used in government. As a high-volume producer, the Federal government needed help in creating a stable environment for planning and co-ordinating these investments. Mergers and consolidations at the turn of the century had helped to eliminate distribution and marketing bottle-necks and these mitigated the initial problems of over-capacity. The First World War had triggered an enormous surge in industrial capacity, so when it ended, the problem of over-capacity reappeared. Plant and equipment in the new business enterprises imposed such high costs, that production at anything less than full capacity severely threatened firms' profitability. Thus, each firm had to somehow co-ordinate the investment decisions with those of other firms.

This problem was only one level removed from that of co-ordinating productive units within a firm. Management techniques applicable to the firm were applied to the economy as a whole. Managerialism thus offered America a set of organizing principles at precisely the time that many Americans sensed a need for greater organization. These principles soon came to shape every dominant US institution. The 'science of management', as expounded by Taylor and Fayol, offered a set of ideas for controlling large organizations. These were principles which appeared to be as universal and immutable as the laws of physics. America needed a generic science of management as a response to a whole set of problems and opportunities generated by the new forms of production.

The 1880–1920 period saw speedy industrialization and was accompanied by a set of ideas emphasizing individual enterprise, self-help and the opportunities offered by industrial and economic expansion. In the philosophical sentiments of the time, success and riches were regarded as the rewards of those who had proved themselves in the struggle to survive. Business leaders emphasized the virtues of character and Christian mission of business enterprises. A slogan of the time was that the 'capitalists of today were the working men of yesterday, and the working men of today will be the capitalists of tomorrow'. Poverty was not held to constitute grounds for claiming assistance. If employees remained in humble, ill-paid positions, this was because of their lack of will-power and modesty of talent.

During this period, management was forced to consider labour as a problem. It was insufficient to bewail inefficiencies and to dismiss those who were conspicuously unfit. Working together, employers developed common principles of management policy and recognized that more refined techniques rather than polemics were what was required. By 1910 the primary emphasis had been placed on the 'man-management problem'. Methods were recommended as to how to increase labour productivity. Stress was placed on the idea that it was in workers' interests to collaborate with their managers' plans and to seek advancement in the enterprise by improving the quality and quantity of their output rather than by joining a union.

Scientific management's emphasis on work specialization, use of predetermined rules for task co-ordination and detailed performance monitoring, allowed an enterprise to employ inexperienced and unskilled workers which was a boon to employers at times of labour scarcity such as the First World War. Additionally it meant that wages could be kept relatively low when labour was more abundant. At the turn of the century, the US labour force consisted largely of uneducated immigrants who were unskilled, had a high turnover and who were frequently in conflict with each other and management.

The growth in size of companies meant that their managements had few existing organizational models on which to base their structural arrangements upon (other than the irrelevant example of the Catholic Church). In the United States firms became so large that the Sherman Anti-Trust Act was thought to be necessary as early as 1890. The Act did little to slow organizational growth and gave management both opportunities and problems. The opportunity was the benefit of the economies of scale. The problem was how to maintain control. The result was that managers needed concepts which allowed them to break these huge concerns into smaller, more controllable sub-units while retaining the economies of scale. Commenting on scientific management, Butler said that:

> It was a child of its age; an age of authoritarianism and an age which had fallen in love with mechanistic concepts of every type. Men everywhere tried to reduce the world to certain fundamental frameworks inside which society would operate, secure in the knowledge that 'natural law' prevailed.
>
> (Butler 1986: 287)

Motivational context

How were ideas such as scientific management and classical management received by managers? Bendix (1963) argued that the 'survival of the fittest' philosophy of scientific management appeared to provide a justification for the absolute authority of individual employers in their own firms, including the authority to weed out the incompetent. This represented an important element in the promulgation of such management ideas. Employers in the United States felt it especially important to assert their right to authority in the workplace, in the light of the dramatic rise in organized labour.

Scientific management at the turn of the century could best be understood in terms of the labour relations of the time (Sofer 1972). The growth of union power had occurred in Britain in the 1860s and 1870s, while in the United States it began on a mass basis only in the 1890s. Such developments were initially hampered by the willingness of immigrants to work for low wages. Between 1897 and 1904, however, union membership in the USA increased between four and five times. In their counter-campaigns, employers attempted to maintain an open shop and sought to repudiate the challenge of the unions to their own central authority. In the management of their own plants they regarded their authority as absolute.

Scientific management and similar ideas of the period made a constant reference to 'natural laws'. These laws offered managers limited options thereby reassuring them that there were only a fixed number of possible actions. The 'principles' upon which these laws were supposed to operate absolved the decision-maker of guilt in the event of failure. The period itself was still heavy with the legacy of eighteenth- and nineteenth-century social and natural philosophers such as Adam Smith, Robert Malthus and Charles Darwin.

All these writers, in their different ways, had seen the world as operating upon certain principles. There had been the principle of the division of labour, of population expansion, of non-intervention in economic affairs and in natural selection. From the 1890s, Taylor codified the four 'great underlying principles of organization' which he claimed determined the format and operation of organizations at every level and in all circumstances. It was in this spirit that both scientific management and classical management ideas were formed.

What managerial strategy and psychological contract between the employee and the company was implicit in this view? The involvement was calculative. The organization bought the services and obedience of the employee for economic rewards. It protected itself against the employee's irrational actions by implementing a system of authority and control. Classical management ideas, for example, based upon the writings of Europeans such as Max Weber and Henri Fayol, can be seen as complementing the 'man-as-machine' theorists. Both groups sought to deal with, and make predictable, the irrational side of human nature.

Authority was held to rest in designated offices or positions and employees were expected to obey whoever occupied that position of authority, regardless of their expertise or personality. As the manipulator of these variables, the manager was meant to counter low morale or production by redesigning jobs or organizational relationships, and by changing incentives or control systems. Employees were expected to do no more than the incentive and control systems encouraged or allowed them.

Scientific management principles were embraced by the unions as well as by management. The unions saw them as a way of preventing despotism in the shop and for controlling the behaviour of their own members. Clear rule definition, explicit job delineation, detailed rules governing wages and working conditions and a grievance procedure based on a highly specialized division of labour, all offered union members a modicum of security against arbitrary action by the company, and a way of monitoring each other's actions. By the 1920s, organized labour was advocating scientific management as enthusiatically as business leaders.

Transfer of rational economic period management ideas and techniques to Britain

A fundamental difference between the adoption of Taylorism in the United States and in Britain was the time lag. While scientific management had repercussions in the USA in the pre-1914 period, it did not have an impact in Britain until the inter-war years. What factors accounted for this time lag of adoption?

Our knowledge of early British responses to Taylorism is based upon data collected by Urwick and Brech (1948) and Levine (1967). This shows that

Taylorism had a relatively small influence on British industry before the First World War, apart from a brief spurt of interest before the outbreak of that war. When the wall of indifference and the lack of understanding was finally breached in the run up to 1914, the reaction was largely hostile.

There are various indications of this lack of response to Taylorism in Britain. First, one can note that technical journals such as *The Engineer* and *Engineering* took little notice of Taylor's first two papers. His crucial paper on Shop Management (Taylor 1903) was totally ignored by all the engineering journals. Second, only one book on scientific management was published in Britain before the end of the First World War. Third, Taylorism was not discussed a great deal at any of the meetings of the professional institutions.

Such rejection was not wholly emotional or based on one person's views. The initial conscious rejection of this American import was due partly to the pattern of demand for many British engineering products which contrasted with that of the United States. In Britain, prior to 1914, there was only a limited mass market and few opportunities for mass production, and hence only a limited need for standardization and specialization of tasks. The war and post-war demand for standardized items like ammunition shells ultimately did replace the past pattern of varied and variable output and thereby made scientific management ideas more relevant.

A second difference which could account for the time lag was the rejection of scientific management ideas by British employers. Opposition came from Liberal and Quaker owners such as Cadbury who felt that it would lead to excessive speeding up, debase the worker and cause serious conflicts between capital and labour. Employers were particularly concerned about the high-wage strategy which was a key element in the US version of scientific management. Such a view was grounded in British class-based notions of appropriate wage levels.

At the turn of the century, engineering employers had sought to reduce wages to combat foreign competition. In Britain, labour tended to be viewed as a residual problem and as an obstacle to the path of technological advance and progress. Pollard (1965) suggested that it was only much later that the new view emerged that the productivity of workers was as important as the productivity of machines, and that it might be worth investing in the development of workers. On the human side, British engineers stressed the high administrative and supervisory costs of Taylorism, and were unconvinced of gaining increased profitability from the application of scientific management ideas in their firms.

Prior to the First World War therefore, the social and economic circumstances in Britain did not favour the adoption of Taylorism. The family-based, entrepreneurial small business dominated and had not, as in the United States, given way to the large corporation. Sofer (1972) wrote that although the rise of British union power preceded the American by twenty or thirty years, the rise of British awareness about new needs and potentialities in labour relations did not come as early as one would have imagined, given the stress on intensive industrialization. In a period dominated by pioneers and founding managers, it was these people who were apt to emphasize the individuality of the workers and the uniqueness of the enterprise rather than to generalize recurring needs. Prior to 1914, the development of new ideas and practices in Britain was not congenial to an integrated theory of organization as it was in the United States. This was one of the major differences between the two societies and it was reflected in the response to scientific management ideas crossing the Atlantic.

The evidence therefore shows that before 1914, British ignorance, indifference and hostility to Taylorism did not result in a widespread shift in employer beliefs. It might be that better established philosophies derived from Nonconformism and the technical training schools meant that there was no real (far less any experienced) need for ideas such as those of Taylor. What then changed in the post-1918 period to make scientific management ideas more relevant and more widely adopted in Britain?

At the company level, the enormous and continuing demands during the war had created stable markets for factories. This led them to develop mass production methods and some standardization. Managers had to staff their factories with unskilled labour, especially women, and this led to the erosion of skill differentials. Moreover, trade unions had gained new status and power, and managers had to consult trade union leaders for the first time. Later, the Depression of the 1920s led to calls for rationalization which referred to efforts to secure the minimum of waste of either effort or material. In Britain, it mainly referred to the large-scale horizontal mergers of firms, and to a lesser extent, to the application of scientific methods of management and control. Through the 1930s these ideas were promoted by Lyndall Urwick who saw rationalization as a natural extension of scientific management beyond its application to individual firms.

Prior to 1914 the continued family framework of many British industries meant that the development of new organizational forms was impeded. Families and entrepreneurs attempted to retain ownership and control as long as possible. In the 1918–28 period, however, corporate capitalism made some headway as a result of industrial concentration. By 1939 corporate capitalism had developed rapidly. 'Rationalized management', as it came to be called in Britain, was promoted by Charles Bedeaux who diffused Taylorist workshop practices and opened the way for the spread of neo-Taylorite systems. The history of scientific management in Britain in the inter-war years is largely the history of the Bedeaux system.

The pressures of the First World War, and the American involvement in that war, led to a transatlantic flow of ideas about management and industrial organization. Technical missions were sent to the United States and these returned with practical experience of Taylorist practices. After the war, scientific management became embedded within broader perceptions of America as a model of industrial productivity and prosperity. A commentator of the time observed that 'Such visions of progress and prosperity acted as cultural conduits by means of which the ideas of Taylorism seeped into the European consciousness'.

It was not until the late 1920s and early 1930s that the problems of the British economy and employers became desperate (and when they sought to lower costs), that a broad and continued interest was created in what scientific management had to offer. Between 1918 and the mid-1920s Taylorite schemes began to filter down to British factory shopfloors with initial attention being paid to time-study and more systematic payment systems. By 1937, 225 companies were using the Bedeaux version of scientific management (Thurley and Wirdenuis 1973).

The rapid spread of this approach through the 1930s in Britain was partly accounted for by the growing number of firms in the new and expanding industries of the period such as food processing, light engineering and motor components. Taylorism was introduced to British shopfloors during a period of high unemployment, short-time working and contracting markets. Such savings on labour costs in a stagnant market could come only from cutting the total hours paid, that is from redundancies. The most likely reason for the ultimate acceptance of work study in the 1940s and 1950s, however, were probably the boom conditions. In these circumstances, increased efficiency led not to redundancies but to higher wages for the increased output in a sellers' market. Thus in the end, Taylorism sneaked into Britain very late being allowed in by workers and their unions under the growth conditions of the Second World War and its aftermath.

SOCIAL PERIOD

Human relations ideas were based on the writings of Elton Mayo and the Hawthorne studies. Schwab and Cummings (1970) commented that an essentially unsupported interpretation of the results was so quickly and widely accepted that the underlying theory was neither questioned nor refined. What was it about that period in the United States that created such a hunger for human relations ideas?

No action is without a countervailing reaction and Taylor's thrust of scientific management generated its own counter-ideology in the form of human relations ideas. This reaction waned over time but it never totally derailed the original ideological thrust which found new allies in the positivism and behaviourism that came to characterize social science and management teaching in the middle years of the century. Anthony wrote that:

The very widespread influence of Elton Mayo's work and the apparent scientific respectability of the Hawthorne experiments had established a reaction to the belief in the techniques of scientific management as sufficient in themselves. The techniques and management principles with which they were associated were rarely questioned, but a belief began to spread that they could be taken too far, and that there were other influences. It was as though a romantic movement in management was beginning to follow the age of reason; reason was never entirely discredited, but it began to be recognized that other forces, some of them dark and mysterious had to be accounted for in exploring and influencing human behaviour.

(Anthony 1977: 223)

That romantic movement reflected several themes which, in Wren's (1973) view, were products of the cultural environment of the period. These were the call for social, human skills rather than technical ones; an emphasis on rebuilding people's sense of belonging through groups and social solidarity in order to overcome the 'confusion of souls'; and a concern with equalizing power through unions, through participative leadership and by fusing the formal organization with the social system of the factory.

Human relations basically held that industrial society was a shaky fabric. Its scale, diversity and constant change meant that it frustrated the basic human desire for intimacy, consistency and predictability in social living. People looked for this in their jobs instead. However, the rationalization of work had resulted in a loss of meaning in the technical aspects of work. Employees now had to focus on social relationships on the job. Lacking a wider certainty and intimacy, they purposely sought to manufacture these at the workplace by means of the informal organization. People were held to be more responsive to the social forces of their peer group than to the controls and incentives of management. Hence, employees' responsiveness to management was seen to depend on the extent to which a supervisor could meet their social needs and needs for acceptance. Mayo's studies initiated a sociological orientation to work relations. The generalizations shown in Table 4.2 summarize what Miller and Form (1964) called the 'core of the Mayo heritage'.

Human relations ideas developed and spread through the United States between the two world wars. The experience of the First World War, continued cycles of boom and bust, and persistent industrial conflict greatly discredited the shibboleths of early *laissez-faire* capitalism. Various intellectual currents had developed which challenged the naive rationalist utilitarian view on which Taylorism was at least partially based. Shortly before the beginning of the 1929 Depression, Magnus Alexander addressed the World Engineering Congress in Tokyo. He spoke about the tendency towards consolidation and association for greater efficiency, careful planning on the basis of diligent research, and concern over the ramifications

Table 4.2 Ideas of the human relations school

Generalization	Drawn from
1 Work is a group activity	All Harvard industrial research studies
2 The social world of the adult is primarily patterned around work activity	Textile mill; relay assembly test room
3 The need for recognition, security and sense of belonging is more important in the determination of workers' morale and productivity than the physical conditions under which they work	Relay assembly test room
4 A complaint is not necessarily an objective recital of facts; it is commonly a *symptom* manifesting disturbance of an individual's status position	Interviewing programme
5 The worker is a person whose attitudes and effectiveness are conditioned by social demands from both outside and inside the work plant	Relay assembly test room; bank wiring observation room
6 Informal groups within the work plant exercise strong social influence over the work habits and attitudes of the individual worker	Bank wiring observation room; metal-working companies
7 The first-line supervisor is the single most important factor in determining the morale and productivity of a work-group	Metal-working companies; Southern California aircraft companies
8 The change from an established to an adaptive society tends continually to disrupt the social organization of a work plant and industry generally	Southern California aircraft companies
9 Group collaboration does not occur by accident; it must be planned for and developed; if group collaboration is achieved, the work relations within a work plant may reach a cohesion which resists the disrupting effects of an adaptive society	Southern California aircraft companies

Source: Miller and Form 1964: 677

and effects of economic life over social progress. The emphasis, in his view, was shifting towards voluntary assumption of social obligations and co-operative effort in the common interest (Hughes 1958).

Just as the engineering purity of Taylor was not followed to the letter by the ever-pragmatic US managers, so too the social philosophy of Mayo was selectively adopted. American capitalists eclectically took advantage of whatever they found of use, first in Taylor's and then in Mayo's prescriptions for industry. Mayo's philosophy was far more alien to capitalists than

Taylor's engineering world view. Indeed, Mayo's theoretical disengagement from the dynamics of profit and competition ran counter to what were owners' and managers' top priorities – the pursuit of profit and corporate survival. So, what then was it about this period in the USA that encouraged the growth of these human relations ideas?

Cultural heritage

A set of new values emerged during the 1940s which were grounded in the cultural heritage of the USA (Sutton *et al.* 1956). These stressed activism, egalitarianism, universalism and social responsibility. They were compatible with human relations ideas and supported and initiated changes in the institutional and motivational spheres. In addition, American society, despite differences in the intellectual outlook of its diverse classes and groups, emphasized the individual, the value of experiential knowledge and of subjective feelings.

By the 1950s the concept of alienation had been given widespread currency through sociology. Its main application was in describing the problems of workers in blue-collar jobs. The problem of control was highlighted by economic expansion and consequent full employment. Massive absenteeism and labour turnover in the United States produced problems of low productivity. Other factors too made it necessary to consider the well-being of workers. Because of full employment there was no longer a queue of substitute workers prepared to take jobs under any conditions. If both trained and untrained workers were to be retained, working conditions had to be considered. This point was impressed upon management by the continuous sabotage of the production line which, with the aforementioned problems, damaged productivity.

It was in the two decades following the Second World War that human relations ideas had their greatest impact upon American managers (Watson 1986). They did not break the grip of scientific management thinking upon job design. However, what they did do was to overlay these now standard work structuring practices with some ameliorating supervisory and welfare practices. The exploitative and de-humanizing edge was taken off Taylorist practices in a way which made them more tolerable and more suited to the new post-war world of full employment. The research evidence and academic credibility of the human relations writers provided a rationale for an element of 'caring' in management which became more acceptable at a time when the older rationales of paternalistic and religious welfarism, which had played a similar role in earlier times, declined.

The Social Man model upon which human relations ideas were based represented a response to the increasing sophistication of a population which in the Great Depression had become aware that the interests of management and the interests of workers were often very different.

Landsberger commented that the quick and uncritical acceptance of Mayo's tentative conclusions on supervisory skills and training manifested 'the widespread craving among business circles for a new management ethic and for an easy, unpainful solution of industrial conflict' (Landsberger 1958, cited in Mouzalis 1967: 206).

The traditional authority of management was suddenly challenged. Management realized that the social context (group) in which individuals were embedded could often influence them just as much as management. Thus management development became a matter of teaching managers about groups, informal organization, social motivation, ascribed authority and democratic leadership. However, did Mayo massage his data to fit with the prevailing views of the time?

Human relations ideas were a response to the practical problems occurring in the stage of industrialization reached by American industry in the late 1920s which had become aggravated by the militancy of labour in the 1930s. What made Mayo unique was his ability to recognize these emerging social problems and to popularize attractive explanations and solutions. In the process he turned himself into a kind of human relations superstar.

Institutional framework

The popularity of human relations ideas in American companies can be linked to the size of organizations, trade union expansion, and worker specialization and training. The increased size of US corporations was accompanied by problems of management control. The bureaucratization of industrial organizations at the time meant an increase in their complexity. Span of control was increased but effective supervision reduced. A new set of management ideas was therefore needed to direct and control the activities of workers since greater amounts of authority and responsibility accrued to lower level supervisors as their companies increased in size.

Turning to labour union expansion, the 1933-7 period in the United States had seen union membership grow from 3 million to seven million. The National Labour Act of 1935 established the right of employees to organize without coercion or interference from management. The most significant aspect of this trend was that it generated a need for specialist management personnel to negotiate labour agreements. From 1933 onwards, therefore, personnel specialists took over much of the adminis-trative and strategic responsibility for labour negotiations. Thus, a new and cohesive management group came into being which would later become a prime consumer of human relations ideas and its associated techniques.

Bendix (1963) noted that unionization forced management to direct its attention to the attitudes and feelings of workers. Management had to deal with workers as people who had legitimate aspirations and opinions. The employers' use of human relations ideas could be seen as an attempt to enlist the co-operation of ˙ orkers and thereby counter the threat of unions while reasserting absolute management authority.

Mayo himself did not tie his human relations ideas to the growth of the union movement at the time. Instead he linked his proposals to the conservative sentiments of business leaders by advocating the non-intervention of government. His ideas therefore struck a positive chord among the very people who were located most strategically to allocate research funds, establish institutes and promulgate his ideology.

During the 1940s and 1950s human relations ideas and techniques posited a social mission for managers which was to recreate within the enterprise, a web of satisfying social relationships that industrialization had destroyed within the wider society. Writing at this time, Drucker (1954) agreed with the human relations view that the business enterprise represented a viable community in its own right. Faced with the problem of legitimizing their own authority at the time, Drucker proposed that such legitimation could be secured by a limited extension of employee decision-making to what he described, with considerable exaggeration, as a 'self-governing plant community'.

Human relations ideas also prospered because they became institutionalized in the major American universities. The Hawthorne studies had provided a stimulus for and gave an impetus to further sociological work in industry. However, Mayo's work was not unique even at that time. Other academics, Whiting Williams and Henri DeMan, were also writing in the behavioural field. The first university course in human relations was offered in 1936. By 1946 it became a required course at the Harvard Business School. Saltonstall (1959) wrote that 'teachers in universities were the first to pick up the Williams and Mayo ideas as worthy of further thought and experimentation'. The major educational institutional support for human relations ideas came at the end of the Second World War, at a time of intense union activity and strikes. Institutes and schools of business were established at the universities of Chicago (1943), Yale (1944), Cornell (1945), Berkeley (1945), Michigan (1946) and Illinois (1946).

The slow but growing influence of psychology and sociology, collectively referred to as the 'behavioural perspective', increased progressively through the twentieth century. It took off rapidly in the 1945–50 period, a time which coincided with the influence of human relations ideas coming from industry. Aronoff (1975) analysed twenty-eight general management textbooks published between 1910 and 1974 in order to trace the increase in the behavioural perspective within the discipline of management. He identified the number of behavioural terms used. His analysis is shown in Figure 4.1. Aronoff's analysis revealed the growth of behavioural science teaching in management schools at American universities. By 1922 at least ten institutions were teaching management. The management textbooks of the 1920s

TOTAL TERMS

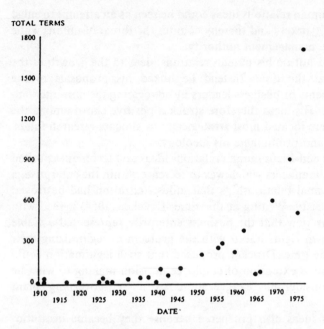

Figure 4.1 Total of behavioural terms per management textbook over time
Source: Arnoff 1975: 761

stressed the importance of employee attitude, concern with the individual's ego and environment. They contained the beginnings of discussions on industrial relations, leadership, motivation, social relations and social structure.

Motivational context

Three main factors oriented the American businesspeople of the time towards human relations ideas (Sutton *et al.* 1956). First, the conflicting demands of their particular position and the broader values of society. Second, the gaps between the demands of social positions and the capabilities of the people who occupied those positions. Third, the inherently conflicting demands which were built into the definition of certain management roles.

Bendix (1963) argued that essential features of the motivational context were managers' needs for achievement, success and career advancement. The strongest advocates of the 'new management' of human relations were the junior managers rather than the senior executives. Human relations ideas represented a way for them to increase their influence and effectiveness within the bureaucratic organization. Human relations ideas, in Bendix's view, became another tool for internal politics and career advancement within the organization.

Mayo's ideas appealed to American managers of the time since they assigned to them a central place in the successful working of contemporary society. Many believed that the relationship between the individual and society had been damaged by industrialization and urbanization. This relationship could be restored, in Mayo's view, by managing organizations in a way that generated a spontaneous collaboration towards a common purpose. Mayo's appeal to managers was also partly based on the contention that their subordinates were illogical; that such uncooperativeness represented a frustrated urge to collaborate; that their demands for money masked a need for managerial approval; and that as managers, they had a historic destiny to be the brokers of social harmony.

It was not only line managers who gave human relations ideas their support. The growth of personnel specialists has already been mentioned. Company trainers and consultants could also be numbered among Mayo's supporters. Training in interpersonal skills seemed to provide a vehicle with which human relations ideas could be applied within the organization. It was upon such courses that management training as a specialist company function built itself within the large corporations. Independent consultants began making a living from this work and still do to this day.

Source: Works Management, August 1989, p. 17

Transfer of human relations ideas to Britain

The period which saw the greatest introduction and diffusion of human relations ideas in Britain was that between 1945 and 1955. It took nearly twenty years for the implications of the Hawthorne experiments to begin to have an impact on British management thinking and practice. Full employment in Britain presented management with difficulties. Among these was the danger of loss of sales from a buoyant market which an industrial dispute could bring and the impracticality of imposing discipline and inducing effort by means of traditional management methods. Management power might have been further limited by the rise in the general standards of education which appeared to encourage a new critical awareness among manual workers. Human relations ideas, wrote Child (1969b), appeared to offer the best way of maintaining and even extending management control in a new socio-economic environment.

The appeal of human relations ideas to British managers was as great as to their American counterparts. It offered them an edifice of scientifically acquired evidence to support the view that it was possible to release the innate enthusiasm of groups for co-operation with management through meeting their members' deeply felt needs for belonging. Child felt that in the 1940s a combination of publicly exposed mismanagement, occurring early in the war, provided an impetus for a review of management. Foremanship became an urgent issue for the management movement. The burden had been placed on the foremen and human relations ideas. The stress on social skills came as an answer to a perceived problem.

Child reported that in the early 1940s only a minority of personnel officers (let alone managers) had heard about the Hawthorne studies. The 'selling' of human relations ideas involved a great deal of propaganda. In 1947, Mayo addressed the Institute of Personnel Management conference. Child argued that the most influential British publication on these famous experiments was the long series of articles by Urwick and Brech which ran in *Industry Illustrated* between November 1944 and July 1946. Since human relations ideas were grounded in educational institutions, research and scholarship, when they did arrive in Britain, they appeared first in management textbooks. J. A. C. Brown's (1954) *The Social Psychology of Industry* was popular among management teachers during the 1950s. Argyle (1972) felt that human relations ideas had their greatest impact on supervisory and management training programmes, even though he felt that it was the personnel rather than the production departments which were most enthusiastic about them in Britain.

Which factors assisted in the transfer and growth of human relations ideas and their associated techniques in Britain? Three main factors may be cited. These were American investment in Britain, the activities of Anglo-American productivity teams, and the development of joint consultation in British industry during this period. Each factor will be examined in turn.

Anglo-American investment in the United Kingdom economy

The investment in the UK by US companies can be said to have created a 'managerial ideas bridge' across the Atlantic. Dunning (1958) surveyed the importance of US investments in the period 1940–53. He reported that in 1940 these investments were £530 million while by 1955 the value of US direct investment in Britain had reached £941 million. This figure was second only to that invested by the USA in Canada and represented 57.7 per cent of US manufacturing investment in Europe as a whole. Some 233 companies were operating as branch units of US companies. In 1954 the ten largest US-financed manufacturers in the UK were Esso Petroleum, Ford Motor, British United Shoe, Monsanto Chemical, Vacuum Oil, Vauxhall Motor, Kodak, Hoover, Standard Telephone & Cable and Goodyear. Other factories which were branch houses of US corporations included Gillette, National Cash Register, Caterpillar Tractor, Elizabeth Arden and Remington Rand.

Dunning felt that no other period had brought with it such a combination of circumstances so conducive to the expansion of American interests. He listed several reasons to account for this. First, the shortage of dollars in the sterling area which deprived US firms of their pre-war sales outlets and induced them to set up manufacturing units in the UK. In this way, they could sell their products for sterling. Second, a growing demand in Britain for US designed and styled goods. Third, the need to develop specific industries also encouraged the growth of postwar American investment in Britain. Finally, US capital had been attracted to those fields in which research and development were of above average significance, and in which the United States had built an important lead during the Second World War.

A unique feature of American-affiliated companies operating in Britain was their centralization of policy. As a matter of principle, both American manufacturing techniques and managerial methods were consciously assimilated and adhered to whenever possible. Dunning reported the very frequent interchanges of personnel that took place between US and UK plants. Special visits were paid by management, production, costing and time-and-motion experts whenever a change of departmental policy in the United States needed to be implemented at UK branch level. Writing some years later in the role of a consultant working at Esso-Fawley, Klein (1976) described how in the late 1960s and early 1970s American consulting teams were detailed to Fawley to prescribe and run management training.

The British subsidiaries of US companies were allowed full and easy access to their parents' manufacturing methods and experiences. Top management methods and business philosophy appeared to be the same in British and American plants, wrote Dunning. Branch facilities benefited from the new knowledge and thereby avoided many mistakes and teething problems in spheres such as training, remuneration of labour, office procedures, costing and budgeting control, work study and inventory control. Following Mayo's teaching, attention was also paid to the role of foremen, in particular to a consideration of their responsibilities, training and their role as the lower strata of management.

The approach and attitude to the key managerial functional areas was looked at through American eyes even though the subsidiary was operating within an alien economic environment. Managing directors had to ensure that their senior plant executives visited their US parent plant frequently to study at first hand the latest management methods being practised.

At the time, human resource management topics were important and US practices in areas such as wage payment systems, profit-sharing schemes, bonus payments, non-financial benefits, informing employees about company policy and suggestion schemes were very much to the fore. Dunning noted that in this sphere, UK companies followed parent company practice, particularly in employee selection and training. A number of large subsidiaries operated special local training schools while senior operatives and staff were sent to the USA for instruction. Burroughs, 3M and Frigidaire all encouraged promising staff to visit their respective parent plants for several months.

Discussing the transfer of 'management technology' across the Atlantic, Dunning (1970) noted that first, if a British firm of the time wanted to move in the direction of US management practices, it had plenty of avenues available to do so (e.g. employing consultants, US technical literature, appointing UK managers with experience of US companies). Second, US management technology was non-proprietary and general, rather than patented and firm-specific. Third, there was the spin-over phenomenon in which the United States passed on both general and system-specific technology to their component suppliers. Executives started their own companies and re-created the organizational and managerial structures, processes and systems.

Finally, it can be noted how American ideas were applied in specific industry firms. Through the normal course of labour mobility, contacts with trade and research associations, customers, suppliers, the transmission of this type of knowledge, and the philosophy behind it was considerable. Thus it was through the American multinationals in the Second World War and post-war era, that the word about modern management ideas and techniques, which of course included human relations ones, was spread.

Anglo-American productivity teams

The second major factor contributing to the transfer of human relations ideas from the United States into Britain were the Anglo-American productivity teams. The teams reported in 1951 that the most significant single factor in America which contributed to high productivity at low cost was efficient management. Even if Britain could not use American production techniques and processes, British firms could assimilate US managerial practices.

The Anglo-American Council on Productivity had been formed in 1948 to arrange for the exchange of information on such issues as production techniques, industrial organization and managerial efficiency with particular reference to conditions in US and UK industries. Between 1949 and 1953 the Council sent 66 teams under the Marshall Plan representing managers, technicians and operators to study the experience of the USA in raising productivity and to see if their methods could be applied to British industry.

The suggestions of these productivity missions were picked up by the National Economic Development Office (NEDO) which, with other bodies such as the Foundation for Management Education and the British Institute of Management (BIM), suggested the establishment of American university-type business schools which initially used much American-based teaching material in the form of case studies and textbooks. The productivity missions promoted the adoption of what they considered to be the secret ingredients of successful American management. These included 'participative' human relations styles of management based on the work of Mayo and the Management-by-Objectives (MbO) system popularized by Drucker (1954).

Joint consultation in Britain

The third major factor contributing to the adoption of human relations ideas in Britain was the move to joint consultation. Management ideas and their associated techniques are closely related. Indeed, the latter are often a more visible expression of the former. In seeking to identify the penetration of human relations ideas in Britain, it is sometimes easier to identify the visible manifestation of ideas in their techniques. One such instance is that of joint consultation councils. These 'works councils' as they were more commonly known, reached their height of popularity in Britain during the 1940s and 1950s.

Initially they were known as joint production committees. These groups were strongly encouraged by the government of the day following the wartime Essential Work Orders (1941). Pucky (1962) felt that an incidental but significant consequence of their establishment was that the 'theory of the infallibility of management' in Britain was severely shaken. Joint consultation was set up in many industries in Britain during the Second World War, particularly in armaments. Their purpose was to obtain greater co-operation from the workers. After the war many firms abandoned them, but they became built into the structures of the nationalized industries in the belief that they would produce a co-operative industrial society leaving collective bargaining to deal with the areas of potential conflict such as wages.

As a technique, these councils had their basis in human relations ideas. They were founded on the belief that individuals would feel better if they were given the opportunity to participate in some way in decisions that affected their jobs or at least be informed about such decisions. Companies wishing to keep their employees satisfied should provide a forum in which they could voice their minor grievances and canvas ideas for improvements. While there might be some issues of contention between employers and workers, there were many more issues of common interest between them.

Joint committees provided the means through which such common ground could be found. There were many matters of administration where the organizing talents of ordinary employees could find expression which might be denied to them unavoidably in everyday work. If the facility to participate and the forum were provided, employees would feel better about working for the company. This would result in lower absenteeism and turnover rates, less conflict, a greater feeling of loyalty and belonging, and higher morale. Finally, it was believed that joint committees provided a context in which management and workers could meet each other in circumstances in which their superior–subordinate role was played down, and their common roles as employees of the firm, equally concerned with its fortune, were stressed.

Joint committees therefore represented an attempt by Mayoite managements to create a platform for management–worker discussions. Their purpose was to demonstrate 'family spirit' and solidarity with the firm. Their failure was due to management's inability to blur successfully its different roles. At one time it was the workers' controller, at the next it was their friend. This changing of hats did not fool the workers, who continued to see the need for trade unions.

The growing post-war affluence in Europe during the 1950s and early 1960s coincided with a marked decrease in working-class radicalism which had been vociferous in the 1945–51 period (Hirszowicz 1981). State intervention, the expansion of large corporations and collective bargaining meant that unions ceased to press for power-sharing or control. Big business and social democratic governments were more concerned during these years with worker apathy and lack of commitment. However, this did not mean that American ideas were applied wholesale. Most were introduced with careful modifications and tailoring.

One of the best known and best documented examples of joint consultation in Britain during the late 1940s and early 1950s was that used by the Glacier Metal Company. At this company, it was the responsibility of the managers to promote industrial harmony, to play down conflicts and tensions, all in the belief that it would lead to the Mayoite promise of industrial efficiency based upon employees' emotional security and a sense of belonging (Jacques 1951; Brown and Jacques 1965). Part of this development came through with Mayoite ideas of group harmony but another part was undoubtedly home grown and re-exported.

PSYCHOLOGICAL PERIOD

Introduction

Although it had its beginnings in the 1940s, the psychological period mainly

Table 4.3 Aspects of the psychological period

Founding fathers	New disciples
Abraham Maslow	Warren Bennis
Frederick Herzberg	Richard Beckhard
Douglas McGregor	Richard Walton
Rensis Likert	Richard Blake and
Chris Argyris	Jane Mouton
Main contribution	
philosophy	empirical research
theory	application techniques
Period of main influence	
1945–65	1965–75

spanned the three decades between 1950 and 1980. It can be divided broadly into two phases. The main characteristics of each phase are shown in Table 4.3. The high point of the psychological period were the 1960s in the USA. The idealism of the 1960s was part and parcel of a time when affluence left room for more liberal methods of management. Among sections of the industrial community, the consensus model of society and organizations held sway. There was held to be no difference between the interests of the individual and the employer provided that the interpersonal skills of managers could be improved (Holloway 1983).

The first phase of the psychological period can be dated as 1945–65. It had its beginnings with the publication of Maslow's seminal article on human motivation (Maslow 1943). Indeed, many observers consider Maslow's concept of 'self-actualization' to be the starting-point for the humanistic approach to organizations. Other authors who had books published in this period included Herzberg *et al.* (1959), McGregor (1960) and Likert (1961).

The founding fathers of the first phase provided the theoretical and philosophical underpinning to a set of therapeutic ideas. Their writings stressed self-awareness, self-knowledge and self-understanding. They emphasized democracy and humanitarianism. The theme was developed by social psychologists, like Kurt Lewin, who had fled from European totalitarianism and authoritarianism. These refugees saw in American society the potential for human fulfilment and democratic involvement of a type that they had previously never envisaged.

As an approach to understanding work behaviour and motivation, the democratic humanist period was distinguished by the way in which more sophisticated psychological assumptions, together with value-based predictions, were introduced into management thinking under the banner of a scientific management programme. For example, Lewin's basic assumption was that people needed to be actively involved in decision-making if they were to be fulfilled and effective in following up the decisions made. Although Lewin died in 1947, the tradition that he established was followed by Likert at the University of Michigan's Survey Research Centre. The message was that democracy paid in management.

The second phase of the psychological period stretched from about 1965 until the late 1970s. It emphasized empirical research and the application of results to the solution of individual and organizational problems. This later strand of the democratic-humanitarian movement held that scientific investigation should seek to realize the potential that people possessed. This thread in American thinking flourished in a variety of forms in the warmth and affluence of places such as middle-class California where it first appeared. It was strange that a creed coming from this particularly rarefied and often self-indulgent quarter of the intellectual world, should have been taken up so much in the traditionally hard-headed world of management thinking and organizational behaviour.

A number of writers sought to list the key assumptions which underpinned the psychological period. Although there are disagreements, the following represent recurring themes from the literature. First, the belief that reality was that which was experienced subjectively as real. The significance of anything was the effect that it had on the individual psyche. Second, anything that might cause even the most minimal emotional discomfort was held to be illegitimate. Third, human personality was believed to be under constant attack by illegitimate, cruel and savage forces.

Not all of these attacks constituted a trauma threat but less extremely, they placed a constraint upon human performance which, if removed, would permit the personality to emerge in a burst of efficiency and productivity. Fourth, anyone could be as good as anyone else if they had the right training. Any differences in performance were only skill differences and were not held to represent differences in character, talent, personality, fundamental belief systems or values. Finally, in determining the truth or validity of anything, new ideas and techniques were held to be better than old ones. Those ideas which were consonant with the advanced and politically popular were better than those which were not. Those which might be derived from the prevailing distortion or misapplication of some psychological principle were better than those which were not. If it felt good to practically everybody involved and if nearly everybody endorsed it, then it was good!

Cultural heritage

To understand the background to the development, growth and adoption of neo-human relations ideas and techniques in American organizations during the psychological period, one needs to examine the influential societal factors of the period, particularly those in the 1965–75 period when these ideas became established. A general humanism can be said to have been ascendant in western culture during the 1960s, especially among middle-class Americans. There was also the impact of the Johnson administration with its dreams of a Great Society and the social indicators movement which sought to measure the quality of life in the USA in general.

Perhaps the predominant factor during this period was the dramatic decline in American self-confidence which, during the period in question, fell to a low ebb. Defeat in Vietnam, economic stagnation, the impact of oil price rises, concerns about the impeding exhaustion of natural resources, all produced a mood of pessimism which spread through those in high circles and through society at large. It led people to lose faith in their leaders.

Following the political turmoil of the 1960s, many Americans retreated to purely personal preoccupations. Unable to effect political changes they opted for psychic self-improvement: getting in touch with feelings, jogging, learning how to relate, and living for the moment (the 'here-and-now'). Elevated to a programme, these activities represented a retreat from politics and a repudiation of, and perhaps a cleansing of the past. The desire was to forget the early 1960s, the riots, the New Left, college campus disruptions, Vietnam, Watergate and the Nixon presidency. Abbe Hoffman, former leader of the Yippies, and Jerry Rubin looked for alternative experiences in the spiritual supermarkets of the West Coast (Lasch 1980; 1985). Rubin (1976) wrote that in the five years between 1971 and 1975 he directly experienced est, Gestalt therapy, bioenegetics, rolfing, massage, jogging, health foods, Tai Chi, Esalen, hypnotism, modern dance, meditation, Silva Mind Control, Arica, acupuncture, sex therapy and Reichian therapy.

The period created what Lasch (1980) termed the 'culture of narcissism'. Additionally, there were aspects of American life itself which fostered and supported such neo-human relations ideas. The freedom from religious superstitition left a gap in the lives of many Americans which came to be filled by the creed of self-love. People hungered not for personal salvation but for the feeling, albeit even a momentary one, of personal well-being, health and psychic security. The inner revolution which began in the late 1960s turned into a full force in the early 1970s. It grew out of an awareness among many Americans that past radicalism had failed to address itself to the quality of personal life or to questions of culture.

Could this be said to be a widespread cultural trend through the United States? Some writers have condemned the psychological or psychic orientation as being the opiate of the upper middle classes. Self-absorption sought to insulate affluent Americans against the horrors around them: the horrors of poverty, racism and injustice. It thereby eased their conscience. Perhaps the 'awareness craze' only addressed the problems of the well-to-do while neglecting those of social groups such as the poor? Lasch (1985) believed that the self-awareness movement grew not out of complacency in

America, but from desperation and that it was not confined solely to the middle classes.

Social questions came to present themselves as personal ones, and these arose from what he called the warlike conditions which pervaded American society from the dangers and uncertainty that surrounded Americans, and from a loss of confidence in the future. While the poor always lived for the present, said Lasch, a desperate concern for personal survival, sometimes distinguished as hedonism, now engulfed the middle classes as well. A sense of well-being become an end in itself, rather than a by-product of some superior commercial goal (Rieff 1987).

Demographic factors also played a part in sustaining the growth of neo-human relations ideas in the period. Rosen (1978) described how the human potential movement spoke relentlessly about 'self' or 'real self', about self-actualization, and the 'whole person'. Where Freud had found a mortgage that could never be entirely paid off, the neo-human relations movement's ideas hinted at a final freedom and a life back in the black. Back (1972) felt that many of the basic tensions in American society which had sparked off the original interest in psychological issues in society in the mid-1940s had, by the 1960s, increased substantially. He cited specifically the existence of a whole generation which had grown up without seeing either the Depression or economic want. These people now crossed the country in search of excitement and viewed life as having a deeper meaning than either material wealth or scientific understanding gave them.

The culture of competitive individualism was retreating during this period. It had carried the logic of individualism to the extreme of a war of all against all. It had promised the pursuit of happiness which, in its turn, had led to a narcissistic preoccupation with the self. In this conception, economic man gave way to psychological man, the final product of bourgeois individualism. While fiercely competitive in his demand for approval and acclaim, psychological man distrusted competition and associated it with an unbridged urge to destroy. Competitive ideologies came to be distrusted while co-operation and teamwork were extolled.

Institutional framework

The main institutional manifestation of the psychological period in American life came in the form of organizational development (OD) programmes in companies. OD programmes were based upon, and put into practice, the ideas of the neo-human relations movement. OD in the United States was originally promoted as a way of encouraging organizational improvement which met both company needs for efficiency and profitability and at the same time provided individual employees with the opportunity for personal growth and the meeting of their social needs.

Some OD writers claimed that they did not consider existing organizational structures as permanent, and that they were ready to recommend technical and policy changes. In practice, there was little modification of structures, and the major thrust of OD came to be upon individual and group change. T-groups and team-building seminars were the most popular techniques. Interpersonal skills training for managers also came to be heavily influenced by the humanistic developments of the period. In the first phase of the period, the legacy of Mayo and the work of Lewin acted to emphasize a social psychological approach which was focused on teams. In the second phase, in the later 1960s and early 1970s, the orientation shifted to individuals and their search for personal growth.

Among the enabling institutional forces of the period was the highly publicized dissatisfaction of the American worker. There was considerable discussion about a 'new breed' of worker who had a disdain for authority, was less interested in work for the sake of it, and had more interest in the elements of work design that would make the job more meaningful and add to the worker's self-fulfilment. The affluence of the period appeared to foster a concern with higher level, self-actualization needs to which employers felt impelled to respond.

Writing from a critical perspective, Marglin (1979) argued that the 1960s and the early 1970s were a period in which worker discontent with work organization reached a zenith. Business magazines ran stories with photographs from Chaplin's film, *Modern Times*, on their covers. Car workers at General Motors went on strike in 1972 complaining not about pay, but about the pace of the assembly line. The US Senate held publicized hearings on *worker alienation* in 1972, and Nixon's Department of Health, Education and Welfare produced a report entitled *Work in America*.

The common theme running through these institutional developments was that work was dull, repetitive and meaningless, especially for the younger generation. The solution that was suggested was greater control of the production process by the workers themselves through job enlargement and even job enrichment. The Vice President of Ford Motors at the time confidentially reported to his fellow executives the astronomical rates of absenteeism, turnover and disciplinary cases. The cause of the problem in his view was too much prosperity. Tight labour markets had obliged the Ford company, and other employers, to take on what they regarded as problem-employees. Given these difficulties, Ford concluded that it had to pay more attention than in the past to the kinds of jobs it offered its workers (Marglin 1979: 478).

Managerial initiatives to humanize work could be seen as a response to the increase in labour costs associated with employee indiscipline born of prosperity. Marglin argued that the evidence of the late 1960s and early 1970s matched that of the post-1973 period. Just as job enrichment and other neo-human relations techniques of work organization had flowered in the expectation of chronically tight labour markets, they had withered away once the pressure was off employers. High and rising unemployment shifted workers' attention away from the quality of work and to the question of just having a job at all.

In response to these industrial concerns, some critics argued that OD consultants offered a mish-mash of 1960s 'flower power' philosophy, anti-authority notions and half-baked concepts such as 'caring-and-sharing', openness and 'letting-it-all-hang-out'. Other commentators felt that neo-human relations ideas offered not a mish-mash, but a coherent set of guidelines backed by a set of implementation techniques. While many OD specialists stood for all sorts of humanistic values, some observers felt that businesspeople wanted to use OD simply to extract more work from employees but more persuasively.

The mood of the time affected organizations in a number of ways. First, it acted to displace politics as the focus of attention. Collective grievances became transformed into personal problems which were considered to be amenable to therapeutic intervention treatments such as counselling. Second, the popularization of psychological modes of thought and the spread of the 'new consciousness' movement added to the quest for spiritual and other panaceas to be used *within* the workplace. Third, the narcissist possessed many traits that led to success in organizations. For example, the manipulation of interpersonal relationships and the discouragement of the formation of deep personal attachments were valued by the corporation. In its turn, the corporation offered narcissists the approval that they needed to validate their self-esteem.

Lasch argued that Whyte's (1957) 'organization man' and the loyalty era had given way to Maccoby's (1976) bureaucratic 'gamesman'. In the age of the executive success game, the narcissist stepped to the forefront. Such people saw the world as a mirror of themselves. They had no interest in external events except inasmuch as they threw back a reflection of their own image. For many people at the time, narcissism represented the best way of coping with the tensions and anxieties of life. The social conditions, wrote Lasch, brought out the narcissistic traits in people.

The sociability of psychological man has already been commented upon. Did the educational and training programmes run under the banner of OD eliminate antagonism and cultivate a 'commercial friendliness'? The American cult of friendliness concealed, although did not eradicate, a murderous competition for goods and positions. Assertiveness training appealed to those who recognized that agility in interpersonal relations determined what appeared on the surface to be achievement. The message was that success depended on psychological manipulation.

The popularization of therapeutic modes of thought, while it may have discredited authority, nevertheless left domination uncriticized. By softening or eliminating the adversarial relationships between subordinates, psychological forms of social control made it more difficult for workers to counter the demands of the organization. The objectives of OD were coloured by these beliefs. OD aimed at creating an open, problem-solving climate in the organization, and supplemented the authority of role and status with that of knowledge and competence. It sought to locate decision-making and problem-solving as close to the information sources as possible. It attempted to build trust and collaboration by increasing self-control and self-direction for people within the organization.

Organizational development began by satisfying the need for companies *to be seen to be* incorporating humanistic values into their processes and structures (Krell 1981). While participants on early OD programmes were educated to recognize their needs as persons in the work environment, management's objectives for participation was to achieve organizational effectiveness. Companies buying an OD package were free to view it as a productivity improving device. Interpersonal effectiveness (and the associated humanistic values) were accepted as a means of achieving this goal.

The absence of religious superstition, together with the decrease in social bonds of kinship, neighbourhood, church and family networks, meant that many people lacked any form of social support or 'normative anchors' which made life tolerable (Lasch 1978). In their place, argued Ouchi and Johnson (1978), the large work organization came to provide the associational ties and cohesion for its people (echoes of Mayo?). In the view of these authors, American companies should attempt to create a complete inclusion of the employee within the company.

Many of the OD techniques based upon neo-human relations ideas such as the family T-group, team-building and counselling, all reflected the notion of 'bringing the family together'. Supervisors received training to be aware of all aspects of an employee's life, and companies organized post-work social events (e.g. Friday afternoon 'beer-busts'). Corporate values were adjusted to reflect employee needs as well as profits.

What about the institutional framework of the later psychological period? From the early 1970s the United States began to experience its worst economic crisis since the Great Depression of the 1930s, as well as a political crisis. Zimbalist (1975) claimed that the post-1945 period of almost uninterrupted prosperity in the US economy came to a halt in the late 1960s. Despite the ever-growing share of total US corporate profits attributable to foreign investments (about 32 per cent by 1974) and the higher profit margins abroad, the overall profit rate for these American corporations began falling from 1965 onwards.

This decline was caused by a number of factors. Among the major ones were the competition between the USA and other advanced nations, notably Japan, the intensifying struggles in the Third World, and the declining productivity gains in the US economy in the post-1965 period, which were lower relative to its major capitalist competitors. American companies' response to these pressures was to introduce labour-saving technology and work intensification and work humanization programmes. Thus OD played a role in providing the 'social technology' with which to implement these changes.

Kanter (1985) analysed the 1960–80 period to identify the topics which preoccupied the American business press in those years. She studied the business periodicals index for the periods 1959–61, 1964–6, 1969–71, 1974–6 and 1979–80. By measuring column inches and citations, she reviewed over 7,000 pages of listings and identified 246 separate topics. She found that in the period, a large number of topics remained relatively stable, with business-fads flying through. Kanter summarized her conclusions by saying that 'the majority of issues growing in importance concerned human resources. . . . There was also considerable attention to executive training and management development' (1985: 45).

Peaking around 1970 and then virtually disappearing were topics which had a 1960s counter-culture flavour. For example, drug problems in industry, group relations, sensitivity training, labour supply and government ownership. There were also discussions about minority employment and automation. The 1970s saw a decline of interest in traditional management style, management rights, work measurement, work sampling and collective bargaining. Topics that grew in importance during the 1970s were related to the struggle to deal with the pressures of a changing competitive environment. These were employee rights, selection, training, supervision, motivation, and the new management style which emphasized teamwork and participation. In these years, human resource management (HRM) rose to prominence. Compensation, incentives, dismissal, outplacement, resignation and employee counselling became popular. Attention was also focused on training and development and affirmative action. While each of these topics was invented and introduced much earlier, the dates indicate when each became firmly established enough in corporate culture to merit the attention of the business press.

Motivational context

What did the OD techniques, based upon neo-human relations ideas, offer managers? There are two answers to this question – a public and a private one. Let us consider the public one first. NHR-ideas had embedded in them certain values, beliefs and attitudes about the nature of people at work. Throughout the century, the view of human beings as simple machines declined, although the law-boundedness of individual behaviour remained a basic presupposition. However, instead of possessing a few law-bounded instincts, individuals came to be seen as driven by a variety of needs. Workers behaved in ways which satisfied their diverse needs. In this context, the manager's job was seen as being to manipulate their behaviour by identifying specific worker needs, and then offering them an incentive in return for work.

Alternatively, the manager could manipulate tasks and environments to influence the creation of new needs, and then to offer need-satisfying incentives. In either case, workers were viewed as being law-bounded but malleable. By developing skills such as expressing feelings honestly and learning how to listen and empathize, it was believed that such a management style would produce less conflict with subordinates who would thus experience commitment to the organization, would become highly motivated and would provide more and better work.

This view was very much in tune with the times as described earlier. In this conceptualization, the manager acted in the role of interviewer, attempting to determine what would challenge the workers, and what their primary need might be. The manager's role was that of catalyst and facilitator rather than controller. Managers motivated and delegated to subordinates and gave them as much responsibility as they felt they could handle.

In this model, authority shifted from the office or the position-holder on to the task itself. Managers became the agents through whom task requirements were communicated. If workers responded to the challenge and were capable of self-discipline (Theory Y), they would see to it themselves that the task was adequately performed. Motivation changed from being extrinsic to intrinsic. The organization provided the opportunity for the employees' existing motivation to be harnessed to organizational goals. The involvement of the worker, in Etzioni's (1961) terms, became moral.

In contrast, the private explanation was that many managers saw in OD a way of improving productivity and profitability. Being the customer who paid the bill, the managers were quite capable of dispensing with the more egalitarian and more humanistic aspects of the OD package with which they did not agree. They had done this years earlier by selecting those aspects of scientific management which they had wanted, while rejecting the others. The application of OD by managers rather than by OD consultants had grown, and the OD consultant supported the changes initiated by general managers. OD ran the risk of encouraging and implementing subtle but pervasive forms of exploitation, curtailment of freedom, control of personality, violation of dignity and intrusion of privacy. All of this would be done in the name of science and of economic and technological efficiency. In the hierarchical fabric of everyday organizational power struggles, OD consultants typically represented the control needs of managements.

While this may have motivated the management of a company to introduce NHR-ideas, one can ask what appeal, if any, the ideas had for workers. Most workers, of course, had no choice in the matter. Some undoubtedly would have looked on cynically as their successors would do ten years later, upon quality circles. However, it is known that many did participate enthusiastically since OD was not only sustained but also flourished in the United States.

Harvey (1974: 24–5) felt that OD represented a religious movement which addressed 'deep feelings of discontent, alienation and loneliness which are met neither by religious institutions, nor other organizations of which we are a part.' He cited the mechanical ceremonies of OD which were entered into without a sense of purpose. In his view, these were unrelated to the organizational problems at hand. Among the rituals he listed were team-building, inter-group sensing, conflict resolution, life planning, T-groups, confrontation meetings, survey research and data collection. He then went on to consider other parallels that OD had with religion such as its liturgy, revival meetings, its Messianic approach, and how it dealt with the 'burnout' among its priest-consultants. Forrest (1984) referred to the neo-human relations development priesthood or the 'lumpen-intelligentsia' who used psychology as the basis for a secular religion of behaviour which acted to legitimize specious training, and which established political and intellectual hegemony for some at the expense of others.

The appeal to those involved came, not least, from the Hawthorne effect itself. The mere involvement of people in OD activities showed that management was paying attention to them. The fact that OD programmes were new and different generated interest in them, irrespective of their focus or content. The underlying values of OD suggested that *everybody* in the organization had something useful to contribute to the effort, had an opinion worthy of respect, and thereby should be able to affect work. The parallels with the quality circle programmes of the 1980s are striking.

Transfer of neo-human relations ideas to Britain

The American NHR-ideas that did come to Britain arrived in the form of OD techniques. Was OD just another package that Americans could sell the 'gullible Brits', as Mant (1986) claimed? One can say that the influence of these ideas in Britain has been minimal. However, one should qualify this by distinguishing between, on the one hand, people-oriented OD techniques such as confrontation meetings and T-groups and, on the other, technological-structural techniques such as job enlargement and job enrichment. While being based upon the same set of neo-human relations ideas, the people-oriented techniques were generally rejected in Britain at both the discussion and implementation levels. The technological-structural techniques, in contrast, were discussed even though they may not have been widely implementing in factories.

Why then were neo-human relations ideas less acceptable to the British than their predecessors? One can examine this question first from the point of view of two American academics and then from that of two British ones. Two American professors, Dubin (1970) and Steele (1977), separately reported the characteristics which they saw in British managers which differentiated them from American ones. There was a high degree of overlap in their conclusions, and these may identify the obstacles to the transfer of certain neo-human relations based techniques into Britain.

Dubin and Steele believed that differences in attitudes to perfectability, class and personal trust were central. Perfectability referred to the belief of American managers that current ways of doing things would eventually be replaced by better ones. They were optimists who considered that the future held promise. In contrast, British managers, they claimed, valued security, reflected in the observation that they must be doing all right if they were still in business. They were pessimists, aware of the costs of change, and required proof that something would work *before* it was adopted. Since such proof could be only supplied after the change, innovations were more likely to be introduced in the USA than in Britain.

The second distinguishing feature noted by these authors was the effect of class. Specifically, the predominantly middle-class British managers placed great weight on people having a 'proper' education. 'Proper' was defined more in terms of where one studied than what one studied. Additionally, in the UK, there was less awareness of a pool of lower-level organizational people capable of being developed into successful managers. These individuals were neglected on class grounds since they did not fit social stereotypes.

Finally, these writers noted the role of personal trust. British managers' primary criterion for valuing their subordinates appeared to be trust and personal loyalty. This was defined as their 'doing the right thing' and being 'sound', especially in the absence of the boss. Trust acted as a pressure to conform in thought and action. Trustworthy employees rarely surprised their supervisors with innovative actions since this would be considered unsound. There was less of this in the United States because of the greater emphasis upon universalistic criteria for selection and evaluation, claimed Dubin and Steele. These criteria were more independent of the particular opinions of the present boss and stressed instead operational and financial achievement. Such universal criteria were necessary because of the greater frequency of job changes at all levels in US companies.

Another pair of academics, this time writing from Britain, Cox and Cooper (1985), also felt that the UK was hostile to OD techniques. They argued that until the 1970s management ideas had flowed unhindered across the Atlantic from America to Britain. They quoted Haire *et al.* (1966), Steele (1977) and Greiner (1977) to support their contention that cultural differences between the United States and Europe at the time prevented the creation of a context for the establishment of the American concept of OD in Europe in general, and within Britain in particular. The British cultural heritage, institutional framework and motivational context were all hostile

Table 4.4 Contrasts between Europe and the United States

Dimension	Europe	United States
Social science tradition	Cognitive Psychoanalytic	Behaviourist Humanist
Model of management	Cognitively complex	Action oriented Behaviourist
Belief in tradition	Tradition valued change regarded with suspicion	Change seen as positive
Suspicion of things	Suspicious and strongly influenced by own culture	Many cultural influences
Political orientation versus openness	Political values	More open values
Class structure	Strong class structure	More classless
Economic situation	Pessimistic	Optimistic

to the adoption of OD. Cooper and Cox (1985) identified a number of key cultural differences of the period. These are shown in Table 4.4.

A closer consideration of the British and American situations at the time is necessary. There were differences in the nature of the demands being placed upon the two countries. While Britain was recovering from the war, the United States focused on the post-war needs of its industry to increase productivity in an expanding economy. The 1960s in Britain represented the first decade when affluence returned to a country ravaged by war. The 1940s and 1950s had been years of hunger, ration cards, cold, reconstruction and reconciliation. By the 1960s, Britain not only had begun to re-establish itself but also was enjoying world prestige. These were the years of the 'Swinging Sixties', the Beatles and Carnaby Street. Misquoted and out of context, Harold Macmillan's phrase that Britain had 'never had it so good' seemed to sum up the attitudes of the day.

The war had created a huge domestic market which was hungry for goods which had not previously been available. Confidence and optimism characterized society and not guilt or self-doubt. At the institutional level, Macmillan's government was succeeded by two Labour administrations under Harold Wilson. In his terms, the white heat of technology would drive Britain forward.

British business remained unconvinced about the value of formal management education (Thomas 1980). The first British business schools were not established until the mid-1960s. British businesspeople were even more suspicious of any in-company, 'touchy-feely' OD programmes run by OD consultants. In the UK the people-oriented technique of the T-group came to represent OD and indeed became synonymous with it. Its excesses provided regular copy for business magazines which have fed the prejudices of their management readers ever since (Rowlandson 1984).

The fragmentation of labour in mass production helped to provide health and prosperity to the shattered nations of Europe. It led to the creation of meaningless tasks which reduced workers to 'happy robots'. In the late 1960s and early 1970s in Britain, the labour problems, shifts in production, and changes in markets, necessitated greater flexibility with an emphasis on quality and reliability. The apparent problem of technocracy and Taylorite strategies reflected in organizational rigidity and inflexibility; expansion of organizational complexity to handle fragmented work; the under-utilization of worker initiative; and the numerous indications of work dissatisfaction. How was this problem to be solved?

Europe, with the exception of Britain, went down the industrial democracy route because of government involvement which reflected itself in the more formal and legalistic approach. In contrast, UK pragmatism let management–union co-operation develop voluntarily with a concern for individual worker involvement in day-to-day decision-making (Mills 1978). The greater involvement of European workers expressed through worker councils in countries such as West Germany and Sweden reflected the new political climate of the time. In EC countries, the principles of industrial democracy were integrated into the mainstream of industrial policy in the community's states in June 1970. This provided for a separation of management functions from those of supervision and control, and declared that worker representatives should constitute one-third of the members on supervisory boards. The fifth directive of the EC Commission, issued in September 1972, proposed the introduction of co-determination in all member countries over a ten-year period.

For ideological and operational reasons British management sought to avoid industrial democracy, especially of worker directors. Experiences in the British Steel Corporation and the Post Office were not in management's view successful. The general lack of confidence in the benefits of worker directors was reflected in the failure to implement the recommendations of the Committee of Inquiry on Industrial Democracy (Bullock 1977).

Reviewing this period, Buchanan (1985) argued that until the late 1970s, the main problem which management was grappling with was the cost of low productivity. This was the period of post-war economic growth. Management was concerned with employee turnover, absenteeism, lateness and sabotage. Their preferred solution led down the path of job-redesign. Hence in Britain, the key neo-human relations ideas which were discussed in those times were those of Herzberg and the techniques of job enlargement and job enrichment. It was believed that these offered simple ways of reducing costs. Buchanan cited the influence of humanistic psychology as contributing to the refinement of work strategies towards autonomous work groups.

As the costs of absenteeism and turnover were recognized, so interest in job design rose, coming to the fore in Britain during the early 1970s. Earlier, during the 1960s, companies such as Volvo, Saab-Scania and Norsk Hydro, as well as Philips and Fiat, had inaugurated programmes of work redesign. The evidence of British interest was shown by the Department of Employment's commissioned review of the field (Wilson 1973) and the formation in 1973 of the Tripartite Steering Group on Job Satisfaction, which included representatives from the government, CBI and TUC. The outcome was a visit to Sweden and Norway, and the establishment of a Work Research Unit within the Department of Employment.

However, investigations of both British and American evidence (Kelly 1982; Jenkins 1983) of studies claiming to show impressive results from job redesign led to questions being asked. Reviewers noted the tendency to report only positive results; the acceptance of management assessment of success rather than use of objective measures (Guest *et al.* 1980); the failure to allow for the 'novelty effect' of the programme among employees; the reduction in performance as one plant of a company learned that redesign was not to be introduced on its site; and the failure to isolate the effect of job redesign from the many other changes that were simultaneously taking place.

The influence of job design did look superficially impressive. While work humanization was supported at the public policy level by several European government's including Britain's, Wall (1982) suggested that its impact on the shopfloor was much less significant. In the cases he studied, many programmes had not progressed beyond the experimental stage; they were often discontinued after a short period; and the implementation of only cosmetic changes accompanied the claim that far-reaching job enrichment was being implemented. Child wrote that:

> The scale and scope of the experiments in job re-design and work restructuring remain extremely limited. There are many minor developments masquerading under the label of job enrichment, but there are possibly no more than a 100 or so European schemes that really enrich jobs significantly.

(Child 1984: 43)

Interest continued in Britain through the 1970s but waned at the end of the decade as rising unemployment increased concern about any kind of working life, regardless of its quality. There was a widespread belief in Britain during the 1970s that improving the quality of working life was an appropriate goal for an affluent, educated industrial society. That belief faded in the face of a worsening economic climate and was never popular with British managers anyway. The concern of management refocused itself on resisting the industrial democracy. That resistance was successful, and many managers today regard autonomous workgroups and job enrichment as quaint relics of a past decade.

ENTREPRENEURIAL PERIOD

In both in the United States and in Britain, the 1980s represented a watershed in business culture. The new culture, it will be argued, provided a fertile ground in which a diverse range of management ideas could flourish. As was mentioned in the previous chapter, a recurring theme of the popular ideas of this period was the notion that the purpose of businesses was to compete with each other for the favours of the customer, who was king.

A series of articles during 1986 in the *Financial Times* (Lorenz, 1986a; 1986b; 1986c; Dixon 1986; Dodsworth 1986a; 1986b; Done 1986; Rapoport 1986) described, and to some extent explained, the rise of the management gurus, including consultant-writers such as Tom Peters, Kenneth Blanchard, Edward de Bono; academic consultants such as Henry Mintzberg, Rosabeth Moss Kanter and Michael Porter; and successful businessmen or hero-managers such as Lee Iacocca, Victor Kiam and Jan Carlzon.

It is still too early to judge whether their ideas will stand the test of time, and become incorporated into standard management textbooks and management practice. Indeed the only objective guide that one has to the popular appeal of these authors and their ideas is the somewhat crude market one of how many books they have sold and how much people are willing to pay to hear them speak at conferences and on in-company seminars.

Books, however, can be a good barometer of attitudes. In the pro-business period of the 1980s, business books were more successful than at any previous time (Freeman 1985: 347). Why should this have been? Some evidence emerged from the *themes* of past best-sellers and the *cultural context* in which they were written. One can contrast this with the anti-business period of past decades. The popular classics of the past were generally critical of business and management. Their bite of satire and pessimism was in tune with their particular times. The *Organization Man* (Whyte 1956) accused business of promoting deadening conformity; *Parkinson's Law* (Parkinson 1957) scoffed dryly at organizational inefficiency; *The Peter Principle*'s (Peter and Hull 1970) critique of the executive ranks fitted the anti-business temper; *Up the Organization* (Townsend 1971) with its pithy notions of how to run a business challenged the status quo. However, the analysis in this chapter takes a broader and more historical perspective, and examines the socio-political and economic issues of the 1980s.

In the United States, the early 1980s were an ebulliently materialistic period during which the United States ended its soul-searching about Vietnam and other social concerns (Dodsworth 1986a). The late 1960s and 1970s had seen Americans concerning themselves with a narcissistic pre-occupation. The turning-point, according to Dodsworth, occurred in 1981, the year that the United States slid into recession. In the preceding four or five years, the country had been riding the crest of an inflationary wave, and was only then brought face to face with its own vunerability, in the face of rising imports of Japanese goods.

According to Forrest (1984), the American character derived from two fundamental themes. First, there was the religiosity of the American consciousness, and second, the belief in the power of human effort to bend the world to human purpose. This ability to create the technology that created the world was reinforced by NASA's success in putting a man on the moon in 1969. Americans ordered their place in the world around the idea that their natures had been forged out of experiences which gave them a special capacity to absorb adversity, and mould out of it a transient good future. No matter what, the Americans could tough it out! It was Napoleon Hill (1966), one of the founders of the 'positive thinking' movement, who pointed out in the 1930s that the word American ended in I CAN!

The reaction to quality circles, introduced by W. Edwards Deming into Japan in the 1950s represented, in microcosm, the American character in action. Their appeal on being imported into the United States in the 1980s lay in the fact that they answered the basic themes in the American consciousness. Quality circles promised redemption from the sin of having fallen from competitive grace in international markets. The act of adoption confirmed that Americans were good and moral people. By providing them with an absolutely elaborate technology of analysis, the circles approach allowed them to operate through a modality in which they still believed was related to their special talents. This was the US faith in technology.

Quality circles also resonated exquisitely with the trendier themes in US life as well. The circle of well-meaning people sitting around applauding each other's efforts provided their participants with feelings of potency and effect. For most of the century Americans felt themselves to have been the masters of technology and of themselves. It was therefore a shock for them to discover that the Japanese, a nation with half their population, had overcome both conventional and nuclear war, and had applied technology so creatively and efficiently that it was able to challenge the United States. What was perhaps even more shocking was the realization that the Japanese might be better than the USA in the ways that Americans admired most, and in which they felt they had a virtual monopoly.

The Japanese–American comparison of performance (to the detriment of the latter) was brought to the attention of US businesspeople by Ouchi (1981) and by Pascale and Athos (1982). Both these works spoke admiringly of Japanese methods, analysed the culture of Japanese companies, and suggested that the US could learn a great deal from Japan. While neither of these books attained blockbuster status, they did sell steadily, and might be said to have sown the seeds for the American riposte and the growth of the entrepreneurial period.

Cultural heritage

The critical factors influencing the entrepreneurial period in the United States can be considered under three main headings, the return of American optimism; the possibility of internal transformation; and media influence on business matters.

Return of American optimism

During the early 1980s the American mood became very bullish, with a strong sense of entrepreneurial pride. Davies (1988) reported a survey conducted by the *Rolling Stone* magazine among America's 'baby boomers' born since the Second World War. The survey reported that this generation saw few heroes in the world of 1988. Martin Luther King and Robert Kennedy, who had been assassinated twenty years earlier, were the most admired figures. President Reagan was admired by 25 per cent of those interviewed. These people saw him as a confident and optimistic leader who dwelt on the nation's strength and virtue, rather than upon its disgrace and failure. At the start of the 1980s, Americans had elected this man to the Presidency. He emphasized competition, individualism and the 'survival of the fittest'.

Reviewing the Reagan presidency, *Business Week* (1988) commented that Reagan gave the nation just what it needed for much of the 1980s. This was a return to stability and optimism, and a respite from emotional turmoil and incessant change that had pervaded the country since the early 1960s. By the end of Reagan's tenure, US foreign policy finally shook off the self-doubt left by Vietnam. He reminded Americans that they had much to feel good about. He chose to fight and win easy battles such as in Grenada and the Gulf of Sidera. Reagan's 'economics of joy', as the magazine described them, were able to succeed where Carter's dismal message of malaise had failed. As a result, the United States experienced its longest peacetime expansion.

Jon Steers, Reagan's former campaign adviser, pointed out after the 1984 election that:

> Reagan has given us one thing the people will cling to regardless of future problems. He has presided over the restoration of our confidence. Blindly

optimistic, fiercely patriotic, and unbending in his loyalty, he is the embodiment of a particular American virtue that says all things are possible, if you will just make them so – that reality is an illusion that came be overcome.

Reagan's own words reflect these point:

> They say the US has had its day in the sun; that our nation has passed its zenith. They expect you to tell your children . . . that the future will be one of sacrifice and few opportunities. My fellow Americans, I utterly reject that view.
>
> (Ronald Reagan, 17 July 1980)

With its back to the wall, battered by competition and criticized for its inadequacy, America swung back on to the attack from the early 1980s. Peters and Waterman's book *In Search of Excellence* (*ISOE*) carried the banner for that attack:

> *In Search of Excellence* touched a chord that ran through the collective consciousness of the country in the early '80s. The national hunger for excellence. President Reagan talked about bringing excellence back, reports on the schools spoke of a lack of excellence, and excellence was the theme of ads countering Japanese competition. Little wonder *ISOE* took off as a national best seller. It was 'the answer', surely we could regain our national position as the preeminent producer of goods for the world . . . *ISOE* just fed the ever present yearning for good news.
>
> (Godfrey 1985: 3)

The book said that there was good news from America. That good management practice was not resident solely in Japan. This was the message that America wanted to hear. When *ISOE* was published in 1982, its timing could not have been better. The American management techniques that had seemed so invincible in the 1950s and 1960s appeared to have lost their impact. Eyes were turning instead to the omnipotent Japanese. *ISOE* dispelled that pessimism about America's ability to compete. It offered new models of good management right in America's own backyard. Americans, by nature, like to think that they can solve their own problems. The book's message that US companies could motivate workers and serve customers just as well as the Japanese made it the best-selling business book at the time.

Both Freeman (1985) and Pierce and Newstrom (1988) suggested a number of additional reasons to account for the popularity of the guru ideas of the time. They argued that the 1980s were a decade in which Corporate America was back in good standing. Pride and hope re-emerged in the business community. It seemed that the time was ripe for a positive vision of business. The business gurus who came along, by chance or design, articulated this vision in a digestible way. After the anti-business era of the late 1960s and early 1970s, after the recession-shocked later 1970s, after being bullied by Japanophiles, after a decade of finger-pointing by management experts, managers were ready for a positive message and simple answers. They were primed to soak up the gospel of made-in-America excellence.

These new epistles to managers shimmered with optimism. They were enthusiastic about the business world. These authors often eschewed the syntax of reservation and qualification, which is common in academic prose. The message was that Corporate America was back in good standing with the public. There was a resurgence of pride and hope in the business community, and the buying public was receptive to business books. Books such as those of Iacocca (1985) expressed confidence in the American business system. They offered reassurance and optimism at a time when US companies had gone through a period of self-doubt and painful reconstruction. Naisbitt emphasized the transition towards an informational society and an entrepreneurial economy. He concluded with a rousing exhortation to the old American go-getting frontier spirit:

> We have extraordinary leverage and influence – individually, professionally and institutionally – if we can only get a clear sense, a clear conception, a clear vision, of the road ahead. My God, what a fantastic time to be alive.
>
> (Naisbitt 1982)

Each book contained different attractive features. Iacocca's appeal was its heroic quality recounting the fairy tale story of a man rising from humble origins to mount a successful industrial rescue. The theme of American Champions which was contained in *ISOE* runs through much of the guru literature. It has a double appeal. At one level it elevated successful businessmen like Stew Leonard into role models, and in so doing, it aggressively reasserted the values of American entrepreneurship and individuality which, in many people's eyes, were the ultimate success fantasy. At another level, the guru books, which were written in a determiningly, unswerving optimistic style, reflected an attitude of change to an era of reassertiveness within the American corporate sector. Management ideas and techniques such as quality circles and corporate culture flourished. Thackray (1986: 114) wrote that 'business and business ideas were the subject of mass entertainment on a scale not known in the US since before the Depression'.

The enterprise culture also affected business school students. Having emerged from the Vietnam era and the concerns of that period, they found that money-making was suddenly in vogue again. The period of introversion seemed to have given way to a new era of greed and avarice. Adam Smith (1989) in his book, *The Roaring '80s* wrote that:

> There are times when getting and spending are very important, and times when public purpose surpasses private interest as the accepted goal. . . . The Reagan years will be remembered as money-value years. . . . It is not only okay to be rich; it is okay to flaunt it.

The high-point of the period was perhaps encapsulated by the phrase, spoken by the character, Gordon Gekko, in the film *Wall Street* that 'Greed is good'. The revival of the money-making ethic established the conditions for the boom in business books and the popularity of their authors.

Possibility of internal transformation

A second influence underlying many of the management ideas promulgated at the time was the notion that a company could become competitive merely by setting its own house in order. That is, it was the master of its own destiny. Authors differed as to how this improvement might be achieved. Nevertheless, a focus on the individual's behaviour inside the firm implicitly assumed that if people were induced to develop their own enterprise, commitment and teamwork, there were no limits to what the company could achieve in terms of growth, profit and market share.

These suggestions made sense, however, only when markets were expanding. *ISOE* was written during a period of recession and became a best-seller just as the Reagan economic era was starting. The same is true of the craze for the entrepreneur. The economic status that the entrepreneur occupied was mostly due to macro-economic reasons. These included American demographics (a bulge of new entrants when the large companies had stopped hiring); industrial upheaval (the spurt of growth in electronics, deregulation, and the first serious opening of the American economy to work markets); the failure of American industrial productivity (which depressed average income per head and caused a revolution in the service economy with 15 million to 20 million new jobs). It became fashionable to be rich and to prove that you could succeed in business. This enthusiasm filtered abroad, and was picked up in Britain, where starting your own business offered an alternative to being unemployed. The impact of these changes, first in the USA and then the UK has been felt and has now passed.

Media influence on business matters

The effect of the media should also be considered. Perhaps for the first time in history, financial and economic issues came to be reported as a matter of course. Some commentators have argued that the media and the large corporations colluded in a strategy to gain publicity for themselves and their managers. Thackray (1987) wrote about a 'credulous media hungry for heroes [which] is more than happy to accept canned realities and pretentions – at least until the bubble bursts.' The collusion from the companies, said Thackray, came from their addiction to publicity which sought to take advantage of a business press which was less than critical of the shortcomings of business.

During the 1980s one found the media puffing up executive egos and rushing into hyperbole. An entire media system developed to support business. This had previously restricted itself to television, film and sports personalities (Rein *et al.* 1987). The age of the entrepreneur was the age of the business celebrity. Steven Jobs, John Welch and Lee Iacocca attained the status of film stars. Galbraith (1983) commented on the modern phenomenon of the synthetic or created personality. Personality was held to be more interesting than organization. It appealed to reporters, television commentators and others who dealt with the exercise of power and who associated it with the walking speaking individual. As a highly practical matter, people could give interviews and appear on television while organizations could not.

The tremendous growth in the circulation figures of the business press and its hunger for content created a temptation for corporations to lower their standards and to take the low road of the cult of personality and the simplification of ideas and processes. Galbraith wrote that:

> Personality traits are attributed to the heads of the organizations that seem appropriate to the power exercised, and this imagery is assiduously and professionally cultivated. It is the principal purpose of much public relations effort . . . presidents of corporations are examples of extensively synthesized personalities; journalists and commentators of the more vunerable sort are persuaded of their unique personal qualities, as are the subjects themselves. . . . Divorced from organization, the synthetic personality dissolves and the individual behind it disappears into the innocuous obscurity from which his real personality intended him.
>
> (Galbraith 1983: 43)

In the entrepreneurial period, the corporations were inclined to overlook the synthetic and to portray large and complex organizations as extensions of the leader's ego. Roger Smith did not just represent General Motors, he was portrayed as fighting its bureaucracy. IBM was portrayed as invulnerable. The decline and departure of the entrepreneurial heroes of the 1980s such as Steven Jobs (Apple Computer) and Donald Burr (People Express) in the United States and Clive Sinclair (Sinclair Computers) and Sir Freddie Laker (Skytrain) signalled a return to business as usual. That is, to competition between oligopolies. The entrepreneurial search was redirected inwards in the form of in-company innovation or *Intrapreneuring* (Pinchot 1985).

Institutional factors

In seeking to explain the appeal of guru ideas, attention is now turned to the institutional level. There are six main factors that can be briefly highlighted to explain the appeal to companies of the ideas of this period. These are the changing corporate environment; corporate social responsibility trends; the failure of personnel management; the decline of trade union pressure; the search for competitive advantage; and the effect of US government legislation on work organization. Each of these will be discussed briefly.

Changing corporate environment

There was a shift of the centre of gravity during this business period away from manufacture towards service, away from supplier towards customer, away from brawn and towards brain (Heller 1990). This occurred against a background of a rapidly changing market environment. The move away from producer-control was facilitated by new technology, deregulation, liberalization and the disappearing frontiers between nations. Old monopolies were destroyed by an abundance of supply and money.

The changed corporate environment of the 1980s was reflected in the emerging new models which concerned the critical management tasks and the context in which people did their work. The infallibility of management and the certainty of management tasks had declined. The perceived potential of the rest of the workforce to contribute to the solution of organizational problems had increased. The theme was that, regardless of organizational level, management had to take other people into account. This included shopfloor workers, customers and suppliers. The employee-involving strategies of the 1980s, such as quality circles, industrial citizenship programmes and intrapreneurship, fitted in well with these organizational change strategies, and allowed the consultant and academic gurus to purvey their wares.

Corporate social responsibility trends

In the United States in 1981, the Business Roundtable issued a statement of corporate responsibility declaring that the managers of corporations were expected to serve the public interest as well as private profit. Four 'constituencies' were identified – customers, employees, communities and society at large, and shareholders. This politicization meant that the management of critical boundary spanning issues became a key role of the chief executive, and the amount of time devoted to this grew significantly. Companies placed an increased premium on people adept at handing corporate relations with the public and government. Like politicians, ambitious executives campaigning for higher office had to project a vote-getting image. This gave the green light for the chief executive who 'fronted' the company, and gave him the opportunity and visibility to become a hero-manager.

Failure of personnel management

Guest (1987) argued that, in the eyes of senior management, personnel management had failed to secure the potential benefits of the effective management of people. The major recession which affected the USA and western Europe in the 1980s resulted in a run-down in manufacturing and consequent unemployment. The question was what contribution could personnel management make to this. Powerless when external economic forces put the survival of the business at stake, this function was seen as an overhead. In the 1980s, articles in personnel journals justified the relevance of personnel management work. In the view of ACAS, the decline in the number of personnel staff represented a change of philosophy which stressed returning as much responsibility as possible to line managers for personnel matters.

The reasons for this can be found in the influences on the development of personnel management, the role of personnel managers within the organization (Legge 1978; Beer et al. 1985; Guest and Horwood 1980) and the prevailing ethos of the time. The political philosophy stressed competition (and implied conflict). In contrast, the personnel tradition of the past, and many personnel policies of the time, were founded on a welfare ethos stressing the principles of fairness and standardization of treatment for specific groups. This was underpinned by collective bargaining which sustained such principles.

The individualistic philosophy of personnel management (which stressed human resource management) questioned the need for old-type personnel specialists (Tyson and Fell 1986). A new approach was needed which established the management of human resources as a mainstream management activity. Human resource management, it was argued, was too important to be left to the marginally located personnel managers. Commentators argued that the emphasis on excellence sought to shore up an establishment threatened by a wide variety of insistent and untidy democratic demands for participation.

Decline of trade union pressure

Both in the United States and in the United Kingdom, the changed political and economic climate resulted in a reduction of union pressure on management. As a consequence, attention turned away from collective and adversarial issues of traditional human relations, and towards individual, co-operative questions of the type that concerned employee relations and human resource management. Trends within the trade unions have reinforced such changes. The growth of organized labour in the 1980s was among the white-collar, especially public sector, employees.

Knowledgeable and educated, these employees were concerned about close supervision and wanted to be left alone to manage their work. This interest led to the bringing of Quality of Working Life demands to the bargaining table. They pushed for flexitime and joint management–labour committees. Many important interest groups converged in their acceptance of more participation at the shopfloor level (Beaumont 1985). That original concern by this group percolated down to shopfloor employees. These ideas were instituted in new work arrangements at Nissan's plant in Tyne and Wear.

Search for competitive advantage

Many companies felt that the way they could achieve a competitive advantage was to seek improvements in the management of people and organizational structures. The emphasis was upon the better utilization of their human resources (Beer *et al.* 1985; Tichy *et al.* 1982). The models of excellence which were presented were influential. The stereotyped Japanese companies and the US excellent companies identified by Peters and Waterman (1982) and Kanter (1985) all practised human resource management. The conclusion reached was that effective human resource management was what excellent companies did. Kanter (1985) noted that fad and fashion played a role in extending more participative work systems. Organizations could be just as fashion conscious as individual consumers. When a few leading ones started to adopt a reform, the rest often quickly followed because they wanted to be seen to be modern as well. In her view, concerns about image were a driving force for executives in the new, more political and more public corporate environment.

Effect of US government legislation

Other innovations and reforms permitted time flexibility and schedule control (Guest 1987). In the United States, federal government and state court decisions have, since the 1970s, supported new employee rights, for example, to privacy, conscientious objection and dismissal.

Motivational context

The final issue to consider is what attracted managers to these ideas as witnessed by book sales, conference attendances and consulting fees. Kanter

(1985) reported that, as a result of the changes taking place in the US economy in the early 1980s, managers felt dislocated and disoriented. They had lost both their sense of supremacy and their sense of control. They found this unsettling, frightening, frustrating and intolerable. They felt at the mercy of change in a world marked by turbulence, uncertainty and instability. Their comfort and success was dependent on those whom they could hardly influence.

For middle managers, the 1980s created changed times and new environments which exerted new pressures that required new insights, skills, orientations and roles. Pressures on their careers from trends in the labour market, declining productivity and foreign competition, all increased career insecurity. The job-holding of women in the United States increased the competition for lower management jobs. Increased schooling led to increased ambitions and a large pool of competition.

Interdepartmental power, as well as individual power, were at stake. Individuals competed with one another inside the company. They sought to improve their unit's bargaining position within the organization. Scarcities increased internal bargaining for resources which affected the daily quality of life, as well as the ability to produce accomplishments that produced net career advantage. Turbulent environments kept shifting the focus of relevance and made whole functions or departments relatively essential or inessential depending on their control over critical issues, as these themselves shifted.

Changes bring opportunities. They allow enterprising consultants to offer change management products and services, thereby turning other people's confusion into profitable business. In such circumstances the market was receptive to ideas and techniques that might 'save the American corporation' or to 'meet the Japanese challenge'. The disruptions of the period created the development of social and organizational techniques for increasing productivity and motivation. Peters (1989) implied that chaos could be managed by the application of 45 prescriptions (see Table 4.5.)

Many of the management techniques played a part in this battle for company attention and resources. Management-by-Objectives (MbO) had, in the past, strengthened the position of line management; quality management emphasized the role of production departments; while corporate culture raised the visibility of human resource departments. These techniques affected the opportunity structure in a company. They signalled which career paths were likely to be significant and which functions would be included in dominant coalitions. Second, they affected the power structure by determining who would have access to resources and information.

Power was also acquired in organizations by struggles to control those issues which preoccupied senior management. New issues crossed old territories. Who should 'own' them? The middle level power struggle in an

Table 4.5 Tom Peters' prescriptions for a 'World Turned Upside Down'

Creating Total Customer Responsiveness

The Guiding Premise	C-1: Specialize/Create Niches/Differentiate
The Five Basic Value-Adding Strategies	C-2: Provide Top Quality, as Perceived by the Customer
	C-3: Provide Superior Service/Emphasize the Intangibles
	C-4: Achieve Extraordinary Responsiveness
	C-5: Be an Internationalist
	C-6: Create Uniqueness
The Four Capability Building Blocks	C-7: Become Obsessed with Listening
	C-8: Turn Manufacturing into a Marketing Weapon
	C-9: Make Sales and Service Forces into Heroes
	I-1-I-10: Pursue Fast-Paced Innovation (see below)
The Evolving Firm	C-10: Launch a Customer Revolution

Pursuing Fast-Paced Innovation

The Guiding Premise	I-1: Invest in Applications-Oriented Small Starts
The Four Key Strategies	I-2: Pursue Team Product/Service Development
	I-3: Encourage Pilots of Everything
	I-4: Practise 'Creative Swiping'
	I-5: Make Word-of-Mouth Marketing Systematic
Management Tactics to Encourage Innovation	I-6: Support Committed Champions
	I-7: 'Model' Innovation/Practise Purposeful Impatience
	I-8: Support Fast Failures
	I-9: Set Quantitative Innovation Goals
The New Look Firm	I-10: Create a Corporate Capacity for Innovation

Achieving Flexibility by Empowering People

The Guiding Premises	P-1: Involve Everyone in Everything
	P-2: Use Self-Managing Teams
The Five Supports (Add Them)	P-3: Listen/Celebrate/Recognize
	P-4: Spend Time Lavishly on Recruiting
	P-5: Train and Retrain
	P-6: Provide Incentive Pay for Everyone
	P-7: Provide an Employment Guarantee
The Three Inhibitors (Take Them Away)	P-8: Simplify/Reduce Structure
	P-9: Reconceive the Middle Manager's Role
	P-10: Eliminate Bureaucratic Rules and Humiliating Conditions

Table 4.5 Continued

Learning to Love Change: A New View of Leadership at All Levels

The Guiding Premise	L-1: Master Paradox

The Three Leadership Tools for Establishing Direction	L-2: Develop an Inspiring Vision
	L-3: Manage by Example
	L-4: Practice Visible Management

Leading by Empowering People	L-5: Pay Attention! (More Listening)
	L-6: Defer to the Front Line
	L-7: Delegate
	L-8: Pursue "Horizontal Management" by Bashing Bureaucracy

The Bottom Line: Leading as Love of Change	L-9: Evaluate Everyone on His or Her Love of Change
	L-10: Create a Sense of Urgency

Building Systems for a World Turned Upside Down

The Guiding Premise	S-1: Measure What's Important

Reconceiving the System Tools of Control and Empowerment	S-2: Revamp the Chief Control Tools
	S-3: Decentralize Information, Authority, and Strategic Planning

Establishing Trust Via Systems	S-4: Set Conservative Goals
	S-5: Demand Total Integrity

Source: Peters 1989

organization was, in part, over the ownership of new ideas which, by definition, could not be fitted into existing functional boxes and which threw the meaning of functional distinctions up into the air to be renegotiated. For example, at which level in the organization should productivity improvement programmes be negotiated and managed? Who should be included in their management?

Transfer of guru theory to Britain

The election of a Conservative government under Margaret Thatcher in

1979 occurred a year before the election of Ronald Reagan to the White House. Both leaders emphasized competition, individualism and the survival of the fittest. Because of the similarity of their outlooks, the background conditions in both countries were equally receptive to the establishment and growth of management techniques based on the ideas of guru writers.

In Britain, the 1980s came to be seen as a period of widespread management innovation. The economic crisis of the 1980s and the pressure from Japan reinforced each other. From the late 1970s the pressure of competition had forced many western corporations, British ones among them, to re-examine their philosophy of job design and control, management style and organization structure, all from the down-to-earth perspective of profits. The cultural climate in which Britain operated during most of the 1980s emphasized utilitarian values, the virtues of self-improvement, and the primacy of enterprise.

The dramatic rise of unemployment in Britain in the early 1980s shifted the economic power to the employers enabling them initially to force through previously unacceptable changes (core working, temporary work, part-timers) amidst a 'climate of fear and uncertainty' (Littler and Salaman 1984). It permitted a shake out of excess labour and the removal of restrictive practices. The 1980s, like the 1930s, spurred some employers to cut wages, extend hours, or impose straightforward labour intensification strategies which involved no attempt at work reorganization. The average annual strike rate in Britain during the 1980s fell to its lowest for 50 years (*The Economist* 1989a).

Summarizing ten years of Conservative government, *The Economist* (1989b) gave the statistics. Productivity in manufacturing industry rose by 5–6 per cent a year on average in 1980–8. Later in the decade, unemployment fell at last to below 2 million (7 per cent of the labour force), while company profits rose to record levels. The top marginal rate of income tax fell from 83 per cent to 40 per cent thereby greatly increasing the rewards for success. Venture capital funds arose to supply entrepreneurs seeking to start their own companies. A booming stock market made it easy for large firms to raise new finance. Summarizing the decade's achievement *The Economist* said that:

> A new ethos and new optimism became apparent in all areas of business, one that seemed to favour ambition, hard work, working breakfasts, short lunches, marketing, buy-outs, restructuring total quality and any number of other buzzwords. Businessmen may not have swallowed all the government's propaganda about the re-birth of enterprise, but they had gradually regained confidence.
>
> (*The Economist* 1989b: 5)

The economic coercion, however, had its limits especially in a situation in which the nature of competition was changing. The new emphasis on quality meant that the reluctant acquiescence of employees had to be replaced by active co-operation. Thus one observed a combination of union-opposed structural changes to work (such as the introduction of a flexible firm structure) being combined with employee commitment strategies (e.g. quality circles, briefing groups, profit-sharing schemes). The change involved a contradictory mixture of job cuts, robots, union opposition and an attempt to engage the enthusiasm and willing involvement of the workforce.

In explaining the adoption of specific management techniques in Britain, Ramsay had earlier argued that one could view such changes from the perspective of perceived environmental threats to management authority. He wrote about 'cycles of control' and argued that techniques such as employee involvement or participation had evolved cyclically:

(a) They seem on each occasion to have arisen out of a managerial response to threats to management authority . . . the initiative is management's and the consequence is, if significant at all, to mollify pressures to change the status quo, not to stimulate its reform.

(b) Each time the schemes emphasise, almost without exception a consensual unitary philosophy, and bear related hallmarks of managerial ideology.

(Ramsay 1977: 496)

In the light of economic developments in Britain from the mid-1980s onwards, one finds the popular techniques reflecting the collaborative theme. Peters and Waterman's suggestion about 'Management by Walking About' was turned into a video training film produced by the Industrial Society. That same organization had earlier promoted one of the most widely adopted management techniques of the 1980s – briefing groups. Finally, the concern with total quality management prompted the use of quality circles.

Elsewhere in Europe, American management guru ideas were being well received. Lorenz (1986a) concluded that, despite all their suspicion of transatlantic influences, Europeans were more open to American ideas than to those of each other. While he felt that the European guru boom would continue, he did not feel that European managers would ever become as fashion conscious as their American counterparts. In particular, he noted the European aversion to emulating the American tendency to go overboard for the latest idea while neglecting the previous one. He concluded that European managements were more cautious about new management ideas. Considering the success of American authored books in continental Europe, Lorenz (1986a) referred to the German situation where there was a feeling of insecurity about which were the right management methods to apply. When in the past everyone had been successful, there was no need for external role models such as Iacocca, but in the 1980s that need did resurface.

French observers also reported a cultural change towards management, making money, and an enterprise culture. French publishing houses successfully marketed the writings of Ouchi (1981), McKenna (1985), Naisbitt (1982), Peters and Waterman (1982) and Bennis and Nanus (1985). They did much to woo French executives away from their previous scepticism of American business concepts. In France, noted Lorenz (1986a), 100,000 copies of *ISOE* were sold in three years. He also reported the greater readiness of the French to learn lessons from others, that is engaging in a search for new answers in an increasingly competitive environment. However, national differences still remained. There was French resistance to some American gurus among those French executives who had received a very rigorous intellectual training. This may account, said Lorenz, for the failure of *The One Minute Manager* (Blanchard and Johnson 1983) which was considered too simplistic. The Germans in contrast were more pragmatic, taking an 'if-it-works-we'll-try-it view'.

The future?

What then of the future? In which direction might the social, political and economic trends turn? Stuart (1986) wrote that new themes in the thinking of managers became more popular as the economic trends which prompted these thoughts touched the lives of more people. An intellectual fad was a reliable, if slightly lagging, indicator of economic activity. He recommended that the first place to look for signs of an up-and-coming fad was in the economy itself.

The Economist (1988b) argued that, after years of being admired, fêted, given its head by politicians and a public desperate for a prosperous way out of the complexities of oil shocks, inflation and unemployment, business would, in the 1990s, be questioned, criticized and perhaps even vilified. To support this contention, it cited some 'straws in the wind'. First, the absence in mid-1989 of business books in the top positions of best-selling American books. Second, the stabilization of applications to American business schools and the rise of applications to law schools. Third, the emergence in Japan of the *datsu-sara* (corporate runaway), managers who dropped out to do their own thing. Fourth, the report of a survey among West Germans in which they placed pollution as the major perceived problem ahead of their 7.75 per cent unemployment rate. Anti-business tendencies, said *The Economist*, were likely to be exacerbated by resentments about the size of executive pay and perks when those people ceased to be regarded as folk-heroes. The growth of the green lobby would stress the part of large companies as environment wreckers, while unemployment would rise and the companies would be blamed for it.

The turning of the pro-business tide might represent the cyclical phenomenon described in this chapter. American suspicions of business have oscillated. There were the anti-trust laws of the 1890s, the New Deal of the 1930s, the rebelliousness of the 1960s. Each occurred after a pro-business period. The next anti-business mood, however, will not, in *The Economist's* view, be general but will instead be focused upon large companies and money dealers such as bankers. The signs, however, are confusing. A single event, such as the Iraqi invasion of Kuwait and the subsequent instability in oil prices, can make prediction impossible.

Rose (1990), writing in *Fortune* magazine, reported the resurgence in America of a new paradigm for viewing the world. Love and caring were back in the workplace. The institutions and ideas of neo-human relations, he felt, were about to make a comeback. New age management was likely to be the flavour of the age. Futurologists and pundits have argued that 1988 marked a watershed. The replacement of Ronald Reagan by George Bush marked a 'kinder, gentler society', a theme to be echoed later by John Major's replacement of Margaret Thatcher. Economically, the stock market crash of 1987, and the subsequent recession, were held to have seen off the 'Gordon Gekko', red braces and car-phone set. Greed was no longer good. Socially, environmental issues were to take centre stage, and the pollution of the Gulf War, together with the plight of the Kurdish people after the Gulf War, raised public concern about environmental and human problems. A period of retrenchment and consensus might follow one of conflict.

Journalists have speculated that the 1990s will in fact see a backlash. Fairley (1991a; 1991b) considered the 1980s an era of conspicuous consumption, and that the 1990s would become a period of self-denial. Life-styles would be pared down, and an element of spirituality added. He dubbed it the *Age of Enlightenment*, in which having *less* was the in-thing. Material possessions did not meet the needs of the soul, and a calmer life-style, as a reaction to merciless materialism, was what was needed. New age proponents claim that humanity is undergoing a shift that will usher in a new order of all-embracing spirituality. The 1980s was a fragmented period, they claim, in which people wanted to be given complete, instant answers, rather than taking the trouble to work things out for themselves.

The backcloth to this new age has been the faltering performance of American business. Superimposed on this has been the speed of computers, communications and global networks. Changes such as deregulation, corporate takeovers, the demise of the Soviet Union and the Gulf War have all made the extraordinary event commonplace. This has led to the vague but growing sense that business has to be conducted differently. This does not, however, mean to be a straightforward return to Lasch's (1980) culture of narcissism.

The current spirituality links the eastern tradition of mind and body synthesis, to a hard-nosed concern for the bottom line. The preparation for combat is seen as demanding mental exercises, meditation and discipline, a sort of martial arts approach. A 'secret army' of businesspeople is being prepared for battle. The lead was taken from the Japanese again who are expected to be the leading industrial nation at the start of the twenty-first century. It has been reported (*Sunday Times* 1991) that some Japanese industrialists were seeking to release their creative powers by tapping into Buddist modes of thought at *alternative think-tanks* held at the Mukta Institute in Tokyo. Here captains of industry met to solve problems through the pursuit of Zen.

Rose reported that in the 1970s, West Coast personal growth philosophies were considered too far-out by American business. The East Coast equivalent, organizational development (OD), prospered however, and indeed flourished in the military under the label of *organizational effectiveness* (OE). Post-Vietnam, a group of officers were tasked to scan the environment for new ideas. One of their slogans became 'Be all you can be', a human potential message that eventually permeated to the US Army's recruitment campaign.

By the 1980s as OE became extinguished, a spin-off called *organizational transformation* (OT) was developed by people who were less concerned with team-building and communication, and more interested in myth, ritual and the spirit, helping managers create a vision that makes corporate goals tangible against a starry universe or earthscope background. The stress of OT was loving each other in a brotherly manner, incorporating spiritual values into work, and doing something physical together. This explains the stress of new age training upon outdoor type courses, and a re-evaluation of work relationships and objectives. It is not clear whether these social, economic and political developments will last long enough through the 1990s to generate a separate and distinctive theme in management ideas.

In this chapter, the historical context of popular management ideas has been considered in a macro-sense. Nevertheless, timing affects the appeal of management ideas in a micro-sense as well. The timeliness of a management idea is a function of the external environment and the manager's current needs and problems. The analysis of the interviews conducted by the author confirms that some ideas, at least, come through a 'window of opportunity', while others may be perceived to have an ongoing relevance. The following comments of the managers interviewed highlight this coincidence of idea-availability and management need:

That stimulated me because I was in the quality business at the time.

Organizational behaviour so topical here today and it's the way we're trying to do it.

Working hard of course to change the leadership style in the company and that is why it is very relevant to us today.

I believe that is probably our greatest need right at the minute.

I think I was ready then to pick up responsibility for total quality management.

Chapter 5

Requirements of managers

INTRODUCTION

This chapter considers how the nature and content of managerial work creates particular kinds of needs which popular management ideas can fill. The author's argument is based on a review of the relevant literature, data obtained from a survey of 115 managers, and in-depth, tape-recorded interviews with a sub-sample of these. The nature of organizational life and managerial work represents the starting-point for an analysis of managerial needs.

Hodgson (1987) identified a number of organizational pressures on managers. These included the emphasis on short-term profits (and hence on short-term thinking); a lack of consistency of purpose; stress on managerial job-hopping; and an individually focused performance review system which used only visible (hard) figures. These factors affected the way in which managers spent their time and how they allocated their priorities. This topic has been extensively researched (Carlson 1951; Marples 1967; Stewart 1967; Mintzberg 1973; Mintzberg 1975; Kotter 1982; Willmott 1984; Hales 1986). The surveys reveal the pressures to which managers are exposed to, and the volume, variety, fragmentation and brevity of their work.

The theoretical work of Abraham Maslow, plus the empirical work mentioned earlier, suggest that managerial needs can be divided into two types: cognitive-intellectual and affective-emotional. The former are further subdivided into predictability and control needs; while the latter are subdivided into social and personal needs. These are summarized in Table 5.1.

The fundamental source of managerial need is twofold. First, the nature of organizational life places responsibility on managers to *perform* and *achieve* in a context where often they neither understand how their actions produce results, nor are able to influence the most volatile element in the organization – other people. Second, partly as a result of this uncertainty, their assessment of themselves is also under downward pressure. A similar low assessment tends to be made of them as individuals, and of management

Table 5.1 Managerial requirements

	COGNITIVE INTELLECTUAL	AFFECTIVE EMOTIONAL	
UNDERSTANDING FOCUSED	predictability needs	social needs	EXTERNALLY DIRECTED
ACTION FOCUSED	control needs	personal needs	INTERNALLY DIRECTED

as a profession. For this reason, the two predominant managerial needs are, on the one hand, for increased predictability and control and, on the other, for increased socal and personal esteem.

Berger and Luckmann (1967) argued that like all species, humans had a need for an ordered, patterned way of life. Since neither biology nor environment predetermined the form that this would take, human beings constructed a world of their own and carefully sought to maintain it against disruption and uncertainty. Modern society, wrote Luckmann (1978), 'confronts the individual with an ever-changing kaleidoscope of social experiences and meanings'. It forces the individual to make choices, decisions and plans. At the same time, this experience of variety and diversity undermines any feeling of certainty since, 'what is truth in one context of the individual's social life many be error in another' (Luckmann 1978). Although as individuals, we might want to be autonomous and independent, we cannot cope psychologically with the permanent burden of critically questioning, analysing alternatives, and working out the full implications of every act.

Becker (1973) wrote about the basic tendency in the human species to seek predictability and the comfort of taken-for-granted assumptions about their world and their circumstances. People looked to their culture to help them with the 'problem of meaning'. On their own, they were unable to make meaningful analyses of the potentially chaotic world in which they had to exist. Hence, they were forced to depend on the meanings made available to them in the social world of which they were a part, which included the organizations for whom they worked. Peters and Waterman (1982) suggested that people would give a great deal to institutions which gave their lives meaning.

This problem of ambiguity is also present at all levels in organizations. Explaining the function of 'bull' in the armed forces, Dixon (1976) argued that it exemplified the general principle which was common to all organisms, namely that of *combating randomness*. Living organisms were complex patterns which existed within the essential disorder from which they came, and to which they would ultimately return. The pattern endeavoured to maintain itself in being and there existed regulators, controls and constraints which functioned to preserve that pattern. They maintained purity and separateness. Life could be construed as a fight for orderliness in the cause of which both voluntary and involuntary behaviour was directed.

According to this theory of entropy reduction, the attraction to and belief in a particular management idea represented a general and necessary propensity on the part of the manager to resist randomness. These management ideas contained within themselves 'theories of the world' which were relatively simple and amenable to control by their users. Other aspects of the organization complemented the process of randomness reduction. For example, maintaining uniformity by written and spoken instruction; clear job descriptions; unambiguous statements of responsibilities depicted in organizational charts; preserving the hierarchy in the company; preserving status differences; separating managers from workers; and delineating what was and was not appropriate behaviour for every situation.

In organizations, it was *people* who featured prominently in managers' work environments. It was they who could make-or-break managers' careers. Because managers stood to lose most, they feared them most. The advent of our affluent industrial society meant that we no longer feared hunger or accidents. The social environment has replaced the material environment as the main area of concern. The manager was at the mercy of people, and not natural forces. Cleverley (1971) argued that a manager's environment was made up basically of relationships with others, which were seen as menacing, incomprehensible and uncontrollable. The human relations world conveyed lurking danger and fatality. It could not be apprehended or controlled by rational or intelligible methods which worked. Management may be defined as 'getting things done through people', but the people were a volatile and unpredictable commodity:

> In the entire environment that surrounds the manager, the most unpredictable, least understood and least controllable factor is the behaviour of the people he manages. Not surprisingly therefore, the subject is shrouded in mystique.
>
> (Cleverley 1971: 96)

In this sphere of human relations, however, managers did not feel that there was a total randomness about their interactions. They did get a sense of some 'tight pattern'. The social experiences of managers left them with a feeling that there was some hidden logic. However, attempts to seize, capture and utilize that logic usually failed. Managers found it impossible to remain passive in the face of this acute and recurrent anxiety which emanated from the sphere of human relationships management and hence searched for guidance.

Table 5.2 Classification by discipline of management ideas mentioned by managers

Category	No.	%
General management	207	55
• Knowledge	94	25
• Skills	113	30
Human relations	91	25
Finance/accounting	50	13
Operations management	15	4
Marketing/business policy	12	3
Total	375	100

The primacy of people–management issues was confirmed by the author's research. Table 5.2 shows that the 115 responding managers from the survey identified a total of 375 management ideas which they had found 'valuable' (3.2 ideas per respondent). Of these, 80 per cent were in the general management and human relations area, confirming that human beings were the least predictable, and hence most uncontrollable aspect of a manager's job.

Since the early 1960s, management thinking has become interested in developing sophisticated systems for managing people successfully. This obsession may be a product of a deficiency in management culture in which there is no concern about people until they become a problem. As soon as a people-problem occurs, the tendency is either to throw money at it (short-term expedient solution), to search for a magic wand (the new system), or to react (in a war-like mode) to pressure from the trade union to resolve the matter. Employees were seen as irrational and hence as not susceptible to the organization's logical control systems. It was not so much that human irrationality reduced the effectiveness of the control systems. Employees followed their own rationalities which differed from those of the organizers (Watson 1986). For much of the time, these two sets of rationales did not coincide.

ACADEMIC SOLUTIONS TO MANAGERIAL NEEDS

The traditional view was that business school academics generated ideas based on their research, and managers used them. In fact, with a few notable exceptions, academics have singularly failed to address, let alone meet the aforementioned management needs. Why should this have been so? The different contexts in which academics and managers work, their different reward systems, and their different perspectives on the same issue can go a long way to explaining why so few management ideas have attained a popular status. Miner (1978) wrote that the business school academic, in the role of a scientist:

'requires that he recognize what is known and is not known in order to state problems for research. He must take every precaution to ensure that his findings, once obtained, are not in error. In contrast, the managerial role does not require the advancement of knowledge but rather the achievement of organizational task and maintenance goals. Time is often a crucial factor in decision-making. Risks and uncertainty are everywhere.

(Miner 1978: 70)

Since 'managers make things happen', management attracts people with personality characteristics which stress getting on with the job, and not with theorizing. The only form of guidance that managers will value comes in the form of a recipe that they can use with the assurance that it will work. In terms of both personal objectives and personality, therefore, those who are charged with generating useful knowledge and those who are required to act upon it, are diametrically opposed. Gurney (Punch 1981) presented the contrast colourfully:

Remember that the professor, the teacher, is paid to be suspicious, sceptical and argumentative. That's our job. . . . And so when a businessman meets a professor, you can see the shutters go over their eyes and their eyes tighten as each faces his mortal antagonist; the man whose life depends on accepting assumptions up against the man whose life depends on questioning them.

Blackler and Shimmin (1984) explained how management researchers and managers perceived, defined and approached the same problems differently. Such differences in their views represented 'contrasting institutionalized systems of values that are expressed in the criteria by which success and failure are judged and the associated behaviour rewarded or penalized'. Their points are summarized in Table 5.3.

Table 5.3 also illustrates that academics will attempt to find data which will elucidate the problem under study in terms of an accepted, conceptual framework which will allow generalizations into the future from their results. In contrast, managers are concerned with short-term actions which will eliminate the specific pressing problem that they are facing. Managers are not concerned that they do not fully understand either the problem's causes or consequences. Academics obtain recognition from their academic peers who evaluate work largely in terms of publications of various kinds. Managers are assessed on the basis of the results that they achieve which are seen clearly by their superiors, peers and subordinates as making a contribution to the company's goals.

Managers make decisions upon incomplete information. To cope with

Table 5.3 Comparison of the value of problem-solving assumptions of academics and managers

	Academics	Managers
Value assumptions:		
• Goal	Understanding	Accomplishment
• Criteria of excellence	Validity	Effectiveness
• Application	Abstract/general	Concrete/specific
Problem-solving assumptions:		
• Time perspective	Long term	Short term
• Methodology	Control inputs for valid explanation	Control inputs for effective influence
Viewpoint:	Objective	Involved
A negative result is:	Information	Failure

Source: Blackler and Shimmin 1984: 69

this situation, research showed that managers paid attention to gossip, speculation and hearsay in their decision-making, and preferred oral to written forms of communication. Agor (1986) showed that senior executives relied on intuitive rather than theoretical reasoning and often instructed subordinates to find data to support their 'gut decisions'.

Lower in the organizations, the pressure to act undermined theoretical modes of thinking. Given a situation and the need to bring about the desired outcome, the manager was likely to ask how this situation was similar to a past one that had been handled in a way which had produced a satisfactory outcome. The manager was less likely to consider the problem in depth, or to enumerate all the possible causes of action. Child (1969a) wrote:

> The manager's life has become much more complicated as the result of his dependence (on psychologists and sociologists) because he is constantly being told about the unreliability of the old saws, clichés, and principles by which he used to direct his affairs.
>
> (Child 1969a: 205)

One consequence of these disparities has been the creation of an informational gap which has been filled by management consultants. Management consultants providing a packaged set of principles and statements are useful in legitimizing strategic choices. Managers need support for their policy choices from empirical sources, but not in a form typically provided by academics. Thurley and Wirdenuis (1989) noted that in Europe a considerable distance had developed between business leaders and the intellectual leaders in the universities and professions. The guru phenomenon, in their view, was a response to the vacuum of intellectual debate. Managers and business people looked to their prophets, and ignored the academic theorists

"Let's be clear on how we operate, Grimstead. I make the decisions and you rationalize them."

© Leo Cullum, 1987

and philosophers who seemed to them to be at best disinterested in business, and at worst positively hostile both to it and to management objectives.

PREDICTABILITY NEEDS

A recurring theme in the social science literature is the search by human beings for predictability, understanding, order and meaning in their lives. *Predictability* is an imprecise concept. Underlying the problem of prediction is the element of chance. Internally, human rationality was bounded and we had to resign ourselves to living with a certain degree of ambiguity, accepting compromises that followed from the realities of unclear criteria and inadequate knowledge. Perrow (1977) observed that most decisions were ambiguous; that preference orders were incoherent and unstable; that efforts at communication and understanding were often ineffective; that subsystems were often loosely connected, and that most attempts at social control were clumsy and unpredictable. Externally, complex social systems were greatly influenced by the vagaries of chance, accident, luck and unintended consequences.

Managers were aware of this. The literature on the organizational world is full of references to insecurity and fear, and as containing ill-understood forces. Barsoux (1989) stated that, for British managers, 'The outcome of any managerial decision is often seen as a lottery, and the manager as the hapless victim of turbulent economic forces. Many managers seem to accept that they are lurching rudderless through life both professionally and in private.' Ouchi and Johnson in their comparative study of companies in the USA (Company A) and Japan (Company J) reported that:

> The only discordant note in the interviews at Company A was the clear and consistent fear of the future. Executives at Company A believe that their future depends entirely on their profitability, and that their profitability has more to do with the state of the economy and the industry than it does with their own decisions and performance, and thus they feel helpless. They appear to cope with this apparently capricious evaluation system by bolstering their professional credentials to increase their marketability with potential employers.
>
> (Ouchi and Johnson 1978: 301)

The great philosopher, David Hume (1757), wrote that 'In proportion as any man's course of life is governed by accident, we always find that he increases in superstition; as may particularly be observed of gamesters and sailors'. A corollary of this is that in considering the range of management activities or managerial roles, those which relate to the most random and unpredictable responses will have the greatest number of rituals, myths and creeds attached to them. Cleverley's (1971) book on managers and magic dealt almost exclusively with people-related activities. Additional chapters concerned themselves with market research and corporate planning issues. These areas contain some most unpredictable elements.

Magico-religious processes developed and thrived in response to randomness and incomprehensibility. The general notion of an organization generating anxieties by its own task which require the adoption of defensive mechanisms on the part of its employees has been extensively documented by the Tavistock Institute researchers (Menzies 1969; Miller 1976: 20). Anxiety-producing situations at work are numerous and include individuals being placed between internal and external organizational demands and ineffective task performance. Rice (1965) listed task requirements and the form of organization as contributing to anxiety at work.

The element of chance thus formed the unstable base for the search for predictability. Oliver (1990), for example, listed some aspects of management ideas which increased their popularity. Among these were its ability to predict events which other ideas could not foretell. In the author's own empirical study, managers mentioned both this predictability issue explicitly, and referred to the value of a management idea in helping them to anticipate the 'key variables in the environment which needed to be considered'. Such forward pinpointing acted to reduce surprise and increased predictability. Specific comments related to 'spotting key facts', 'recognizing problem areas' and 'avoiding mistakes'.

In the light of the failure of business academics to offer them predictability, where have managers turned? Religion and magic have traditionally offered people a way of making sense of the inexplicable. Unlike previous eras, there is now no common religion to provide an overarching framework of meaning which puts everything into perspective. Most worrying for managers was a lack of any widely shared or seriously accepted ideology or vision which decreed how things should be arranged. Dubin wrote:

> We live in a highly secular world. The morality of the Judeo-Christian tradition is no longer the consensual boundary within which practical decisions are taken in the operation and management of work organizations. Secular man, even though he is an executive and decision-maker, is very much in need of moral guidelines within which to take his decisions. . . . Today's rational decision-makers avidly seek moral justification for their actions and are only too ready to see the new morals in the scientific theories of applied behavioural scientists. . . . Once this phenomenon is recognized, it becomes easier to understand how simple theories can often be widely accepted by practitioners at the very moment that they come under questioning and dispute amongst scientists.
>
> (Dubin 1976: 22)

Forrest (1984) argued that one of the fundamental themes of the American character was the essential religiosity in the American consciousness. Popular management ideas have been described as the 'new religion' which is reflected in the quasi-religious nature of much management education with its priests and followers. Harvey (1974) likened organizational development (OD) to a religious movement. He argued that it contained both its Old Testament prophets (McGregor, Likert) and New Testament prophets (Blake, Beckhard, Walton). The faithful quoted the scriptures (Argyris, Chapter 2, verse 14). Its ceremonies and rituals were performed as OD techniques (T-groups, team-building, life planning, confrontation meetings). It had a liturgy ('Blessed are those who collaborate for they shall inherit the organization'). It even possessed a seminary training for its priesthood ('I graduated from the Grid seminar in Toledo').

Additional features which Harvey noted included revival meetings, techniques for dealing with priest 'burn-out' and a messianic approach to both success and failure. More recently, Oliver (1990) described the images of religious conversion in Eli Goldratt's Just-in-Time seminar, which included a testimonial by a recent convert, a recognition by the audience of its inadequacies (sinfulness), and the promise of redemption. All this was supported with the debunking of existing frameworks, their replacement with his assessment of good and bad (ideas), and finally the warning of the dangers of false prophets.

Watson (1986) commented that independent-mindedness and the sheer unpredictability of human beings produced a strong and widespread inclination by managers to resort to magic, myth and panaceas which, in turn, lead to the mystification of the very idea of 'management' itself. Feeling vulnerable, managers invented myths, established creeds and clung to rituals so as to avoid the 'dark inhumanity of randomness and chance'. Cleverley (1971) cited the research findings of the anthropologists, Lucy Mair and Sir James Frazer, to argue that much managerial behaviour was essentially irrational, even though there was a widely held belief that managers were or ought to be, rational creatures.

Many parts of managerial behaviour fulfilled a magico-religious purpose. Management had its own system of taboos and was essentially ritualistic, ceremonial and magical in nature. Behaviour met either the *instrumental* needs of managers (to influence and control their environment including the people in it) or *expressive* needs (those directed at releasing some kind of inner conflict, settling unease or expressing emotion). Often a single behaviour met both types of needs.

Miner (1982) argued that many managers had turned to moral guidelines as the Protestant ethic declined in significance. As religious adherents had received simple guidelines (ten commandments; mortal and venial sins), so too the popular management ideas offered their followers simple directions for actions together with an appended social philosophy, as Exhibit 5.1 shows. The latter related to the nature of humans who were seen as fundamentally irrational (scientific management and human relations) or fundamentally amenable to change (neo-human relations and guru theory). Managers chose the ideas which most closely reflected their attitudes. Miner saw these management ideas as being similar to religions but possessing the added sanctions of science.

The parallels with other aspects of life are instructive. Ashworth (1980) felt that the gap created by the demise of traditional religion was filled by 'popular science'. This consisted of writings on the occult, UFOs (unidentified flying objects), spoon-bending and so on. These satisfied readers' needs for an orderly social world. Knowledge and beliefs were part of the human mind's innate propensity to combine opposing categories and ideas into understandable structures. These formed myths or stories which we told ourselves about the world in order to explain it. Popular science began where religion and science ended, claimed Ashworth. It overcame the deficiencies of the two for the individual by resolving them into a hybrid which provided a satisfactory social myth. The popular self-help magazines in psychology promised to allay such anxieties, as did certain people-management ideas. Most of these did not contain any genuine knowledge or information which was not available to common sense.

In the absence of hard and fast universal rules there are alternatives available. Managers can choose from 'distilled wisdom', 'secrets of success' and crude empiricism ('It worked foi them, it'll work for you!'). What these three offer is certainty and the peace-of-mind to be gained by buying a product or service that has been debugged and which has had any problems ironed out. Numerous management products are marketed on the basis of their successful track record. The new customer gains the benefits of revisions and improvements. In the case of *'distilled wisdom'*, the customer is given the illusion of buying cheaply into a bank of knowledge, as the following examples from training course brochures show:

> Since its inception in 1974, LDL [Leadership Development] has invested thousands of hours, and hundreds of thousands of pounds in researching the sales process. The results are included in this seminar and are yours for £39 plus VAT.
>
> *(Close That Sale!* brochure)

> In two days you can learn from 25 years of experience.
>
> *(Effective Negotiating* brochure)

Karrass's *Effective Negotiating* course brochure invites participants to 'learn the secrets of effective negotiating'. There is a tension here. Secrets may be perceived as threatening ('powerful medicine'). Seminar participants see the secret being possessed by the seminar leader, but dispensed in such a way that it can be understood by the faithful followers who will not be frightened away. The religious undertones in the advertising copy are unmistakable, in one case making the point by denying it:

> There is nothing mysterious or metaphysical about the Liberating Leadership concept. It is based on a few straightforward procedures and behaviours, allied to a simple theoretical foundation. Simple, straightforward. However, doing it well and consistently is often difficult.
>
> *(Liberating Leadership* brochure)

> It sounds simple and it works.
>
> *(Time Manager International* brochure)

The popular management ideas are those which can convey the illusion of a predictable and certain world to the manager. The less popular ones are those which stress relativism. Academic writings are, by tradition, filled with qualifications and disclaimers which can confuse and generate additional uncertainty in the reading or listening audience. The sovereignty of evidence, within the empirical theory of knowledge, paints a picture of a cold and insubstantial world (Gellner 1985). We know what we know because of the evidence we have available to us. Everything is conjectural. New evidence may abrogate it or transform our world. Thus, the world is not solid enough for individuals to lean on or to support themselves.

Exhibit 5.1 Examples of guru guidelines offered to managers

Eight Principles for Excellence

One: A bias for action: a preference for doing something – anything – rather than sending a question through cycle and cycles of analyses and committee reports.

Two: Staying close to the customer – learning his preferences and catering to them.

Three: Autonomy and entrepreneurship – breaking the corporation into small companies and encouraging them to think independently and competitively.

Four: Productivity through people – creating in *all* employees the awareness that their best efforts are essential and that they will share in the rewards of the company's success.

Five: Hands-on, value driven – insisting that executives keep in touch with the firm's essential business.

Six: Stick to the knitting – remaining with the business the company knows best.

Seven: Simple form, lean staff – few administrative layers, few people at the upper levels.

Eight: Simultaneous loose-tight properties – fostering a climate where there is dedication to the central values of the company combined with tolerance for all employees who accept those values.

Source: Peters and Waterman 1982

The Ten Commandments of How To Succeed in Business

The Wisdom of the Seventies

To outpace the economy in sales and profit growth, you'd better find the most fashionable and rapidly expanding industries.

Size is just as important as sector. Find and penetrate the biggest markets.

Achieve economies of scale by moving down the experience curve.

Low price yields high share.

A. Find a good business and stay with it
B. Diversify. Become a conglomerate.

Your employees are bureaucrats. waiting to be told what to do – so tell them.

The company's mission is to create wealth for shareholders.

The New Tradition

It doesn't matter. There are winners in every sector – doughnuts, glue, and textiles as well as software, health care, and telecommunications.

You're better off if you create and develop niches.

Create new experience curves through innovation. Let competitors work their way down the ones you just made obsolete.

Value wins.

Don't stay where you are but don't go everywhere, either. Edge out – into related products or related markets or both.

Give your employees values and a vision. Make them shareholders: They will behave like owners because they *are* owners.

The company's mission is to create an institution, leave a legacy, make a difference. Well managed, the company will create wealth as a by-product.

If it ain't broke, don't fix it.

Fix it or it will break.

Successful executives are cool, rational, professional managers.

Successful leaders are obsessed with the business. Justifiably, they have at least as much faith in their own instinct and intuitions as they do in facts and analyses.

Successful companies are run by quirky entrepreneurs who are disorganized and undisciplined.

Successful companies are run by people who have their priorities straight, their values clear, their direction tight, and a strong grasp of the culture.

Source: Clifford and Cavanagh 1986

Deming's fourteen points

1 Create constancy of purpose toward improvement of product and service, with the aim to become competitive and thus to stay in business and to provide jobs.
2 Adopt the new philosophy. We are in a new economic age. We no longer need to live with commonly accepted delays, mistakes, defective materials and defective workmanship.
3 Cease dependence on mass inspection to achieve quality. Require instead statistical evidence that quality is built in.
4 End the practice of awarding business on the basis of price tag alone.
5 Improve constantly and forever every activity in the company, to improve quality and productivity, and thus constantly decrease costs.
6 Institute modern methods of training and education on the job, including management.
7 Institute supervision. The aim of supervision should be to help people and machines and gadgets to do a better job.
8 Drive out fear, so that everyone may work effectively for the economy.
9 Break down barriers between departments.
10 Eliminate slogans,exhortations, and targets for the workforce asking for zero defects and new levels of productivity. Such exhortations only create adversarial relationships, as the bulk of the causes of low quality and low productivity belong to the system and thus lie beyond the power of the workforce.
11 Eliminate work standards that prescribe numerical quotas for the day. Substitute aids and helpful supervision, using the methods to be described.
12 a) Remove barriers that rob the hourly worker of his rights to pride of workmanship. The reponsibility of supervisors must be changed from sheer numbers to quality.
   b) Remove the barriers that rob people in management and in engineering of their right to pride of workmanship. This means, *inter alia,* abolishment of the annual or merit rating and of management by objective.
13 Institute a vigorous programme of education and retraining.
14 Create a structure in the company that puts everyone in the organization to work at company-wide quality improvement.

Source: Hodgson 1987

Qualifications tend to be absent in the popular management seminar literature and in management gurus' public presentations. Certainty is conveyed through the presentation of procedures, step-by-step guides and golden rules. The vision of success is often forcefully projected as the overcoming of chaos and ambiguity. The management ideas are offered as part of a solid, non-conjectural, support-providing world. The techniques which spring from the ideas are intended to supply this made-to-measure commodity for managerial consumption. A good example of this approach in the dealing-with-people area is offered by *The One Minute Manager* (*TOMM*) (Blanchard and Johnson 1983).

Thomas (1989: 22) argued that the success of *TOMM* could be attributed to the emerging 'domain assumptions' of management, which he listed as including the idea that managing was getting people to do what you wanted them to do; that it involved the easy acquisition and application of simple, universal, no-cost behavioural techniques that worked; that effective management required emotional labour; that self-control was a key feature of successful management; that what was good for employees was good for the organization and vice versa; and that effective management was based on the ethic of honesty. This theme of certainty runs through the book.

Thomas contended that *TOMM* set up what he called a 'congenial resonance' in its management readers. Some elements of it accorded with their assumption ground, while denying others. Above all, *TOMM* seemed to deny the very thing that management educators had, over the history of management education, wished to assert. Namely, that there were no simple, universally effective, ethically unquestionable, behavioural techniques of management. Managers shared a belief that there *was* an answer, that a cure must exist for any corporate malaise. Geller's point, made earlier, was that managers did not experience total randomness in their interactions with others, but that they were failing to grasp the underlying logic of the 'tight pattern'.

The author's interviews revealed the phenomenon of revelation. This is the notion of individual conversion, in a quasi-religious way. The manager moves from scepticism to true belief in the management idea, despite at times harbouring initial scepticism and suspicion. The change is sudden, dramatic and total. Past errors (of thought and action) are confessed. The (new) true way is confirmed by a rejection of the notion that alternative strategies might be possible. The 'Paul-on-the-road-to-Damascus' syndrome is captured in some of the subjects' language. Revelation is experienced as 'a bit of an eye-opener', 'like a penny dropping', 'like a veil being lifted', as something that is a 'whole new way of thinking' and 'kind of illuminates'. That which is revealed varies. The reasons for past (inexplicable) failures in the company may be revealed. Alternatively, a fundamental shift in perspective may occur as to how to proceed in order to attain a desired future goal or objective.

An example of this from the world of sport is the German Tennis Federation's coaching strategy which is based on the observation that players spend most of their time on court *not* playing tennis. On a clay court, the average rally is 3.5 strokes, while on grass it is 1.8. For 70 per cent of the time the player is between points (Bailey 1991). In business, the idea of Materials Requirements Planning (MRP) is a good illustration of a figure–ground switch. In trying to reduce costs, many managers focused on labour costs. As a management idea, MRP reminded them that, in many organizations, these represented only 20 per cent of the total cost, while materials accounted for over 70 per cent.

Such a revelation does not appear to come from the provision of utterly new, previously unavailable knowledge. Rather, the effect of the idea is to produce a shift in perception on the part of the manager. The psychologist's figure–ground concept is the best analogy. It is not that there is anything new in the picture. What changes is the way that the different elements in it are highlighted. The concept of figure–ground can explain why, once revealed, such management ideas are treated as simultaneously significant (in the words of subjects as 'impressive', 'weighty' or 'mighty') and also as insignificant ('trite', 'common sense' and 'a truism'). This process of repositioning the non-threatening 'old' idea, rather than imposing the intimidating 'new', may account for manager appeal and acceptance.

CONTROL NEEDS

The opposite of predictability is uncertainty and chaos, and perhaps most importantly, a lack of *control*. Asked what the secret of successful automotive management was, a senior General Motors executive replied, 'Control. Dealer control. Product control. Labour control' (Gordon 1987). The goal of controlling one's life in general, and work life in particular, is widely sought but rarely attained. The manager's future is dependent on the performance of others. The predictability sought is provided by belief systems, models or mind-maps which are offered by a continuous stream of management ideas. These ideas can only be implemented with techniques which claim to help managers exercise such controls. Predictability focuses on understanding, while control involves 'doing with understanding'. The former is therefore a passive requirement, while the latter is an active one. The two are closely related: both concern the cognitive needs of managers.

Do managers seek techniques? An analysis of information sought by managers from the British Institute of Management's information services (Blagden 1980) revealed that 24 per cent of enquiries were about management techniques with which to control operations. This was the most sought after data. Personnel topics received 49 enquiries (16 per cent of the total). Classifying external information sought by American managers, Keegan (1974) found that management principles and techniques ranked top with

120 queries representing 16 per cent of the total. This was followed by technical queries (10 per cent), financial and credit questions (10 per cent) and government legislation questions (7 per cent). Managers on both sides of the Atlantic appear to share a common interest in techniques. The main information sources on techniques are books, journals, courses, seminars and conferences.

Management techniques have a special attraction for managers who have a *product* view of knowledge which equates the possession of knowledge about a subject with the possession of technique. The growth of 'how to' publications is a testimony to managerial needs in this area. 'Ask executives what they want by way of improving literature and most call for a richer menu of management techniques' (Heller 1986: 324). He felt that they could not have enough of barely comprehensible inventions such as Monte Carlo simulation, management by exception, statistical sampling or linear programming.

Even the popular hero-manager books, which have achieved a huge success in their own right, have often been repackaged with a technique focus. Following the publication of *Iacocca: An Autobiography* (Iacocca 1985), there came *The Iacocca Management Technique* (Gordon 1987). Following Clutterbuck and Goldsmith's (1985) *The Winning Streak* came *The Winning Streak Check Book* (Clutterbuck and Goldsmith 1986). The evidence seems to suggest that managers believe that the technique is the way to knowledge. Management ideas which therefore offer techniques will be more highly valued.

Some of the most popular forms of management training offered by training companies or consultants stress tools. Their advertising literature about short seminars and courses emphasizes personal and interpersonal techniques. Such offerings include seminars such as 'Time Manager International', 'Liberating Leadership Team', Leadership Development's 'Close that Sale!', Karrass's 'Effective Negotiating' and the one-day seminars from CareerTrack with titles such as 'Management Skills for Technical Professionals' and 'How to Set and Achieve Your Goals'.

Attendance at these seminars is substantial if the firms' advertising literature is to be believed. The 'Close That Sale!' seminar claims 59,000 participants from 70 companies. Time Manager International claims that 28,000 people participated in its worldwide series of seminars during 1986. Finally, Effective Negotiating claims a worldwide participation rate of 150,000. Such courses are usually of one day's duration. They are offered at a low fee and attract a high attendance, often of over one hundred people. They feature a 'high-energy' presenter and offer their audiences 'tested techniques' and 'proven skills', as the following samples from their advertising leaflets illustrate:

An outline of the principles, procedures and behaviours that add up to a

Liberating Leadership. . . . A number of ideas and techniques that you can start to apply during the day itself.

('Liberating Leadership' programme)

This remarkable seminar sets out to provide a stream of ideas to develop selling ability.

('Close That Sale!' seminar)

The objective of the Management Effectiveness Seminar is to internalize the skills, knowledge and beliefs of 3-D Theory of Managerial Effectiveness in such a way that they become part of the manager's day to day worklife.

('Management Effectiveness' seminar)

The limit on the numbers of attendees makes it possible for each one to benefit from specific, usable ideas and methods . . . so the information, the ideas and the techniques you learn are all directly applicable to real situations, and you can put them to use immediately.

('Effective Negotiating' seminar)

Cleverley (1971) argued that the buying of techniques by managers met both instrumental and expressive motives. The manager who bought the latest technique and the consultant or company which supplied it, both acted in the secure belief that they were doing something beneficial for the individual recipient, company and economy. Thus the purchase and adoption or consumption decision fulfilled an *instrumental* need. Additionally, the purchase and use of some management technique by managers represented an expression of their solidarity with the group to which they belonged. It thus also fulfilled an *expressive* need.

An important aspect of buying behaviour is what can be called the *individuality-community* aspect. This refers to the phenomenon of managers and trainers wanting to be seen to be using some new technique, *both* before and at the same time as everyone else. They want to be ahead of the latest fad and inside of it at the same time. Becker (1973) argued that people were driven by an essential dualism. They needed both to be part of something and to stand out, to be at one and the same time conforming members of a winning team and to be stars in their own right. The former represented the need to express individuality, while the latter involved the need to submerge in the safety of the crowd. People wished to do both. This paradoxical situation did create a problem but it was not insoluble.

The ritual expression of community can be found in the advertising literature for techniques which claims that millions of managers have benefited from technique A or technique B. The ritual expression of individuality comes from selecting a particular version of that technique B and customizing it. Thus, in a year in which time management or stress counselling are popular, there are likely to be a wide range of different

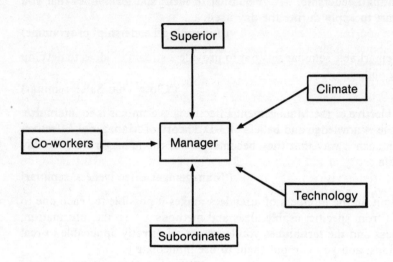

Figure 5.1 Reddin's route to effectiveness through five situational variables
Source: Reddin 1986: 259

approaches to or packages on these themes. In the field of clothes, while there may be a predominant fashion theme, there will be a range of clothing within that theme.

From this analysis one can conclude that the most popular management techniques will be those that emphasize those aspects of managers' environments over which they have control, and hence which they can influence. They will de-emphasize or ignore those variables over which managers lack control. For this reason, one finds little reference to the 'environment' in anything other than a general way. This is because the environment represents a source of uncertainty and unpredictability which can engender in the manager feelings of powerlessness and anomie.

Advertising materials for some management ideas emphasizes this point. Figure 5.1 shows Reddin's 3-D Theory of Managerial Effectiveness. This defines the manager's situation in terms of five key variables which, to varying degrees, are all within the manager's control. The marketing copy tells managers that how well they respond to these situational elements or how well they change their demands will have a direct bearing on their effectiveness. In this theoretical formulation, managerial effectiveness arises from the situation and is within the control of managers if they 'choose and use the right behaviour'.

The managers in the interviews conducted by the author made reference to a theme which might be labelled *empowerment*, which refers to the feeling of increased power to attain success. The literature review suggested that management ideas which were perceived to offer managers increased power and control over their work and environment were the most popular. The data showed that empowerment was felt by a number of managers, and was experienced as enabling them to make changes in their organizations.

Empowerment was also experienced as directing a manager's attention to those aspects or topics where actions are likely to produce the greatest benefits. One manager stated that 'it helps me to deal with quality and helps me change staff's behaviours'. A management idea can empower by replacing the muddling-through (non-purposeful activity) approach of those who have a problem and are 'lost', with an objectively analysed direction for action (a 'driving vision'). 'It's valuable because it means I can focus on the measures for . . .' said a respondent, while another saw his favoured management idea providing 'aspects that we could focus on and get some leverage out of'. On occasions, the idea gave managers the wherewithal to make changes. At other times, empowerment was experienced as permitting managers to function independently, giving them control over their own actions and results, and thereby reducing their dependence on others.

One can identify recurring similarities in the language used by those interviewed. The predominant word used was *focus*. In photographic terminology, the subject of the photo is brought into sharp focus. The surroundings are intentionally blurred to avoid distraction. Such isolation is a prelude to action. The deployment of resources over a narrow area or upon a specific identified target is likely to increase effectiveness. A production manager talked about 'getting right to the heart of things' and valued the way the idea enabled him 'to direct all that energy' effectively. Oliver (1990) had separately commented upon a management idea's promise of offering its user a greater quantitative precision over the competing ideas on offer.

Operationally, managers perceived that their actions, based on the prescribed elements of the idea, would produce the consequences that they desired. Managers described the sequences of activities which were developed from their favoured management idea. Such a sequence was held to 'make sense'. It was thereby defined as 'simple' by them. Internally, the managers appeared to achieve an understanding of the proposed causal chain, and may have therefore experienced a sense of relief from that comprehension. A manufacturing manager felt that to be valuable to him, a idea had to be:

> logical, it would have . . . to be something that we had not thought of before but, when you were exposed to it, it would have to make sense, you know, kind of advance your understanding, but fit in with, once you were aware of the concept, 'Yes I can see that type of thing', as opposed to 'Well, you may say that, but I just can't relate to it'.

Management ideas experienced as logical have another benefit, one which goes back to Frederick Taylor and scientific management. The notions of logic and common sense (with which it is often linked) carry with them a spurious objectivity. Within the organizational context, the aim is to achieve controlled performance towards collective goals. For the most part, this process requires management direction and carries the possibility of conflict. However, if an idea can be sold as being logical, that is, as possessing a rational and justification of its own (somehow independent of management or workers), then the chances of acceptability are increased while those of conflict are reduced.

Such perceived logic can reside in the idea techniques themselves. One manager described how one such technique impressed him 'with its objectivity'. It was accepted by those on whom it was used. He said, 'the folks themselves really said that's captured me, that's me to a tee, yup, I wouldn't argue with that, whereas my heart was in my mouth a little bit, because I thought the people would cry foul and this ain't fair'. Cognitively, managers seek ideas and techniques which can help them to understand and anticipate what is going on in their organization and its environment.

SOCIAL NEEDS

The right-hand side of Figure 5.1 deals with the affective or emotional needs. These can be related to Maslow's (1943) category of esteem needs. Maslow divided this category into two dimensions. The first were the externally directed social needs. These pertained to how individuals felt that other people viewed them, that is the esteem they were accorded by others. Dimensions such as reputations, prestige, recognition, attention, importance, appreciation and legitimation were those described by Maslow.

It involved enhancing managerial status through confidence-building measures. Watson (1986) argued that British managers were typically afflicted with insecurities and anxieties which stemmed from the incongruence between their high status as 'wealth creators', and their low status as non-professionals. The anxieties also resulted from their responsibility for controlling the uncontrollable (especially other employees) and from the absence of any clear definition of their role. Mangham and Silver (1986) reported that 'to articulate the skills, abilities and competences required of managers, produces different answers, not only between companies but within companies'.

In the past, managerial status has been challenged by the ambiguity experienced by managers in being at one and the same time both bosses and company employees. They were asked to control others yet were themselves controlled. The nineteenth-century company acts created a caste of non-owning managers who sought recognition in their own right. This is a process which has been extensively documented by Child (1969a). If managers have been seeking their occupational identity, it is not surprising that texts and seminars which provide a strong concept of management will be positively received.

In Britain, the status of business people and managers has not been historically high. In the past, entry into the professions, notably medicine, the law and the church, was preferred. The Civil Service has been favoured over commerce or industry. Mant (1979) observed that what he called 'British binary thought' divided jobs into clean, respectable U-category ones, and dirty, disreputable, non-U-category ones. In Mant's view, managers were in the latter grouping. Accountancy was perhaps one of the few areas in which professional ambitions and business concerns came together. This low social standing of business people was also true of the United States, but to a lesser extent and in a different way. Gilkes, President of the publishing house, The Free Press, noted:

> The role of the corporation in American life was underestimated and undervalued for more than 50 years. It played the villain in the melodrama that American social analysts promulgated to describe what they thought was social and economic reality in America.
>
> (Knowlton 1989: 62)

However, by the 1980s, American business found itself in the cultural mainstream and the nation's newest celebrities were the managers in the corporate world. Cummings (Pierce and Newstrom 1990: 338) felt that best-sellers provided an apology, rationale or the positioning of American management as something which was not just on the defensive with regard to world competition. The writings acted to raise the social status of management.

The issue of managerial social insecurity and defensiveness is a constant theme in the literature. Watson (1986) argued that much of what was written and said about management was concerned to justify it or to give legitimacy to managerial work. Perhaps the outstanding modern contribution to the task of legitimizing the role of management in western society was made by Drucker. His book, *The Practice of Management* (Drucker 1954) was subtitled 'A study of the most important function in American society'. In the book he wrote that 'The manager is the dynamic, life-giving element in every business'. In this role he felt that managers' activities had ramifications beyond their office walls since management would remain a basic and dominant institution as long as western civilization itself survived. According to Drucker, managers had two tasks. They had to create a whole that was larger than the sum of its parts. Second, they had to harmonize, in their decisions and actions, the requirements of the immediate and the long-term future. These tasks were somewhat vague, just as the precepts of any new religion tended to be vague.

Child (1969a) argued that management thought had two functions. Its technical function was concerned with the practical means of carrying out tasks. Its legitimatory function was primarily linked to the securing of social recognition and approval for managerial authority and the way it was used. To the extent that the execution of the technical aspects of management (e.g. setting up payment systems) involved persuading others to go along with it, Watson felt that everything that managers or their spokesmen said or wrote about their activities was coloured by the constant concern to defend their authority. The right to manage and maintain legitimacy, in his view, had to be constantly re-established. Such social inferiority surfaced only in the 1970s when the financial advantage associated with managerial work diminished, and when management's right to manage was challenged by legislation, trade unions and employees. Mant discussed the 'professional management movement' and felt that managers needed:

> a body of arcane knowledge on which they are based and which distinguishes them from other callings. If the agents of the owners needed legitimation for what they were up to, then they needed a 'profession' of the tradition type without a science. So the hunt was on for some set of 'principles' of management to justify the existence of the profession in the first place.
>
> (Mant 1979: 51–2)

It is argued that there is an ongoing need for managers to reinforce their image by acquiring social standing. Managerial action cuts across many widely held liberal democratic values such as liberty, fraternity, freedom of choice and defence against exploitation. In terms of what managers do on a daily basis, these values are ignored and personal self-guilt generated. Such 'unethical' managerial behaviour in a socio-cultural context generates existential discomfort which seeks release.

The original purpose of the search for management principles, according to Mant, was not to maximize profit but to legitimize the manager's role. This represented a reversal of the traditional process by which professions have developed. Baker identified the psychological benefits of having such a body of management theory:

> the identification of management, organization of administration as a distinct function to be studied in its own right. . . . The practical achievement was to make men think and apply themselves to the problem of management and organization, *and to give those who did so some feeling of pride and self respect.*
>
> (Baker 1972: 31, added emphasis)

Mant (1979: 53) argued that the managerial literature went beyond the mere description and categorization of management tasks and engaged in manufacturing, 'a mythology about executive work, sedulously nourished by the management consultants, business school professors and so on. Executives like the myth and are prepared to pay good money to have it reinforced.'

The myth that Mant referred to concerned the rational, scientific decision-making, building-on-facts, leadership-based-on-knowledge-not-force approach. That part of the mythology of management has been called a 'well-organized guild or church that sustains itself'. It does not have to rely on the published works of authors in order to be sustained and promulgated. The ideas of management have a definite role both within management practice and within academic business school activity.

Child discussed the importance of creating a theory of management which underpinned the practice of management, the importance of having educational institutions to teach it, and the need for a British Institute of Management to confirm a quasi-professional status upon its members. 'Industry Year' (1986) had the slogan 'Industry Matters', which confirmed the belief that not enough people in Britain felt that it did. The Chartered Manager Initiative launched in the late 1980s took this process one step further, certifying that managers *did* possess certain unique skills and knowledge.

The ambiguities themselves derived from the large-scale social and economic context of management. The effect was to complicate the situation in which managers found themselves. At a basic level it manifested itself as managerial insecurity. Thus one can argue that writers, theorists and management consultants offer a variety of 'images of managerial work' which act to reassure managers, reduce their insecurity and justify their position.

Watson (1986) distinguished the images of management as art, science, magic and politics (Figure 5.2). The *management-as-science* view was based upon the belief that there was a body of knowledge, either in existence or awaiting discovery, which could be learned and acted upon to achieve effectiveness. Scientific management was perhaps the prime exponent of this view, although it was shared with classical administrative theory. *Management-as-art* emphasized that managerial ability was a matter of intuition, wit and personality. Management was seen as involving the undefinable (and hence unteachable) qualities which are associated with the notion of leadership. Leadership skill, this school stated, could be developed although not taught. To have an art is to possess and practise in-born talents. Much of the hero-manager branch of guru theory rests upon the proposition that these great men possess the qualities lacked by the majority of the readers. The management development movement's starting-point is the belief that everybody innately possesses leadership potential which needs to be developed. Mintzberg (1973) argued that managerial work was not done by

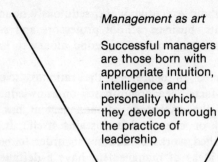

Management as art

Successful managers are those born with appropriate intuition, intelligence and personality which they develop through the practice of leadership

Management as science

Successful managers are those who have learned the appropriate body of knowledge and have developed an ability to apply acquired skills and techniques.

Management as magic

Successful managers are those who recognize that nobody really knows what is going on and who persuade others of their own powers by calling up the appropriate gods and by engaging in the expected rituals.

Management as politics

Successful managers are those who can work out the unwritten laws of life in the organizational jungle and are able to play the game so that they win.

Figure 5.2 Management as art, science, magic and politics
Source: Watson 1986: 29

procedures prescribed by scientific analysts but by 'intuitive' seat-of-the-pants approaches.

The *management-as-magic* school sees the role of management to control the mysterious elements around, especially human beings. It involves occasionally resorting to ritualism and following the behavioural scientists. The ritualism comes from the application of principles whose effectiveness is unknown. They cite research and theory to support their views. Finally, *management-as-politics* sees management as concerned with manipulating symbols, rituals, myths and other cultural devices to weld together the efforts of human beings into a coherent whole. This is viewed as political behaviour. Managers are involved in power relations with those whom they manage. They are in competition for scarce resources with fellow-managers. Large parts of the excellence-corporate culture school of guru theory stress this theme (Peters and Waterman 1982; Deal and Kennedy 1982).

From this perspective, the criticism by managers and organizations of the relevance of MBA programmes can be viewed somewhat differently. So too can the explanation for popularity of courses such as time management. One can argue that the former are in fact *too* relevant. Participating in extended MBA-type programmes may be threatening. These offerings are based on research and the objective assessment of manager performance. Exposure to this might seriously undermine managers' positive perceptions of themselves. Such programmes threaten to identify their weaknesses, highlight their deficiencies and leave them with negative feelings that what they are doing is wrong and that they must start anew. What must such programmes stress instead if they are to be popular?

From the evidence of attendance numbers, it appears that they should offer a positive image of the management role. Popular courses such as Time Manager International (TMI) focus on the individual manager and emphasize success. The TMI brochure offers a 'feeling of satisfaction . . . [that] is almost beyond description'. Such course-running companies can be seen as primarily selling psychological well-being. The vehicle for this may be a time management course, an interpersonal skills course, or indeed a course on any topic provided that it projects the image of the manager as *essential* (a person indispensable to the well-being of the organization); *resourceful* (possessing desirable personal qualities); and *successful* (highly effective in the job already).

Analysis of manufacturing industry in 1984 reported that British production chiefs tended to be preoccupied with patching-up activities. These included chasing up overdue supplies, cannabalizing components, urging quality-control departments to pass what had previously been judged to be defective bought-in parts, rescheduling jobs and organizing overtime to catch up. The quality valued in the British manufacturing culture was *resourcefulness* which might also be called 'structured indispensability'. This was a process in which managers created crises, the solving of which confirmed their indispensability to the running of the system.

Allan Katcher, an American psychologist, asked senior US executives what they would least want their subordinates to know about them. In nineteen of the twenty cases the answer was the same. They feared that their junior staff would come to know how inadequate the chiefs felt in their jobs (Dixon 1986d: 14). Thus, one can argue that the growth in the popularity of management guru books and seminars, far from being linked with an up-turn in managers' confidence, in fact represents a response to widespread self-doubt among executives, even among those at the top.

Past management writers stressed rationality and implied that to excel, managers had to virtually become gods. Since few could achieve perfection the majority were doomed to a state of inadequacy. The advertising literature of the popular Liberating Leadership Team Programme, in contrast, contains examples of positive communication and psychological massaging:

> Bold. Far seeing. Thoughtful. Honest. Persistent. Effective and Open to Ideas! Someone very close to you has all these and many other great leadership qualities. Who can that person be? It's you of course!

> During the taster day we will introduce you to: Your own excellent ideas about what a good leader does and does not do.

> Just think what wonderful leaders and people we would be, if only we could realize all those innate capabilities, put them to work for ourselves and our organization.

> It's a puzzle, all of us have difficulty in doing justice to the qualities we have that would make us leaders.

In the literature review, the initial notion of the legitimation of management was expressed in terms of an idea's role in giving managers a legitimate status within the workplace, and perhaps confirming their indispensability to the work process. Such a notion of legitimation was most attractive in the past when industrialization and the replacement of the entrepreneurial owner with the hired manager made the role of management more tenuous than it is now at the end of the century. One can see these issues in the writings and ideas of the scientific and administrative management schools.

It may be that legitimation is still relevant today but at a personal rather than organizational level. It is the legitimation of a manager's own views to others in the organization, rather than the legitimation of the managerial role in society. When a well-known management author is perceived to affirm a manager's views and actions, this can act to raise the manager's self-esteem. When such views have been publicly voiced, the self-confirmation brought about by the official voicing of an idea may also raise the manager's social standing. One manager said that the idea he valued 'was good because it confirmed some of the thoughts I had that . . . it was good to have some authoritative reference'.

PERSONAL NEEDS

There was a second aspect of esteem which was internally directed and which focused on individuals' personal feelings about themselves (self-esteem). The relevant dimensions proposed by Maslow were strength, achievement, adequacy, confidence and independence. These issues related to individuals gaining reassurance or reaffirmation about their own views of themselves. This was particularly relevant if, for some reason, such personal worth was challenged. Articles in the business press report companies' attempts to create *spiritual warriors* through 'new age training' and 'transformational' business seminars. One human technology consultant commented that:

> Like the shamans and magicians of the past, we provide structured opportunities for people to access, in a coherent way, their potential for creating the life they want.
>
> (*International Management* 1991: 42)

These spiritual warriors aimed to develop 'respect for and contact with the divine in all things and explicitly in his or her self'. The focus of this work, according to one of the trainers involved, was upon the spiritual, emotional and creative aspects of clients. Apart from outdoor-type activities, trainers used the American Indian Medicine Wheel, the book of prophecies and mysticism, and the *I Ching*. Much of past and present management training appears to relate to gaining the feelings of strength, achievement, adequacy, confidence and independence that Maslow identified.

Such needs may also be met by managers just being with the hero-managers or consultants whom they want to be like and whom they admire. The books of many of these writers possess little that cannot be found in an introductory management textbook. The managers attending the seminars run by the top presenters have often already read their book, and know what the person will say. It is the fact that the ideas contained within them are expounded by a successful chief executive of a multi-million corporation that give them their value. The appeal of these gurus for the management audience must therefore lie more in *them* as individuals than in their message. Cleverley referred to these gurus as the *sorcerers* of management, claiming that:

> Managers seek recourse to unorthodox sources of power and knowledge. And since their culture is semi-literate, they seek help chiefly from sorcerers who have developed their own salvation through profit. They call them consultants.
>
> (Cleverley 1971: 59)

The need for reaffirmation of a positive self-image can explain why as much attention is paid to the management evangelists as to their messages. The status of the idea presenter is often more important than the message being conveyed. This is true whether the presentation is in writing or verbal. In the case of the latter, the guru on the platform speaks the rhetoric of success with the language of conviction, a point which will be discussed in greater depth in Chapter 7. The personality of the presenter is a critical aspect on the seminar circuit as the following adverts stress:

> It is almost impossible for someone to listen to him and not get more sales as a result. . . . His dynamic approach, his drive, his enthusiasm transmits itself to the audience and never fails to influence them.
> (Brochure description of Robin Fielder, leader of the 'Close That Sale!' seminar)

> Since then over 150,000 professionals have benefitted from Dr Karrass' unrivalled knowledge, and his unique ability to identify, formulate and communicate the practical skills of negotiating.
> (Brochure description of Dr Chester Karrass, leader of the 'Effective Negotiating' seminar)

Managers may search out the management gurus to receive their guidance in the same way as believers might look to their religious leaders. Much has been written about management charisma. Some of the modern management gurus such as Drucker, Deming, Peters and Kanter possess a charismatic quality in the eyes of their followers. De Vries (1988) defined charismatic leadership as a gift of grace possessed mainly by prophets who appear at historical moments of distress. Charismatic leadership, he felt, had a salvationistic or messianic quality.

Charismatic leadership, uncertainty and unpredictability go together. Because of the ambiguity and complexity of life's events, we choose guru leaders to help us make order out of chaos. These leaders become the outlets for assuming responsibility for otherwise inexplicable phenomena. Weber argued that charismatic leaders rose to prominence in periods of psychic, physical, ethical, religious, political or economic distress. Stable, well-functioning societies had less need of their services. Charismatic leadership was the result of a need for order (Bryman, 1992).

The power of the gurus comes from their ability to articulate the issues of the business world. Paradoxically, in providing 'deliverance', truly charismatic leaders have tended to be revolutionary, and have came into conflict with the established order. Gurus solve this paradox by claiming to create order out of disorder, and by providing their followers with new systems of coherence and continuity.

Managers can become susceptible to a guru's ideas by the process of projection. The charismatic phenomenon of the guru is created as much by the managers as by the guru himself. It is based on managers' personality dynamics. Although they appear to be passive spectators, managers are, in fact, the true creators of the image of the idealized manager, that is the charismatic guru leader. The image of this person is carried about within the psyches of all managers, in one form or another. Gurus are legitimized by the perceptions of their followers. Projective processes seem to play a major role in myth-making and the symbolic actions from which these perceptions emerge (Schiffer 1973). These attributional projective processes lead to leaders becoming the recipients ('containers') of other people's ideals, wishes, desires and fantasies (Bion 1959). They become imbued with mystical, charismatic qualities by their followers. The business media also play their role in this process.

Frequently the management seminars are identified by their developer's or promulgator's name ('Spend a Day with - -'). The companies may send their executives to sit at the management guru's feet and hope that they have the right money and are there at the right time to buy what the guru is selling. To the guru, faith is more important than fact, and image and symbolism are as important as reality. Often management gurus may tell half truths. They may exaggerate a point since it is image that matters most. To the guru, if it feels good it is good. For them, the bottom line is the 'happiness sheet' that the participants fill in at the end of the day. They may rationalize this by claiming that faith itself is what drives change.

There are few wonder workers or magicians to mediate between the individual manager and the uncontrollable forces in the organizational world. In the past, before the thirteenth century, one could create one's own saints until Rome took this practice under its control. Perhaps the same practice continues in management. Thomas (1978) argued that saints were what people wanted. They did not just intercede with God for you (leaving the outcome to Him), but they actually performed the trick themselves, and that was magic! Andre (1985) argued that the management guru believed both in himself and his orthodoxy. More than a mere salesman, the guru was his own convert. He exulted that 'I have seen it with my own eyes! People have told me how effective I am! I am the way, the truth and the consultant!'

One way to meet the manager's need for personal psychological well-being was to create folk heroes who might be elevated to star status. Klein's (1959) work in psychoanalytical theory argued that normal adults, when they experienced situations of persecutory anxiety, reverted to earlier patterns of behaviour and used the processes of projective and introjective identification to defend themselves against the anxiety. Managers who felt concerned about their self-esteem or their self-worth might focus on a successful manager like Iacocca, Harvey-Jones or Scully. Since managers wanted to be like their successful heroes, they identified with them and introjected them, splitting off the bad parts and projecting these on to others.

Ritti and Funkhouser (1987: 128) argued that the existence of leadership was frequently inferred from behaviour it presumably caused. This was the way that great leaders tended to be defined. Leadership was one of humanity's most cherished myths. Historical recountings of leadership are embellished and purified in our mythologies. Business magazines powerfully portrayed that myth with larger-than-life leaders being held to be single-handedly responsible for prosperity, resurrection, achievements and problems in organizations. According to these authors, the leadership myth is 'enacted' within the culture of the organization by all participants. Participants perceive and interpret events selectively to support the myth of management efficiency (i.e. the ability to produce results). Leaders contribute to the process of enactment by paying attention to symbol and ritual.

The same process may occur between managers, consultants and academic gurus. Byrne (1986) reported on a type of executive seminar called a 'skunk camp'. The similarity between his description of it and a religious retreat is instructive. The 'holy man' leading this event was Tom Peters, the co-author of one of the world's best-selling business books. The cost to each participant's company was $4,000 and at this particular event the day began with a group jogging session. Following a communal breakfast, the members gathered in the conference room 'waiting for enlightenment'. Byrne reported:

> In walks our rumpled leader. Head down, hands in the pockets of his brown shapeless cords, he paces relentlessly. His voice climbs to the treble clef as he runs through the litany: 'Dehumiliate . . . Get rid of your executive parking spots. . . . Get everybody on the same team. . . . There are two ways to get rich: superior customer satisfaction and constant innovation'.
>
> (Byrne 1986: 45)

Byrne's description has similarities with one reported by Oliver (1990) of a Just-in-Time seminar run by Eli Goldratt (co-author of the book, *The Goal*):

> Goldratt appeared punctually at 9.15 a.m., and in contrast to all the delegates who were wearing suits, he wore neither a jacket nor a tie and was wearing a skull-cap and open-toed sandals. He began by saying he had no pre-prepared slides or any notes. . . . The expression the 'cost world' was used to denote old order and the 'throughput world' to denote the new one. . . . Towards the end of the session, Goldratt threw out the question, 'Where shall we begin the improvement?'. The audience responded with a chorus of cries of 'Us', 'Ourselves' and other similar expressions.
>
> (Oliver 1990: 15)

Oliver highlighted the imagery of religious conversion in Goldratt's session which was evident in his style of presentation, dress and mode of audience response. It also included de-bunking 'false ideas' and their replacement with his beliefs; the presentation of contrasting philosophies as 'different worlds' (one 'good' and the other 'bad'); and finally, an attack on a competing Just-in-Time author-guru as a 'false prophet'.

It was mentioned earlier that seminar participants do not appear to be troubled that the ideas being presented by the speaker often all appear in his book. This phenomenon can be observed elsewhere. Concert-goers attend performances of works they know well. In a radio interview, Cliff Richard revealed that in every live performance he included old hits which he sang in exactly their original form. Experiments with rearrangements were not well received. He said that the original songs linked the audience's mind with some significant event or experience in their lives, and that in order for them to relive it, it had to be sung in exactly the same way.

Managers may attend Tom Peters' seminars to become immersed in his personality. In fact, if he was not to say what they may have already read, they would come away disappointed. Lorenz (1986c) wrote that 'managers still pay repeated visits in their thousands to sit at [the guru's] feet, or buy his latest book. One executive at a leading multinational talks of needing his "Drucker fix" every two or three years.'

One is therefore left to explain why managers should wish to attend a workshop, conference or seminar at which the guru will 'perform' even though they have already read the book and know what the guru will say. In Oliver's (1990) account of the J-I-T seminar, 90 per cent of Goldratt's audience claimed to have read his book. The notion of a 'guru fix' is a common metaphor. It stresses that it is the guru's performance itself that is valued. Koestler (1964: 307) suggested that the watching of illusions on stage (e.g. a guru performance) had a cathartic effect on the watchers. It enabled them to free themselves from their personal anxieties by identifying with the personae in the story, and thereby allowed them to achieve a certain self-transcendence which was peace-inducing.

The aim of the guru may be seen to share his experience and make others participate in it. The intrinsic value of illusion derives from its transferring the watcher's attention which is lured away from the 'here and now' to the 'there and then', that is to a plain remote from self-interest. The attention is lured by heroes and victims which attract the audience's sympathy and with whom they partly identify. In so doing, they temporarily renounce their preoccupations with their own worries and desires. Participating in the illusion inhibits a person's self-asserting tendencies and allows the self-transcending tendencies to unfold. The effect is cathartic.

Conrad (1985) argued that not only seminars, but also some books (such as Peters' writings) have this capacity. Their appeal is in their *mythos*, that is their capacity to transport readers symbolically from a world of everyday experience to a mythical realm. The book's appeal for managers, in this context, comes not from the useful tips that it may offer them but rather from the fact that, while reading it, they are living in the aura of success.

Illusion then is the simultaneous presence and interaction in the watcher's mind of two universes, one real and the other imaginary. The cathartic effect comes from the balancing of both spheres in the mind. The audience perceives the hero as Tom Peters and the successful manager whom he describes – at the same time. It is this precarious suspension of awareness between the two plains which facilitates the flux of emotions from the here-and-now to the there-and-then.

Once interest is deflected from the self, it will attach itself to something else. The falling level of self-assertive tension automatically allows the self-transcending impulses to dominate. The *creation of the illusion* itself (the process) has a cathartic value quite separate from the product (the content) of the presentation which may be judged to be cheap or uninspiring. Indeed from videos it can be judged that the presentation is more akin to a revivalist meeting (generating emotion and adulation) than to a closely reasoned argument (supported by research) found in the presenter's books. The books themselves act as a springboard for their writers. The books lead their audiences to desire to meet their authors at first hand. The process helps subjects to actualize their potential of self-transcending emotions thwarted by the dreary routines of mundane existence. This seems to explain why just *being there*, at the guru's presentation, is separate from, and additional to, obtaining his ideas. The presentation sessions of the gurus have been described as 'experiences'.

The self-transcending impulses are focused on identifying with the narrator or the subjects he describes. Introjection is the term used by psychologists to describe the process by which individuals take chunks and patterns of other people's existence into their own. They suffer and enjoy vicariously the emotions of those with whom they have become entangled. The emotions generated are vicarious ones derived from the spectator's participation in another person's existence. This is a self-transcending act. Self-transcending emotions which create the cathartic effect assume a double meaning. First, the concentration on the guru's performance rids the watcher's mind of the 'dross of its self-centred trivial pre-occupations'. Second, it provides a harmless outlet for the emotions so generated.

These points suggest that managers attend guru presentations pay to get a buzz. Koestler (1964) pointed out that it is the *stimuli of the illusions and not the emotions that are all that are bought* when managers buy a ticket for the performance. The sequence of the stimuli are cunningly designed to trigger off their latent participatory emotions which would otherwise remain frustrated if an outlet were not provided. It is the managers who supply everything else. They buy a ticket to the illusion in which success and power are theirs. They enter into a self-transient state in which they identify with the images that the guru has projected. Having aroused their dominant self-transient potential and having provided them with an outlet, the managers can return to reality, and get on with their tasks.

Two final points are relevant in this context. First, the need to participate (in the illusion) remains something more imperious and intense for humans, more than the thirst for knowledge or the desire for conformity with the claims of reason. Second, the use of the images provided by the gurus can impede the recognition of where reality ends and illusion begins. This phenomenon is not limited to participating in management guru seminars or conferences. It extends to the watching of plays in the theatre and soap operas on television. Knowing what will happen in the end (the punch-line of the joke, that the police will arrive in time, what the guru will recommend) does not prevent the audience experiencing the emotions of fear, anger, joy or satisfaction, and displaying the corresponding bodily symptoms. Paradoxically, it may actually enhance the experience. This capacity of human beings to live in two universes simultaneously (one real, the other imaginary), and to blur the line, is well known.

The most valued guru trick, however, is the ability to make accurate predictions based on one's knowledge and skill. To the layman this is perceived as magic. Kantrow (1980) commented that Drucker's ability to foretell the future was remarkable. The continued appearance of instant gurus, each with his own personal gospel and proprietary lexicon, suggests that managers have a need for such a service. In recent years, Pinchot (1985) has talked of intrapreneurship; Kennedy (Deal and Kennedy 1982) of corporate culture; and Adizes (1979) of consensus-building meetings and brainstorming sessions.

Why do these managers need to see and talk to these gurus in the flesh even though they have read and are familiar with their ideas already? What does such personal contact offer them that cannot be obtained from these other sources? Lorenz (1986b) suggested that the process of reading preceded learning about the idea. The best-sellers gave a company an idea about what it might work on. This was reinforced by idea transmission mechanisms such as workshops. However, for senior staff, the process may be reversed. Comparing the relative impact of gurus' books with their seminar and conference appearances, Berry argued that most top European executives read business books only *after* they had been electrified by a guru's presentation.

At this point in the argument one might draw upon Freud's concept of the libidinal process of *identification*. This is the process whereby someone wants to be like someone else (de Board 1978: 18). In the process of identification, the person wishing to be like the other person introjects that person into his ego. Identification by introjection can explain the bonding that is formed between a manager and the management guru. The manager first accepts the guru, and then his ideas. In this context, the personal dimension – 'feeling the flesh' – is crucial, and reading about it is not a substitute.

It is through the guru or his disciples that the magic is worked. One can see evidence of this in the elevation of management principles or goals when they come to be worshipped. Cleverley (1971) claimed that MbO and participation were two such principles. In his view, they have been transformed into beneficent spirits. However, malevolent spirits also existed in the form of *bad organization, poor communication* and *weak marketing*. The role of the sorcerer (or his apprentice) was to use his medicine to drive out these bad spirits, which were often used as fashionable scapegoats to explain otherwise unaccountable misfortunes.

In this process, the presence of the guru appeared to be an indispensable element in the ritual in the way that a priest led a ceremony of exorcism. It was not sufficient for an acolyte to say his master's words. These must be uttered by the sorcerer himself. Commenting on a seminar by de Bono, a manager said that 'One seminar by de Bono teaches you more than reading his books'. Kantrow's (1980) view on Drucker was that 'One can learn more – and much more deeply – from watching him think than from studying the content of his thought.' Since it is impossible to watch a person's thought processes, one can assume that it was the physical presence at a Drucker seminar that was valued.

Customers paying to attend a seminar also have an investment in not demystifying the products of their chosen 'saint'. In accepting the person, they also accept his prescriptions for action or his package (if he has one to sell). They thus save themselves the time and trouble of picking over and analysing it in detail. Since many of the available prescriptions are based on behavioural science research or else represent a social philosophy, most company trainers lack the theoretical background or expertise to evaluate them objectively. Additionally, they may lack the power to 'disagree'. By accepting the guru-figure they obtain a warm feeling. If the solution is successful, many people will be put through it. If it fails they will continue their search for another guru. The failure of a package or approach does not rock their faith that there is a holy grail to be found.

The religiosity of the whole experience is reflected in the currently fashionable management concepts of corporate spirit, soul of the organization, and the vision of management. Perhaps most significant is the popularity of corporate culture whose existence is contemplated like that of an individual's soul (Does it exist? Of what is it composed? Can it be changed/redeemed? What are the myths, rituals and heroes that have formed it?).

Cleverley (1971) distinguished between sorcerers who used a body of systematically acquired knowledge whom he labelled *medicine men* and those whose power was supernatural whom he gave the title *witch doctors*. One would place nearly all management consultants and academics in the former category, whereas the hero-managers occupy the latter category. The major difference between the two classes is that in the case of the former, their power resides in knowledge and not in the individual. In the second case, that of the witch doctor, the power resides in the individual himself. Cleverley made a number of observations about the use of consultants. He wrote that managers, while dealing with complexity and chaos, needed to cling to the belief that someone, somewhere knew the answers. He cited the anthropologist, Lucy Mair, who wrote:

> They may be sceptical about the genuineness of particular practitioners, but everyone believes there are genuine ones somewhere; in times of real trouble they could have no hope without this belief.

(Mair 1962)

Hastings (1989) wrote about senior executives who were presiding over the transformations of their organizations which were occurring at such a speed and to a degree unknown before. Uncertainty was the order of the day, and high levels of it caused severe stress. Speed of change could lead to work overload, which reduced feelings of control. Not knowing, and therefore not being in control, was a deeply disturbing experience for many top executives. The need to find someone who knew what was going on itself created its own consequences.

The first of these was a faith in outsiders. Considering non-technical problems, Cleverley (1971) argued that while a manager might doubt his own power and ability, he rarely doubted that of another person, at least when that person was first engaged. The manager assumed that the outside specialist possessed more power for no other reason than that he was from outside. A consultant's power was held to be greater if he worked outside of his country of origin. Foreign magic was more mysterious, and therefore more powerful, than the domestic variety.

The second consequence was the stress upon no-surprise solutions. Cleverley argued that it was the type of consultant's answer that was required by the manager (rather than the problem) which dictated the choice of consultant or consultancy firm. Thus, rather than solving a performance problem, the company might select an Arthur Anderson solution or a McKinsey solution. Sorcerers tended to specialize and the all-purpose consultant was a rarity. It was inherent in the nature of knowledge gained by study and experience, that the sorcerer should be a specialist.

Third was the belief in the existence of the holy grail. The failure of a consultant or a package, far from demotivating management, could energize them to double their efforts for a 'better' consultant or a 'better' solution. Cleverley (1971) offered an explanation for this seemingly paradoxical situation which merits detailed quotation:

> More often the manager believes that the really efficacious technique is

still around the corner. Somewhere – in work study, in industrial engineering, in behavioural science, in autonomic systems, in decentralization, in planned management development, in one of a hundred other fashionable phrases – he must be able to find the true secret. And so he reads success stories, listens to successful speakers, analyses case studies, attends conferences and seminars. Not always is he credulous, frequently he is cynical. But even where the cynicism is not simply a cloak to cover confusion or a refusal to admit lack of understanding, it is normally only the result of an inner belief that he himself already knows the truth.

There is really no better argument for my basic thesis than the existence of this pattern of behaviour despite all empirical evidence. It conjures up . . . [a picture of] addicts who cluster around roulette tables, obsessed with the attempt to discover the system that will ensure they make their fortunes. . . . Unfortunately for their sense of objectivity the roulette-players, like the managers, have the occasional visible evidence of success. Some roulette players are bound to win, even among those who play systems. And each example of a successful player provides the kernel for the building of fresh legends to sustain the hopes of the addicts.

Similarly some businessmen are bound to succeed. Our society and our economy are structured in that way. And every company that succeeds, every entrepreneur that makes a fortune, provides further evidence for the belief that there must be a road to success, even if it is only the road of hard work and long hours. This, more than anything else, is the pathetic fallacy of the managerial group.

(Cleverley 1971: 230–1)

Both management techniques and consultants add legitimacy and support for what a manager may want to do. In addition to providing a knowledge solution, the consultant also gives a chosen approach his blessing and 'the mystical force of the right name'. In a sense, he gives the manager the permission to go ahead. He justifies the manager's choice and shifts some of the responsibility for possible failure off the manager. Among the factors that Oliver (1990) identified as influencing conversion and resistance to new management ideas were the characteristics of their inventors. In his view, the inventor's reputation, nationality and personality all played a part. Of course, both consultants and their packages are replaceable.

The author's interviews with managers, concerning which management ideas they found valuable, revealed yet another set of recurring themes. These were labelled *challenge*, *correspondence* and *integration*, which were all important at the personal level. Some management ideas were experienced as challenging. That is, as opposing taken-for-granted ways of thinking and doing things. One manager referred to 'opening himself up', 'letting yourself take a look at a few things in spite of the preconceived notions that you might have' and 'dropping barriers'. Underlying these comments there seemed to be the notion of individuals taking a risk to escape from some sort of mental cage that they had constructed for themselves. The ideas and their associated tools acted temporarily to bring people together in new ways. One commented that it 'forced people to really look hard at what was required of them'. Davis (1971) had argued that challenges to taken-for-granted assumptions generated reader interest. When a management idea challenges your beliefs, then you tend to take notice of it.

The notion of *correspondence* is perhaps best expressed in terms of a link. The establishment of that link by the subject imbued the idea with innate value and gave the subject confidence in its use. It may be a link between an idea itself and an individual's perceived practices and beliefs. An interviewee explained 'I found that . . . [the idea] . . . fascinating, but then again it was compatible with the way I like to think I'm doing business'. This comment is particularly instructive since it reminds us that correspondence is with a subject's self-image, and not necessarily the reality. Another respondent said that 'it's something that you think you always do and we certainly didn't do it in such a rigorous way'.

Some new ideas are experienced as 'striking a chord' in a person and 'harmonizing with their thinking', that is, creating an inner resonance with something already known or experienced by the subject. There is an analogy here with the body's immune system which defends it from disease. This resonance appears to permit an idea to penetrate the individual's defences which might be expected to reject it. The resonance acts to define the idea as 'common sense' and thereby as not representing a threat to the person's self-image. Thus new applications of old (accepted) ideas represent another version of this common sense.

In his description, a production manager stressed his commitment to and comfort with a scientific approach to technical work and management. Discussing the new idea of Total Quality Management (TQM), he explained how it corresponded with and could be incorporated into his preferred scientific approach. He also expressed the view that 'the two have come together very well I think'. Alternatively, the correspondence may be between the management idea and some memorable experience of failure or success in the past. A financial manager mentioned that 'I could relate back to when I naively set up committees'.

Furnam and Singh (1987) reported the selective-recall hypothesis which suggested that people remembered information better that was congruent with their attitudes. Their attitudes and beliefs act as a sort of organizing framework that supports the encoding and retrieval of attitude-supporting material. The correspondence may be with the company's culture, including its value system. A manager said that 'We all agree on this [idea] . . . [it] has been to our mind the most satisfying of recent years and I like to think it matches up with most people's values'. Also at the organizational level, in the words of a subject, the idea 'represented an attractive way of looking at the need for change'. Thus, while individuals and companies may acknowledge the need to be challenged in order to change, some approaches are preferred to others.

There is an interesting apparent contradiction in what has just been reported. Respondents valued ideas which challenged their existing views *and* those which corresponded with their existing views. How might such a contradiction be explained? Managers will tend to resist the introduction of new concepts which threaten to invalidate their existing frames of reference. Our existing picture of the world provides us with a sense of security. It allows us to make things 'hang together in some sort of sense'. We each cherish our own cognition, ideology or *Weltanschauung*. When a bit of data comes along that does not fit, it calls into question our whole cognition. Thus we each check our knowledge against our existing cognition before deciding whether to accept it or not.

Students and managers alike will not accept information that causes them a great deal of trauma to make it 'fit'. However, Brickman (1980) proposed that discoveries (new ideas) emerged from a region in which we disbelieve them, to a zone where we find them interesting, to a zone in which we find them obvious, and then finally, into a further region in which we become oblivious to them. Initially threatening ideas could thus become common sense.

The key point for aspiring gurus is that they should not try to sell any ideas which, given where the audience stands, are too outlandish for them to accept (Davis 1971). Ries and Trout (1986: 32) felt that the mind had no room for the new and different unless it was related to the old. For this reason, they recommended that if one had a new idea or product, then it was better to tell the customer what it was *not* rather than what it was (horseless carriage, unleaded petrol). Butler (1986) hypothesized three possible responses when people checked a piece of information against their existing knowledge or bank of common sense. These are shown in Table 5.4.

This explanation suggests that a new management idea can be both challenging and at the same time corresponding. It should be new, but not so new that it does not relate to something already known. The problem for management gurus is to achieve this difficult blend. Many management ideas have failed to achieve popularity because they were either too challenging or too obvious.

Finally, turning to *integration*, some managers experienced a feeling of closure as disparate insights, theories and experiences became integrated by means of a management idea. A feeling of satisfaction was achieved as the subjects had the opportunity to restructure their existing knowledge and integrate it into a whole which was more meaningful for them. One manager commented that 'I like it because it brings together all the various

Table 5.4 Human responses to new information

1 Already known ——————►	redundant information —►	no learning takes place
2 Too radical ————►	reject it, usually finding some reason for discrediting the infor- mation in order to defend existing view of world in the face of attack	—►no learning takes place
3 New but involves only a limited re- arrangement of world ———————————————————————————►		learning takes place

Source: Butler 1986: 97

theories and models'. It allowed him to 'integrate all the various models' which he had come across'. Another explained that the value of the idea came 'only when I was able to put it in the context of a threat to the company'. A sales manager valued a book which put all the issues together, 'in a rather nice way, so that stimulated me again'. Gestalt research has shown how satisfying such closure is for individuals.

The discussion in this section highlights the importance of the unconscious and perhaps irrational aspects of behaviour. To explain the adoption of certain management approaches and packages in these terms necessitates drawing upon psychoanalytical theory. The main authors in the field are Freud, Klein and Bion. The relevant concepts are identification, the unconscious, anxiety and defence systems. The field consists of theories and concepts rather than experimentation. Miner (1980) argued that hitherto in organizational behaviour, there had been a greater emphasis placed upon the charting of the domain of conscious, rational decision-making than upon the unconscious and the irrational. He attributed this preference to the relative ease of measurement in the conscious domain. However, he felt that this represented a clear gap which needed filling.

CONCLUSION

Manufacturers have been encouraged to be customer- rather than product-oriented. Henshel (1975: 103) said that people would work for predicted states they approved of and against those that they detested. Ideas that related to forecasted futures which managers found appealing would be selected and preferred to those which they found repellent. Successful gurus have matched their ideas to the needs of managers. This chapter has revealed managerial needs for predictability, control and esteem. Some successful gurus have worked with content theories of motivation to appeal to the majority of managers. In the management idea design phase, they have incorporated, whether consciously or unconsciously, many of the attributes valued by managers.

The first of these managerial needs was *predictability*. That need was met by a management idea explaining their environment to them and thus making it less confusing and threatening. If the idea succeeded in its task, managers experienced a feeling which can be called *revelation*. After the revelation, they gained a clearer and more accurate vision of their work environment. Operationally, the search for a potential new management fad involved identifying some commonplace aspect of the organizational milieu which was simultaneously well-known and yet ignored by company management. Who would have thought that the management of time would secure guru status and millionaire wealth for at least one American and one Dane? The focus of attention may be some aspect of nature (time) or an unlikely part of the organization. *Fortune* magazine featured an article on the problems and potential offered by the company mailroom (Farnham 1989). Alternatively, the focus may be upon an undesired management habit. A business magazine recently reported that a consultant would work with managers to rearrange the items cluttering their desk and so help them to clear it (desktop management guruship?).

The guru identifies the opportunity offered to meet the aforementioned managerial needs, and then invests it with hitherto unconsidered potential. This procedure was earlier described as 'figure–ground shifting' and examples from tennis and materials management were cited. Operationally, successful management ideas do not usually offer new, hitherto unavailable knowledge. Instead, they restructure and reprioritize that which is already known so that it is perceived differently (but not too differently) by managers.

A review of the more popular 'new' management ideas of the 1980s shows that many of them represent new wine in old bottles. The total number of bottles remains the same, but each is refilled with new contents. The bottles themselves are grouped differentially by kind. The personal topics have the greatest number of different types, and the choice diminishes as one moves away from the individual, out towards the team and then out again towards the organizational level. The implication of this is that a management idea which addresses an individual's inner or outer self is likely to have the greatest impact. The continuing appeal of the Dale Carnegie books and their imitators over decades supports this view. Figure 5.3 summarizes the main topic areas.

Interviews with managers drew attention to the value placed by them on macro-ideas which integrated into a single whole (previously held separate) mini-ideas. To help the manager achieve this satisfying feeling of integration, future management ideas should not only repackage an idea towards the left of Figure 5.3 but also integrate it with one or two others from the adjacent columns. Quality circles, one of the most popular management

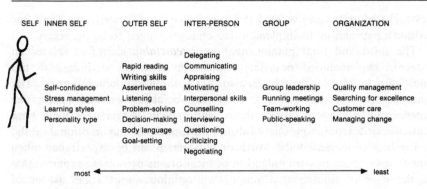

SELF	INNER SELF	OUTER SELF	INTER-PERSON	GROUP	ORGANIZATION
			Delegating		
		Rapid reading	Communicating		
		Writing skills	Appraising		
	Self-confidence	Assertiveness	Motivating	Group leadership	Quality management
	Stress management	Listening	Interpersonal skills	Running meetings	Searching for excellence
	Learning styles	Problem-solving	Counselling	Team-working	Customer care
	Personality type	Decision-making	Interviewing	Public-speaking	Managing change
		Body language	Questioning		
		Goal-setting	Criticizing		
			Negotiating		

most ◄───► least

Figure 5.3 Management ideas classified by personal impact

ideas of the 1980s, successfully integrated elements of group leadership, team-working, problem-solving, interviewing, delegating and public speaking. Integration, once again, involves the notion of creating a non-threatening 'new' idea from a set of known, non-threatening 'old' ones.

The second management need identified was for *control* and developed naturally from the first. The issues here go beyond the question of understanding the environment, and move to shaping it. Valuable management ideas in this context were those which were able to guide managers to the really important issues which needed addressing. This was labelled *empowerment*. It appears that managers wanted the guru to identify for them which of the myriad factors in their environment were the crucial ones (and thus which needed to be focused and acted upon), and thereby distinguish those that could be safely ignored. The management guru unequivocally and assuredly said to managers, 'Pay attention to this, but not to that. This will get you to where you need to go better and faster.' It is here that the guarded disclaimers (ifs and buts) of traditional business school academics contrast with the confident, unambiguous (but not necessarily any more correct) assertions of the management gurus.

Managers also want permission from the guru to go ahead and implement the action. This may be either to gain extra confidence and support for their actions, or perhaps to absolve them from the final responsibility should something go wrong. Having highlighted the organizational processes which managers need to focus on, the next imperative for the gurus is to ensure that their idea possesses the associated techniques which managers will perceive as likely to bring about the desired changes. These will be considered in greater depth in the next step.

Second, ideas which possessed associated techniques with which to intervene to bring about changes were valued by managers. They were seen as *logical*. Having had their view of their organization and its problems restructured, managers wanted the knowledge, confidence, tools and 'consultant's permission' to implement the changes judged to be necessary.

restructured, managers wanted the knowledge, confidence, tools and 'consultant's permission' to implement the changes judged to be necessary.

The third and final management need that was identified related to esteem. This included not only the worth or value attributed to the individual by him or herself, but also that accorded to them by others. The analysis in the chapter referred to meeting social and personal needs. The interviewed managers talked about legitimation. Advertisers have long known that a product purchase fulfils both functional and emotional needs.

Feelings of increased self-worth or self-esteem can be experienced when one's views or actions are judged to be meritorious by outside experts. This is the case of finding that one's own opinion about some aspect of management is confirmed by a well-known management writer or speaker. The distinguishing feature is that only the manager realizes that the 'expert agrees with him'. Since the expert is perceived to legitimaize the manager's previously held views, he and his writings are accorded increased value.

Earlier it was suggested that by promoting the ideas of a hero-manager or consultant guru, managers identified themselves with that admired individual. Teenagers identify with, and 'live through', their pop idols. One can speculate that a similar process may occur here. Both the American and British business press reports the activities of managerial and entrepreneurial heroes who are written about and revered. A constant diet of such articles over the years must indicate that this is the type of copy that management readers of these journals enjoy.

Social esteem, in contrast, refers to the positive assessment made of the individual by others. These may be professional colleagues or senior managers inside or outside of the organization. It is not possible to recommend explicitly how the guru can take cognizance of the self-esteem need when designing the management idea (since individual managers will have their own set of personal managerial beliefs which are hidden from the guru). The social esteem needs, however, revealed by the literature review and protocol analysis, are more transparent and are thus capable of a greater degree of manipulation.

The guru can create a management-idea product whose adoption will be perceived by managers as offering them the possibility of social-esteem enhancement. How might this be done ? Social esteem can be gained by emulating others, that is adhering to the group norms. If the norm is to introduce quality circles, then managers can show solidarity with their opposite numbers by committing their company to the same idea. Hence, our guru should cite examples of similar applications in other companies, and explain that great benefits were obtained in a short time. Success of implementation can also give managers an opportunity to boast about their achievements.

Social esteem can additionally be gained if managers present themselves as the idea champion. In a number of organizations, the promotion of the latest management fad by managers has been used to help them gain company-wide visibility in the promotion stakes. Management-idea championing can represent a low-risk way of signalling to those with the power to promote that managers are not adverse to change, do not mind challenging established views, but that while they are prepared to look critically at the system in which they work, they will unduly 'rock the organizational boat'.

Further esteem can be gained if the idea is not of the black-box variety, that is if it offers (and is seen to offer) the championing managers scope to make their own unique contribution to it. This in turn gives them greater ownership of the idea in the perception of others. It might be thought that this is a high-risk strategy, since the idea may fail to yield the expected benefits. As was pointed out earlier, assessments of success and failure tend to be very vague in this area, and all parties concerned have a vested interest in not admitting to failure.

This chapter has argued that the nature of managerial work in organizations creates a number of cognitive and emotional needs among those who occupy positions of responsibility in such institutions. One way in which such needs can be gratified is through the embracement and promotion of certain management ideas and their application through their associated techniques. These needs are constant and, in a way, are never satisfied. Temporary resolution is affected by a change in circumstanaces which pushes the situation for the manager into disequilibrium. It is for this reason that demand for management ideas is likely to continue, at least in competitive capitalist societies.

Chapter 6

Promotion of management ideas

INTRODUCTION

How does a management idea become transformed into a marketable commodity? Business school academics play a relatively small but nevertheless important part in bringing management ideas to the attention of a management audience. Of much greater importance now is the marketing of these ideas by their developers and companies which sell the associated idea products.

In 1924 researchers from the Industrial Health Research Board in Britain, studying women at work, discovered that 'the social conditions of work were found to have significant (but not emphasised) consequences, boredom being less likely to arise when operatives worked in groups rather than alone' (Wyatt *et al.* 1928). Given this finding and the date of its publication, why are human relations ideas associated with Mayo, Roethlisberger and Dickson, and why has no one ever heard of Wyatt, Fraser and Stock?

This chapter takes a marketing perspective and examines the part played by the product developers and marketeers in turning a basic management idea into a popular one, by advertising and selling it. It demonstrates that the activities of product development and promotion play a crucial role in transforming a management idea into a popular one. Such transformational activities can be effective only if the management idea possesses innate characteristics which allow it to be transformed from a mental state into different types of physical products which can then be sold to and consumed by customers. The short-hand term given for this process of transformation is *productivization*.

There are four main types of management-idea-based techniques (excluding traditional consultancy advice). These are the *teaching device*, the *training event*, the *organizational development (OD)-type intervention* and the *system-wide programme*. These four types of techniques are not equivalent but represent progressively deeper and more permanent influences upon the organization. The term used to describe this process is *structuralization*. Thus management idea popularity is partly a function of the degree of structuralization that it can achieve with a company through its associated techniques. The adoption of management-idea-based techniques is influenced by their active promotion. Of particular importance are the processes of *branding*, *advertising* and *product development*.

STRUCTURALIZATION

In his analysis of the labour process, Littler (1982) argued that management ideas should be considered not as ideologies but rather as *forms of work organization* or *sets of principles underlying work organizations*. Viewed from this perspective, scientific management, human relations, classical management and similar idea systems can be considered as significant sets of design criteria which are used to structure work. As such, they have continued to exert a major influence on managerial thinking and organizational design right through to the present day.

Littler offered a three-level framework which he termed the levels of structuralization. The first level was called *employment relations*; the second was *structure of control*; while the third level was *work design, division of labour and technology*. His basic argument was that those management ideas which possessed the greatest number of structural implications, and which also achieved widespread management appeal, had the greatest chance of progressing through the levels before finally establishing themselves permanently within the organization structure and its processes. While there was a tendency for changes at all three levels to go together, a management idea could be effective at the first level while leaving the others unaffected.

Littler's contribution offers a useful way of thinking about the differing impact of the various management ideas and also provides a framework within which to examine the role of middlemen or entrepreneurs who disseminate management ideas. To do this, however, it is first necessary to modify and extend Littler's original formulation to fit in more directly with the subject of this book.

Level 1: individual understanding

An innate feature of a popular management idea appears to be its inherent communicability. Thus the first level of impact is that managers should understand the idea (but not necessarily how it can help them to do their job better, or what they should do differently). Most management ideas fail to achieve even this first level of structuralization, because of their intrinsic complexity or because of the failure of their authors or promoters to communicate them effectively.

Level 2: individual action

The individual action level involves the basic management idea being developed beyond the comprehension level of the manager, into a set of propositions explaining how it can benefit managers and explaining how they should adjust their own behaviour. The impact of the idea will thus be greater since a way will have been developed to 'put knowledge into action'.

Level 3: group action

Group action level penetration implies that the management idea has an impact upon a wide number of company employees because the behavioural changes are not only targeted upon a few individuals but are also designed to affect groups and teams. The idea therefore becomes more widely applied throughout the organization.

Level 4: organizational action

This level of structuralization is achieved when the idea becomes institutionalized within the company as a whole and ceases to be dependent on the discretion of individuals or groups for its continued application. Such institutionalization occurs when the idea becomes incorporated into the planning processes, budgets, reward and review systems of the organization. Procedural proposals which are the basis of action have been found to be particularly valued by practitioners (see Weiss and Bucuvalas 1980: 251).

Assuming that the management idea possesses an innate potential to achieve the fourth level of structuralization, what factors determine the idea's progress through other levels? In Chapter 2 a *management idea* was defined as a mental state of understanding (a research finding, theory, principle, tip, personal idea or saw). This was contrasted with the term *management idea technique* which referred to a means which either assisted in the communication of the management idea or enabled it to be translated into action at the individual, group or organization level. Management idea techniques are vehicles of idea transfer and are of four types. Each of the four levels of structuralization described earlier has its own associated management techniques.

To achieve the first level of structuralization, the production of a *teaching device* is important. Onward progress to Level 2 necessitates the availability of a *training event* of some kind. Continued movement to Level 3 requires the establishment of some *organizational development (OD)* intervention targeted at a number of individuals or groups. Finally, the achievement of Level 4 structuralization, equivalent to the permanent institutionalization of the idea in the company, calls for a long-term, wide-ranging *system-wide programme* based upon a reappraisal of organizational functioning. The four revised levels of structuralization are shown in Table 6.1.

Table 6.1 Structuralization levels and their associated delivery modes.

Level	Impact	Delivery mode
1	individual understanding	teaching device
2	individual action	training event
3	group action	OD-intervention
4	organizational action	system-wide programme

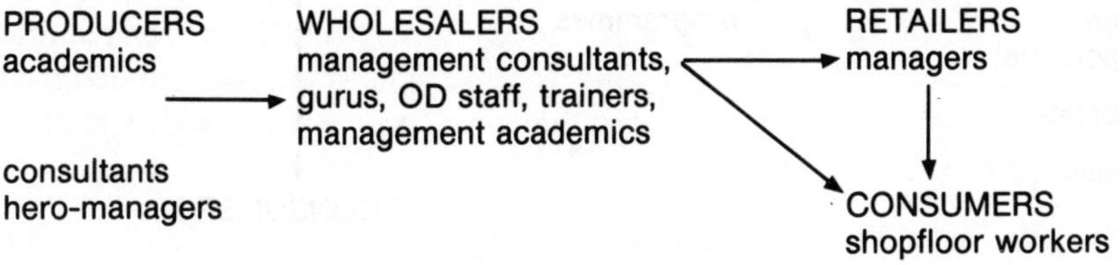

PRODUCERS   WHOLESALERS   RETAILERS
academics   management consultants, ⟷ managers
           ⟶ gurus, OD staff, trainers,
                   management academics

consultants
hero-managers   CONSUMERS
                                                  shopfloor workers

Figure 6.1 Relationships in the generation and productivization of management ideas

Productivization

This four-level framework, based on Littler's ideas, provides a means with which to examine how management ideas become established within an organization. In particular, it permits the examination of the role of middlemen in the process of translating a management idea into a product or a service capable of being marketed, sold and consumed. This process is labelled *productivization*, and can be defined as the process of taking an idea relevant for managers (such as a theory or a research finding) and changing it into a form that can be sold to, and consumed by, an organizational customer.

One can argue that the management wholesaler takes the raw material of the academic, consultant or hero-manager in a way similar to which a dairy products company buys bulk milk from a farmer. That milk is then transformed into a number of different dairy products. At this stage value is added and the products are destined for different markets. Figure 6.1. summarizes this relationship.

Many entrepreneurs have an idea which they turn into a product or service. Excluding traditional individual consultancy, four separate types of products can be distinguished. These are the teaching device, the training event, organization development, the intervention and the system-wide programme. Their relationships are depicted in Figure 6.2.

Teaching devices

A teaching device is an aid to help learners to understand some piece of

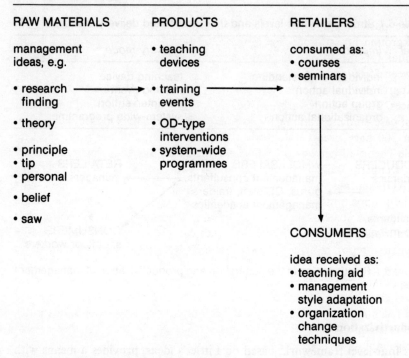

RAW MATERIALS	PRODUCTS	RETAILERS
management ideas, e.g.	• teaching devices	consumed as: • courses • seminars
• research finding	• training events	
• theory	• OD-type interventions	
• principle • tip • personal	• system-wide programmes	
• belief		
• saw		

CONSUMERS

idea received as:
• teaching aid
• management style adaptation
• organization change techniques

Figure 6.2 Range of products produced from management ideas

knowledge. It is made up of a content element and a delivery element (teaching/learning technique). The device assists in the process of communicating the idea. At a basic level, each idea represents a conceptual framework which can be used for purposes of analysis. For example, a case description or a real life work problem such as lateness and absenteeism can be analysed using Herzberg's or Maslow's theories of motivation. Students use such frameworks to analyse the case situation in order to locate the causes and go on to make recommendations. The story description in the case represents the content element of the device, while the classroom case discussion constitutes the delivery element.

More sophisticated teaching devices might include a self-completion questionnaire (instrument) which would identify students' responses. The purpose of these teaching devices is to assist the tutor, involve the students and communicate the idea so that it is fully understood by the listeners. Training devices vary in their design and effect. Some are included in textbooks, student workbooks and tutors' manuals and can be used free with no further payment. The widespread teaching of certain management ideas, such as those of Herzberg and Peters already mentioned, provides an opportunity for management training materials companies to produce, market and sell teaching devices based upon those ideas. Such teaching device packs include the instrument itself for the student to complete; background notes about the theory; comparative test scores, and a user's manual for the tutor. Such commercially produced instruments sell at between £5.00 and £15.00 per item.

Apart from instruments there are many other delivery systems or teaching devices. These include various kinds of aptitude, personality and vocational tests; case studies; training films; role plays; simulation games and so on. Over 300 have been catalogued (Huczynski 1983). For example, the Life Cycle Theory of Leadership, which was originally developed by Paul Hersey and Kenneth Blanchard, was renamed Situational Leadership Theory (LEAD), and has spawned a wide range of spin-off teaching devices.

The propositions of the hero-managers are unlikely to achieve even the first level of structuralization. Some are 'unteachable' in the sense that educationally there is little that a teacher can do with a personal anecdote other than report it. These types of management ideas are thus unlikely to progress to higher levels unless teaching devices are developed to assist in their communication. In contrast, the management ideas contained in Peters and Waterman's (1982) book on excellence have been supplemented with teaching devices such as video and audio-tapes on the eight attributes of excellence; case studies of the excellent companies; and instruments to assess employees' perceptions of company excellence.

Training event

A training event is defined as a vehicle which seeks to put into practice the management ideas of an individual or group. Such an event may be run by the idea-developer personally, franchised to a training company, or may be developed independently by a company. The 'skunk camps' described by Byrne (1986) were residential programmes run by Tom Peters' company and taught by him. During these seminars he conveyed the management ideas contained in his book, *In Search of Excellence* (Peters and Waterman 1982).

A training event may be developed around research findings. The original research by Bill Byham on managerial careers led to the development of assessment centres. This work was later packaged into videos, workbooks, role plays and tutor's notes. Byham founded a company, Development Dimensions International (DDI), to market a range of off-the-shelf, ready-to-use management courses. Perhaps the best-known example of a management development programme based on a management idea is Blake and Mouton's Grid Management Seminar. Developed by Robert Blake and Jane Mouton, it was based on their theory concerning organizational effectiveness and change that appeared in their book (Blake and Mouton 1964).

In order to be productivized into a training event, the management idea must contain a number of clearly defined elements or principles which are capable of being standardized, taught and franchised. Other examples of training events are the 'One Minute Manager Seminar' and 'Time Manager International'.

Organizational development (OD) intervention

While using the term 'organizational' in its title, the majority of OD interventions seek to change individual or group behaviour rather than to tamper with the company structure, technology or objectives. The inability or reluctance of OD interventions to affect these aspects of a company is what distinguishes this third level of structuralization from the fourth. OD interventions are typically directed at work teams or entire departments. Perhaps the best-known set of such interventions are those based upon neo-human relations management ideas. Developed originally in the United States in the 1960s, OD is now used as a generic term and has incorporated the Quality of Work Life programmes of the 1970s.

System-wide programme

These are long-term, wide-ranging programmes which not only impact upon people, whether individually or in groups, but also involve changes to technology, work organization, financing, inventory control, reward systems and so on. Past examples of system-wide changes have included the implementation of Taylor's scientific management principles. More recent ones include the implementation of the 'Deming Way' at the Ferraro plant of General Motors, and the attempts by various companies to apply Just-in-Time and Total Quality Management principles.

The four idea-techniques – teaching devices, training events, OD interventions and system-wide programmes – all represent means through which management ideas penetrate behaviour in organizations and company processes. Table 6.2 gives examples of each of the main management idea families.

Peters and Waterman's (1982) book, *In Search of Excellence*, has formed the basis of an incredibly successful marketing effort, and represents a case study in successful merchandising. Diaries, calenders, skunk camps and television documentaries have followed from it. Unlike consultants, the process of productivization for academics, involves them becoming entrepreneurs. Watson (1980) used the label 'social science entrepreneurs' to refer to those engaged in such activities. He said that writers such as Gellerman, Blake and Mouton, Herzberg and Reddin were criticized by purists:

> their work is designed to sell, whether in the form of books, management seminars, training films or consultancies. Like the task splitting scientific managers with whom they so passionately take issue, their work is

Table 6.2 Management idea families and their associated products

Management idea family	Teaching device	Training event	OD intervention	System-wide programme
Bureaucracy	Readings on Weber	Case	Role analysis exercise	Organizational designs incorporating bureaucratic principles
Scientific management	Assembly-line production game	Operations and methods course	Time-and-motion study	Work simplification
Classical management	Readings on Urwich. Gulick, Fayol	Organizational charting	Management-by-Objectives (MbO)	Job definitions and descriptions
Human relations	Team-work exercises	Interpersonal skills courses for supervisors	Management intervenes in informal organization to create and sustain consent	Creating a sense of community in the workplace
Neo-human relations	Human relation experiential exercises	Laboratory (T-group) training	Blake and Mouton's grid management	Job enrichment
Guru theory	'Pillars of Excellence' instrument	Tom Peters' 'skunk camp'	Quality circles	Total Quality Management (TQM)

reductionist, partial, evangelistic and sociologically highly inadequate on the explanatory level with its underplaying of structural, situational, cultural and economic factors. It is ultimately simplistic by a judicious mixing of simplistic assumptions and pseudoscientific jargon it has made itself highly marketable.

(Watson 1980: 38)

MARKETING

Once the management idea has been productivized, marketing becomes important. Reduced to its basics, successful marketing depends upon customers being aware of the products on offer; finding the products conveniently available (place); and judging the product attributes in terms of price and performance to be capable of satisfying their needs. Promotion, place, price and product represent the key aspects of the 'marketing mix'. To the potential buyer, management-idea-based products represent a cluster of value satisfactions. Customers will attach value to a product in proportion to its perceived ability to meet their needs. The predictability, control, social and personal needs of managers were considered in chapter 5. Levitt (1980) argued that products are always combinations of the tangible and the intangible. They are often complex symbols denoting individual or company status, taste, rank, achievement, aspiration and even 'being smart'.

A product was a promise whose commercial substance resided as much in the proposer's reputation (or 'image') and the product's meticulous packaging, as in its physical content. Thus the product represented the total package of benefits that customers received when they purchased a teaching device, a training event, an organizational development intervention or a system-wide programme. This chapter therefore goes on to focus on three crucial aspects of marketing which appear to affect the popularity of a management-idea-based device, event, intervention or programme. These are its branding, promotion and product development.

Branding

A brand is a name, term, sign, symbol, design or a combination which is intended to identify the goods or services of one seller or a group of sellers, and to differentiate them from those of competitors. A *brand name* is that part of a brand which is utterable. Well-known brands include Coca-Cola and Ford. A *brand mark* is that part of a brand that can be recognized but which is not utterable. It may be a symbol, design or distinctive colouring or lettering. McDonald's yellow-on-red 'Golden Arches' device above its restaurants is a brandmark. Finally there is a *trademark* which is a brand, or that part of a brand, that is given legal protection. It gives the owner the exclusive right to use the brand name and brandmark. The term branding is

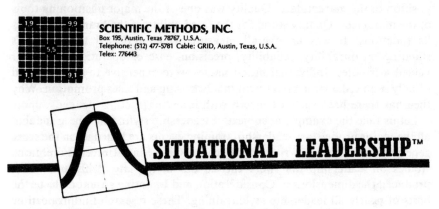

SCIENTIFIC METHODS, INC.
Box 195, Austin, Texas 78767, U.S.A.
Telephone: (512) 477-5781 Cable: GRID, Austin, Texas, U.S.A.
Telex: 776443

Exhibit 6.1 Examples of brands in training devices and events

used to refer to the process of establishing brand names, marks or trade names for a product. One can find examples of branding in the field of training devices, management programmes, training devices and OD techniques.

Blake and Mouton's Grid Development programme is historically noteworthy as being among the earliest examples of brand-naming. Kahn (1974) complained about this, saying that their company, Scientific Methods, Inc., 'had registered the term as a mark or brand-name, the very antithesis of scientific conceptualization'. Exhibit 6.1 shows some of the best-known brands in the field of training events, and includes that owned by Scientific Instruments Inc.

There are numerous reasons for branding. These apply as much to management-idea products as to other goods and services. A brandmark might be required for identification purposes or to simplify handling. Alternatively the producer may want to emphasize a certain quality level to protect unique product features from being imitated. The producer may want to emphasize a certain quality level in the offer and make it easy for satisfied customers to find the product again. Finally, the producer may see the brandname as an opportunity for endowing the product with an inherent superiority that may create the basis for price differentiation (see Kotler 1980).

Ultimately, the brand has an informational value to buyers by allowing them to shop in a market which has hundreds of different items. The brand serves as a useful expression for a whole collection of attributes and properties associated with a product and enables the purchaser to obtain products which satisfy highly specific wants without having to resort to a detailed description of them.

In developing a brand, the manufacturer had to establish the brand's quality level as well as other attributes that would support its targeted position in the marketplace. Quality was one of the major positioning tools of the marketeer. Quality stood for the rated ability of the brand to perform its functions. It was an overall measure which reflected the product's standing on durability, reliability, precision, ease of operation and other valued attributes. Individual brand names were expensive to establish and usually required a large investment in advertising and sales promotion. Why then has there been such a concern with branding?

Let us take the example of subject of leadership style. One can argue that all the major proprietary leadership training events are based upon the same generic product. Many writers consider the Ohio State University research studies on leadership that were carried out in the late 1940s and which produced the dimensions of Consideration and Initiating structure, to be the basis of nearly all leadership style training. These research findings can be considered to be an undifferentiated product (Bryman 1986).

In the case of Situational Leadership, the function performed by the 'subordinate maturity' variable in the theory was to provide a focus that distinguished this leadership model from the many similar ones (Graeff 1983; Nicholls 1986). More often, however, differentiation of leadership training events is achieved by having the developer-seller's name in the title. For example, Adair's 'Action Centred Leadership', Blake and Mouton's 'Grid Management' seminar, Reddin's '3-D Theory of Leadership Effectiveness' seminar and Hersey and Blanchard's 'Situational Leadership' course all represent differentiated versions of a similar product. Their differences are sustained through branding.

Promotion

Let us now consider the promotion of productivized idea-products in a little more depth. An analysis of the way in which teaching devices, training events, OD interventions and system-wide programmes are packaged and promoted shows that they stress different features.

Promoting teaching devices

These self-standing teaching devices are neither complete management training events nor OD interventions. They include role play exercises, video films and case studies. Their promotion is targeted at management trainers or lecturers who use these teaching materials. The advertising copy stresses a number of benefits which are similar to those one gets with ready-to-eat meals. It is upon these that the marketing effort can be concentrated. These are ease of preparation; professional presentation; guarantee of success; and ease of consumption.

Ease of preparation means that the tutor can buy as many of these devices as are needed for the class. Little prior work is needed and orders can be phoned in. Professional presentation refers to the fact that the device itself, whether instrument, case study or video package, is professionally produced. Exhibit 6.2 gives an example of the completeness of an instrument called POIS which is sold by University Associates and also contains part of an editorial from another catalogue of training devices sold by Organizational Development and Design.

Guarantee of success is the third positive attribute of a teaching device. Tutors are offered products which 'have been tested and which work'. The experience of past users and the step-by-step tutor's guide all give confidence that the process will be successful. Finally, ease of consumption is more a feature of the idea content than of the teaching device itself. It is the ease with which the basic ideas can be depicted and presented. Four of the most communicable sets of management ideas (McGregor, Maslow, Herzberg, Berne) are shown in Exhibit 6.3. Each has had numerous teaching devices designed around it.

Promoting training events

In Britain, to a greater extent than in the USA, theoretical ideas tend to be dismissed. Indeed, sayings such as 'only of academic interest' and 'all right in theory but not in practice' capture the pervading anti-theory attitude. A brochure by the CareerTrack company assures the potential participants of a One Minute Manager training event that 'You won't have to buy into any big theory'. The following is a description of a video-based training device which appeared in a Gower Training Resources catalogue:

> New supervisors almost always face a difficult task when they first step onto the management ladder. They need practical advice and guidance that they can implement immediately – and get results. *The last thing they need is to have their heads filled with theories about managing people* . . . [name of film] is a how-to film. *There's not a management theory in sight* – instead it focuses on a few basic skills that all supervisors need and can use.
>
> (Gower 1988: 9, original emphasis)

Thus, an anti-theoretical approach to the promotion of the event would tend to be a marketing feature in the British context. The emphasis would be placed on 'common sense', 'learning-by-doing' and learning from fellow managers rather than from 'fancy experts'. The American market could probably cope with a greater level of theoretical sophistication as the success

Trainer's Package for the Kipnis–Schmidt POIS

This packet includes the key element in this user-focused series . . . the *Trainer's Manual*. This essential tool contains everything you need to include the POIS in your programmes. Background and information to prepare your theory input and lecturettes • ideas and guidelines for administering, scoring, interpreting and processing the information from the scales • guidelines for incorporating or designing a workshop around the instrument itself.

An excellent resource as well as an introduction to the POIS materials, the **Trainer's Package** also contains a copy of each of the instruments—*Influencing Your Subordinates (Form S)*, *Influencing Your Manager (Form M)*, and *Influencing Your Co-Workers (Form C)*—as well as a copy of the Respondent's Guide.

SOLD AS A SET ONLY

Each time trainers stand in front of groups, they put their reputations on the line. 'You're only as good as your last presentation,' is an adage trainers are well aware of. Having spent most of my adult life as a teacher and trainer, I know the feeling. I personally want to communicate something of significance, get people to change their behavior *and look good in the process.*

That's our underlying motivation at Organization Design and Development. We want you 'to look good in the process,' while changing people's behavior and communicating something of significance! With that in mind, each item offered in our catalog is carefully tested and designed to meet those requirements. Our spring issue is fairly bursting with new and exciting components for your programs.

Exhibit 6.2 Advertisement for a teaching device

of the Grid Management events and Situational Leadership Theory teaching devices shows.

Promoting OD-type interventions and system-wide programmes

Since OD interventions sometimes snowball into system-wide programmes, for purposes of analysing how they are promoted, the two can be considered jointly. An analysis of the research and promotional literature suggests that four factors can enhance the chances of successfully promoting an OD intervention. The promotional literature should not stress a diagnosis of the customer's problem but should instead emphasize the nature of the solution being offered; it should explain that the customer has total control over the programme; the intervention should be presented as capable of being phased or limited in its application; and it should emphasize practice at the expense of theory. Let us consider each of these issues in turn.

First, why should the intervention or programme be low on customer problem diagnosis but high on the solution offered? Interventions and programmes not only represent benefits to the customers but are also alternative solutions to their problems. The customer will favour one solution over another. Some types of solution will be preferred because they will be better understood, be less risky, make the adopter look smart or whatever. One of the purposes of clear branding is to allow customers to select their preferred solutions. The recurring theme is one of giving managers control and choice. Indeed, Krell (1981) argued that the ability of a product to accomplish change or learning was secondary. What product design needed to emphasize, in his view, was simplicity and ease of sale. Customers responded more positively when offered *results* rather than *processes*. Nevertheless, as will be argued, some aspects of the process also represent selling points.

Krell (1981) felt that interventions and programmes should look complete and be light on diagnosis. It was the purchasers who wanted to do their own diagnosis and who chose their preferred prescription or solution. They would not be buying it otherwise. The individual consultants and consulting companies often have a preferred solution approach or a standardized analysis technique. Thus customers can buy the type of the solution that they desire. Some may select an approach which differs little from the training events described earlier. One consultant may tend to see organizational problems as rooted in inadequate leadership and team performance. He will therefore recommend a leadership training event or an OD team-building activity. Consultants often specialize and their specialisms are known to their customers.

In their role as management idea wholesalers, consultants can increase the attractiveness of their offerings by standardizing either the problem solution or the process of the solution, and frequently both. Hill (1971) observed

Maslow's hierarchy of human needs:

- SELF-ACTUALIZATION
- EGO-STATUS
- BELONGINGNESS
- SAFETY
- BASIC SURVIVAL

MANAGER'S THEORY

ASSUMED ATTITUDE OF EMPLOYEES TOWARDS:	THEORY X	THEORY Y
ORGANIZATIONAL OBJECTIVES	Indifferent to them	Will work toward them if they perceive rewards associated with doing so
RESPONSIBILITY	Will avoid it if possible Prefer to be directed	Will accept responsibility if they are rewarded for acting responsibly Capable of self-direction toward objectives that are valuable to them
WORK	Dislike all forms of work Will avoid if possible	Consider work as natural as play if they associate rewards with working
REWARDS	Want money and security More pay will produce more work	Behave in ways that seek to satisfy a variety of needs
APPROPRIATE MEANS FOR DEALING WITH EMPLOYEES	Coercion, pressure. threat of punishment Well-specified tasks and close control Pay and monetary incentives	Establish a work environment in which employees can realize recognition, challenge. satisfaction of achievement, etc.

Theory X and Theory Y comparison

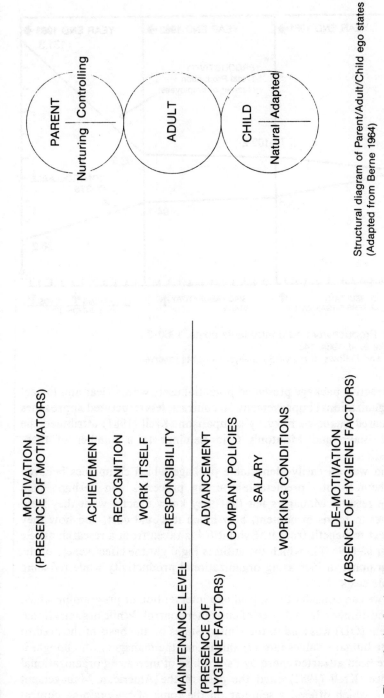

MOTIVATION
(PRESENCE OF MOTIVATORS)

ACHIEVEMENT

RECOGNITION

WORK ITSELF

RESPONSIBILITY

ADVANCEMENT

MAINTENANCE LEVEL

COMPANY POLICIES

(PRESENCE OF
HYGIENE FACTORS)

SALARY

WORKING CONDITIONS

DE-MOTIVATION
(ABSENCE OF HYGIENE FACTORS)

The motivation/hygiene concept

PARENT
Nurturing | Controlling

ADULT

CHILD
Natural | Adapted

Structural diagram of Parent/Adult/Child ego states
(Adapted from Berne 1964)

Exhibit 6.3 Examples of frameworks of popular management ideas

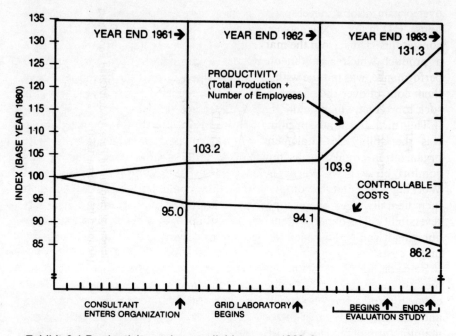

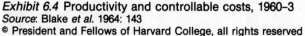

Exhibit 6.4 Productivity and controllable costs, 1960–3
Source: Blake *et al.* 1964: 143
© President and Fellows of Harvard College, all rights reserved

that an attractive package presented potential users with a clear and logical path to organizational improvement. In contrast, less structured approaches often appeared vague or risky by comparison. Krell (1981) attributed the success of Blake and Mouton's Grid Seminar to a number of these characteristics.

The Grid was an easily identifiable package which companies believed allowed them to buy predictable training processes and perhaps even predictable results! Managers felt that they knew exactly what they were going to get in terms of content, how much it would cost, and how they could expect to benefit from it. Exhibit 6.4 is taken from a research article by Blake *et al.* (1964) in which the authors highlight the effectiveness of the Grid Programme in increasing organizational productivity while reducing controllable costs.

Second we can consider the appeal of a intervention or programme which offers the customer a high degree of customer control. While organizational development (OD) was sold in the United States on the basis of the need to incorporate humane values into organizations, the managers who bought it might have been attracted more by its promise of increasing organizational performance. Krell (1981) cited the case of the American Management Association which offered a seminar on the topic of maintaining control over organizational development consultants. Companies even created in-house OD units to take over or oversee the work of independent OD consultants. Thus, from the marketing point of view, the aim was to develop a product which simultaneously met a company's need for improved performance, was in tune with the humanistic values of the period, and gave them control over the change process. There existed a lucrative market for such a product which could achieve all these objectives.

The third and final appealing feature of an intervention or programme was the ability to implement it on a phased or limited basis. The organization could buy as much or as little of it as it required or was comfortable with. M. Warner (1984: 62) felt that the appeal of the Quality of Working Life interventions was that they could be applied ad hoc and incrementally. Another appealing feature of any product was its reversibility. The damage of an unsuccessful programme could be limited by aborting it and getting back to the point of departure without incurring any major costs (excluding the financial ones which were relatively minor).

Some employee participation programmes were not perceived by companies to meet this reversibility criterion. While the consultants felt the company could return to square one, the organizations were less convinced and shunned many such programmes. Kanter quoted a Hewlett-Packard manufacturing manager who described participation as 'a lobster trap. Once you're in it, it's hard to get out. I'm saying it's worth it, but look at the risks realistically' (Kanter 1985: 241).

What organizations feared most was buying a product which, if unsuccessful, trapped them into a fiasco. The manager stood to lose if a particular programme did not work, but had literally no choice but to remain fully committed to it, even in the face of failure (Staw 1980: 74). Kanter (1985: 221) identified a range of other characteristics of innovations which, in her view, made them particularly attractive to potential buyers. These are identified in Table 6.3.

The well-known marketing principles apply as much to the selling of these different management-idea products, as to other products and services. First, whenever a market opens up, new sellers will seek to enter it. The market for devices, events, techniques and programmes appears to be virtually insatiable. The entry fee needed to participate is relatively low. It consists of a basic management idea which is capable of being pro-ductivized. Here one can draw parallels with dieting (F-Plan, Cambridge Diet), keeping fit (jogging, aerobics), parenting (Dr Spock approach) as well as the fashion fields of clothes and shoes. These products and services often have a quasi-scientific basis and are frequently associated with a cult figure or guru. The most successful authors and practitioners can become millionaires. Each product tends to focus on a single dominant theme such as fibre, meditation or exercise.

Commenting on the process by which a theory or technique becomes

Table 6.3 Characteristics of OD and system-wide interventions which gave them 'manager-appeal'

Aspect	Explanation
trial-ability	they could be demonstrated on a pilot basis
reversible	company could return to pre-experiment status in the event of failure
divisible	could be introduced in steps or stages
consistent	consistent with sunk costs and built upon prior resource experience
familiar	consistent with successful past experience
concrete	tangible, discernible
congruent	fitted the organization's direction
publicity value	offered visibility for company if succeeded

established, Gellner (1985) explained that at the start of its promotion, big 'pump-priming' claims were essential if it was to take off. Once the idea become institutionalized, the vested interests connected with it, plus the overall impetus, acted to project and protect it. At this point, the intervention could downgrade or even disclaim any doctrinal pretensions. In the field of management, any technique that showed the slightest sign of success tended to be rapidly and effectively advertised by its consumers. In this way, in a short time, the 'sacred fire' was stolen and spread through the hands of those who had seized it.

In passing, one can note the importance of 'word-of-mouth' advertising (Dichter 1966). The 'problem' of uncritical and indiscriminate application of management ideas is exacerbated, not only by potential customers actively seeking to make purchases of such items, but also by the predilection of successful users to do impromptu adverts on behalf of the management idea technique and the consultant or consulting company which sold it. Word-of-mouth advertising appears to be an important form of communication in the decision to purchase management-idea products. Preedy (1987) put it thus:

> Buying consultancy is rather like buying a suit; you ask your contacts about suppliers, prices and quality, and you listen for satisfaction that seems to fit your need. You can buy off-the-peg solutions, or you can get them tailor made, but there are similar opportunity costs in both courses.
>
> (Preedy 1987: 21)

Product development

In marketing, the product life cycle (PLC) concept (see Figure 6.3) holds

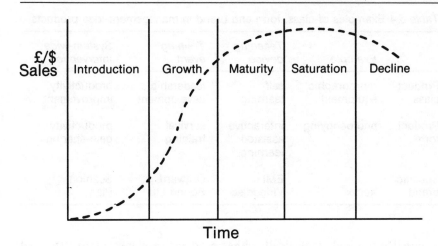

Figure 6.3 Product life cycle

that products go through stages of development determined by consumer demand. Five stages are identified: introduction, growth, maturity, saturation and decline. Marketeers have used the concept to help identify where in the cycle a company's products are. It allows them to pinpoint those which need replacing, revamping, relaunching or discontinuing. Marketing writers counsel caution in the use of this concept and quote examples of products which do not fit the theory. Nevertheless, the PLC does offer a useful framework within which to consider a key aspect of management idea techniques.

In using the PLC concept it is important to distinguish between the life cycle of a product *class*, the product *form* and the specific *brand*. This is because each one of the three tends to follow a different life cycle pattern. The life cycle of a product class tends to be longer than either the form or the brand. Table 5.5 clarifies the differences by comparing a tangible product with comparable examples of teaching devices, training events and system-wide interventions.

Some management-idea entrepreneurs have made use of this concept. There is evidence to suggest that they have analysed their product, the current market, the nature of the industry and the competition. There are a number of teaching devices, training events, OD interventions and system-wide programmes which were originally developed in the 1960s, and which continue to be sold in the 1990s. In order to discuss and illustrate these ideas systematically, it is useful to use Ansoff's (1968) product-market matrix which is shown in Figure 6.4.

The matrix is helpful for organizing one's thoughts, although it is in fact

Table 6.4 Examples of class, form and brand in management-idea products

	Example	Teaching device	Training event	System-wide intervention
Product class	reprographic equipment	self-learning	leadership development	productivity improvement
Product form	photocopying	interactive assisted learning	survival training	productivity gain-sharing
Specific brand	Xerox	EMI Videodisc	Outward Bound Ltd	Scanlon Plan

impossible to divide realistically either products or markets into either old or new, since both are frequently developed. Hence there are many intermediate points along each dimension. The four cells shown should be considered as extreme points of a matrix with numerous additional cells in between. Nevertheless, one can consider each quadrant and give examples from the field of management-idea-based techniques.

MARKETS

	Old	New
Old	(1) Selling more to increase market share	(2) Repackaging of existing product to make it acceptable to new customers; also franchising.
New	(3) Product innovation or upgrade based on perceived customer needs	(4) True innovation

PRODUCTS

Figure 6.4 Product market mix and mangement-idea products

Quadrant 1: old products in old markets

This involves the continued selling of existing products to existing customers. The hope is to attract more customers from these old markets.

Quadrant 2: old products in new markets

In the management-ideas field, many developers use franchising. Franchising is a form of marketing and distribution by which one company grants another the right to use any tangible or intangible possession it owns for the purposes of trade, in return for some benefit. The possession in question may be a patent, recipe, trademark or business method which cannot be obtained without legal action. For the granter of the franchise, the benefit it yields is expansion for a low investment and the receipt of fees, royalties or profits. A franchisee can benefit from initial training, ongoing support, and centralized marketing and purchasing.

Once the product has been successfully developed and marketed, it is available for franchising. In the case of a management course, the first step is for the owning company to license the franchisee. This may be a training company which will offer the courses under licence in one country, or it may be a manufacturing company which buys a licence to run a course 'in-house'. In the case of the former, the training company acts as an agent for the owning company. Thus the Adizes Institute has licensed the Danish Management Centre in Copenhagen to use the Adizes Method for Synergistic Management. Busvine Associates Ltd run in-company and public seminars. When they use Reddin's 3-D Managerial Effectiveness (see Exhibit 6.5) materials on these they pay the latter a royalty.

Quadrant 3: new products in old markets

Blake and Mouton's Grid Development events serve as a good illustration of the strategy of adapting an existing product to fit a new market. Their company, Scientific Instruments, Inc., segmented its market for the Grid Management events. The original Grid event was undifferentiated. They must have judged there to be different markets or market segments which exhibited the same broad characteristics. These segments formed different markets which warranted the development or customization of the basic product. Exhibit 6.6 shows how Scientific Instruments, Inc., segmented their training events by occupation and managerial level. The initial extension of the general Grid Management event was to senior managers, junior managers and supervisors, and then to salespeople, nurses, academic administrators, estate agents and social workers

The later extension of Grid Management events occurred not in terms of its content (management style issues applied to different groups), but of the instrument-backed learning device. These applications were to fields such as stress management, critiquing (feedback) and marital relationships. Thus the teaching device used in the Grid Management events (i.e. the twin axis model plus the instrument) which previously had been the vehicle to convey the theory of leadership (the means to an end), now became an end in itself.

Grid Management events were originally launched in the mid-1960s. At

FOR A.T.M. MEMBERS' INFORMATION

THE 3-D MANAGERIAL EFFECTIVENESS SEMINAR
designed by Dr. Bill Reddin
and the subject of the article in the Autumn edition of MEAD
"TWENTY YEARS OF TRANSNATIONAL EXPERIENCE"
is run in-company and publicly in the UK

BUSVINE ASSOCIATES LTD will run public seminars at
Oxford or Kenilworth on the following dates in 1986 & 1987

1986
September 28 – October 3
October 26 – October 31
November 23 – November 28
1987
January 18 – January 23
February 15 – February 20

1987
March 22 – March 27
April 26 – May 1
May 31 – June 5
June 28 – July 3
September 27 – October 2
November 8 – November 13

If you want to discover more about our planned change and
development consultancy work which uses the Managerial
Effectiveness Seminar and the associated 3-D Managerial
Effectiveness Concepts – please contact

MICHAEL FORRER   **ROBERT BUSVINE**

BUSVINE ASSOCIATES LTD
9 PEMBROKE ROAD
SEVENOAKS KENT TN13 1XR
Telephone: 0732-453125

3-D

IN ASSOCIATION WITH W.J.REDDIN AND ASSOCIATES

Exhibit 6.5 Advertisement for a licensed training event

The Managerial Grid

The Social Worker Grid

The Grid for Sales Excellence

The Marriage Grid

The Real Estate Sales Grid

Grid Approaches to Managing Stress

Grid Approaches for Managerial Leadership in Nursing

The Academic Administrator Grid

The New Managerial Grid

Management by Principles

Making Experience Work: The Grid Approach to Critique

The New Grid for Supervisory Effectiveness

Corporate Excellence Through Grid Organization Development

The Versatile Manager: A Grid Profile

Exhibit 6.6 Product development of the Managerial Grid

that time, Scientific Methods, Inc., saw the product in the growth stage, and must have worked actively to counter the usual pattern of decline and saturation taking place by introducing product innovation on a regular basis. Part of this is reflected in their publications stream which was concerned with revamping the basic Managerial Grid concept. The original book on which the Grid programme was based was published in 1964 and entitled *The Managerial Grid* (Blake and Mouton 1964). Four years later, the same authors wrote *Corporate Excellence Through Grid Organization Development* (Blake and Mouton 1968). This was followed by *The New Managerial Grid* (Blake and Mouton 1978) and by *Managerial Grid III* in 1986 (Blake and Mouton 1985). Their publication stream continues.

Quadrant 4: new products in new markets

There are four major product invention strategies available to those who sell new teaching devices, training events, OD interventions or system-wide programmes in new markets. First, there is the *guru strategy* where an academic, consultant or manager writes or ghost-writes a book which then becomes the basis of a product line which includes seminars, video and audio-tapes and workbooks. Second, the *research strategy* involves going down the research and development route to generate original, research-based management ideas which are then developed into one of the four techniques. Third, there is the *revision strategy* which involves taking existing management-idea-based techniques (devices, events, interventions or programmes) making revisions to them, and then selling them under your own brand name. Finally, there is the *development strategy* in which consultants take existing management ideas which have not been previously productivized, and develop their own branded techniques out of them. Let us consider each of these in turn.

Guru strategy

In the guru strategy, the book is the starting-point. It has to be a best-seller since this brings its author's name to the attention of a wide audience. The book itself can be a major source of income for the author. *In Search of Excellence* and *The One Minute Manager* have sold millions of copies, earning their authors large sums in royalties. The original book creates an audience for the public training events. These may be video-taped or audio-taped and sold as teaching devices.

Research strategy

The research strategy is well illustrated by the original work of Kepner-Tregoe. This company was founded by Drs Charles H. Kepner and Benjamin B. Tregoe and was based on their work on problem-solving. The approach was described in their original book, *The Rational Manager* (Kepner and Tregoe 1965). During the 1950s both authors worked for the Rand Corporation in California on advanced airforce defence systems. Following a period of conceptualization, empirical research, testing and simulation, Kepner and Tregoe discovered fourteen concepts relevant to the process of problem-solving and decision-making. After five years of work on this topic, the Rand Corporation did not wish to pursue this line of inquiry, and so the two researchers left the company to set up their own consultancy. They have developed programmes for senior, middle and junior managers, sales managers, supervisors and public sector companies. They train and license managers to act as course leaders to conduct in-house Kepner-Tregoe seminars and they monitor these to maintain standards.

Revision strategy

The revision strategy takes an existing topic of managerial interest and develops or adapts what already exists. This is then sold as a different product. An example of this is the topic of team member roles. In the late 1970s Meredith Belbin conducted research into the characteristics of teams which were most successful in business games. He concluded that teams whose members possessed certain complementary traits had the greatest

Source: Margerison and McCain 1984

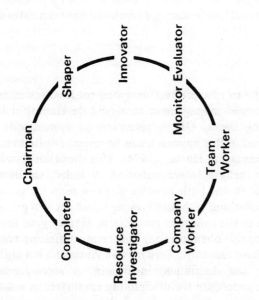

Exhibit 6.7 Example of a revision strategy: Team Roles
Source: Belbin 1981

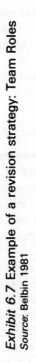

chance of winning. His ideas were published in a book (Belbin 1981) which formed the basis of a series of workshops on the subject organized by the British Association for Commercial and Industrial Education and taught by him.

The topic of complementary team member characteristics was investigated by Margerison and McCann (1984). These writers described how they conducted their own independent research to produce their own set of group member role labels. The 'Belbin 8' model and the Margerison and McCann 'Team Management Wheel' model are shown in Exhibit 6.7. Their Team Management Resource consists of a number of products including a book (*How to Lead a Winning Team*); a teaching device (The Margerison-McCann Management Index); a training event for managers (based on the instrument and focused on team-building); and a training event for trainers (to instruct company training staff as to how to run courses using this approach). This revision strategy on the topic of group member roles has a long tradition going back to the work of Benne and Sheats (1948) and Bales (1950).

A better known and equally spectacular product revision concerns Hersey and Blanchard's 'Life Cycle Theory of Leadership'. This was renamed 'Situational Leadership' and then acronymized to LEAD (see Exhibit 6.8). LEAD spawned a great variety of spin-off devices including a profile, instrument, handout, poster, film and simulator. Like Blake and Mouton's 'Grid Management' programme, whose approach (two dimensions and a grid) has been applied to other contexts such as marriage and stress management, the Situational Leadership approach too has been extended to parenting.

Development strategy

The development strategy to new product development involves taking an existing but unproductivized management idea, and developing it into a teaching device, training event, OD intervention or system-wide programme. Two illustrations of this approach can be given. The first involves a piece of academic research by Harvey (1974). This drew the conclusion that groups could often behave in ways that all its individual members opposed. He argued that it was both possible and common for groups of people to agree about something without knowing it and act as a group in a way which was opposed to the collective group view. Harvey gave the label 'The Abilene Paradox' to this phenomenon. This research finding has been developed into a video-based teaching device by an American management training film company and distributed in Britain. A second example involves research into a procedure for disciplining employees in a manner which places responsibility on them to change their own behaviour. The label given to this approach is 'Discipline Without Punishment'. The

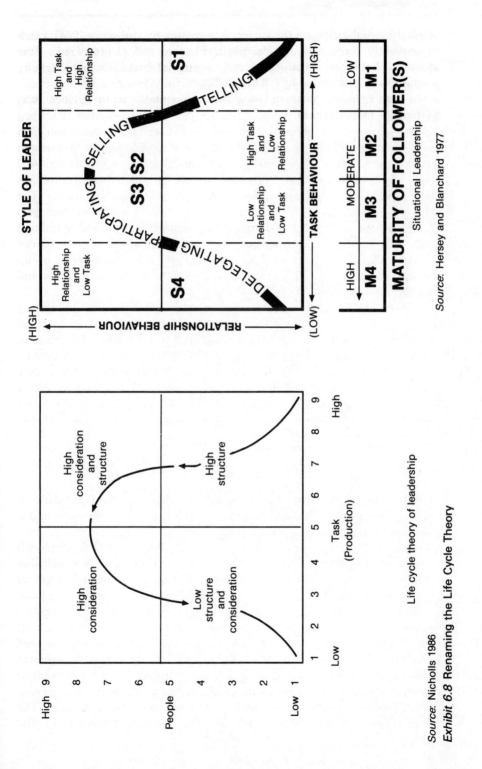

STYLE OF LEADER

RELATIONSHIP BEHAVIOUR

(HIGH)

High Relationship and Low Task

High Task and High Relationship

Low Relationship and Low Task

High Task and Low Relationship

(LOW)

TASK BEHAVIOUR ⟶ (HIGH)

PARTICIPATING

SELLING

TELLING

DELEGATING

S3 S2

S1

S4

MATURITY OF FOLLOWER(S)

Situational Leadership

HIGH	MODERATE		LOW
M4	M3	M2	M1

Source: Hersey and Blanchard 1977

High consideration and structure

High consideration

High structure

Low structure and consideration

People

High 9
8
7
6
5
4
3
2
Low 1

1 2 3 4 5 6 7 8 9
Low   Task   High
         (Production)

Life cycle theory of leadership

Source: Nicholls 1986

Exhibit 6.8 Renaming the Life Cycle Theory

original journal article on the subject was written by Huberman (1964) and subsequently elaborated by Campbell, Fleming and Grote (1985). The approach has been transformed into a a video-based teaching device, produced and distributed by CRM/McGraw-Hill video. As a training event it has been renamed 'Positive Discipline' and is marketed by Performance Systems of Dallas, Texas.

Chapter 7

Public presentation of management gurus' ideas

INTRODUCTION

To complete our understanding of what distinguishes a popular management idea from an ordinary one, in addition to considering the content of the ideas themselves, how they meet management needs, the time of their launch and their promotion, it is also necessary to pay attention to the process of their public communication by their inventor or promoter.

Historically, the role of the idea presenter has been important. Frederick Taylor gave a public presentation of his ideas on scientific management in New York's Grand Palace in 1914 which was attended by 69,000 people (Reich 1984). However, the best documented public presentation of his ideas was at the Congressional hearings concerned with the adoption of scientific management at the Watertown Arsenal in Massachusetts in 1911. Elton Mayo, the driving force behind the promulgation of human relations ideas, was a regular speaker at conferences of business people. At these events, he spent as much time promoting governmental non-interference in business, as his own ideas about management.

It is true that, in its traditional form, the public lecture as a means of mass communication and influence has greatly declined, if not completely disappeared. Jesus preaching to the multitudes, John Wesley on the hillside, Adolf Hitler at the Nuremberg rallies. The sight of British politicians undertaking a punishing round of speeches in church halls up and down the country at election time is largely a thing of the past. Indeed, the appearance of a mass lecture of the traditional variety, such as Billy Graham's evangelism at Wembley Stadium before an audience of thousands of listeners, is such a rarity that it is deemed worthy of press coverage.

Nevertheless, while public speaking as a mass communication mode has been supplanted by the electronic media, the public speech is still required. Prime ministers still speak to millions from the rostrum at their annual party conference, but now through television. If the listeners cannot come to the speakers, the speakers will go to their audience through television, video-tape or audio-tape. Most of the modern gurus have produced these types of audio-visual training materials. Some have even had a mini-TV series of their own. Interestingly, our assessment of the credibility of the speaker's ideas, beliefs and pronouncements seems to be largely dependent on how he or she comes over on these occasions, even though there is no logical relationship between what they say and how they say it.

In a study of communication, Mehrabian (1968) estimated that audiences in general devoted 50 per cent of their attention to how presenters *spoke*, 42 per cent to how they *looked* and only 8 per cent to what they *said*. This finding is particularly relevant to the world of management. Gowler and Legge (1983) argued that management had an oral tradition. The importance of this has been stressed in the research findings of Mintzberg (1973), Stewart (1976) and T. R. V. Davis and Luthans (1980). All these writers have demonstrated what a great part oral communication plays in a manager's job. Their data suggest that between a half and three-quarters of a manager's time is devoted to giving and receiving information in a non-written mode. Stewart (1976: 92), for example, reported that 'management is a verbal world whose people are usually instructed, assisted and persuaded by personal contact rather than on paper'. The ideas of some management writers, such as Rosabeth Moss Kanter, are held to be more accessible by listening to her 'in the flesh' than by reading her books (*Personnel Management* 1986: 19).

Not only do managers appear to prefer to be told things, rather than having to read them for themselves, but also they appear to place the responsibility on the speaker to entertain them while communicating the information. Salaman and Butler (1990) listed the traditional assumptions made by management educators and trainers as to the conditions under which managers learned. Managers preferred learning-by-doing, valued experience, and expected the topic to have an obvious, practical and immediate application. Paradoxically, these authors claimed that while in one sense the approach was active (doing things), in another sense it was passive. Managers-as-learners expended little effort to discover the relevance, application or practicability of the general propositions offered to their personal situation or problem. A sort of 'fast food' approach to learning was offered in which the tiresome preparation was eliminated, but perhaps the goodness was removed as well?

Most significantly, Salaman and Butler noted that this placed the responsibility for the success of any learning event as much (if not more) on the trainers as on their material. They wrote that:

> It defines the trainers as performers, absolutely central to the delivery and success of the material, and rewards them appropriately. Form may be as important as content in a milieu where success – as re-employment – depends on audience appraisal and a high need for certainty and technique.
>
> (Salaman and Butler 1990: 185)

John Wesley, the Methodist preacher of the late nineteenth century, offers a historical case study in effective public-speaking skills executed in a religious setting. Performance-wise he was effective, converting thousands of listeners, and building up an effective structure which perpetuated his teachings, and which is still in existence today.

The idea that there may be some connection between what Wesley did on a cold and windy hillside some two hundred years ago, and what the management guru does in a centrally heated, luxurious hotel auditorium in the late twentieth century, may seem absurd. Even more bizarre might appear the link between a guru's presentation and the brain-washing techniques used in different parts of the world in the post-1945 period of the Cold War. This chapter will argue not only that there is a great similarity between these different approaches, but also that given their effectiveness, they tend to be used, in a modified form, by many management platform presenters.

Since the end of the Second World War, the public visibility of management idea presenters has steadily increased. The proponents of neo-human relations, which was the dominant management idea of the 1960s and 1970s, were the business school academics and consultants. They were joined in the 1980s have by the hero-managers. During the 1980s both achieved (perhaps temporarily) pop star ratings, and were able to fill auditoria with managers eager to listen to them. Some of the audience members were attracted by the speaker's reputation, and read his book only after they had seen and evaluated his performance.

While managers may be drawn to a seminar by the guru's reputation, they may not necessarily be sufficiently convinced to go on to implement his ideas. From the guru's perspective, it is in his interest to make a convert, since this can mean additional in-company speaking engagements or consultancy opportunities. How can the speaker persuade the members of his audience to his way of thinking if they are not already predisposed to it?

A realistic aim of the guru's persuasive communication is not that his ideas should necessarily and immediately modify the *actions* of his audience, but that they should alter their *beliefs, attitudes* and *feelings* towards his suggestions. Psychologists confirm that these aspects of the listener's personality are quite capable of being changed by persuasive speaking. Changes in these, in turn, can lead ultimately to changes in the listener's *behaviour*. The psychological literature offers ample guidelines on how to change attitudes, while philosophical writings offer us insights into *rhetoric* – the art of speaking effectively. Suggestions from both these sources will be garnered and focused on the question of how to influence managers successfully in a public-speaking situation. Aristotle, the Greek philosopher, was among the first to acknowledge that *how* something was said had a great influence on whether the idea was adopted or not. Indeed, he distinguished between three modes of persuasive appeal which were based on *ethos* (source credibility), emotional appeal and logical proof. Aristotle wrote that:

> Of the modes of persuasion furnished by the spoken word there are three kinds. The first depends on the personal character of the speaker; the second on putting the audience into a certain frame of mind; and the third on the proof or apparent proof, provided by the words of the speech itself. Persuasion is achieved by the speaker's personal character when the speech is so spoken as to make us think him credible. . . . This kind of persuasion, like the others, should be achieved by what the speaker says, not by what people think of his character before he begins to speak. Secondly, the persuasion may come through the hearers, when the speech stirs their emotions. . . . Thirdly, persuasion is effected through the speech itself when we have proved a truth or an apparent truth by means of the persuasive arguments suitable to the case in question.
>
> (Aristotle, *Rhetorica*, in McKeon 1941)

Aristotle's reference to *mode* of persuasion has already been discussed in Chapter 2 which focused on management idea content. Here the preferred contents of ideas were discussed, as well as which forms of presentation best 'convinced' management audiences. Hence, this chapter will focus on the first two modes, the speaker's character and the emotional reponse of the audience.

SPEAKER'S CHARACTER

Aristotle referred to 'ethos' or the perceived character of the speaker. He felt that behaviour that revealed a presenter to his audience as being of high character, intelligence and goodwill acted to create a persuasive influence. Operationally, ethos was defined as expertness, trustworthiness and personal dynamism. Let us consider these three factors in that order.

Expertness

What do we know about perceived expertness? Kuhn (1970) cited the case of a research paper written by a well-respected writer on electro-dynamics whose name had been accidently omitted from it when the paper was first circulated. It was regarded as a hoax among fellow scientists until its authorship was revealed whereupon it became accepted. Speakers' reputations affect the audience's perception of the truth and value of the content of their ideas.

A more controlled and more famous experiment, known as the 'Dr Fox Lecture', was carried out at the University of Southern California's Medical School (Naftulin *et al.* 1973). It was given by a Dr Myron Fox to a group of psychologists, psychiatrists, administrators and educationalists. Their response was unanimously favourable. They described the presenter as 'knowledgeable' and the presentation as 'excellent'. In fact, 'Dr Fox' was an actor who had been given a fictitious curriculum vitae and been trained to give the lecture. Although based on a real article, the lecture itself was filled with contradictory statements, double-talk and *non sequiturs*. The researchers were interested in studying the effects of personality on the ratings of lecturers. They concluded that presentation was more important than content, and often there was only the illusion that anything had been learned. Kuhn's and Naftulin *et al.*'s findings confirm the adage that one has to 'know to see' rather than 'see to know'.

Trustworthiness

Turning now to trustworthiness, Aristotle's notion does have an intuitive appeal. Discussing the ethos of ex-President Ronald Reagan, Morrow wrote that:

> He discovered what it means to be 'together' with an audience, to stand on stage and capture the people. Acting, when it achieves the right harmonics between performer and audience, is a work of almost intimate leadership. The actor enters into the minds of others and leads them through the drama, making them laugh or cry, making them feel exactly what he wants them to feel. It is a powerful and primitive transaction, a manipulation, but at its deepest level, a form of tribal communion. The 'Great Communicator' has come to communicate with the American people on the tribal level.
>
> (Morrow 1986: 8)

What Morrow was describing was the concept of *identification* from psychoanalytic theory which Burke (1962) explained in the following way:

> A is not identical with his colleague B. But insofar as their interests are joined, A is identified with B. . . . Yet at the same time, he remains unique, an individual locus of motives. Thus he is both joined and separate, at once a distinct substance and consubstantial with another.
>
> (Burke 1962: 544–5)

To use an analogy from the physical world, when two tuning forks of equal frequency are placed near each other, one struck, placed alongside the other and then, after a time, stopped, a sound can be heard from the unstruck one. This is called 'sympathetic vibration' and requires the two bodies to have identical resonant frequencies. Humans may have similar psychological resonant frequencies. Research on personality shows that we are most influenced by our closest friends and relatives. At management seminars, there may be a tendency for the audience members to respond to the speaker since both will share broadly common categories and strategies in thinking about the world of work. Effective speakers will adapt themselves, and attempt to speak the language of their listeners.

Politicians have traditionally been keen for their audiences to perceive them as trustworthy, expert and dynamic. At least part of that perception is created by their physical appearance, that is how they look and how they speak. In Morrow's view, Ronald Reagan's ability to appear as authentic to his audience was one of his greatest strengths. This is why the American people tended to trust Reagan, even though they may have not agreed with his principles.

One thing that successful politicians and management gurus have in common is a clear, umambiguous set of strongly held beliefs. To persuade others, effective speakers have first to believe themselves. Morrow noted, 'There's an old rule in Hollywood that when your face is up there on the screen in close-up, if you don't believe the line you're speaking, the audience will know it, and they won't believe it either'. Tom Peters, the most successful and among the most highly paid business speakers, is typically referred to as an *evangelist*, *missionary* or *revolutionist*.

The possession or absence of an unqualified belief or mission determines both the language and mode of presentation that the speaker can use. The believer can come over as involved, forceful and exciting. The sceptic, typically a business academic presenting research findings with disclaimers and guarded generalizations, often comes over as detached, reticent and boring. The believer repeats the same message to different audiences, while the academic tends to present different messages to the same audience.

It may be that a crucial difference between vibrant oratory based on belief and guarded research findings is that the former appeals to the emotions, while the latter addresses itself to the intellect. Horace Walpole commenting on John Wesley's preaching style commented, 'evidently an actor is Garrick. He spoke his sermon so fast, that I am sure that he has often uttered it, for it was like a lesson. There were parts and eloquence in it; but towards the end, he exalted his voice, and acted very ugly enthusiasm' (Knox 1950: 84, note 1).

Knowing about the importance of perceived authenticity, how does one establish it? Reagan did it through his public performances on television. *Looking* sincere was important. The use of the hidden transparent tele-prompter screen allowed him to look directly at his audience and the television viewers. Margaret Thatcher and other politicians at party conferences have extended the use of the technique. The increased eye-contact with the use of these 'sincerity machines' helps speakers appear more authentic and trustworthy.

Personal dynamism

The third aspect of Aristotle's ethos was personal dynamism. Was this not an innate personality feature that one either possessed or did not? Interestingly, Atkinson (1984) discovered that spell-binding oratory, often referred to as speaker dynamism or charisma, boiled down to a limited number of behavioural (and hence learnable) speaking techniques which have been known for over a thousand years. These techniques, in turn, reduced to one dominant strategy.

That strategy is simply not to use a script when speaking. To the audience, the absence of speaker notes implies that the presenter is speaking spontaneously. The speaker is therefore perceived to be more genuine or authentic. The decision not to use a script has a number of other persuasion-enhancing spin-offs. Freed from notes, speakers can add emphasis with carefully co-ordinated head, hand and arm movements. These are particularly important when presenting to a large audience. Speakers are also able to sustain longer continuous eye-contact with their audience, monitoring and responding to their listeners. Keeping them constantly under surveillance is also a means of keeping their attention. The use of body language clearly signals to the audience the effort that speakers have put, and are putting, into the delivery of their speech.

If the first recommendation is not to use a script, then the second is not to use glasses. Few of the great orators in history have worn glasses. Hitler needed glasses, but wore them only in private. For his public speeches he discarded them and had his speech headings typed in half-inch type. Why should glasses be avoided? Atkinson (1984) explained that humans are the only primate species in which the irises are framed by visible areas of whiteness. He claims that the evolutionary significance of this has to do with the communicative importance of our eyes. The whites of our eyes make it relatively easy for audience members to track even slight speaker eye-movements over large distances.

Using examples from one of the Labour Party's most charismatic speakers, Tony Benn, Atkinson illustrates the power of eye contact. He contrasts this with the case of the late Oxford philosopher, A. J. Ayer who, after an accident, had to wear dark glasses when lecturing. He found it difficult to keep the attention of his large student audience. Heritage and Greatbatch (1986) studied the part played by speech delivery (intonation, timing and gestures). They concluded that elements of delivery were used by successful speakers to inhibit or encourage applause ('work the audience'). Techniques identified included gazing at the audience at or near the point of message completion; delivering more loudly than surrounding speech passages; delivering with greater pitch or stress variation; markedly speeding up or slowing down; and using a variety of non-verbal gestures.

These research findings go some way towards explaining the variability of audience response to some of today's management gurus. Accounts of a Henry Mintzberg seminar held in London reported that he talked 'with expressionless eyes behind thickish lenses fixed somewhere on the back hall' (Foster 1989: 75). Many managers, consultants and academics have viewed and compared the video-taped presentations of Tom Peters, Rosabeth Moss Kanter and other American gurus. On the basis of his research, Atkinson would probably advise both Henry Mintzberg and Michael Porter to replace their glasses with contact lenses if they wanted to gain the maximum impact upon a large audience.

EMOTIONAL RESPONSE OF AUDIENCE

After speaker ethos, Aristotle's second mode of persuasion concerned the emotional response of the audience. He said that persuasion may come *through the hearers* when the speech stirs their emotions. Having paid for their tickets, one can assume that the managers in the audience are positively disposed or at least interested in the gurus and what they have to say. Here one might separate speakers' 'performance' from their ideas or prescriptions. Managers can enjoy the former without being committed to the latter. Financially, it is in the gurus' interests to turn at least a percentage of their audiences into converts, since this increases the opportunities for in-company presentations and consultancy work. Gurus therefore need not only to entertain, but also to convert the unbelievers to their views. How should they go about it?

It is useful to start thinking about this at the macro-level. Most audience members will already hold views on the subject of the presentation – be it leadership, organizational structures, innovation, quality or whatever. The guru has therefore to unhook them from their existing view or beliefs, convert them to his thinking, and then reinforce his ideas so that they are sustained in his absence. If that description sounds familiar it is because it describes the change model from the organizational development (OD) literature which was popularized by Kurt Lewin (1951). The term 'popular-ized' is used advisedly, since it will be shown that Lewin re-presented and relabelled a strategy which was developed long ago.

Lewin recognized that a person's attitude to himself, to other individuals and to other groups is central to him. It is likely to be integrated with his self-concept and personality. Schein and Bennis (1965: 275) wrote that 'Dilemmas and disconfirmations arise from . . . and in turn produce powerful emotional responses and arouse what might be called "social anxiety" or anxiety about basic sense of identity'. They went on to say that such attitudes are likely to be strongly held and would resist change. If one seeks to change such strongly held attitudes, then Lewin recommended a model which consisted of three phases – unfreezing, changing and refreez-ing. The first two phases created the conditions necessary for change to take place, while the third stabilized what change has occurred. The key mechanisms are as follows:

Phase 1 Unfreezing
  (a) lack of confirmation or disconfirmation
  (b) induction of guilt anxiety
  (c) creation of psychological safety by reduction of threat or removal of barriers to change
Phase 2 Changing
  (a) scanning the interpersonal environment
  (b) identification with a new model or idea
Phase 3 Refreezing
  (a) personal – integrating the new responses into the rest of the personality and attitude system
  (b) relational – integrating new responses into ongoing relationships and organizational practices

Lewin's view was that attitude change began by creating in a person the feeling of disequilibrium. Subjects were provided with information that challenged their image of themselves or what was unexpected. This left them feeling uncomfortable, anxious, guilty, or all three. However, for change to occur, some element of psychological safety had to exist or be offered in the situation. If not, the person would become even more rigid and defensive. The process being described here is an emotional and not a cognitive one.

In this period of manufactured disequilibrium, subjects would begin to seek new information about themselves and their situation, and redefine their beliefs on these matters. In the case of the management presentation, new information would be obtained from reading books, listening to tapes and finding out what others were doing. Subjects would also identify with some particular person whose beliefs seemed to them to be more viable. In Lewin's terminology, the changees started to see themselves from the perspective of another person or a range of other people. As their frame of reference shifted, they developed new beliefs to issues such as leadership, organizational structures, innovation and quality. The new beliefs led to new feelings which could result in new behaviours. If these new feelings and responses matched up with the manager's personality and attitudes, or if they were confirmed or reinforced by other managers, then they would be incorporated by the manager. Lewin's theory is well known to business consultants, and even some managers, but where does it originate from?

In his book, Sargent (1961) examined the techniques of indoctrination, brain-washing and thought control. He discussed these in terms of political re-education in post-revolutionary Soviet Union, China and North Korea. However, the techniques that Sargent discussed were merely elaborations of those used by John Wesley in the eighteenth century. Wesley's Journal of 1739–40 describes the basic techniques he used to make converts. An analysis of these reveals that Lewin was renaming methods used by Wesley some two hundred years ago, and described by Aristotle earlier still. Let us now examine the three phase change process in operational terms.

Unfreezing

The first step involves creating high emotional tension in the prospective convert. This is what Lewin referred to as *unfreezing*. Wesley sought to convince his listeners that a failure to achieve salvation would condemn them to eternal hellfire. A sense of urgency increased the prevailing anxiety which, through the effect of suggestibility, could infect the whole group or gathering of listeners.

Aristotle had taken the trouble actually to identify the emotions which, if touched upon by a speaker, would motivate his audience. He listed anger, love, fear, pity and envy. Scheidel (1967) reported that contemporary social science studies indicated that a moderate level of fear appeal was the most effective in producing a change in the audience's attitude. Atkinson (1984) had emphasized the role of the listeners in creating a persuasive setting in which they would *contribute to their own persuasion*. Persuasive speaking was thus a two-way process in which both the speaker and the listener contributed to the ultimate effect. Detailed accounts of Wesley's preaching report high states of emotional excitement among his congregations, leading in some instances to cases of temporary emotional collapse. Sargent reported that:

> These phenomena often appeared when he [Wesley] had persuaded his hearers that they must make an immediate choice between certain damnation and the acceptance of his own soul-saving religious views. The fear of burning in hell induced by his graphic preaching could be compared to the suggestion we might force on a returned soldier, during treatment, that he was in danger of being burned alive in his tank and must fight his way out. The two techniques seemed startlingly similar.
>
> (Sargent 1961: 18–19)

The emotional tension generated in the listeners by the preaching was so powerful that it disrupted their existing beliefs and perhaps eliminated past learning. The thought of everlasting hellfire affected the nervous system of Wesley's audience, while Ivan Pavlov, the great Russian psychologist, found that the fear of death by drowning in the Leningrad flood of 1924 wiped out his dogs' learned responses. In his writings, Tom Peters gives a detailed description of the failings of American business. It can be argued that his presentations create a similar tension in the minds of his influential audience, and thus established the conditions in which unfreezing could take place.

Sargent contended that the main reason for the failure of post-Weslyan preaching in Britain was the fashion to solely address the congregation's intellect, while failing to stir up strong emotions. He contrasted this with highly emotive religious events in the southern states of the United States and the Carribbean. For conversion to occur, he argued, subjects had to have their emotions worked up until they reached an abnormal condition of anger, fear or exaltation. It was only in this state that old beliefs, attitudes and, ultimately, behaviour patterns could be disrupted and new ones implanted. Since this point is so central, it is worth exploring in a little more depth.

The human nervous system is normally in a state of dynamic equilibrium between excitation and inhibition. If subjected to excessive stimulation (e.g. by John Wesley's or Tom Peters' preaching), it can pass into a state of excessive excitation or excessive inhibition. At this point, the brain becomes temporarily incapable of its usual intelligence functions. Sargent (1961: 41) described the high state of excitation created in the general population by the Fall of France, the Battle of Britain and the Blitz during the Second World War. In this state, large groups of people were temporarily able to accept new and sometimes strange beliefs without criticism. Critical facilities may have become inhibited in these states of anxiety hysteria, which also have the effect of increasing the state of suggestibility. Historically, these psychological processes have been used to indoctrinate ordinary people into both religious and political beliefs. It may be that a similar process may be operating at management guru seminar presentations.

The conclusion to be drawn is that the successful platform gurus are able to induce some kind of nervous tension in their audience or stir up sufficient feelings of anger or anxiety, to secure the potential converts' undivided attention, and possibly increase their level of suggestibility. The key here is to increase or *prolong the stress* in people, thereby altering their thinking processes, impairing their judgement, and increasing their openness to suggestibility. In this state, the conversion, when it comes, will happen quite unexpectedly for the subject. Roused to a pitch of indignation and anger, subjects suddenly break down and accept everything demanded of them – the need to innovate, to care for the customer, to emphasize quality, to involve employees, or whatever. Past conditioned behavioural patterns are reversed and the 'cortical slate wiped clean'. James (1914) noted that Wesley's own interviews with his converts revealed that their deliverance from sin had been instantaneous, and that the change had been wrought in a moment.

A period of intense anxiety, depression, self-questioning and indecision can precede final sanctification. Such 'softening-up' processes contribute to the disturbances of the brain functions which occur when stresses become too great, and when a protection mechanism comes into play. The intellect acts as a defence against the emotions as the old adage, 'Don't let your heart rule your head' states. Therefore, in the guru presentation context, the intellect represents an obstacle to successful conversion. Rather like the high-tech 'smart' missile which avoids enemy fire and guides itself unerringly to its chosen target, the guru's message must avoid the audience members' intellectual defences, and zero in on their emotions. Morrow summarized the essence of Ronald Reagan's appeal rather elegantly:

> Reagan overrides the print press and captures the electronic image-making tools. The image, without the mediation of language, feeds directly into the [viewer's] brain. Reagan goes directly into the American bloodstream, the American consciousness.
>
> (Morrow 1986: 8–9)

Thus Aristotle, Wesley, Lewin and Sargent all agree that the first phase of the change process involves unfreezing potential converts from their past beliefs by mounting an emotional assault on their brains. The primary objective is not to change their behaviour, but to change their attitudes and beliefs.

What evidence is there to suggest that successful platform gurus actually do this? Currently, primary data are unavailable. Even secondary sources, such as the detailed accounts of successful management guru presentations, are scarce. Thus, all that can be done is to review any existing partial secondary accounts of guru presentations for any evidence that these change processes may be in operation.

The most comprehensive report of a management guru presentation is provided by Oliver (1990) and consists of an account of a 'Theory of Constructs' seminar conducted by Eli Goldratt. Goldratt is a highly influential international management consultant. He is the co-author of *The Goal* (Goldratt and Cox 1989), a book that has been read by thousands of managers. Goldratt's ideas and techniques for improving the management of operations have been adopted by many companies. Goldratt represents a highly successful idea inventor and presenter. The intention is to study Oliver's account of Goldratt's seminar, in order to analyse his presentational techniques which appear to be so successful.

We are looking for any evidence to suggest that Goldratt addresses his comments at the audience's emotions and not just at their intellect, following in the tradition of Wesley. Oliver reports Goldratt's reference to an old order which he labels the 'cost world', and a new order called the 'throughput world' (which emphasizes JIT, TOC and total quality). Goldratt draws contrasts for his listeners between these two worlds to help them decide in which of the two they are currently located. He asks them questions as to whether their company produces goods and services or money; whether or not it is 'infatuated' with quality; the extent to which intangible benefits are calculated as investment decisions; and the extent to which managers in the audience respond to training rather than their intuition. Finally, Goldratt asks listeners to assess the percentage of time that they spend on crisis management. 'Any manager who spends more than 30% of his or her time putting out fires . . . is a cost world person', he says (Oliver 1990: 18).

Earlier, the slightly obscure point made by Atkinson (1984) was reported that the persuasive process was not one-way – from the persuader to the persuadees. Rather, the context was created within which the audience participated in their own self-persuasion. It was concluded that the process of successful persuasion was in fact two-way. One can argue that Goldratt's 'two world' contrast with the questions invites audience members to self-locate themselves in these two categories produced by the speaker. In this way, audience members participate in their own self-persuasion. Goldratt's response to the audience's comment that he had sold them his idea of the Theory of Constraints was 'No, you sold it to yourself' (Oliver 1990: 25).

Before moving to the change phase, one further point merits comment. This is the overriding theme of the guru presentation as a quasi-religious experience, a point which will be developed later. In the the unfreezing phase of the public presentation, this manifests itself in two ways. First, the eternal contrast between damnation and salvation, hellfire and heaven, sin and grace, good and evil. Into this traditional counterpoint, Goldratt's cost world and throughput world fit neatly. One finds it too in an account of a Henry Mintzberg presentation (Foster 1989: 74). Mintzberg talked about the *old world* ('we all thought we knew, until 1973, how to make strategy'), and the *new world* ('we have no techniques for predicting discontinuities, we can only extrapolate').

The second observation is the presentational style of the speaker. Earlier in the chapter, it was suggested that one consequence of being able to play the role of missionary (a believer in and promulgator of his own ideas) was that speakers were able to come over much more forcefully to their audience. A journalist attending another Goldratt seminar (Management Today, 1984) commented on his 'hectoring style'. An analysis of Tom Peters' videos, widely available in the UK, shows him preaching with fire and often shouting at a large audience – a spectacle which John Wesley would have found familiar. Such a presentation style is based on personal belief. Both Goldratt and Peters believe in the ability of their ideas to improve organizational performance. This allows them to speak in an evangelical style, which is something that distinguishes them from traditional academics.

Changing

Having unfrozen the audience's existing ideas and beliefs, the guru has then to change them. Festinger (1957) suggested that once a tentative explanation had taken hold in a person's mind, information to the contrary produced not corrections, but elaborations of the new explanation. Thus, once unfreezing and replacement occur, change starts rolling. But what exactly is it that is being changed? It was noted earlier that it was not so much behavioural change that was expected, as changes in managers' attitudes and beliefs. These, in their turn, led to changes in what they did and how they behaved. The effect of persuasive speaking can be viewed as a change in people's 'object of judgement' and or the way that they 'structure their categories'. Simply put, the audience member sees and assesses the same things and ideas differently.

Scheidel (1967) argued that it was not so much that, for example, managers made a new judgement on the importance of customer satisfaction as a result of attending a Tom Peters' presentation, but that rather they made a new assessment or judgement of the customer. The concept, category or set of feelings associated with the notion of *customer* were changed. In other words, it was the 'meaning' of the customer for the persuadee that was being modified.

Oliver (1990) also wrote about the 'shock value' of unsuspected events. The shock that this study revealed was in terms of the paradigm shift. It is the notion of individual conversion, in a quasi-religious way. This was discussed earlier (pp. 184–5). The psychologist's 'figure–ground' concept was used to explain the fact that while there was not anything new in the picture, what had changed was the way that the different elements in it were perceived. The concept of figure–ground can explain why, once revealed, such management ideas are treated as simultaneously significant (in the words of subjects as 'impressive', 'weighty' or 'mighty') and, also as insignificant ('trite', 'common-sense' and a 'truism'). This process of repositioning the non-threatening 'old', rather than imposing the intimidating 'new', may account for manager appeal and acceptance.

Persuasion results from changes in the beliefs and attitudes towards propositions held by listeners. These represent modifications in the concepts and associations which make up the proposition, and thus modifications in attributed meanings. The final outcome of this change sequence is in the manager's object of judgement. Thus the ends or goals of persuasive speaking are changes in the belief and attitude components of category systems, and the resulting modification of those systems. The new beliefs and attitudes, however, have to offer their holders superior methods of achieving results, and a better means of realizing their perennial needs.

Cleverley (1971: 102) identified nine reasons for changing beliefs. These were drawn directly from Firth's (1959; 1967) work on the changing religious beliefs of the natives on tl e Polynesian island of Tikopia. First, there was the economic benefit. As known experts in the field, they hoped to increase their prospects of advancement. Irrespective of their belief in the idea, they expected to be treated better by their superiors. Second, there was a conviction about the truth of an idea. Managers may be persuaded intellectually by the logic or empirical basis of the teaching. This is necessary but not itself sufficient. Third, there was comfort, that is accepting the idea not because it was thought to be correct but because it seemed to offer a more pleasant life. Fourth, there was conformity to external authority. Managers were impressed by outsiders who claimed to know the true way of doing things. Fifth, there was obedience to internal authority, that is adopting an idea because the boss had. Sixth, there was the hope of attaining increased status through conversion. Managers wanted to be seen at the forefront of organizational progress. Seventh, there was the attraction of corporate life, the feeling of fellowship created by sharing esoteric jargon and attending seminars and courses. Eighth, there was the magnetism of a mass movement which allows you to be part of a community. Finally, there was the unease at division in the community. Managers may dislike 'rocking the boat'. Hence they outwardly conform to a set of beliefs not genuinely held, in preference to appearing to be dissenters.

How is this change of belief achieved? Broadly speaking, push-and-pull factors operate. From the push perspective, John Wesley's sermons, while vividly depicting the horrors of eternal hellfire, also offered listeners an escape route from this induced mental state. A key aspect of the change phase is the *identification with a new idea*. Hellfire, company failure and redundancy are presented as being the result of a *rejection* of the offer of eternal salvation which is to be won by faith, JIT or a customer care programme. Emotionally disrupted by the described threat, managers can be rescued from the ever-lasting torture by confessing their sins and and accepting the new gospel. Salaman and Butler (1990: 185) concluded that what managers valued above all was 'certainty tied to prescription'.

A pull-factor operates to complement the push factor. The acceptance by the manager of the newly acquired view is positively reinforced. For example, managers experience a release of tension that follows the acceptance of the new position; they value the comfort of having re-established their cognitive balance (after the unpleasant cognitive dissonance experienced while being torn between the old and new views). Managers are pleased at being associated with a prestigious advocate like Peters, Kanter or Harvey-Jones and they hope for future personal gain through the organizational visibility that they will gain in advocating the new idea. All of these factors act as reinforcing rewards which, at least in the short term, will fix or set the modified viewpoint in the manager's head.

Having noted that both push-and-pull factors operate to facilitate the change, the various steps involved will be now considered. The actual change in the head is achieved as a result of a triple process of *receiving*, *focusing* and *associating*. A detailed understanding of the mechanics of these processes is important since all three can be manipulated, and one's persuasive power can thereby enhanced.

Receiving

Scheidel (1967) used the term 'receiving' to refer to the process by which a speaker's persuasive message is acquired by the listener. It includes the transmission of symbolic cues, and the modification of the message by the listener who filters and complements it. The definition implies that listeners themselves contribute much to the message that they ultimately receive. Thus the persuader and persuadee in Scheidel's terms are 'co-creators' in the situation.

The message that leaves the speaker's lips is *filtered* and complemented by the audience members. Experiments on selective perception show that listeners tend to remember material that favours their own position. The message will be filtered by listener needs, expectations and prior knowledge. A second form of message modification involves the *completing* of messages. We tend to prefer to see events as complete wholes. We not only filter out some parts, but also add something to the messages which we receive. Third, building on the previous point, we each have a tendency to *generalize* in our search for internal consistency and completeness. Managers can be persuaded by two or three special company case studies at a business seminar; they will generalize the point by adding other related cases. Humans strive for order in their existence as Chapter 5 showed.

Filtering, completing and generalizing are all essential features of the listening behaviour since without them, verbal communication would become extremely cumbersome. Speakers in their turn must always rely upon the listeners to supply some of the missing data. This knowledge is useful. The filtering process can explain why there may be a lack of response to the guru's message among those who are opposed to his viewpoint – they just don't receive his message! Completing can partly explain the response of his idea-supporters in the audience – these require only the slightest of stimulations to move them to change.

Gurus will add greatly to their persuasion if they package their idea-message into a form which is complete, that is whose parts are coherent and mutually consistent. Gurus can expect that, as their message is received by listeners, it will be narrowed and the parts that stand out the most will be emphasized and receive most of the audience's attention.

Focusing

Focusing refers to the way that a persuasive speech is organized and its elements emphasized. Focusing produces the restructuring of categories in the listeners' heads, and creates changes in their objects of judgement. A fascination with persuasive speech has led to the production of many studies and guides to effective presentation. The techniques of public speaking were first considered by the Greeks, who called the subject *rhetoric*. The Romans, in their turn, referred to *oratory*. Politicians and others who speak to persuade for a living, have consistently woven different types of discourse together, so as to gain the interest of as wide an audience as possible, for as long as possible.

Great orators from history include Adolf Hitler, Winston Churchill, John F. Kennedy, Fidel Castro and Martin Luther King. All of these seemed to have the ability to captivate their audience, inspire groups and mobilize mass opinion. Part of this success comes from their innate personality: the behaviourally modifiable parts of this have already been discussed in the section on the character of the speaker. Many British politicians, including prime ministers, perhaps because they lack innate charisma, have undergone public speaking training run by image consultants. The rest of this section examines how a speech's content, structure and delivery affects its persuasive impact on its target audience.

Larsen (1976) reported that Hitler took lessons in elocution and rhetoric, and trained himself to speak in a certain pattern, with note headings and not a full script. He spoke in paragraphs, and in passages a few minutes long. He began each passage in a moderate tone, then rose in pitch and volume. The last few words he bellowed out in an impassioned roar. This was the signal for the crowd to burst into applause. He shot out his right hand, with lifted finger, as though he had not yet finished his argument, while in fact looking at his piece of paper in his left hand to note the next topic heading. Then, when the applause subsided, he began his next passage in exactly the same manner.

Hitler paid great attention to propaganda as described in his book, *Mein Kampf*. He noted that effective propaganda involved understanding the emotional ideas of the masses and finding a psychologically correct form of gaining the audience's attention and heart (Andersen 1988). Effective propaganda was limited in length to a few points, and needed to be repeated until people understood it. Thus the essential features of effective propaganda were the same as those of effective advertising – emotional appeal, simplicity and repetition. It had to be applied uniformally and continually. Larsen's and Andersen's assessments provide a way of identifying the behaviours of the rostrum presenters who can successfully persuade.

An obvious starting-point for such research is the courtroom where the barrister seeks to persuade the jury. Although the process was researched by Atkinson and Drew (1979), the problem remained that juries listened to the proceedings in complete silence, and therefore gave little or nothing away in the form of audible responses to those passages in the advocate's talk that made an immediate and favourable impact on them. It was partly for this reason that Atkinson (1984) switched his attention to situations in which the audience gave a clear and unambiguous audible response – the conferences of British political parties.

The fundamental problem that faces all public speakers, be they politicians, management gurus, trade union leaders or university lecturers, is the immense potential that they have for boring their audiences. The talk in their speeches, seminars, conference presentations and lectures goes on for a very long time as compared to most other forms of human communication. However, it is not just an issue of time duration. As important is the fact that, on these occasions, the normal turn-taking of normal conversations is suspended. Human communication values brevity and succinctness, and normal talk involves balanced interaction between the speakers. The person who monopolizes a conversation is treated as a bore. Atkinson (1984) noted that in terms of their typical duration, speeches and sermons represented an intolerable imposition on the patience of their listeners, unless of course, the speakers, through their performance, proved otherwise.

Apart from breaking the established mores of social communication interaction, what is the problem with prolonged, public speaking? Fundamentally it is that formal presentations do not offer their listeners the opportunity to speak, which weakens their basic incentive to pay attention. The onus is therefore put on the speaker to 'attract, sustain or upgrade the attentiveness of audience members who might otherwise be inclined to go to sleep' (Atkinson 1984: 11).

It was noted earlier that the absence of a script and of glasses permitted speakers to establish eye contact with their audience, keep them under constant surveillance, and thereby maintain their attention. In addition, some public speaking events provide the audience with an opportunity to express applause, and such applauding can act as a substitute response for those deprived of the opportunity to speak. The audience therefore communicates and hence participates, not by speaking, but by clapping, cheering, whistling, booing and even shouting slogans.

The presentations of management gurus are not usually punctuated by interspersed applause in the way that those of politicians are. However, an analysis of party political speeches can reveal ways in which management ideas can be 'packaged' for presentation, so as to elicit 'silent applause' and the approval of the audience. Whether applauding actively or silently, the audience can become involved in the guru's presentation by looking for verbal and non-verbal cues given by the speaker, as to when it is their turn to participate mentally or verbally. These indicate to the audience when to express surprise, to smile or to laugh out loud. Searching for these cues to make the appropriate reaction, represents an example of audience participation, and thereby maximizes audience response.

Atkinson (1984) analysed the complex rules of rhetoric, including allegory and antithesis, metaphor and metonym, periphrasis and pleonism.

His findings were clear and unambiguous. He argued that audiences were most likely to respond to two types of speaker statements. First, those which were verbally constructed to *emphasize* and highlight their contents against the surrounding background of speech. Second, those statements which *projected a clear completion point* to the audience, for the message in question. To achieve such a response from the audience, Atkinson recommended the use of *claptraps*: a claptrap was a trick, device or language designed to catch applause. By using a claptrap the presenter instructed an audience, in a step-by-step manner, towards a precise moment in the very near future, when all were to do the same thing at the same time. Among the most well-known and explicit claptraps are 'Ready, steady, . . . ' and 'Hip, hip, . . .'. The former leads to a race start, while the latter evokes a co-ordinated audience cry of 'Hooray'!

To be successful, claptraps have to help a speaker 'work the audience'. Used simultaneously or in sequence, they allow the speaker to co-ordinate the activities of a large number of audience members, not all of whom will be paying attention to what the speaker is saying. By synchronizing verbal and non-verbal signals, the speaker gives the audience a high chance of spotting at least one of the claptraps, so that the audience react (applaud) together on cue. Speakers have to make it clear to their listeners that they have launched into the final stage of their message sequence, at the end of which a reaction or applause from the audience is required. Second, the speaker has to supply them with enough information, to enable them to anticipate the precise point at which the message will be completed.

Research by Atkinson (1984) of actual oral performances at political conferences suggests that there are only a few effective claptrap devices. Half of all outbursts of applause were accounted for by only two claptraps. Heritage and Greatbatch's (1986) study of 476 political speeches attested to the conclusion that audience responses were strongly influenced by the rhetorical construction of political messages. It also confirmed that, of the seven rhetorical devices discovered, the same two were most effective in producing a spell-binding speech.

The most used verbal formation was the *two part contrast* (TPC) or antithesis, which accounted for one-third of all the applause elicited. This format often comes in the form of contrasts such as 'day and night', 'us and them' and 'young and old'. The making of a contrast between items is an adaptable and widely used technique for packaging and delivering applaudable messages. It was extensively described by the Greeks and Romans. Some well-known TPCs are:

Our task is not to fix the blame for the past, but to fix the course for the future. (John F. Kennedy)

All animals are equal, but some are more equal than others. (George Orwell)

Your problem is not delegating down, but getting your subordinates to delegate up.

An employee gets the boss he deserves. A manager gets the employee he deserves.

The second most effective claptrap was found to be the *list of three* (LOT), which accounted for 15 per cent of applause-eliciting verbal formats. The attraction of the three part list is in its air of unity or completeness. Among the well-known LOTs in history are the following:

Never in the field of human . . . has so much been owed by so many to so few.

Try, try and try again.

Liberty, equality and fraternity.

Successful claptraps are achieved by careful choice of words, stress on words, expert timing, and the use of pauses. For example, in a LOT, Atkinson recommended delivering the first list item with a rising intonation, while the termination of the utterance should be marked by a falling intonation. He offers very detailed descriptions of how words like 'now' and 'however' should be used. Changes in intonation, hand movements to stress words, and finger-pointing are all part of the repertoire.

Heritage and Greatbatch (1986) concluded that the audience's positive reaction was to the verbal structuring of the speech, rather than to any increased general positive response to its content. These findings, as well as those of Atkinson (1984) and Mehrabian (1968), support the general proposition that *how* presenters spoke was as (if not more) important than *what* they are actually said.

A significant conclusion of these investigators was that spellbinding oratory and the guru's 'charisma' were not the result of supernatural powers, but involved mastering a relatively small number of powerful technical skills such as the creation of TPLs and LOTs. These were used in quick succession, and were combined with secondary claptraps such as *puzzle-solution*, *headline–punchline*, the *combination, position-taking* and *pursuit*. Speakers could achieve maximum impact by carefully co-ordinating their verbal and non-verbal cues and their intonational and rhythmic signals in order to produce an invitation to applaud. The very best orators have also developed the skill of 'speaking through the applause' for even greater effect.

The problem of securing and holding an audience's attention increases as its size increases. Increased size progressively restricts both the complexity of the ideas that can be communicated, and the linguistic forms that are available to the speaker with which to convey them. The techniques of being simple and obvious may be the only ones available for use with a large audience. It is a truism that the greatest impact comes from the speaker saying the right thing, at the right time to the right audience in the right place. There is, however, no formula that will show the speaker how to articulate the sentiments that catch the mood of the audience being addressed with greater than average precision. This requires innate sensitivity. There is no data on how to 'get the pulse right'. However, once the audience's sentiments have been revealed, we know how the speech can be most effectively formulated and delivered. The TPL and LOT principles appear to be valid for the written as well as spoken word as an analysis of the content of advertising slogans, nursery rhymes and the Communist Manifesto illustrates.

Application

For people to change, they have to identify with the new model. In Oliver's (1990) account of the Goldratt seminar, the two regimes (cost and throughput) were described as different worlds separated by a psychological gulf. Value assessments became attached to them as labels of 'good' and 'bad' as the presentation progressed ('Why is something as good as improvement resisted?', 'Why is it that something so good encounters something so bad as emotional resistance?').

Once Goldratt had finished criticizing earlier models which he considered unsatisfactory, he replaced them with his own ideas. Of the exercises completed by the thirty or so participants, only one or two of them were judged to have given the 'correct' answer. Goldratt appeared to imply that to change, i.e. to move to his 'Throughput World', the managers in the audience would have to change as people:

> It will not be easy to move from a cost world to a throughput world. We have to throw away much of what we have learned over the last thirty years. . . . We've met the enemy, it is us!
>
> (Oliver 1990: 21)

Goldratt's question of where the improvement will begin was greeted with a chorus of 'us' and 'ourselves'. At this point in his account, Oliver's description of his previously reserved audience changes. They appear to become more involved and vocal:

> He then asked his audience if they wanted him to tell them how to make the necessary changes in their companies. The majority cried out 'Yes', but this time there were three or four cries of 'No, no, let us work it out for ourselves'.
>
> (Oliver 1990: 23)

In the change phase of Lewin's framework, the new model identified with can either be conceptual (e.g. Goldratt's Theory of Constraints) or human (a convert as a role model). Sargent (1961) noted that under conditions of induced excitation, the audience's tendency towards sympathy and imitation increased. Discussing the non-conformist revival, Edwards (1829) reported that 'The clergy, when in the course of their sermons, they perceived that persons were thus seized, earnestly exorted them to confess their sins'. Oliver reported that

> As the seminar resumed after lunch, Golratt introduced a large coloured gentleman to the audience. . . . The gentleman introduced himself as Emerson, and then proceeded to describe what Goldratt's ideas had done for his company.
>
> I work for a multinational company based in Southampton. Before we encountered Eli's ideas four years ago we had a turnover of $55,000,000. In the light of his ideas we made an investment of just $3,000,000. Within about a year our turnover was up to $77,000,000 and today it stands at $98,000,000.
>
> My company proves that you can make these things happen. . . . How do you transition your thought patterns from the cost world to the throughput world?
>
> (Oliver 1990: 20)

Oliver's report of Goldratt's seminar suggests that the latter is applying the techniques designed to get his audience to identify with his ideas. Although this example is set in the context of business seminar on manufacturing strategy, the techniques themselves appear to be those which have been effectively used from time immemorial.

Associating

The final aspect of the change process in which a listener's category system is restructured, is referred to by Scheidel (1967) as associating. This involves relating the personalities of the persuader and persuadee. Different versions of consistency theory by Osgood and Tannenbaum, Heider, Newcomb and Festinger (see Brown 1965) all hold that humans have a tendency to seek consistency in their cognitions. Any imbalance or dissonance triggers actions to redress the balance. However, these theories do not explain *how* this force leads to a change in position.

Scheidel claimed that an association of beliefs and attitudes can lead to a restructuring of concepts and categories in the listeners' minds which, in turn, will lead them to change their actions. For example, persuasion may occur when the persuadee associates a concept being advanced (e.g. customer care) with a concept they already favour (e.g. increased profits).

A second form of association is that of expert testimony. The film, pop or sports star promoting a product is an example of persuasion by association. When Tom Peters proposes customer care, the category (Peters) is brought into association with another category (customer care). Managers may have a set of beliefs about Peters (honest, reliable, expert, trustworthy, unbiased). However, they may know little about customer care, and this category is vague and incomplete. However, the excellence seminar has strongly associated the category 'Peters' with the category 'customer care'. The latter category will thus begin to take on some of the meaning of the former category. Thus, managers will come to consider customer care favourably because they view Peters favourably.

This transfer has been facilitated by people's natural tendency to seek harmony, congruity and symmetry in their associations. For managers to attribute high value to Peters, and low value to the concept of customer care that Peters promotes, would create in them a disequilibrium. Managers would be forced to lower their estimation of Peters. It is easier for them to regain their balance by raising their assessment of customer care. Thus, the need for balance provides the impetus, while the association of the two somewhat disparate categories (Peters and customer care) provides the situation for the persuasion. The meanings of each of the two categories become modified. It is in this process of modification that one finds the occurrence of persuasion.

A third form of association involves bringing together two concepts that the audience might favour equally, and showing how they conflict. A manager may favour strict employee direction and high profits. A persuasive speech, extolling the virtues of employee participation, might demonstrate how employee non-involvement can reduce profits. Association is the key element in the change phase. As the ideas of the persuader are associated with the ideas of the persuadee, the latter's mental categories are restructured and persuasion occurs. When the two respond similarly to the concepts and strategies of the persuasive message, and when they similarly focus on the various states of the case, persuasion takes place.

Refreezing

The third and final phase of the change process as described by Lewin involved making the change permanent. Having induced stress in people and thereby unfrozen them, eradicated their old ideas and implanted new ones, the task is to reinforce and permanently fix the change. Lewin called this refreezing, while Scheidel (1967) referred to it as *resolving*, referring to 'the process by which the re-structured categories are reinforced and thereby learned. Resolving accounts for lasting effects of persuasive speech'.

As time passes following a persuasive speech, the tendency is for the listeners to slide back, and revert back to their original beliefs and hence behaviours. The change processes of receiving, focusing and associating which have been described here occur *during* the speaking event. Once that ends, and information reception ends, the emphases and associations also end, as does the persuasive influence. If the persuading effects are to last, therefore, the listener must *learn* some aspects of the re-structured belief and attitude system. Learning theory tells us that behaviour patterns which are reinforced by rewards tend to be repeated.

Take, for example, the case of a manager who listens to Tom Peters acclaiming the importance of customer care. At the moment of the Peters' presentation, the manager's mental category of 'customer' may become restructured. This may occur because previously unknown facts are presented from a reliable source like Peters; or because an association occurs as the listener identifies with customer care; or Peters emphasizes some values that the manager holds; or because Peters' own prestige has an effect on the manager. Some or all of these factors will combine to restructure the meaning of the 'customer' for the manager, and produce a persuasive effect. As time passes, however, the influence of the last two factors which involve Peters' presence will reduce. The emphasis is lost, and the speaker becomes separated from the message in the mind of the manager.

The first two influencing factors continue, however, perhaps because listeners valued the knowledge, and this value reinforced their retention of the information provided on customer care. Our manager may also possess a strong social value, and has a need for belonging which reinforces his newly experienced association with the idea of customer care. In either case, the manager's new pattern of thinking, because it fulfils some existing need or desire, will be rewarded. Anything that meets persuadees' needs or motives represents an adequate reward for implementing the new idea in the refreezing phase. Through reinforcement, part of the persuadee's experience may be learned. As with any learning, new experiences will undergo extinction or will fade as time passes unless such experience is repeated, and occasionally reinforced. The effect of these rewards is to fix (by learning) some aspect of the guru's idea, as it is presented. This is another definition of refreezing.

Follow-up methods are important to secure follow-up gains. Once the conversion has taken place, these should be used as soon as possible thereafter. It is in this process of refreezing that is most often neglected. Potentially popular management ideas are allowed to dissipate. In contrast, Wesley divided his converts into groups of no more than twelve. These classes met on a weekly basis under an appointed leader. Initial problems relating to their conversion and future mode of life were discussed, while fear of punishment was branded as a consequence of failure to repent. Once converted, love rather than fear was used to consolidate the gain. At these meetings, members who were not found to be sincere repenters would be expelled from both the class and the Methodist Society. The power of Methodism during the eighteenth and nineteenth centuries can be attributed to these class meetings, according to Piette (1938).

Wesley's class meetings themselves derived from early Christian practice, the basis of which was the Jewish faith. This was controlled partly by the Presidents of the Sanhedrin, and partly by means of the Temple services and the synagogue system (Sargent 1961: 200). Communists divided converts into small groups or cells which were responsible to the higher Party officials. At the end of Billy Graham's preaching, the audience are invited to come down and meet counsellors. Emerson, in Oliver's (1990) account of Goldratt's Theory of Constraints seminar, also announced that he was forming a TOC club in the UK to establish a forum in which people interested in TOC could meet and exchange experiences. Perhaps it is not accidental that the spread of the Just-in-Time philosophy in Britain has been accompanied by the creation of JIT Clubs holding regular meetings. Throughout history, these arrangements, each in their different ways, have all sought to provide a follow-through that is necessary not only to make converts but also to keep them.

Chapter 8

Succession of management fads

INTRODUCTION

Managerial needs are rarely if ever satisfied, due to the nature of organizational life. The search by managers for valuable ideas is in fact encouraged rather than diminished. The changes in fashion in ideas can be explained with reference to the process of management fad displacement. The organizational problems which create the needs remain broadly constant. Thus the so-called 'new' solutions offered (management ideas and their associated techniques) tend to be similar to those which preceded them. Thus, 'old' products can be easily displaced with little psychological pain to managers, because the new ones are so similar. This final chapter considers the changing fashions in management ideas. It examines how seemingly contradictory management ideas happily coexist, and then accounts for the process of management fad creation and replacement. This is seen as the consequence of a complex interaction between management idea consumers and suppliers which operates at a number of different levels.

The author contends that the nature of organizational life in capitalist economies, coupled with the information gap between business academics and managers discussed earlier, will ensure that the cycle of management fads will continue to be with us for the foreseeable future. Virtually all of the management ideas and techniques that have been and continue to be developed are based upon the six families of management ideas presented in Chapter 2. These can be considered as the intellectual bank from which the producers of management ideas make withdrawals in order to produce what, ultimately, may become the management fad of the future.

A literature review reveals that widely differing and often mutually incompatible families of management ideas such as scientific management, human relations and guru theory continue to exist alongside each other. Are not their prescriptions contradictory? One might have expected that, with the possible exception of some historical interest, the newer ideas would replace older ones. However, a review of any management textbook or training course brochure will reveal that this has not happened. This phenomenon was observed by Woodward. Commenting on the coexistence of classical administrative management and human relations she said that:

> At first sight it appears that the approach of the traditional social scientist [human relations theory] is in conflict with the approach of the classical management theorist. Certainly two bodies of knowledge have been built up which to a considerable extent cancel each other out.
>
> (Woodward 1965: 243)

Eight explanations have been offered to account for the continued coexistence of these different management ideas. These explanations are labelled wave, ideology, performativity, complementarity, territorial, marketplace, investment and non-criticism.

EXPLANATIONS OF COEXISTENCE

Wave

The wave explanation for the coexistence of competing management ideas was offered by Watson (1986). He noted the practice of presenting management ideas as belonging to successive historical 'schools', each of which 'comes along' to discredit or displace what went before. This process of discreditation and displacement, however, did not mean the obliteration of what had been presented earlier. These older ideas in management thought continued to have a major impact on management thinking and practice.

The reason for their continued presentation was the belief that the older ideas contained insights found valuable by managers and management teachers. Ideas from the past thus remained current long after their successors had hoped that they might have been buried. New ideas were like new waves upon the shore. They arrived and appeared to cover up those which had preceded them. The impact of each new wave, however, did not replace the impact of the wave that had preceded it. According to Watson, the waves clashed and merged with each other. Their effect on the shoreline was a function of this combined clashing and intermingling.

Ideology

The ideology explanation of management idea coexistence was proposed by Anthony:

> A great deal of management education, that part of it concerned with behavioural science, is in fact, theocratic, it is designed to establish a unity of purpose and of values largely by providing managers with a common language, and a system of concepts. Management education is

truly ideological in the sense that it aims to influence behaviour by inculcating beliefs and expectations.

(Anthony 1977: 261–2)

The dissemination of a management ideology by way of management education, said Anthony, had two latent effects. It helped to promote the internal solidarity of management, and it justified its authority over subordinates. He felt that the ideological function of management education could account for the astonishing absence of controversy in management education. In Anthony's view, many of the major contributions were based on uncertain theory, applied by questionable logic, to unrelated circumstances. Much of what passed for behavioural science in his estimation did not fulfil the most elementary validity of scientific method. The theories of science stood as long as researchers failed to *overthrow* them. In contrast, management theorists advanced theories which they claimed had been 'proved' as a result of some hasty search for evidence that might *support* them. C. W. Mills (1959) wrote how management ideology was justified:

> The whole growth of ideological work is based on the need for vested interests lodged in the new power centres to be softened, whitened, blurred, misinterpreted to those who serve the interests of the bureaucracies inside and to those in its sphere outside.

(C. W. Mills 1959: 154)

Anthony went on to argue that the methodological problems of behavioural science management ideas were compounded by the vulgarization of these ideas by consultants and their simplification by teachers. They had been processed into a form that could be transmitted to managers who totally lacked a behavioural science background. Perhaps this gives us an additional clue for the lack of controversy between ideas. It would be difficult to find another field of educational activity in which intelligent and sometimes educated minds were so harmoniously disposed. There may be an occasional disagreement about educational methods in management education but rarely about basic doctrine.

Performativity

Lyotard (1984) argued that the legitimation of scientific research lay increasingly in the concept of *performativity*. This view was grounded in the belief that the primary role of research was to create wealth and to furnish industry with methods and techniques that could be commercially exploited. This represented a shift away from the stress on falsification (as emphasized by Popper 1959), away from the testing of each scientist's hypothesis, and away from debating the truth in relation to some referent of 'reality'. Instead, the discussion came to focus primarily on methods and techniques and the results which they generated. The results were pieces of information which existed in a limbo and lacked any theoretical context. The emphasis of techniques over questions led ultimately to a concern not with whether a statement was true or false, but with *what it is worth*.

The truth of a statement took a backseat and attention was shifted instead to defining and debating the performativity of the idea-technique. The methods which were the means to an end (and which were developed to test the validity of ideas) became instead ends in themselves. Attention turned away from a consideration of the validity of the ideas, and towards their techniques (e.g. time-and-motion study, organizational charting, human relations training). Lyotard (1984) himself wrote about the 'merchantalization of knowledge':

> The relationship of the suppliers of knowledge and the users of knowledge, to the knowledge that they supply and use, is now tending, and will increasingly tend to assume the form already taken by the relation of commodity producers and consumers to the commodities that they produce and consume – that is, the form of value. Knowledge is and will be produced in order to be valorized in a new production: in both cases, the goal is exchange. Knowledge ceases to be an end in itself, it loses its 'use-value'.
>
> (Lyotard 1984: 4)

Complementarity

The complementarity explanation for the coexistence of management ideas was put forward by Woodward (1965), who stated that with the growth of management education, the social sciences contribution had come to be seen as complementing rather than contradicting classical administrative management. She noted that 'the human relations movement, which developed out of the Hawthorne studies, did not question the ideas of the classical administrative approach, but took the view that modification had to be superimposed to allow for the fact that people act in response to other pressures' (Woodward 1965: 243).

She argued that if the rules of classical administrative management did not work it was due to a failure of implementation or to the workers' ability to disrupt the carefully laid organizational plans. Thus, both sets of ideas were required. Managers needed to know about human behaviour *in order to* implement and make classical administrative management rules work. Managers looked to the human relations writers to help them do this. Thus, classical administrative ideas provided managers with the basic goals, while human relations ideas contributed to the process of their implementation. The two were seen as complementary.

Territorial

The territorial explanation of coexistence was proposed by Woodward (1965) who considered it at the intellectual rather than the practical level. She argued that the phenomena to be explained by organizational theory were different from those to be explained by social science. By organizational theory she meant management theory which was held to focus on macro-organizational issues. Woodward equated social science with human relations ideas which she considered to be concerned with micro-political issues.

A second intellectual territorial separation occurred between the formal organization area (considered the proper concern of management or organization theorists) and the informal organization area (considered the proper subject for the social science theorists, that is the human relationists). This system of academic separation resulted in the writers from one school of thought not referring to the contributions of those from the other school. Social scientists at the time appeared to be prepared to accept informal organization as their own area of study. The analogy that can be made here is to the notion of non-competing groups in the labour market. The ideas do not displace each other because they are not perceived to be overlapping.

Marketplace

The marketplace explanation of coexistence sees any management education, training and development technique taking its place alongside existing ones, rather like a product on the supermarket shelf. The continued demand for a technique is based on customer acceptance and satisfaction. As with soap powder, the customers like the widest choice.

Academics argue that the true test of a management idea should not be customer acceptance but the extent to which, in the case of a theory, standards such as correspondence to facts, coherence, parsimony, pragmatism and plausibility are attained. In such a context, the relationship between any two theories becomes an adversarial one. In the scientific environment heated debates can occur as new theories based on research evidence come to challenge and refute existing ones.

Settle (1971) argued that the key constituent of science was criticism. This critical-mindedness appeared to be lacking in the field of management education. In the absence of a critical tradition (one in which error and weakness were sought out), erroneous systems are readily excused, protected and perpetuated. The nature of scientific endeavour has been summarized in the following terms:

social science operates on the basis of standards, which apply to the definition of problems and terms, and to the collection, analysis and interpretation of data. Those standards are designed to achieve objectivity and repeatability of research, and are similar to the standards applied by natural scientists.

(Huczynski and Buchanan 1982: 193–4)

Korman and Vredenburgh (1984) pointed to the failure of the 'self-correcting characteristics of scientific theory-hypothesis-testing model' in management research whereby the process of ongoing research disconfirmed existing weak theories, and replaced them with better ones. They wrote that management theories which were supported by little or no evidence continued to dominate the management literature and continued to be written about and to influence the thinking of students and practitioners.

In management much is made of 'proven' ideas and techniques. The Popperian requirement of falsification is difficult to achieve. The two orientations, those of the researcher and the manager, are diametrically opposed here. The complexity of the research has made it easy for contradictory findings to be questioned and discounted. Existing management theories tend to command the 'high ground', and are difficult to attack and dislodge. Consultants can claim that these theories have not really been disproved. Pinder (1977) commented on the low quality of social science research in general and expressed doubts as to whether theories of motivation deserved application in organizations at all.

Investment

The investment explanation of coexistence was offered by Korman and Vredenburgh (1984), who wrote about the personal investment of individual researchers in their previous writings. There were also the consultants who developed the different techniques around the management ideas, and who needed to continue to sell their 'product' (in the form of training events or OD interventions) in the marketplace. Once created, the management idea left the sphere of influence of its producers (usually the academics) and entered the world of management technique wholesalers and retailers. Knight (1975) made the point that once research findings were turned into a message and a marketable package, they were taken out of the research arena where ideas develop by being tested and disproved.

The productivization process turned the management idea into a product. A great deal of 'value-adding' took place as college lecturers developed teaching devices such as notes, handouts and exercises to teach the material. Meanwhile, management consultants 'packaged' the ideas with detailed documentation, and promoted them with glossy and expensive advertising. Not only did all this represent a significant investment of time and money among those involved, but also for many it represented their livelihood.

Thus the self-correction process represented a threat to be resisted since it could reduce the life cycle of their product. Lorsch (1979) commented on how each set of ideas or each technique becomes almost a fad with its strong advocates promulgating its early successes. Then, as a growing number of companies tried the techniques, and as reports of failure and disappointment mounted, the fad quickly died. This often repeated pattern has not, however, caused managers to lose interest in trying other management ideas which they believed could help them.

Non-criticism

How does the lack of criticism of management ideas contribute to management idea coexistence? Business school academics, traditionally the producers of most management ideas are, according to Koontz (1961), unwilling to understand each other. They are reluctant to criticize each other's ideas since it is not good selling practice 'to knock a competitor'. Koontz attributed their reluctance to integrate one set of ideas with another to the walls created by the learned disciplines, to the fear that someone or some new discovery may encroach on one's professional or academic status, or to a fear of professional or technical obsolence. He urged such 'cultists' to look at the approach and content of other views and exchange and understand them.

The critique that can be made of Koontz is that he ignores the product nature of management knowledge. There are significant marketing advantages to having one's product incompatible with that of another company, as the manufacturers of the early personal computers knew. It locks the consumers into their system. It may be that at a later point in time, compatibility becomes an advantage and an open system standard in management ideas becomes established. Becker (1973) argued that even where integration was sought, the process itself tended to create differentiation:

I have had the growing realization over the past few years that the problems of man's knowledge is not to oppose and to demolish opposing views, but to include them in a larger theoretical structure. One of the ironies of this creative process is that it partly cripples itself in order to function. I mean that usually, in order to turn out a piece of work, the author has to exaggerate the emphasis of it, to oppose it in a forcefully competitive way to other versions of truth; and to get carried away by his own exaggeration, and his distinctive image is built upon it.

(Becker 1973: xi)

The retailers of the knowledge – the managers – actively seek out panaceas and, despite repeated disappointments continue to believe that social science is capable of producing magical solutions. Andre (1985) contrasted those managers who acted primarily on the basis of science with those who acted on faith. The former looked to the accumulated knowledge of management science, not for answers but for ideas and approaches. The latter group acted on faith and adopted a particular management idea or technique because it was advocated by someone in authority or whose views they respected. These managers, said Knight (1975), wanted to be told exactly what was right and wrong, with total self assurance in words of one syllable. Guion (1975) wrote about the gullibility of managers who acted on ideas without any requirement of evidence of whether or not it would work. The essence of gullibility lay in the managers' inability or unwillingness to seek out and evaluate the available evidence or to note its absence.

These managers made little effort to seek alternative ideas. Their optimism about creating a better organization by the use of the technique was based upon their faith in the authority figure who commended it, be it a hero-manager, consultant guru or academic guru. Such a human engineering approach, while leading managers to perpetual disenchantment, also condemned them to wait continually for the next management idea to come along.

The question of whether the management idea was effective or not was relevant only if the main purpose of the exercise was an *instrumental* one. Even then, few managers who were responsible for the purchase of a management technique or the engagement of a consultant were going to admit that they had made a mistake if the technique or adviser failed to live up to expectations. However disastrous the consequences, managers were likely to say that the company had 'got what it wanted out of it'. Similarly, no consultant was going to admit that he had totally failed.

Management technique failure is less important (or irrelevant) in a situation where *expressive* goals are sought. The act of calling in consultants or the purchase of the management technique itself may be sufficient to resolve managers' inner conflict or settle their unease. Such a purchase can reassure them and reinforce a view of themselves as active and fully paid up members of the business community. Whether the bought-in technique actually achieves any measurable improvements is seen as either irrelevant or as a bonus.

The criticisms that have been made of the most popular management ideas have merely been ignored. Blackler and Brown (1980: 162) gave the example of the criticisms that were made of job design theories. These were largely ignored by their developers. These authors cite the criticisms made by Braverman (1974) and Fox (1976) who argued that the job design changes typically proposed did not greatly affect the quality of workers' lives. These comments have prompted little response from the job design consultants.

Whichever explanation is the crucial one, one can see these different pressures working together to maintain in place the wide range of different management ideas, rather than acting to sort, sift and replace them. Attention now turns to an explanation of how the techniques based on these ideas emerge and re-emerge as management fads.

SUCCEEDING MANAGEMENT FADS

Much has been written about the way in which management ideas and their techniques have come in and gone out of fashion. Often they have been dubbed panaceas, fads or flavours-of-the-month. Byrne noted that:

> Today, the bewildering array of fads pose more serious diversions and distractions from the complex task of running a company. Too many modern managers are like compulsive dieters, trying the latest craze for a few days, then moving relentlessly on.
>
> (Byrne 1986: 61)

Commenting on this almost aimless rush for instant solutions through the use of ever more ephemeral business fads, T. R. Horton (President of the American Management Association) said:

> If you tell me I can avoid a cold by taking half a pound of vitamin C, I'll want to believe you, even if it only gives me indigestion.
>
> (quoted in Byrne 1986: 54)

Pascale (1991) argued that management ideas had acquired the 'velocity of fads' in the post-1945 period. He attributed this to the ascendance of *professional management*, which was based upon the premise that a set of generic concepts underpinned management everywhere. Such presumed universal concepts diminished the reliance upon the bottom-up management wisdom that had been prominant in pre-war times, and lent itself to the mass marketing of 'managerial techniques' in the style of the packaged goods industry. Pascale assessed the influence of the various management fads since 1950: these are shown in Figure 8.1.

Of the four types of idea-based techniques – devices, events, interventions and programmes – teaching devices have been relatively stable, while system-wide programmes are rare. It is the training events and the OD interventions that have shown the greatest degree of variability over time. It is necessary to account for their rise and fall.

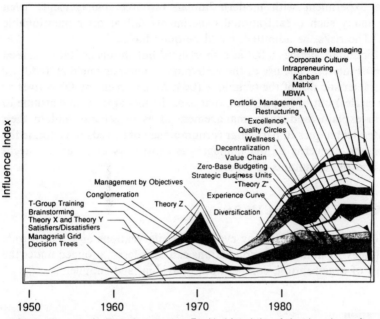

One-Minute Managing
Corporate Culture
Intrapreneuring
Kanban
Matrix
MBWA
Portfolio Management
Restructuring
"Excellence"
Quality Circles
Wellness
Decentralization
Value Chain
Zero-Base Budgeting
Strategic Business Units
"Theory Z"
Experience Curve
Diversification

Management by Objectives
Conglomeration
Theory Z
T-Group Training
Brainstorming
Theory X and Theory Y
Satisfiers/Dissatisfiers
Managerial Grid
Decision Trees

Influence Index

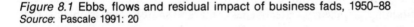

1950   1960   1970   1980

* Curves shown are for illustrative purposes. Empirical foundation of chart based upon frequency of citations in the literature. However, increased interest in business topics in the past
decade tends to exaggerate amplitude of recent fads when compared to earlier decades. As a
result, the author has modified curves to best reflect relative significance of trends over entire
period.

Figure 8.1 Ebbs, flows and residual impact of business fads, 1950–88
Source: Pascale 1991: 20

Despite the interest in the timeless procession of business and management fads in the United States and Britain, no convincing explanation of
the phenomena has yet been produced. The popular business press has
long acknowledged the existence of management fads. However, its attitude to them has been ambivalent. At different times it has reacted
positively to them, congratulating their producers for developing and
promoting innovative ideas. At other times it has criticized them for
opportunism and selling their customers short.

Byrne (1986: 41) took a critical view and quoted one manager, who
stated 'last year it was quality circles . . . this year it will be zero
inventories. The truth is, one more panacea and we will all go nuts'. Byrne
felt that fads were counterproductive. Their bewildering array represented
a serious distraction from the complex task of running a company. He
likened many modern managers to compulsive dieters, trying the latest
craze for a few days, then moving relentlessly on. In contrast, Lee (1971)
was positive and congratulated American top management on its willing-

ness to experiment with modern human resource management, 'even though many such organizational experiments fail or offer questionable results.' The risks, he admitted, could be quite high.

One dictionary defines a fad as a short-lived but enthusiastically pursued practice or interest. The use of the verb 'pursue' reminds one that 'faddism' is a characteristic not of the technique (be it Management-by-Objectives or quality circles) but of its pursuers, that is of the managers who consume it. Thus, to explain faddism in management ideas in general, and in their associated techniques in particular (programmes) one needs to examine the motives and concerns of the managers-as-consumers of ideas and techniques and of consultants-as-sellers.

MANAGERS-AS-CONSUMERS

Why do managers buy training events, OD interventions and system-wide programmes? A number of explanations can be offered, grouped under the headings of organization, competition, individual and suppliers.

Organization

At the organizational level, four explanations can be offered to account for changes in management fads. First, the new idea can be perceived as a solution to a critical company problem. The objectives of managers running companies within a capitalist economy are broadly the same (e.g. profitability, efficiency, effectiveness, market share). The problems that they face have generally remained the same both between companies and over time (e.g. low output, low quality, high costs, absenteeism, turnover, union demands). What has changed is managers' *perception* of the intensity of certain problems, leading at times to panic. For example, in the United States, the growth of unionization under Roosevelt's 'New Deal' demanded a company response in the form of the popularity of human relations management ideas and their associated techniques. Once the short-lived problem had been overcome and the union threat declined, so did human relations ideas and techniques.

Pascale (1991) felt that in the face of sagging fortunes, companies were notably more willing to experiment with new ideas. Indeed, he even suggested that the shelf life and consumption of business fads could be used as an indicator of managerial panic. The 1960s and 1970s represented the psychological period which was dominated by neo-human relations ideas and the predominance of OD techniques. Figure 8.2 illustrates the declining share and comparative advantage of some major US companies in this period which could have opened them up to management fads.

Specific and intensely felt organizational problems might be regarded as

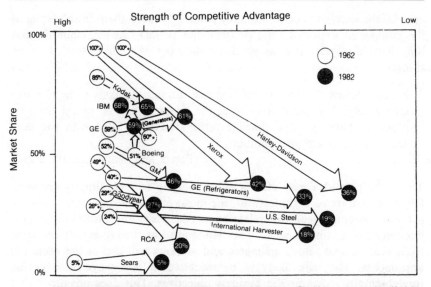

Markets defined as follows: Xerox: plain paper copiers; Harley-Davidson: motorcycles, Kodak: photographic film; IBM: mainframe computers; GE (General Electric)$_1$: generators; GE$_2$: electrical appliances (refrigerators); GM: passenger cars; Boeing: commercial widebody jet aircraft; RCA: color TVs; Goodyear: OEM ties; U.S. Steel: finished steel; International Harvester: farm tractors; Sears: mass-market retailing.

Figure 8.2 Market share and comparative advantage: trends in thirteen key industries, 1962–82
Source: Pascale 1991: 19

the crests of waves in a sea of swirling flatness. The management techniques designed to solve these different and specific problems will themselves be specific and short lived, and will thus attract the charge of faddism. Of the twenty-seven fads highlighted by Pascale (Figure 8.1), two-thirds were spawned during the 1980–90 period. This coincided with a period of intense competition with Japan and other emerging south-east Asian economies.

Second, the new idea can act as an internal motivational device. It has been argued that companies use training events, interventions and programmes to keep their employees motivated. In the 1930s Mayo discovered that the act of paying attention to workers affected their performance positively. There are numerous past examples of people programmes which were launched in a blaze of publicity so as to gain employee interest. Motorola's 'Participative Management Programme', Data General's 'Pride Teams' and Honeywell's 'Positive Action Teams' are all examples. These people programmes involve incentives, training or 'hoop-la', and undergo continuous retuning. In their research, Peters and Waterman (1982) were surprised by the number of people-programmes that they found and the frequency with which they were replenished and refurbished. They reported that service-incentive programmes were changed at least once a year by the excellent companies they studied to 'keep them fresh'. None of the companies expected their programmes to last forever, claiming that they had life cycles just as products did, but that these tended to be shorter:

> No one device . . . even in the best institutions – is likely to be effective indefinitely. The point is to treat the problem as one would the new product challenge. The pipeline must always be filled with the next score of candidate programmes.
>
> (Peters and Waterman 1982: 242)

Third, the new idea may offer a novel solution to a continuing problem. Given the nature of organizations, the message that the company wants to get over to employees will relate to the necessity for profitability, productivity and quality of work. This will tend to be fundamentally the same from year to year. Both managers and workers will tire of the same old approaches. They are likely to be receptive to new ways of achieving fundamentally the same old business objectives. This does not mean that the old approaches are incorrect, only that they may be seen as boring. Managers seek new answers to old questions that do not depend on past explanations. From this perspective, the termination of a technique, or more accurately its exhaustion over a period of time, is not considered as unusual and to label it a failure may be inaccurate.

Fourth, the management idea can be a vehicle which assists organizational change. Management techniques generally seek to produce not only behavioural changes but also attitudinal ones. An intervention technique such as a quality circles programme might have a higher order objective than just reducing the reject rate. For example, the aim might be to achieve flexible manning. Where the purpose is to achieve a major organization change oriented to the future, it would be incongruous for the company to use an old intervention from the past in order to motivate those affected by the change or to implement the change itself. New techniques were needed for new changes. However, Pascale (1991) noted that overwhelmingly, companies lacked a grasp of the larger context in which these ideas had to be embedded. By introducing them in a piecemeal manner and by changing them too frequently, they sowed the seeds of the techniques' own destruction.

Competition

First, a fear of the competition may encourage idea adoption. Kanter (1985: 181) suggested that organizations were forced to pay attention to and experiment with anything, however strange, that might offer a solution to the many problems that beset them. To ignore any potential source of ideas meant giving the competition an advantage. Grayson and O'Dell (1988) explained that managers were under pressure to show that they are 'doing something' and techniques such as employee involvement programmes provided excellent material for slide presentations at quarterly meetings. Newstrom echoed the same point:

> organizations are clearly searching for something – anything, that will help to increase the effectiveness of their supervisory, managerial and executive staffs. This phenomenon (desperate searching) has been reinforced by mounting pressure placed on organizations by the demand for productivity improvements and the impact of the economic recession of recent years.
>
> (Newstrom 1985: 3)

What is seen as the appropriate solution is decided by imitation at the national or organizational levels. In the 1970s the former West Germany and Sweden were promoted as models to be emulated. At the same time, Ford and ICI, both large unionized companies, were also considered to have discovered the secrets of success. By the 1980s Japan had become the country to be emulated while the small, non-unionized companies were seen to be the way forward.

A second variant on the competition theme was when a company wished to promote an image of itself as go-ahead – in the eyes of its customers or employees or both. In such circumstances it would not make sense for it to adopt a previously tried intervention. Instead it would be searching to pick up the latest idea ahead of its competitors. It could then claim to have been far-sighted by being among the pioneers with respect to the introduction of some technique.

Third, a company may want to match the competition in terms of any possible advantage accruing from some new technique. This explanation is not concerned with benefits (actual or potential) but with customer perceptions. The success of the technique itself is irrelevant. Instead, the company considers how a customer might view it if it is *not* seen to be using a technique. Thus a company may introduce a quality circle programme to signal to its customers that it is concerned with quality. Its motivation is not to be seen to be ignoring this fashion, irrespective of whether or not it works.

Individual

First, a new idea may act as a career enhancer. Any technique based upon an idea will be introduced into an organization by a 'champion' who promotes its adoption. The effect of this is that the visibility of the person doing the championing is increased within the company. Moreover, this demonstrates to others that this individual is both creative and actively seeking improvements. Thackray (1986) reported that one of the effects of increased interest in corporate culture was that it significantly raised the status of the human resource management department and that of personnel teams. Overnight these individuals became culture managers and interpreters. Technique implementation stimulates empire building which can help managers to advance their careers. It increases the opportunities for minions to rise to heights which, under normal circumstances, would be beyond their capabilities. It also gives them the opportunity to ingratiate themselves with their superiors (Jones and Kirby 1985).

Second, idea support may represent a managerial defence. Heller (1986: 310) argued that no management could be blamed for failure due to lack of knowledge. However, no management could be excused for a failure to implement an available technique which could be learned by sitting at the feet of the relevant guru. While managers may not be apostles of enlightened management, they could qualify as enlightened executives, and thus cover themselves against the charge that they had not found out the current wisdom, evaluated or implemented it experimentally. Ritti and Funkhouser summarized the point:

> Place yourself in the position of a mid-level manager of an organization. Things aren't going too well for you. Productivity is lagging. What could be the problem? Something *you* haven't done? Certainly not! No, it's those employees out there. They're just not motivated. So the answer is to start up a motivation programme. That ought to do the trick. And look what you accomplish with this. First, the problem is acknowledged and officially identified as a problem of individuals, not of the management system. Next, you can pat yourself on the back for having taken corrective action. Crisp, hard-hitting decision-making. You've gotten yourself a big name 'motivation consultant' (talk funny, make money) and you'll put a programme in place. There, that should take care of it.
>
> (Ritti and Funkhouser 1987: 63)

Third, the idea may be seen as offering quick results to difficult problems. Mayer described the 'panacea conspiracy':

> Many of today's managers, though they may deny or not realize it, are members of a flourishing movement I call 'the Panacea Conspiracy'. These managers typically promoted into management from such technical specialties as engineering or law, or finance, have little managerial know-how. Most don't have the time, interest, or awareness needed to learn their new craft, but they are anxious to produce immediately. What they are looking for, although they may profess to know better, are quick-fix solutions to dynamic complex problems.
>
> (Mayer 1983: 23)

The panacea conspiracy involved the buying managers and the selling consultants colluding with each other over the outcomes of their association. While the consultants may have seen the solution of the problem as essentially a long-term one, they recognized managers' lack of knowledge (or desire to acquire the necessary knowledge), their disinterest in the subject, and their lack of commitment to putting in the sustained effort required. According to Mayer, the consultants rationalized that, since the managers were not ready to deal with what really needed to be done, any gimmick was worth trying which might trigger their interest, bring progress, impress them, or make them grateful to the consultants or make them feel valued and secure.

Mayer implied that the adoption of a technique by this type of manager was a defensive act, that is defending themselves against their ignorance. It might equally represent a form of pseudo-participation with respect to employees. Mant (1979: 55) wrote that 'managers constantly sought new techniques since workers have wised up to one [technique] . . . and need outfixing with something a lot cleverer. . . . It is an alluring message for the naturally exploitative executive who wants to sleep at night.' Williamson (1978: 6) wrote in a similar vein, saying that 'the more people grasp one theory, the more urgent it becomes to manufacture a different model, fast, so that you are still ahead in the great race to be ahead.' Pascale (1991) noted that one of the unintended consequences of the mass marketing of fads has been the fostering of superficiality. In his view, it has become professionally legitimate in the United States to accept and utilize management ideas without an in-depth grasp of their underlying foundation, and without the commitment necessary to sustain them.

Fourth, the adoption of the technique offered the manager an insider-status. This explanation of adoption has also been described as 'me-too-ism'. Managers and trainers who adopt new training devices or interventions can be seen to be up-to-the-minute. The concept of reference group is central here. Such groups either directly or indirectly influence a person's behaviour or attitude. According to marketing theory, in the introductory phase of the product life cycle, the decision to buy the new product is heavily influenced by others. In the market growth stage, the group influence is strong on both product and brand choice. In the product maturity stage, brand choice and not product choice are heavily influenced by others. In the decline stage, group influence is weak on both.

Thus the sellers of management products are likely initially to target those individuals who are opinion formers in their relevant groups. Once ICI, IBM and similar companies have adopted a quality awareness programme, the remaining companies follow suit. The manager had to be up on all the latest terms and be abreast of all the newest enthusiasms. When someone used the latest catchphrase over the lunchtable or at a conference, he had to recognize it and be able to respond in kind. However, such a

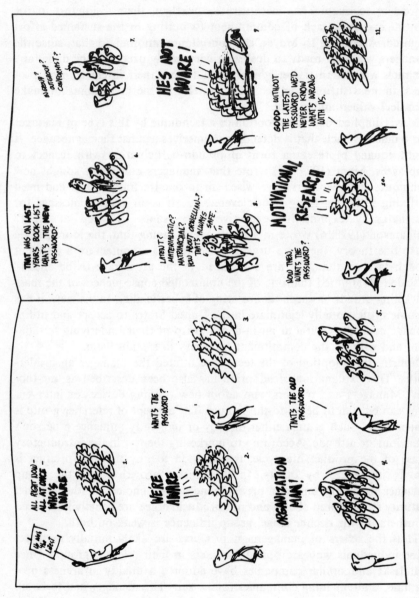

Source: Jules Pfeiffer, *Sick, Sick, Sick*, 1959

response need not imply understanding.

Finally, Dixon (1987: 214) identified the reduction of boredom as a crucial (albeit in his view a self-destructive) motive. The relation of boredom to arousal, curiosity, exploratory activity and information overload are relevant. The unexpected-in-life does much to reduce boredom. Dixon argued that a great source of the unexpected are people. Being unpredictable, they can do a lot of different things, and in a different order. Being a rich source of information, the control of their activities constitutes a boredom-reducing goal for the manager. When we are not discussing the weather, most of us are talking about other people. Interest in people reduces boredom in life.

Mayer (1983) argued that panaceas usually did little more than produce more panaceas, each with their own proponents, literature and markets. Those attracted by the latest trick promoted it, and the more successful panaceas became stylish. Eventually however, their shortcomings became evident and they either faded away or some parts of them became incorporated into the day-to-day fabric of the organization. Campbell argued that:

> The fads centre around the introduction of new techniques and follow a characteristic pattern. A new technique appears on the horizon and develops a large stable of advocates who first describe its 'successful' use in a number of situations. A second wave of advocates busy themselves trying out numerous modifications of the basic technique. A few empirical studies may be carried out to demonstrate that the method 'works'. Then the inevitable backlash sets in, and a few vocal opponents begin to criticise the usefulness of the technique, most often in the absence of data. Such criticism typically has very little effect. What does have an effect is the appearance of another new technique and a repetition of the same cycle.
>
> (J. P. Campbell 1971: 565–6)

CONSULTANTS-AS-SUPPLIERS

What part do suppliers play in the continued replacement of one management idea by another? The topic can be considered under the heading of planned obsolence and of searching and deciding on techniques.

The first explanation that can be offered is planned obsolence. A producer can enter the management idea market with the confidence that a particular product which is selling well today will be displaced at a future time. This involves totally withdrawing the product, and replacing it with something else. Thus some wholesalers currently promoting 'wellness programmes' acknowledge the limited time application of their product. The president of the PA Executive Research Group estimated that wellness programmes would have a two to three year life cycle. One can contrast this strategy with the relaunching of an old product (The NEW Management Grid) or extending its target population. Forrest was cynical about this process, while Peters and Waterman described it in depth:

> The progress of the 'behavioural sciences' is inexorable and accelerated. You are unlikely to keep up. Should you threaten to catch up, we will define what we gave you as passé and give you something new. Should we run out of new stuff, which is not very likely, we will change the name of something we have already promoted to you as 'the answer', and which we have displaced with some 'new answer', and then give it to you again.
>
> (Forrest 1984: 54)

> Our objective is first and foremost to have a steady flow of new products. Then, once we hit, we expect to dominate the niche, sometimes for three or four years. During that stretch we price according to full value to the customer. We're providing both a tool that is some kind of labour saver and we expect the market to pay what it's worth. Sure we create an umbrella. But when others come in with approximations, perhaps at lower cost, rather than fight them for share, we usually give in – that is, get out. Because by then we're developing the next several generations of products for the market and others.
>
> (Peters and Waterman 1982: 184)

Gellner (1985: 205) offered an explanation of the relationship between success and failure and between truth and fallacy in his examination of the psychoanalytic movement. He explained that truth was not an advantage in producing a burning belief in a theory or idea. Truth was unpatentable. Once it was revealed, and once the important secret of effectiveness became revealed, the attempt to protect and monopolize it became impossible. However, while truth might be unpatentable, a type of falsehood which contained some genuine attraction and genuine offence, was self-patenting, and constituted the elements of which a strongly held and popular belief system was made.

Applying Gellner's ideas to two management interventions – A and B – one might find that intervention A produced a productivity increase in 80 per cent of companies who used it by a publicly testable method. In contrast, intervention B achieved only a 20 per cent success rate by an esoteric, invisible and unspecifiable method which was accompanied by some emotional activity. It was likely, argued Gellner, that intervention A would spread rapidly, but the publicity of the method ensured that no magic would be attached to it. It could be freely emulated by anyone. It generated no offence and no transference. Interventions such as management-by-objectives, job enrichment and quality circles might come into this category.

In contrast, intervention B generated both offence and transference. It made its enemies among disappointed clients who did not fall into the lucky 20 per cent for whom it worked. Those in the fortunate group not only would be grateful, but also would become bound to the intervention and its practitioners. The lucky 20 per cent cannot be identified in advance. Since intervention B was untestable it tied adherents to their implementing consultants by faith. If they spread the word, 20 per cent of those whom they contacted would become converts. Given the consequences of exponential growth, the intervention B 'movement' would grow, despite feeling under attack, and just like the Christians persecuted in Roman times, this would help morale and attract disciples. Thus the ability of an intervention to arouse emotional opposition seems to be of crucial importance. Intervention A with its 80 per cent success rate would become common property and would engender no movement at all.

Second, suppliers offer managers relief from the need to extensively search for solutions. Heller (1986) concluded that certain techniques could work wonders in individual companies at particular times. In his view, this was because they suited the way in which individual managers liked to act in particular markets. The successful techniques used in one company, he felt, could paralyse another. Yet managers beset by corporate ailments, reached out for techniques (events, interventions and programmes) formed in a different context as if these were antibiotic, cure-all, wonder drugs. So the question is asked, how extensively do managers search for the techniques based upon management ideas, and where do they obtain their information about their efficacy?

In Britain, according to Blagden (1980), managers read 7.8 hours per week. Their main reading was the *Financial Times* and *Management Today*. These two publications were read by more managers than all the remaining ones put together. The Blagden research supported March and Simon's (1958) notion of limited search as it applied to management ideas and techniques. The narrowness of the reading suggested that managers scanned their environment for techniques in a limited way. Janis and Mann (1977) also supported this conclusion, arguing that individuals tended to avoid cognitive strain by considering a restricted number of alternatives and frequently only one. Acceptability was decided on the basis of whether the choice was 'good enough'. Simple decision rules were used such as 'consult an expert and do what he says'. This non-vigilant decision-making strategy was used when the decision was reversible. We cannot cope with all the available information since we lack the cognitive capacity to do all the calculations and make a decision. Becker suggested why this should be so:

Source: The Economist, 4 May 1991, p. 23

The man of knowledge in our time is bowed under a burden he never imagined he would have, the over-production of truth that cannot be consumed. For centuries man lived in the belief that truth was slim and elusive and that once he found it, the troubles of mankind would be over. And here we are in the closing decades of the twentieth century choking on truth.

(Becker 1973: x)

Naisbitt (1982), in his analysis of global trends, noted the proliferation in the variety of everything from foods to religious cults. His book appealed to readers who had encountered the complexity of the world, and sought collective identity and reassurance (Neal and Groat 1984). Shoppers had so many options to choose from that they could hardly stand the process of having to decide. The variety on offer, with all its intricate trade-offs, created such a a paralysis for the consumer that any solid system of dogma that could simplify and provide an authoritative base for deciding felt like liberation (Berg and Smith 1987: 8). Perhaps there may be a social link betweeen the emergence of dogma and the proliferation of variety.

Managers rarely possessed the requisite insight to know the meaning of choosing one option rather than another. There was therefore anxiety associated with keeping so many options open. In the field of complex human interactions there was little theory at any level of generalization that had a predictive value. Paradoxically, wrote Anthony, the more responsible and influential the general manager became, there was:

> precious little theory to help him cope with confusion and complexity. What is available to him is a ready battery of consultants' advice, of educational programmes compounded of recipes and simplifications, distillations of general explanations of human behaviour, catalogues of the best way to 'handle' people, select them, promote them, motivate and control them. None of these may relate to the constantly shifting situation and the arcane complexities that confront him, but the advice is to hand, it is simple, it provides comfort, and above all it is appropriate to his understanding.
>
> (Anthony 1987: 258)

What happens when there is a pressure to decide but a lack of available guidance? Ambiguity, like pain, is not a comfortable situation. Thus any opportunity to obtain relief, even if temporary, would be welcomed and grasped. This could propel managers into choosing a collectivist solution. By following others and emulating what others did, they could both reduce the burden of choice, and dissipate the responsibility for failure. In the context of the organizational world, the 'Deming Way' or the 'Management Grid Approach' can be seen as providing such a unified set of principles which can guide managers through the numerous choices or might even make choosing unnecessary. One might argue that the reliance on a single authority (a management guru) in the light of massive ambiguity of options represented another response to variety 'gone mad'.

A second finding was that once the search for a tool had been simplified and limited information obtained on each alternative, the decision process itself was simplified. Disproportionate weight was given to certain variables. Four such tests or decision rules were used by managers. Under pressure they would make accept–reject decisions on the basis of only one criterion. Clearly, such extreme simplification had consequences for the entire marketing and buying process. For example, it would appear that vendors of management packages must keep their positioning strategies simple by providing their customers with strong and uncomplicated propositions. Detail was dysfunctional. Managers fought to stop themselves being deluged by details.

Schwenk (1986) in his empirical study of how managers processed information, identified the various simplifying strategies or rule-of-thumb biases which were used to reduce the amount of information needed to be considered in decision making. He discovered that a disproportionately large amount of weight was given to vivid anecdotal information about individuals and companies and a small amount to pallid statistical information (Borgida and Nisbett 1977). The message to influencers was that they should use anecdotal information which was both vivid and salient; which was consistent or which presented a consistent picture, and which would discourage decision-makers from seeking any other information. Thus, John De Lorean, the American businessman who sought money from investors to establish a motor car company to produce a sports car, attempted to increase the salience of information about himself, so as to encourage a kind of representativeness heuristic which reduced listeners' motivation to seek out and use other types of data with which to evaluate him and his project proposals.

Schwenck (1986) also discovered that large volumes of anecdotal information relating to a particular choice, increased decision-makers' confidence in their choice by increasing the number of reasons for confidence available in memory. A consultant or company seeking to sell a management tool or technique should take positive action to create and maintain commitment to a course of action by the potential customer (the prospect). Since the vendor controlled much of the information received by the prospect, he could manipulate this information to increase the prospect's confidence in a course of action and his commitment to it. Companies selling management tools could provide a large amount of vivid, anecdotal information about themselves thereby producing a consistent picture of themselves in the prospect's eyes, and drawing the attention away from statistical information about the probability of success with a tool such as a quality circle or a training course.

The provision of this type of information could encourage the representative heuristic among the prospects, and would tend to make them overconfident in their decisions. By focusing on information about the consultant or the vendor company, the prospect would get an 'illusion of control' over the circumstances. This in turn would lead to higher levels of commitment to the course of action. Initial evidence suggests that package-adopting or consultant-engaging managers use a satisficing rather than a maximizing decision approach. There is relatively little in the way of either detailed evaluation or comparative research. Impulse-buying appears to be frequent. Discussing how the management consultant Ichak Adizes came to be involved with Bank of America, Byrne noted that:

The banker [Armacost] was introduced to the Yugoslavian-born consultant by board director Charles R. Schwab in 1983 via cassette tape. Armacost, says Adizes, listened to his 'Adizes Method Audio Series' until 2 a.m. one night and was so impressed that he arranged a retreat with the consulting whiz for top management.

(Byrne 1986: 47)

Casey and Pierce offer a similar description of how Arnold Weinstock of GEC adopted action learning as the favoured management development approach for his company:

> In the autumn of 1973, I watched Revans on television illustrating the theories and practice of action learning. He and I met subsequently and embarked on an action learning programme for some managers in GEC.
>
> (Weinstock in Casey and Pierce 1977: ix)

Armacost and Weinstock are examples of people who acted primarily on their own faith in the product. As believers, they may have made little effort to seek alternatives. In their minds they may 'test' one approach with another but only in terms of its face-validity and intuitive appeal. This description of consumer motives suggests that fads are cyclical in their nature and that faddism is in fact a good thing given the purposes that consumers put the techniques to. There appear to be a finite number of solutions on offer. There are only so many ways in which organizational performance can be improved. These basic solutions are frequently updated, branded and claimed to be 'new', but are in fact reformulatedversions of the six management idea systems described earlier in Chapter 2, and whose coexistence was explained in this chapter.

Technical solutions started with scientific management and continued through computerization, quantitative management, zero-based budgeting, robotics, materials requirement planning, and Just-in-Time working. *Structural* solutions started with bureaucracy and classical administration management and have extended to diversification, centralization, matrix management, decentralization, conglomeration and restructuring. *Employee-focused* solutions began with the human relations ideas and were succeeded by neo-human relations, management-by-objectives, T-groups, job enrichment, 'management-by-walking about' and quality circles. *Customer-focused* solutions were concerned primarily with delivering better quality products and services to consumers and represent perhaps the only true innovations in management techniques in the last seventy years. These have taken the form of customer care programmes, vendor improvement programmes, and company-wide quality improvement programmes.

One therefore finds old, modified techniques being offered to solve organizational problems. Quality circles, for example, can be seen as a modified version of the employee-focused technique of worker involvement. Peters was reported as saying about his book that:

> there's absolutely nothing new whatsoever between the covers. It was a

translation of ideas and materials that had been around for up to 50
years. All it added was brilliant timing and packaging.

(Peters in Lorenz 1986b: 8)

It can be observed that the failure of successive techniques does nor appear
to deter organizations from seeking new ones. Indeed, in some circumstances, failure may increase rather than decrease such a search. Peters and
Waterman, who were responsible for releasing numerous fads on to the
market, reflected critically that:

> Ten years ago it was job enlargement. Before that it was the seemingly
> ubiquitous organizational development movement replete with
> teambuilding, T-groups, conflict resolution and managerial grids. The
> bones of these programmes are scattered on America's low productivity
> desert. . . . most . . . [of the programmes] will turn out to be duds, just
> as do new product ideas. If job enrichment does not work at the
> Milwaukee plant, try seven other programmes that are working in other
> plants, or that have worked at other plants.
>
> (Peters and Waterman 1982: 241–2)

For the purposes for which they are used, the replacement, sometimes a
rapid replacement, of techniques is necessary. This assumes that such
techniques have objectives other than merely performance improvement.
Even in this area there are forces which will lead to their eventual
replacement. Watson (1986) commented upon the 'paradox of consequences' which held that all personnel procedures contained the seeds of
their own destruction. This was because they all involved the human
element. Individuals and groups brought their own values, interests and
aspirations to bear upon any activity with which they became involved, for
example, quality circles.

Management had constantly to monitor and modify personnel systems
to avoid too high a degree of entrenchment and inflexibility as people
established a personal or sectional stake in the pattern which had been set
up. They thus compromised the effectiveness of the procedure as a means
of fulfilling managerial purposes since it did not coincide with their own
interests. Thus for example, a new wage payment system might bring order
to the bargaining activity of a company. But unless it was monitored and
revised, it could create particular expectations among individuals and
groups which might become major constraints on the organizational
changes which would be required later.

This meant that there would never be the right technique or system.
Whatever intervention was introduced, it would have to be modified,
adjusted or replaced as its internal contradictions broke through. Henstridge (1975) pointed out how in the personnel management field, a
succession of reasons was given by practitioners as to why certain pro-

cedures and policies had been initiated, altered, adjusted, dropped, or made more flexible. The explanations were of the following type: 'We tried this but it did not work', 'we had to think of something to deal with that', 'we do it this way here because', 'we had trouble with the unions so'. Managers feel themselves forced or pressured into developing a unique, contingent approach to meet the problems of the particular situation.

Marglin (1979) offered an explanation of the succession of management fads from a Marxist perspective. He argued that conflict was inherent in the private ownership of the means of production. Specific manifestations of such conflicts in the work situation required institutional changes to allow the system to function. Since the basic features of capitalism had to be respected (e.g. division of labour; organizational hierarchy; top-down control) the solutions that could be offered to address these problems were necessarily limited. The solutions proposed addressed the problems only at the surface level. For example, dealing with the symptoms rather than the causes. Moreover, they tended to change the *form* of the problem for management rather than to resolve it in any fundamental sense. The solution to one problem tended to exacerbate other problems, or created a totally new one. The process according to Marglin was a dialectic one. Problems led to solutions which led to new problems.

CONCLUSION

This book has addressed itself to the issue of the sociology of management knowledge application. The findings of the research have highlighted a range of cognitive and structural factors that appear to contribute to the high valuation of certain management ideas. Perhaps the book has contributed to the development of the *sociology of management idea application*. It was Robert Merton who, in 1949, called for a systematic study of the factors that either impeded or facilitated the application of applied social science for the purposes of practical action. Merton's own study considered the cultural, organizational and political dimensions which inevitably affected utilization. The purpose of this study was to make a contribution to the relevance, scope and utility of a small, albeit important, segment of social science research that was concerned with management and organizations. Merton highlighted the need for an applied social research on applied social science.

Holzner (1978) contrasted the classical sociology of knowledge as being concerned with the social bases of intellectual productions. In contrast, a sociology of knowledge application, in his view, should be concerned with the social consequences of knowledge (Holzner and Marx 1979). It is important to understand the different frames of reference with which people perceive knowledge and the discrepancies between the frames of reference of knowledge producers and knowledge users. The focus of a sociology of knowledge application, argued Holzner (1978), should be the analysis of the organizational arrangements for knowledge production and use, and those which encouraged optimal learning. He identified five major issues for consideration. These are listed as sets of questions taken from his writings. They are included in the hope that they may provide a stimulus to others who might wish to investigate the subject.

SOCIAL SCIENCE ENTERPRISE

As social science enters the management sphere and influences the manner in which managers perceive and think about what they do, the type of research that is carried out is obviously important. One needs to know what kind of research is undertaken and what conditions shape its nature. How do social scientists in the industrial and organizational sphere select the research that they do? What are the personal, social, structural and political conditions which shape its nature? To what extent do the disciplines and fashions of the disciplines themselves reward certain types of investigations and inhibit others? To what extent do discipline research methods shape the nature of the questions asked and the directions of the inquiry? To what extent are the political and ideological proclivities of social scientists the determining factors? To what extent do social scientists expect their work to influence managerial action? Through which channels do they expect such influences to flow? When do they expect it to have such an effect? How does this expectation affect their work and how they do it? When they consider themselves as pure scientists, detached critics or management advisers, what kind of research do they do and where do they publish it? What is the effect of their institutional auspicies? The source of their funding? Their own status?

TRANSMISSION OF SOCIAL SCIENCE RESEARCH

The general focus here is upon the way in which knowledge relevant to management and organizations is communicated to managers. What are the channels through which such information flows? Which audiences are reached by different channels? Once research and theory findings are abstracted or summarized from journal articles and books for managers by trainers, consultants and lecturers, what biases and distortions are introduced? Are there differences in the clarity and cogency of the different information channels? How long does it take for a new management idea to get through to managers? What factors affect the time lag? How are the differences and contradictions in the different management ideas resolved, explained and communicated?

RECEPTION TO RESEARCH AMONG MANAGERS

How interested and active are managers in finding out about current management ideas? What accounts for the differences in their interests? How do managers evaluate ideas and what criteria govern the attention that they pay to ideas and techniques? What are the properties in techniques and packages that they value that lead them to adopt and implement? How important for them is the source of the ideas and techniques? How important for acceptance is the channel through which they hear about the idea or technique?

EFFECTS OF SOCIAL SCIENCE RESEARCH ON MANAGEMENT ACTION

Here the main issues relate to the circumstances under which managers draw upon social science in taking action. What form of idea do they tend to use – data, generalizations, concepts or theories? How closely do managers' understandings of the social science that they use, approximate to the meanings that the social scientists seek to convey? How do they use their knowledge of social science? What contribution does social science make (compared with other sources of knowledge) to the actions that managers take? What are the consequences of applying social science to the work that managers do? Are company programmes that are based on social science knowledge more effective or efficient than those which are not? Is the quality of decisions improved?

TO WHOSE BENEFIT?

The final area concerns whether it is only managers in an organization who use social science or unions which use such ideas to oppose management action. When managers use ideas and techniques, in what circumstances does it benefit them and when does it benefit non-managerial groups? Under what circumstances does the use of social science buttress existing company policy, and when does it support and guide change?

This book has sought to make a contribution to the sociology of knowledge application. Knowledge is only one component that enters in managerial policy and decision-making, but it has a sinuous and pervasive effect. Managers do with what they know. Managerial and organizational social science represents only one component of knowledge yet, under certain circumstances, it can carry a special authoritativeness. This is because it is presumed to have a systematic and objective hallmark of science. It also provides a powerful vocabulary that shapes the way in which problems and issues are defined and conceptualized. Despite charges of jargon, social science has become the language of discourse in which managerial policy and action are discussed and carried on.

The book also acts as a warning to managers as consumers of management ideas. Over the last hundred years many management ideas based on organizational theories and research have proved effective. They have helped to increase productivity and have raised employee job satisfaction. Other ideas, however, have had the opposite effect. This study should also appeal to the aspiring management guru. By analysing popular management idea elements and conditions, it offers a step-by-step guide to the manager, management lecturer or consultant who wishes to achieve guru status.

References

Abrams, M. (1981) 'A Manager's View of Management Development', *Management Education and Development*, vol. 12, part 2, pp. 113–15.

Adizes, I. (1979) *How to Solve the Mis-management Crisis*, New York: Dow Jones-Irwin.

Agor, W. H. (1986) 'The Logic of Intuition: How Top Executives Make Important Decisons', *Organizational Dynamics*, Winter, pp. 5–18.

Albrow, M. C. (1970) *Bureaucracy*, London: Pall Mall.

Andersen, R. (1988) *The Power and the Word*, London: Grafton/Collins.

Anderson, D. G., Phillips, J. R. and Kaiable, N. (1985) *Revitalizing Large Companies*, Working Paper, Cambridge, MA: MIT Press.

Andre, R. (1985) 'The Scientist, the Artist and the Evangelist', *New Management*, vol. 2, no. 4, Spring, pp. 16–21.

Ansoff, H. I. (1968) *Corporate Strategy*, Harmondsworth: Penguin.

Anthony, P. D. (1977) *The Ideology of Work*, London: Tavistock.

Anthony, P. D. (1986) *The Foundation of Management*, London: Tavistock.

Anthony, P. D. (1987) 'In Defence of the Inappropriate', *Management Education and Development*, vol. 18, part 4, pp. 255–9.

Argyle, M. (1953) 'The Relay Assembly Test Room in Retrospect', *Occupational Psychology*, vol. 27, pp. 98–103.

Argyle, M. (1972) *The Social Psychology of Work*, Harmondsworth: Penguin.

Argyris, C. (1957) *Personality and Organization: The Conflict Between System and the Individual*, New York: Harper & Row.

Argyris, C. (1962) *Interpersonal Competence and Organizational Effectiveness*, London: Tavistock.

Argyris, C. (1964) *Integrating the Individual and the Organization*, New York: Wiley.

Argyris, C. (1970) *Intervention Theory and Method*, Reading, MA: Addison Wesley.

Argyris, C. (1972) *The Applicability of Organizational Sociology*, London: Cambridge University Press.

Argyris, C. (1973) 'Personality and Organization Theory Revisited', *Administrative Science Quarterly*, vol. 18, pp. 141–67.

Aristotle, *Rhetorica*, translated and edited by W. Rhys Roberts, McKeon, R. (ed.) in (1941) *The Basic Works of Aristotle*, New York: Random House.

Aronoff, C. (1975) 'The Rise of the Behavioural Perspective in Selected General Management Textbooks: An Empirical Investigation Through Content Analysis', *Academy of Management Journal*, vol. 18, no. 4, pp. 753–66.

Ash, M. K. (1984) *Mary Kay on People Management*, London: Futura.

Ashworth, C. E. (1980) 'Flying Saucers, Spoon-bending and Atlantis: A Structural

Analysis of New Mythologies', *Sociological Review*, vol. 28, no. 2, May, pp. 353–76.

Atkinson, J. M. (1984) *Our Masters' Voices*, London: Routledge.

Atkinson, J. M. and Drew, P. (1979) *Order in Court: The Organization of Verbal Interaction in Judicial Settings*, London: Macmillan.

Auletta, K. (1984) *The Art of Corporate Success*, New York: Putnam.

Aupperle, K. E., Acar, W. and Booth, D. E. (1986) 'An Empirical Critique of *In Search of Excellence*: How Excellent are the Excellent Companies?', *Journal of Management*, Winter, pp. 499–512.

Avis, W. (1986) *Take a Chance to be First*, New York: Collier Macmillan.

Back, K. W. (1972) *Beyond Words*, New York: Sage.

Bailey, E. (1991) 'Science Runs on to Court', *Daily Telegraph*, 24 June, p. 17.

Bales, R. F. (1950) *Interaction Process Analysis*, Reading, MA: Addison Wesley.

Baker, R. J. S. (1972) *Administrative Theory and Public Administration*, London: Hutchinson.

Barnard, C. (1938) *The Functions of the Executive*, Cambridge, MA: Harvard University Press.

Barsoux, J.-S. (1989) 'Muddle Management', *Management Today*, December, p. 128.

Bartell, T. (1976) 'The Human Relations Ideology: An Analysis of the Social Origins of a Belief System', *Human Relations*, vol. 29, no. 8, pp. 737–49.

Batra, R. (1988) *Surviving the Great Depression of 1990*, New York: Dell.

Beaumont, P. B. (1985) 'The Diffusion of Human Resource Management Innovations', *Relations Industrialles* (Canada), vol. 40, no. 2, pp. 243–56.

Becker, E. (1973) *The Denial of Death*, New York: Free Press.

Beckhard, R. (1969) *Organizational Development – Strategies and Models*, Reading, MA: Addison Wesley.

Beer, M., Spector, B., Lawrence, P., Quinn Mills, D. and Walton, R. (1985) *Human Resource Management: A General Manager's Perspective*, Glencoe, IL: Free Press.

Belbin, R. M. (1981) *Management Teams: Why They Succeed or Fail*, London: Heinemann.

Bendix, R. (1963) *Work and Authority in Industry*, New York: Harper & Row.

Benne, K. and Sheats, P. (1948) 'Functional Roles of Group Members', *Journal of Social Issues*, vol. 4, pp. 161–8.

Bennis, W. and Nanus, A. (1985) *Leaders: The Strategies for Taking Charge*, New York: Harper & Row.

Berg, D. N. and Smith, K. K. (1987–8), 'The Management Paradox in the Education Process', *Organization Behaviour Teaching Review*, vol. XII, pp. 1–15.

Berger, P. and Luckmann, T. (1967) *The Social Construction of Reality*, Harmondsworth: Penguin.

Bernardin, H. J. and Alvares, K. M. (1976) 'The Managerial Grid as a Predictor of Conflict Resolution Method and Managerial Effectiveness', *Administrative Science Quarterly*, vol. 21, pp. 84–94.

Berne, E. (1964) *Games People Play*, Harmondsworth: Penguin.

Beyer, J. M. and Trice, H. M. (1982) 'The Utilization Process: A Conceptual Framework and Synthesis of Empirical Findings', *Administrative Science Quarterly*, vol. 27, pp. 591–622.

Bion, W. R. (1959) *Experiences in Groups*, London: Tavistock.

Blackler, F. H. M. and Brown, C. A. (1980) *Whatever Happened to Shell's New Philosophy of Management?*, Aldershot: Saxon House.

Blackler, F. and Shimmin, S. (1984) *Applying Psychology in Organizations*, London: Methuen.

Blagden, J. F. (1980) *Do Managers Read?*, Cranfield, Bedfordshire: British Institute of Management/Cranfield Institute of Technology Press.

Blake, R. R. and Mouton, J. S. (1964) *The Managerial Grid*, Houston, TX: Gulf Publishing.

Blake, R. R. and Mouton, J. S. (1968) *Corporate Excellence Through Grid Organization Development*, Houston, TX: Gulf Publishing.

Blake, R. R. and Mouton, J. S. (1969) *Building a Dynamic Corporation Through Grid Organization*, Reading, MA: Addison Wesley.

Blake, R. R. and Mouton, J. S. (1978) *The New Managerial Grid*, Houston, TX: Gulf Publishing.

Blake, R. R. and Mouton, J. S. (1985) *The Managerial Grid III*, Houston, TX: Gulf Publishing.

Blake, R. R., Mouton, J. S., Barnes, L. B. and Greiner, L. E. (1964) 'Breakthrough in Organizational Development', *Harvard Business Review*, vol. 42, pp. 133–55.

Blanchard, K. and Johnson, S. (1983) *The One Minute Manager*, Glasgow: Fontana/Collins.

Blau, P. (1955) *The Dynamics of Bureaucracy*, Chicago, IL: University of Chicago Press.

de Board, R. (1978) *The Psychoanalysis of Organizations*, London: Tavistock.

de Bono, E. (1971) *Lateral Thinking for Management*, Harmondsworth: Penguin.

de Bono, E. (1986) *Tactics: The Art and Science of Success*, London: Fontana.

Borgida, E. and Nisbett, R. (1977) 'The Differential Impact of Abstract vs. Concrete Informationon Decisions', *Journal of Applied Social Psychology*, vol. 7, pp. 258–71.

Bowers, D. (1973) 'OD Techniques and Their Results in 23 Organizations: The Michigan ICL Study', *Journal of Applied Behavioural Science*, vol. 9, pp. 21–43.

Braverman, H. (1974) *Labour and Monopoly Capital*, New York: Monthly Review Press.

Brickman, P. (1980) 'A Social Psychology of Human Concerns', in Gilmour, R. and Duck, S. (eds) *The Development of Social Psychology*, London: Academic Press.

Brown, H. (1980) 'The Individual in the Organization', in Salaman, G. and Thompson, K. (eds) *Control and Ideology in Organizations*, Cambridge, MA: MIT Press.

Brown, J. A. C. (1954) *The Social Psychology of Industry*, Harmondsworth: Penguin.

Brown, R. (1965) *Social Psychology*, New York: Free Press.

Brown, W. and Jacques, E. (1965) *Glacier Metal Papers*, London: Heinemann.

Bruck, C. (1989) *The Predator's Ball: How the Junk Bond Machine Started the Corporate Raiders*, New York: Simon & Schuster.

Bryman, A. (1986) *Leadership and Organizations*, London: Routledge.

Bryman, A. (1992) *Charisma and Leadership in Organizations*, London: Sage.

Buchanan, D. A. (1989) 'Principles and Practice in Work Design: Current Trends; Future Prospects', in Sisson, K. (ed.) *Personnel Management in Britain*, Oxford: Blackwell.

Buchanan, D. A., Boddy, D. and Sutherland, J. (1985) *Technical Change Audit*, Paper presented at the MSC Workshop on the Management of Technological Change, Sheffield, 23–24 September, unpublished mimeo.

Bullock (1977) *Report of the Committee of Inquiry on Industrial Democracy*, Cmnd 6706, London: HMSO.

Burke, K. (1962) *A Grammar of Motives and a Rhetoric of Motives*, Cleveland, OH: Meridian – World Publishing Company.

Burnham, J. (1962) *The Managerial Revolution*, Harmondsworth: Penguin.

Burns, T. and Stalker, G. M. (1961) *The Management of Innovation*, London: Tavistock.

Business Week (1984) 'Who's Excellent Now?', 5 November, pp. 76–8.

Business Week (1986) 'Editorial', 20 January, p. 100.

Business Week (1988) 'America After Reagan', 1 February, pp. 40–7.

Butler, G. V. (1986) *Organization and Management: Theory and Practice*, Englewood Cliffs, NJ: Prentice Hall.

Byrne, J. A. (1986) 'Business Fads: What's In and What's Out', *Business Week*, 20 January, pp. 40–7.

Campbell, D. N., Fleming, R. L. and Grote, R. C. (1985) 'Discipline Without Punishment – At Last', *Harvard Business Review*, July–August, vol. 85, no. 4, pp. 162–4, 168, 170, 174 and 176.

Campbell, J. P. (1971) 'Personnel Training and Development', *Annual Review of Psychology*, vol. 22, pp. 565–602.

Caplan, N. (1977) 'A Minimal Set of Conditions Necessary for the Utilization of Social Science Knowledge on Policy Formulation at the National Level', in Weiss, C.H. (ed.) *Using Social Science Research on Public Policy Making*, Lexington, MA: Lexington Books.

Carey, A. (1967) 'The Hawthorne Studies: A Radical Criticism', *American Sociological Review*, vol. 32, no. 3, pp. 403–16.

Carlisle, E. (1985) *Mac – Managers Talk About Managing People*, London: Pan.

Carlson, S. (1951) *Executive Behaviour: A Study of the Workload and Working Methods of Managing Directors*, Stockholm: Stronbergs.

Carlzon, J. (1987) *Moments of Truth*, New York: Harper & Row.

Carnegie, D. (1983) *How to Develop Self-Confidence and Influence People by Public Speaking*, Tadworth, Surrey: Worlds Work Ltd.

Carroll, D. (1983) 'A Disappointing Search for Excellence', *Harvard Business Review*, November–December, pp. 78–88.

Carter, R. K. (1971) 'Clients' Resistance to Negative Findings and the Latent Conservative Function of Evaluation Studies', *American Psychologist*, vol. 6, pp. 118–24.

Casey, D. R. (1983) *Crisis in Investing: Opportunities and Profits in the Coming Great Crash*, New York: Simon & Schuster.

Casey, D. and Pearce, D. (1977) *More than Management Development*, Aldershot: Gower.

Child, J. (1968a) 'British Management Thought as a Case Study within the Sociology of Knowledge', *Sociological Review*, vol. 16, pp. 217–39.

Child, J. (1968b) 'Industrial Management', in Parker, S. R., Brown, R. K., Child, J. and Smith, M. A., *The Sociology of Industry*, London: Allen & Unwin.

Child, J. (1969a) *British Management Thought*, London: Allen & Unwin.

Child, J. (1969b) *The Business Enterprise in Modern Industrial Society*, London: Collier Macmillan.

Child, J. (1984) *Organization*, London: Harper & Row.

Clark, J. V. (1960–1) 'Motivation in Work Groups: A Tentative View', *Human Organization*, vol. 13, pp. 199–208.

Clegg, S. (1975) *Power, Rule and Domination: A Critical and Empirical Understanding of Power in Sociological Theory and Everyday Life*, London: Routledge.

Clegg, S. (1979) *The Theory of Power and Organization*, London: Routledge.

Clegg, S. and Dunkerley, D. (eds) (1977) *Critical Issues in Organizations*, London: Routledge.

Clegg, S. and Dunkerley, D. (1980) *Organization, Class and Control*, London: Routledge.

Cleverley, G. (1971) *Managers and Magic*, London: Longman.

Clifford, D. K. and Cavanagh, R. E. (1986) *The Winning Performance: How America's Midsize Companies Succeed*, London: Sidgwick & Jackson.

Clutterbuck, D. and Crainer, S. (1988) 'The Corporate Sages', *Business*, September, pp. 84–95.

Clutterbuck, D. and Crainer, S. (1990) *Masters of Management*, London: Macmillan.

Clutterbuck, D. and Goldsmith, W. (1985) *The Winning Streak*, Harmondsworth: Penguin.

Clutterbuck, D. and Goldsmith, W. (1986) *The Winning Streak Check Book*, Harmondsworth: Penguin.

Cohen, H. (1983) *You Can Negotiate Anything*, New York: Bantam.

Conrad C. (1985) 'Review of *A Passion for Excellence*', *Administrative Science Quarterly*, vol. 30, no. 3, pp. 426–8, cited in Guest, D. (1992), 'Right Enough to be Dangerously Wrong: An Analysis of *In Search of Excellence* Phenomenon', in Salaman, G. (ed.) *Human Resource Strategies*, London: Sage.

Cooper, C. L. (1977) *Organizational Development in the UK and USA: A Joint Evaluation*, London: Macmillan.

Cooper, C. and Hingley, P. (1985) *The Change Makers: Their Influence on British Business and Industry*, London: Harper & Row.

Coser, L. A. (1956) *The Functions of Social Conflict*, London: Routledge.

Cox, C. J. and Cooper, C. L. (1985) 'The Irrelevance of American Organizational Sciences to the UK and Europe', *Journal of General Management*, vol. 11, no. 2, Winter, pp. 27–34.

Crosby, P. (1979) *Quality is Free*, New York: Mentor.

Crozier, M. (1964) *The Bureaucratic Phenomenon*, London: Tavistock.

Dale, E. (1965) *Planning and Developing the Company Organizational Structure*, New York: American Management Association.

Daniel, W. W. (1973), 'Understanding Employee Behaviour in its Context: Illustrations from Productivity Bargaining', in Child, J. (ed.) *Man and Organization*, London: Allen & Unwin.

Davies, H. (1988) 'Life Without Heroes', *Daily Telegraph*, 30 March.

Davis, M. S. (1971) 'That's Interesting: Towards a Phenomenology of Sociology and a Sociology of Phenomenology', *Philosophy of Social Science*, vol. 1, pp. 309–44.

Davis, R. C. (1957) *Industrial Organization and Management*, New York: Harper & Row.

Davis, T. R. V. and Luthans, F. (1980) 'Management in Action: A New Look at their Behaviour and Operating Modes', *Organizational Dynamics*, Summer.

Deal, T. E. and Kennedy, A. A. (1982) *Corporate Cultures*, Harmondsworth: Penguin.

Deming, W. Edwards (1986) *Out of the Crisis*, MIT Centre for Advanced Engineering, Boston, MA: MIT Press.

Dichter, E. (1966) 'How Word-of-Mouth Advertising Works', *Harvard Business Review*, November–December, pp. 147–66.

Dickson, J. W. (1981) 'Participation as a Means of Organizational Control', *Journal of Management Studies*, vol. 18, no. 2, pp. 159–76.

Dixon, M. (1986a) 'Ancient Wisdom with a Novel Twist', *Financial Times*, 7 July, p. 14.

Dixon, M. (1986b) 'The Pundit Who Shuns Ivory Towers', *Financial Times*, 28 July, p. 12.

Dixon, M. (1986c) 'Riding on an Unusual Hobby Horse', *Financial Times*, 4 August, p. 14.

Dixon, M. (1986d) 'Why There are Still No Sure Answers', *Financial Times*, 29 September, p. 14.

Dixon, M. (1988) 'Intuition Wins Over Intellect', *Financial Times*, 25 March.

Dixon, M. (1989) 'Intuitive Feelings', *Financial Times*, 28 March.

Dixon, N. F. (1976) *On the Psychology of Military Incompetence*, London: Futura.

Dixon, N. F. (1987) *Our Own Worst Enemies*, London: Jonathan Cape.

Dodsworth, T. (1986a) 'Why America is Just Wild about Wisdom', *Financial Times*, 30 June, p. 14.

Dodsworth, T. (1986b) 'The Parable of the One Minute Pundit', *Financial Times*, 14 July, p. 14.

Done, K. (1986) 'Preaching What He Practises', *Financial Times*, 15 September, p. 14.

Dowling, W. F. (1973) 'Conversation with Rensis Likert', *Organizational Dynamics*, vol. 3, pp. 23–38.

Drucker, P. F. (1954) *The Practice of Management*, New York: Harper & Row.

Drucker, P. F. (1976) 'The Coming Re-discovery of Scientific Management', *The Conference Record*, vol. XIII, no. 6, June, pp. 23–7.

Dubin, R. (1970) 'Management in Britain: Observations of a Visiting Professor', *Journal of Management Studies*, vol. 7, pp. 183–98.

Dubin, R. (1976) 'Theory Building in Applied Areas', in Dunnette, M.D. (ed.) *Handbook of Industrial and Organizational Psychology*, Chicago: Rand McNally.

Dunning, J. H. (1958) *American Investment in British Manufacturing Industry*, London: Allen & Unwin.

Dunning, J. H. (1970) *Studies in International Investment*, London: Allen & Unwin.

Economist (1988a) 'Middle Managers Face Extinction', 23 January, pp. 59–60.

Economist (1988b) 13 February, p. 63.

Economist (1988c) 'In the Land of the Blind . . .', 25 June, pp. 106–7.

Economist (1989a) 'Backlash Against Business', 15 April, pp. 13–4.

Economist (1989b) 'The End of the Beginning: A Survey of Business in Britain', 20 May (forty-page special feature).

Economist (1990) 'Bold as a Lion', 16 June, p. 157.

Edwardes, M. (1985) *Back from the Brink*, London: Pan.

Edwards, J. (1829) *A New Narrative of the Revival of Religion in New England with Thoughts on that Renewal*, Glasgow: Collins.

Eilon, S. (1985) *Management Assertions and Aversions*, Oxford: Pergamon.

Etzioni, A. (1961) *A Comparative Study of Complex Organizations*, New York: Free Press.

Etzioni-Halevy, E. (1985) *The Knowledge Elite and the Failure of Prophecy*, London: Allen & Unwin.

Fairley, J. (1991a) 'The Age of Enlightenment', *Sunday Times Magazine*, 24 March, pp. 13–18.

Fairley, J. (1991b) 'Dawning of the New Age', *Sunday Express Magazine*, 4 August, pp. 16–19.

Farber, S. (1982) 'Material and Non-material Work Incentives and Practices', *Review of Radical Political Economics*, vol. 14, no. 4, pp. 29–39.

Farnham, A. (1989) 'What Goes on in your Mailroom', *Fortune*, 27 February, pp. 71–3.

Fayol, H. (1949) *General and Industrial Management*, translated by P. Straws, London: Pitman.

Festinger, L. A. (1957) *A Theory of Cognitive Dissonance*, Evanston, IL: Row Peterson.

Fincham, R. and Rhodes, P. S. (1988) *The Individual, Work and Organization*, London: Weidenfeld & Nicolson.

Firth, R. W. (1959) *Social Change in Tikopia: A Re-study of a Polynesian Community after a Generation*, London: Allen & Unwin.

Firth, R. W. (1967) *Tikopia: Ritual and Belief*, London: Allen & Unwin.

Follett, M. P. (1949) *Freedom and Co-ordination*, London: Management Publications Trust.

Ford, H. (1922) *My Life and Work*, London: Heinemann.

Forrest, D. (1984) 'Self-destructive HRD', *Training and Development Journal*, December, pp. 53–7.

Foster, G. (1989) 'Mintzberg's Strategic Force', *Management Today*, April, pp. 74–6.

Fournet, G. P., Distefano, M. K. and Pryer, M. W. (1976) 'Job Satisfaction: Issues and Problems', *Personnel Psychology*, Summer, pp. 165–83.

Fox, A. (1966) *Industrial Sociology and Industrial Relations*, Royal Commission on Trade Unions and Employers Associations, Research Paper 3, London: HMSO.

Fox, A. (1974) *Man Mismanagement*, London: Hutchinson.

Fox, A. (1976) 'The Meaning of Work', in *People and Work*, Block 6, Unit 6, Milton Keynes: Open University Press.

Freeman, F. H. (1985) 'Books that Mean Business: The Management Best Seller', *American Management Review*, vol. 10, no. 2, April, pp. 345–50.

Friedlander, F. (1965) 'Comparative Work Value Systems', *Personnel Psychology*, vol. 18, pp. 1–20.

Friedlander, F. (1976) 'OD Reaches Adolescence: An Exploration of its Underlying Values', *Journal of Applied Behavioural Science*, vol. 12, pp. 7–21.

Friedlander, F. and Brown, L. D. (1974) 'Organizational Development', *Annual Review of Psychology*, vol. 25, Palo Alto, CA: Annual Reviews, pp. 313–41.

Furnam, A. (1990) 'Commonsense Theories of Personality', in Semin, G. R. and Gergen, K. J. (eds) *Everyday Understanding*, London: Sage.

Furnam, A. and Singh, A. (1987) 'Memory for Information about Sex Differences', *Sex Roles*, vol. 15, pp. 479–86.

Galbraith, J. K. (1983) *Anatomy of Power*, Boston, MA: Houghton Mifflin.

Garfield, C. (1986) *Peak Performance: The New Heroes in Business*, London: Hutchinson.

Garner, L. (1989) 'Breaking through the 180 Second Barrier', *Daily Telegraph*, 4 January, p. 11.

Gellner, E. (1985) *The Psychoanalytic Movement*, London: Paladin.

Geneen, H. S. (1985) *Managing*, London: Grafton.

Godfrey, J. (1985) 'Excellence Re-visited', *The New Management*, vol. 2, no. 4, Spring, p. 25

Goldratt, E. M. and Cox, J. (1989) *The Goal*, Aldershot: Gower.

Goodlad, S. (1976) 'On the Social Significance of Television Comedy', in Bigsby, C. W. E. (ed.) *Approaches to Popular Culture*, London: Edward Arnold.

Goodman, R. A. (1968) 'On the Operationality of the Maslow Need Hierarchy', *British Journal of Industrial Relations*, vol. 6, pp. 51–7.

Gordon, M. M. (1987) *The Iacocca Management Technique*, London: Bantam.

Gouldner, A. W. (1954) *Patterns of Industrial Democracy*, New York: Free Press.

Gower (1988) *Gower Training Resources: Complete Catalogue of Training Films*, Aldershot: Gower.

Gowler, D. and Legge, K. (1983) 'The Meaning of Management and the

Management of Meaning: A View from Social Anthropology', in Earl, M. (ed.) *Perspectives in Management*, London: Oxford University Press.

Graeff, C. L. (1983) 'The Situational Leadership Theory: A Critical View', *Academy of Management Review*, vol. 8, pp. 285–91.

Graicunus, V. A. (1937) 'Relationship in Organization', in Gulick, L. and Urwick, L. (eds) *Papers on the Science of Administration*, New York: Institute of Public Administration, New York: Columbia University.

Grayson, C. J. and O'Dell, C. (1988) *American Business: A Two Minute Warning*, London: Macmillan.

Greiner, L. E. (1977) 'Reflections on OD American Style', in Cooper, C. L. (ed.) *Organizational Development in the UK and USA: A Joint Evaluation*, London: Macmillan.

Gribben, R. (1989) 'Caring 1990s Will Drop Thatcherism Say Forecasters', *Daily Telegraph*, 15 November, p. 3.

Guest, D. E. (1987) 'Human Resource Management and Industrial Relations', *Journal of Management Studies*, vol. 24, no. 5, pp. 503–21.

Guest, D. and Horwood, R. (1980) *The Role and Effectiveness of Personnel Management*, London: London School of Economics.

Guest, D. R., Williams, P. and Drew, P. (1980) 'Workers' Perceptions of Change Affecting the Quality of Working Life', in Duncan, K. D., Gruneberg, M. M. and Wallis, D. (eds) *Changes in Working Life*, Chichester: Wiley Interscience.

Guion, R. M. (1975) 'Gullibility and the Manager', *Personnel Administrator*, January, pp. 20–3.

Gumpert, R. A. and Hambleton, R. K. (1979) 'Situational Leadership – How Xerox Managers Fine Tune Managerial Styles to Employees', *Management Review*, vol. 68, no. 12, pp. 8–12.

Hackman, J. R. and Oldham, G.R. (1980) *Work Design*, Reading, MA: Addison Wesley.

Haire, M., Ghiselli, E. E. and Porter, C. W. (1966) *Managerial Thinking: An International Study*, New York: Wiley.

Halberstam, D. (1987) *The Reckoning*, London: Bantam.

Hales, C. P. (1986) 'What Do Managers Do? A Critical Review of the Literature', *Journal of Management Studies*, vol. 23, no. 1, pp. 88–115.

Hall, D. T. and Noughaim, K. E. (1968) 'An Examination of Maslow's Needs Hierarchy in an Organizational Setting', *Organizational Behaviour and Human Performance*, vol. 3, pp. 12–35.

Hall, D. (1985) 'Making the Most of Top Managers', *Management Today*, January, pp. 37 and 40.

Harvey, J. B. (1974) 'Organization Development as a Religious Movement, *Training and Development Journal*, vol. 28, March, pp. 24–7.

Harvey-Jones, J. (1988) *Making it Happen*, Glasgow: Collins.

Hastings, C. (1989) 'Lonely Managers', *Eurobusiness*, vol. 1, no. 4.

Hayes, R. and Abernathy, W. (1980) 'Managing Our Way to Economic Decline', *Harvard Business Review*, vol. 58, pp. 67–77.

Heller, R. (1986) *The New Naked Manager*, London: Coronet.

Heller, R. (1990) 'Now Here's What You Ought to Do', *Business Life*, British Airways Magazine, October, pp. 32–6.

Henshel, R. L. (1975) 'Effects of Disciplinary Prestige on Predictive Accuracy', *Futures*, vol. 7, pp. 92–106

Henstridge, J. (1975) 'Personnel Management – A Framework for Analysis', *Personnel Review*, vol. 4, pp. 47–53.

Heritage, J. and Greatbatch, D. (1986) 'Generating Applause: A Study of Rhetoric and Response at Party Political Conferences', *American Journal of Sociology*, vol. 92, no. 1, July, pp. 110–57.

Hersey, P. and Blanchard, K. H. (1969) *The Management of Organizational Behaviour: Utilizing Human Resources*, Englewood Cliffs, NJ: Prentice Hall.

Herzberg, F. (1966) *Work and the Nature of Man*, Cleveland, OH: World Publishing Company.

Herzberg, F. (1968) 'One More Time: How Do You Motivate Employees?', *Harvard Business Review*, vol. 46, pp. 53–62, January–February.

Herzberg, F., Mausner, B. and Snyderman, B. (1959) *The Motivation to Work*, New York: Wiley.

Hill, N. (1966) *Thinking and Growing Rich*, 3rd edn, Hollywood, CA: Wiltshire.

Hill, P. (1971) *Towards a New Philosophy of Management*, Aldershot: Gower.

Hirszowicz, M. (1981) *Industrial Sociology: An Introduction*, Oxford: Martin Robertson.

Hitler, A. (1969) *Mein Kampf*, translated by R. Manheim, London: Hutchinson.

Hodgson, A. (1987) 'Deming's Never Ending Road to Quality', *Personnel Management*, July, pp. 40–4.

Holland, P. (1989) 'Poem', *Management Education and Development*, vol. 20, no. 1, p. 96.

Holloway, W. (1983) 'Fitting Work: Psychological Assessment in Organizations', in Henriques, J. *et al.* (eds) *Changing the Subject*, London: Methuen.

Holzner, B. (1978) 'The Sociology of Applied Knowledge', *Sociological Symposium*, vol. 21, pp. 8–19.

Holzner, B. and Marx, J. H. (1979) *Knowledge Application: The Knowledge System in Society*, Boston, MA: Allyn & Bacon.

Homans, G. C. (1951) *The Human Group*, London: Routledge.

Honour, T. F. and Mainwaring, R. M. (1982), *Business and Sociology*, London: Croom Helm.

Horn, C. A. (1983) *Essays in the Development of Modern Management*, Boston, MA: Institute of Management Services/Beacon.

Horton, T. R. (1986) *What Works for Me: 16 CEOs Talk about their Careers and Commitments*, New York: Random.

Huberman, J. (1964) 'Discipline Without Punishment', *Harvard Business Review*, July–August, pp. 62–8.

Huczynski, A. A. (1983) *Encyclopedia of Management Development Methods*, Aldershot: Gower.

Huczynski, A. A. and Buchanan, D. A. (1982) 'Management Development and Social Science: Complementary or Conflicting Endeavours?', *Management Education and Development*, vol. 13, no. 3, pp. 191–200.

Hughes, H. S. (1958) *Consciousness and Society: The Reorientation of European Social Thought, 1890–1930*, New York: Vantage.

Huizinga, G. (1970) *Maslow's Need Hierarchy in the Work Situation*, The Netherlands: Wolters-Noordhoff nv. Groningen.

Hume, D. (1757) *The NaturalHistory of Religion*.

Iacocca, L. with Novak, W. (1985) *Iacocca: An Autobiography*, London: Sidgwick & Jackson.

International Management (1991) 'Disciples of the New Age', March, pp. 42–5.

Jacques, E. (1951) *The Changing Culture of a Factory*, London: Tavistock.

James, B. G. (1985) *Business Wargames: Business Strategy for Executives in the Trenches of Market Warfare*, Harmondsworth: Penguin.

James, W. (1914) 'Tyerman's Life of Wesley', in *Varieties of Religious Experience*, London: Longmans Green.

Janis, I. L. and Mann, L. (1977) *Decision-making: A Psychological Analysis of Conflict, Choice and Commitment*, London: Collier Macmillan.

Jenkins, D. (1983) 'Quality of Working Life: Trends and Directions', in Kolodny, H. and Van Beinum, H. (eds) *The Quality of Working Life and the 1980s*, New York: Praeger.

Jones, B. (1985) 'Review: Littler, C.R. (1982) *The Development of the Labour Process in Capitalist Societies'*, *Journal of Management Studies*, vol. 22, no. 1, pp. 103–6.

Jones, R. and Kirby, S. (1985) 'Cult Management and the Theory of the Four Orders', *Management Monitor*, vol. 4, no. 2, pp. 3–7.

Kahn, R. L. (1974) 'Organizational Development: Some Problems and Proposals', *Journal of Applied Behavioural Science*, vol. 10, pp. 485–502.

Kakar, S. (1982) *Shamans, Mystics and Doctors*, London: Allen & Unwin.

Kanter, R. M. (1985) *The Change Masters: Corporate Entrepreneurs at Work*, London: Allen & Unwin.

Kantrow, A. M. (1980) 'Why Read Peter Drucker?', *Harvard Business Review*, January–February, pp. 74–82.

Katz, D. and Lazarsfield, P. F. (eds) (1955) *The Part Played by People in the Flow of Communication*, Glencoe, IL: Free Press.

Katz, D., Maccoby, N. and Morse, N. C. (1950) *Productivity, Supervision and Morale in an Office Situation*, Detroit, MI: Darrel Press.

Kaufmann, B. E. (1984) 'Reply', *Industrial and Labour Relations Review*, vol. 37, no. 2, January, pp. 269–72.

Kay, W. (1985) *Tycoons: Where They Come From and How They Made It*, London: Pan.

Keegan, W. J. (1974) 'Multi-national Scanning: A Summary of Information Sources Utilized by Headquarters Executives in Multi-national Companies', *Administrative Science Quarterly*, vol. 19, pp. 411–21.

Kelly, J. (1980) *Organizational Behaviour*, Homewood, IL: Richard D. Irwin.

Kelly, J. E. (1982) *Scientific Management, Job Re-design and Work Performance*, London: Academic Press.

Kepner, C. H. and Tregoe, B. B. (1965) *The Rational Manager*, New York: McGraw Hill.

Kiam, V. (1987) *Going For It: How to Succeed as an Entrepreneur*, London: Fontana.

King, N. (1970) 'Clarification and Evaluation of the Two Factor Theory of Job Satisfaction', *Psychological Bulletin*, vol. 74, no. 1, pp. 18–31.

Klein, L. (1976) *The Social Scientist in Industry*, Aldershot: Gower.

Klein, M. (1959) 'Our Adult World and its Roots in Infancy', *Human Relations*, vol. 12, pp. 291–303.

Knight, K. (1975) 'The Role of Research in the Real World', *Personnel Management*, December, pp. 14–33.

Knowlton, C. (1989) 'The Buying Binge in Business Books', *Fortune*, vol. 119, no. 4, 13 February, pp. 61–3.

Knox, R. A. (1950) *Enthusiasm: A Chapter in Religious History*, Oxford: Clarendon Press.

Koestler, A. (1964) *The Act of Creation*, London: Hutchinson.

Koontz, H. (1961) 'The Management Theory Jungle', *Academy of Management Journal*, vol. 4, no. 3, pp. 174–88.

Koontz, H. (1980) 'The Management Theory Jungle Re-visisted', *Academy of Management Review*, vol. 5, no. 2, pp. 175–87.

Korman, A. K. and Vredenburgh, D. J. (1984) 'The Conceptual, Methodological and Ethical Foundations of Organizational Behaviour', in Gruneberg, M. and Wall, T. (eds) *Social Psychology and Organizational Behaviour*, Chicago, IL: Wiley.

Kotler, P. (1980) *Marketing Management*, 4th edn, Englewood Cliffs, NJ: Prentice Hall.

Kotter, J. P. (1982) 'What Effective Managers Do', *Harvard Business Review*, November–December, pp. 156–67.

Kramer, H. (1975) 'The Philosophical Foundations of Management Rediscovered', *Management International Review*, vol. 15, nos 2–3, pp. 47–55.

Krell, T. C. (1981) 'The Marketing of Organizational Development: Past, Present and Future', *Journal of Applied Behavioural Science*, vol. 17, no. 3, pp. 309–29; Comment by C. P. Alderfer (pp. 324–5); Comment by R. T. Harris (pp. 326–7); Response by T. C. Krell (pp. 328–9).

Kuhn, T. S. (1970) *The Structure of Scientific Revolutions*, Chicago: University of Chicago Press.

Landsberger, H. A. (1958) *Hawthorne Revisited*, New York: Cornell University Press.

Langer, E. J. (1983) *The Psychology of Control*, Beverly Hills, CA: Sage.

Lanners, E. (ed.) (1977) *Illusions*, London: Thames & Hudson.

Larsen, E. (1976) *Weimar Witness*, London: Bachman & Turner.

Lasch, C. (1980) *The Culture of Narcissism: American Life in an Age of Discontinuity*, London: Sphere.

Lasch, C. (1985) *The Minimal Self: Psychic Survival in Troubled Times*, London: Picador.

Lawler, E. E. and Suttle, J. L. (1972) 'Causal Correlational Test of the Need Hierarchy Concept', *Organizational Behaviour and Human Performance*, vol. 7, pp. 265–87.

Leavitt, H. J. (1975) 'Suppose We Took Groups Seriously . . ..', in Cass, E. L. and Zimmer, F. G. (eds) *Man and Work in Society*, London: Van Nostrand Reinhold.

Lee, J. A. (1971) 'Behavioural Theory vs. Reality', *Harvard Business Review*, vol. 49, pp. 20–28 and 157–9.

Lee, R. (1987) 'The Use of "Appropriate Theory" in Management Education', *Management Education and Development*, vol. 18, part 4, pp. 247–54.

Lee, R. and Piper, J. A. (1986) 'How Views about the Nature of Management can Affect the Content of Management Education Programmes: The Advance of the Political Approach', *Management Education and Development*, vol. 17, part 2, pp. 114–27.

Legge, K. (1978) *Power, Innovation and Problem Solving in Personnel Management*, London: McGraw Hill.

Levine, A. L. (1967) *Industrial Retardation in Britain*, London: Weidenfeld & Nicolson.

Levitt, T. (1980) 'Marketing Success Through Differentiation – Of Anything', *Harvard Business Review*, January–February, pp. 83–91.

Levy-Leboyer, C. (1986) 'Applying Psychology or Applied Psychology', in Heller, F. (ed.) *The Use and Abuse of Social Science*, London: Sage.

Lewin, K. (1951) *Field Theory in Social Science*, New York: Harper.

Likert, R. (1961) *New Patterns of Management*, New York: McGraw Hill.

Likert, R. (1967) *The Human Organization: Its Management and Values*, New York: McGraw Hill.

Littler, C. R. (1982) *The Development of the Labour Process in Capitalist Societies*, London: Heinemann.

Littler, C. R. and Salaman, G. (1984) *Class at Work*, London: Batsford.

Lomax, D. (1986) *The Money Makers: Six Portraits of Power in Industry*, London: BBC Publications.

Lorenz, C. (1984) 'Same Name But Different Job', *Financial Times*, 14 May, p. 9.

Lorenz, C. (1986a) 'Europe Warms to Business Punditry', *Financial Times*, 2 July, p. 18.

Lorenz, C. (1986b) 'The Passionate and Unrepentent Crusader', *Financial Times*, 18 August, p. 8.

Lorenz, C. (1986c) 'The Grand Old Man of Provocative Punditry', *Financial Times*, 1 September.

Lorenz, C. (1987) 'The Man Who Put Cash Cows Out to Grass', *Financial Times*, 20 March, p. 18.

Lorsch, J. W. (1979) 'Making Behavioural Science More Useful', *Harvard Business Review*, March–April, pp. 171–81.

Luckmann, B. (1978) 'The Small Life Worlds of Modern Man', in Luckmann, T. (ed.) *Phenomenology and Sociology*, Harmondsworth: Penguin.

Lupton, T. (1976) ' "Best Fit" in the Design of Organizations', in Miller, E. J. (ed.) *Task and Organization*, New York: Wiley.

Lyotard, J.-F. (1984) *The Postmodern Condition: A Report on Knowledge*, Manchester: Manchester University Press.

Lyttle, J. (1991) 'Pandora's Music Box', *Daily Telegraph*, 1 August, p. 15.

McBurnie, T. and Clutterbuck, D. (1987) *The Marketing Edge*, Harmondsworth: Penguin.

Maccoby, M. (1976) *The Gamesman*, New York: Bantam.

McCormack, M. H. (1984) *What They Don't Teach You at the Harvard Business School*, Glasgow: Collins.

McGill, M. E. (1988) *American Business and the Quick Fix*, New York: Henry Holt.

McGregor, D. (1960) *The Human Side of Enterprise*, New York: McGraw Hill.

McGregor, D. (1967) *The Professional Manager*, New York: McGraw Hill.

McKenna, R. (1985) *The Regis Touch: Million Dollar Advice From America's Top Marketing Consultant*, Reading, MA: Addison Wesley.

McKeon, R. (1941) *The Basic Works of Aristotle*, New York: Random House.

Mair, L. (1962) *Primitive Government*, Harmondsworth: Penguin.

Management Today (1984) 'OPT's Prophet of Profits', December, p. 12,.

Management Today (1985) 'Business Schools Learn their Lesson', December, pp. 73–6 and 95.

Mangham, I. and Silver, M. (1986) *Management Training: Context and Practice*, Bath: School of Management, University of Bath.

Mant, A. (1979) *The Rise and Fall of the British Manager*, London: Pan.

Mant, A. (1986) 'Leadership – the Second Coming', *Personnel Management*, December, pp. 38–41.

March, J. G. and Simon, H. A. (1958) *Organizations*, New York: Wiley.

Margerison, C. J. and McCann, D. J. (1984) 'Team Mapping – A New Approach to Managerial Leadership', *Journal of European Industrial Training*, vol. 8, no. 1.

Marglin, S. A. (1976) 'What Do Bosses Do?', in Gorz, A. (ed.) *The Division of Labour*, Brighton: Harvester.

Marglin, S. A. (1979) 'Catching Flies with Honey: An Inquiry into Management Initiatives to Humanize Work', *Economic Analysis and Workers Management*, vol. 13, pp. 473–85.

Margulies, N. and Raia, A. P. (1973) *Organization Development: Values, Process and Technology*, New York: McGraw Hill.

Marples, D. L. (1967) 'Studies of Managers: A Fresh Start?', *Journal of Management Studies*, vol. 4, pp. 282–99.

Maryles, D. (1984) 'The Year's Best Selling, Hard Cover Top Sellers', *Publishers Weekly*, 16 March, pp. 27–30.

Maslow, A. H. (1943) 'A Theory of Human Motivation', *Psychological Review*, vol. 50, no. 4, pp. 370–96.

Maslow, A. H. (1954) *Motivation and Personality*, New York: Harper.

Matheson, M. T. (1974) 'Some Reported Thoughts on Significant Management Literature', *Academy of Management Journal*, vol. 17, pp. 386–9.

Mayer, R. J. (1983) 'Don't Be Hoodwinked by the Panacean Conspiracy', *Management Review*, June, pp. 23–5.

Mayo, E. (1933) *The Human Problems of an Industrial Civilization*, London: Macmillan.

Mayo, E. (1949) *The Social Problems of an Industrial Civilization*, 2nd edn, London: Routledge.

Mehrabian, A. (1968) 'Communication without Words', *Psychology Today*, vol. 2, pp. 53–5.

Meindl, J. R. (1982) 'The Abundance of Solutions: Some Thoughts for Theoretical and Practical Solution Seekers', *Administrative Science Quarterly*, vol. 27, pp. 670–85.

Meindl, J. R. and Ehrlich, S. B. (1987) 'The Romance of Leadership and the Evaluation of Organizational Performanace', *Academy of Management Journal*, vol. 30, no. 1, pp. 91–109.

Meindl, J. R., Ehrlich, S. B. and Dukerich, J. M. (1985) 'The Romance of Leadership', *Administrative Science Quarterly*, vol. 30, pp. 78–102.

Menkes, V. (1987) 'Big Bang for Publishers', *Business*, May, pp. 163–4.

Menzies, I. E. P. (1969) *The Functioning of Social Systems as a Defence Against Anxiety*, Centre for Applied Social Research, Tavistock Institute of Human Relations, London.

Merton, R. K. (1949) 'Patterns of Influence', in Lazarsfield, P. F. and Stanton, N. (eds) *Communications Research*, New York: Harper.

Merton, R. K. (1957) *Social Theory and Social Structure*, Glencoe, IL: Free Press.

Mikes, G. (1984) *How to be a Guru*, Harmondsworth: Penguin.

Miles, R. E. (1975) *Theories of Management: Implications for Organizational Behaviour and Development*, New York: McGraw Hill.

Milgram, S. (1974) *Obedience to Authority*, London: Tavistock.

Miller, D. C. and Form, W. H. (1964) *Industrial Sociology*, New York: Harper & Row.

Miller, E. J. (ed.) (1976) *Task and Organization*, Chichester: Wiley.

Miller, G. A. (1956) 'The Magical Number Seven, Plus or Minus Two: Some Limits on Our Capacity for Processing Information', *Psychological Review*, vol. 63, pp. 81–97.

Miller, G. A. (1967) *The Psychology of Communication: Seven Essays*, Harmondsworth: Penguin.

Mills, C. W. (1959) *The Sociological Imagination*, London: Oxford University Press.

Mills, T. (1978) 'Europe's Industrial Democracy: An American Response', *Harvard Business Review*, November–December, pp. 143–52.

Milne, A. A. (1926) 'Introduction', in 'The Red House Mystery', in *Four Great Detective Novels*, London: Oldhams.

Miner, J. B. (1978) *The Management Process: Theory, Research and Practice*, New York: Macmillan.

Miner, J. B. (1980) *Theories of Organizational Behaviour*, Hinsdale, IL: Dryden Press.

Miner, J. B. (1982) *Theories of Organizational Structure and Process*, Hinsdale, IL: Dryden Press.

Mintzberg, H. (1973) *The Nature of Managerial Work*, New York: Harper & Row.

Mintzberg, H. (1975) 'The Manager's Job: Folklore and Fact', *Harvard Business Review*, vol. 53, July–August, pp. 49–61.

Montgomery, D. (1979) 'Immigrant Workers and Managerial Reform', in Montgomery, D. (ed.), *Workers Control in America*, New York: Cambridge University Press.

Mooney, J. D. and Riley, A. C. (1931) *Onward Industry*, New York: Harper & Row.

Morita, A. (1987) *Made in Japan: Akio Morita and Sony*, Glasgow: Collins.

Morrow, L. (1986) 'Yankee Doodle Magic', *Time*, 7 July, vol. 128, no. 1, pp. 6–10.

Mouzalis, N. (1967) *Organization and Bureaucracy*, London: Routledge.

Naftulin, D., Ware, J. and Donnelly, F. (1973) 'The Dr Fox Lecture: A Paradigm of Educational Seduction', *Journal of Medical Education*, vol. 48, pp. 630–5.

Naisbitt, J. (1982) *Megatrends*, New York: Warner.

Neal, A. G. and Groat, H. T. (1984) 'Review: Naisbitt, J., *Megatrends*', *Contemporary Sociology*, vol. 13, no. 1, pp. 120–2.

Nelson, D. (1975) *Managers and Workers: Origins of the New Factory System in the United States: 1880–1920*, Madison, WI: University of Wisconsin Press.

Newstrom, J. W. (1985), 'Management Development: Does It Deliver What It Promises?', *Journal of Management Development*, vol. 4, no. 1, pp. 3–11.

Nicholls, J. (1986) 'Beyond Situational Leadership: Congruent and Transforming Models for Leadership Training', *European Management Journal*, vol. 4, no. 1, pp. 41–62.

Noble, D. F. (1977) *America by Design: Science, Technology and the Rise of Corporate Capitalism*, New York: Knopf.

Nord, W. (1974) 'The Current Failure of Applied Behavioural Science: A Marxist Perspective', *Journal of Applied Behavioural Science*, vol. 10, pp. 557–78.

Nord, W. (1977) 'Job Satisfaction Reconsidered', *American Psychology*, vol. 32, pp. 1026–35.

Nowotny, O. H. (1964) 'American vs. European Management Philosophy', vol. 42, no. 2, March–April, pp. 101–8.

Ohmae, K. (1987) *The Mind of the Strategist: Art of Japanese Management*, Harmondsworth: Penguin.

Oliver, N. (1990) 'Just-in-Time: The New Religion of Western Manufacturing', Proceedings of the British Academy of Management Conference, Glasgow Business School, 9–11 September.

O'Toole, J. (1985) *Vanguard Management*, New York: Doubleday.

Ouchi, W. G. (1981) *Theory Z: How American Business Can Meet the Japanese Challenge*, Reading, MA: Addison Wesley.

Ouchi, W. G. and Johnson, A. M. (1978) 'Type Z Organization: Stability in the Midst of Mobility', *Academy of Management Review*, April, pp. 305–14.

Parker, W. E. and Kleemeir, R. W. (1951) *Human Relations in Supervision and Management*, New York: McGraw Hill.

Parkinson, N. (1957) *Parkinson's Law*, Harmondsworth: Penguin.

Pascale, R. T. (1991) *Managing on the Edge*, Harmondsworth: Penguin.

Pascale, R. T. and Athos, A. G. (1982) *The Art of Japanese Management*, Harmondsworth: Penguin.

Patzig, W. D. and Zimmerman, D. K. (1985) 'Accuracy in Management Texts: Examples in Reporting the Works of Maslow, Taylor and McGregor', *Organizational Behaviour Teaching Review*, vol. 10, no. 2, pp. 39–47.

Payne, R. (1970) 'Factor Analysis of Maslow-type Need Satisfaction Questionnaire', *Personnel Psychology*, vol. 23, pp. 251-68.

Perrow, C. (1973) 'The Short and Glorious History of Organizational Theory', *Organizational Dynamics*, Summer.

Perrow, C. (1977) 'Three Types of Effectiveness Studies', in Goodman, P. S., Pennings, J. M. and Associates (eds) *New Perspectives in Organizational Effectiveness*, San Francisco, CA: Jossey-Bass.

Personnel Management (1986) 'PM Diary', August, p. 19.

Peter, L. J. and Hull, R. (1970) *The Peter Principle*, London: Pan.

Peters, T. J. (1989) *Thriving on Chaos*, London: Macmillan.

Peters, T. J. and Austin, N. (1985) *A Passion for Excellence*, London: Collins.

Peters, T. J. and Waterman, R. H. (1982) *In Search of Excellence*, New York: Harper & Row.

Pfeffer, J. (1977) 'The Ambiguity of Leadership', *Academy of Management Review*, vol. 2, pp. 104-12.

Pfeffer, J. (1981) 'Management as Symbolic Action', in Cummings, L. and Staw, B. (eds) *Research in Organizational Behaviour*, Greenwich, CT: JAI Press.

Pfeiffer, J. (1959) *Sick, Sick, Sick*, London: Collins.

Pierce, J. L. and Newstrom, J. W. (1988) *The Manager's Bookshelf*, New York: Harper & Row.

Pierce, J. L. and Newstrom, J. W. (1990) *The Manager's Bookshelf*, 2nd edn, New York: Harper & Row.

Piette, M. (1938) *John Wesley in the Evolution of Protestantism*, London: Sheed & Ward.

Pinchot, G. (1985) *Intrapreneuring*, New York: Harper & Row.

Pinder, C. (1977) 'Concerning the Application of Human Motivation Theories in Organizational Settings', *Academy of Management Review*, vol. 2, pp. 384-97.

Pollard, H. R. (1974) *Developments in Management Thought*, London: Heinemann.

Pollard, H. R. (1978) *Further Developments in Management Thought*, London: Heinemann.

Pollard, S. C. (1965) *The Genesis of Modern Management Thought: A Study of the Industrial Revolution in Great Britain*, London: Arnold.

Popper, K. R. (1959) *The Logic of Scientific Discovery*, London: Hutchinson.

Porter, M. (1985) *Competitive Advantage: Creating and Sustaining Superior Performance*, New York: Collier Macmillan.

Preedy, J. (1987) 'What You Should Expect from Consultants', *Personnel Management*, January, pp. 20-3.

Presthus, R. V. (1961-2) 'Weberian v Welfare Bureaucracy in Traditional Society', *Administrative Science Quarterly*, vol. 6.

Pucky, W. (1962) *Management Principles*, London: Hutchinson.

Pugh, D. S. (ed.) (1984) *Organization Theory: Selected Readings*, Harmondsworth: Penguin.

Pugh, D. S. and Hickson, D. J. (1976) *Organizational Structure in its Context: The Aston Programme I*, Aldershot: Gower.

Pugh, D. S., Hickson, D. J. and Hinings, C. R. (eds) (1983) *Writers on Organization*, Harmondsworth: Penguin.

Punch, M. (1981) *Management and Control of Organizations; Occupational Deviance; Responsibility and Accountability*, Leiden/Antwerp: H. E. Stenfert Kroese.

Quinn, R. E. and McGrath, M. R. (1982) 'Moving Beyond the Single Solution Perspective: The Competing Values Approach as a Diagnostic Tool', *Journal of Applied Behavioural Science*, vol. 18, no. 4, pp. 463-72.

Ramsay, H. (1977) 'Cycles of Control: Worker Participation in Sociological and Historical Perspective', *Sociology*, vol. 11, pp. 481-506.

Ramsay, P. (1987) *The Corporate Warriors: The Battle of the Boardroom*, London: Grafton.

Rapoport, C. (1986) 'A Rarity in his Own Land', *Financial Times*, 21 July, p. 8.

Reddin, W. J. (1970) *Managerial Effectiveness*, New York: McGraw Hill.

Reddin, W. J. (1986) 'The 3-D Managerial Effectiveness Seminar (MES) – Twenty Years of Transnational Experience', *Management Education and Development*, vol. 17, part 3, pp. 257-70.

Reich, R. B. (1984) *The Next American Frontier: A Provocative Programme for Economic Renewel*, Harmondsworth: Penguin.

Rein, I. J., Kotler, P. and Stoller, M. R. (1987) *High Visibility*, London: Heinemann.

Rice, A. K. (1965) *Learning for Leadership*, London: Tavistock.

Rieff, P. (1987) *The Triumph of the Therapeutic: Uses of Faith After Freud*, Chicago: University of Chicago Press.

Ries, A. and Trout, J. (1986) *Positioning: The Battle for your Mind*, New York: McGraw Hill.

Ritchie, B. and Goldsmith, W. (1987) *The New Elite*, London: Weidenfeld & Nicolson.

Ritti, R. R. and Funkhouser, G. R. (1987) *The Ropes to Skip and the Ropes to Know*, New York: Wiley.

Roberts, J. (1984) 'The Moral Character of Management Practice', *Journal of Management Studies*, vol. 21, no. 3, pp. 287-302.

Roberts, K. H., Walter, G. A. and Miles, R. E. (1971) 'A Factor Analytic Study of Job Satisfaction Items Designed to Measure Maslow's Need Categories', *Personnel Psychology*, vol. 24, pp. 204-20.

Robinson, J. (1985) *The Risk Takers: Portraits of Money, Ego and Power*, London: Allen & Unwin.

Roethlisberger, F. J. (1941) *Management and Morale*, Cambridge, MA: Harvard University Press.

Roethlisberger, F. J. and Dickson, W. J. (1964a) *Management and the Worker*, New York: Wiley.

Roethlisberger, F. J. and Dickson, W. J. (1964b) 'Introduction', in Mayo, E. *The Human Problems of Industrial Civilization*, New York: Wiley.

Rose, F. (1990) 'A New Age for Business', *Fortune*, 8 October, pp. 80-6.

Rose, M. (1978) *Industrial Behaviour: Theoretical Developments Since Taylor*, Harmondsworth: Penguin.

Rosen, R. D. (1978) *Psycho-babble*, New York: Atheneum.

Ross, L. (1977) 'The Intuitive Psychologist and his Surroundings', in Berkowitz, L. (ed.) *Advances in Experimental Social Psychology*, vol. 10, New York: Academic Press.

Rowlandson, P. (1984) 'The Oddity of OD', *Management Today*, November, pp. 90-2.

Rubin, I. M. (1986) 'Helplessness: Today's Management Myth', *Eurobusiness*, November, pp. 47-52.

Rubin, J. (1976) *Growing (Up) at Thirty Seven*, New York: M. Evans.

Ruff, H. J. (1979) *How to Prosper during the Coming Bad Years*, New York: Times Books.

Salaman, G. (1978) 'Towards a Sociology of Organizational Structure', *Sociological Review*, vol. 3, pp. 519-54.

Salaman, G. (1981) *Class and Corporation*, Glasgow: Fontana/Collins.

Salaman, G. and Butler, J. (1990) 'Why Managers won't Learn', *Management Education and Development*, vol. 21, part 3, pp. 183–91.

Salancik, G. R. and Meindl, J. R. (1984) 'Corporate Attributions as Strategic Illusions of Management Control', *Administrative Science Quarterly*, vol. 29, pp. 238–54.

Saltonstall, R. (1959) *Human Relations and Administration*, New York: McGraw Hill.

Sargent, W. (1961) *The Battle for the Mind*, London: Pan.

Scheidel, T. M. (1967) *Persuasive Speaking*, Glenview, IL: Scott Foresman.

Schein, E. H. (1978) *Career Dynamics: Matching Individual and Organizational Needs*, Reading, MA: Addison Wesley.

Schein, E. H. and Bennis, W. G. (1965) *Personal and Organizational Change through Group Methods*, New York: Wiley.

Schiffer, I. (1973) *Charisma*, New York: Free Press.

Schwab, D. P. and Cummings, L. (1970) 'Theories of Performance and Satisfaction: A Review', *Industrial Relations*, vol. 9, no. 4, October, pp. 408–30.

Schwab, D. P. and Heneman, H. G. (1970) 'Aggregate and Individual Predictability of the Two Factor Theory', *Personnel Psychology*, vol. 23, pp. 55–66.

Schwenk, C. R. (1986) 'Information, Cognitive Biases and Commitments to a Course of Action', *Academy of Management Review*, vol. 11, no. 2, pp. 298–310.

Settle, T. (1971) 'The Rationality of Science Versus the Rationality of Magic', *Philosophy of the Social Sciences*, vol. 1, pp. 173–94.

Sharpe, T. (1984) 'The Day I Saw John Fenton or "By the Inch, It's a Clinch" ', *Management Education and Development*, vol. 15, no. 1, pp. 14–6.

Simon, H. A. (1958) *Administrative Behaviour*, London: Macmillan.

Simon, H. A. (1969) *The Science of the Artificial*, Cambridge, MA: MIT Press.

Smith, A. (1989) *The Roaring '80s*, New York: Summit Books.

Smith, C. (1989) 'From Greed to Green in the 80s', *The Indy*, 21 December, p. 8.

Smith, J. H. (1975) 'The Significance of Elton Mayo', Foreword to Mayo, E., *The Social Problems of an Industrial Civilization*, 2nd edn, London: Routledge.

Sofer, C. (1972) *Organizations in Theory and Practice*, London: Heinemann.

Staw, B. M. (1980) 'Rationality and Justification in Organizational Life', in Staw, B. M. and Cummings, L. L. (eds) *Research in Organizational Behaviour*, Greenwich, CT: JAI Press.

Steele, F. (1976) 'Is Organizational Development Work Possible in the UK Culture?', *Journal of European Training*, vol. 5, no. 3, pp. 105–10.

Steele, F. (1977) 'Is the Culture Hostile to Organizational Development: The UK Example', in Mirvis, P. H. and Berg, D. N. (eds) *Failures in Organization Development and Change*, New York: Wiley.

Stephenson, T. (1985) *Management – A Political Action*, London: Macmillan.

Stern, J. P. (1985) *Nietzsche*, London: Fontana.

Stevenson, T. E. (1975) 'Organizational Development: A Critique', *Journal of Management Studies*, vol. 12, pp. 249–65.

Stewart, R. (1967) *Managers and their Jobs*, London: Macmillan.

Stewart, R. (1976) *Contrasts in Management: A Study of Different Types of Managers' Jobs*, London: McGraw Hill.

Storey, J. (1983) *Managerial Prerogative and the Question of Control*, London: Routledge.

Storm, R. (1990) 'Spiritual Warriors Attack the Boardroom', *The Independent on Sunday*, 13 May, p. 28.

Strauss, G. (1973) 'Organization Development: Credits and Debits', *Organizational Dynamics*, vol. 1, no. 3, pp. 2–18.

Stuart, D. (1986) 'Big is Back – and Beautiful', *The World in 1987*, London: Economist Intelligence Unit.

Sunday Times (1991) 'Welcome to Technopolis', 16 June, pp. 36–43.

Sutton, F. X., Harris, S. E., Kaysen, C. and Tobin , J. (1956) *The American Business Creed*, Cambridge, MA: Harvard University Press.

Tannenbaum, R. and Schmidt, W. H. (1973) 'How To Choose a Leadership Pattern', *Harvard Business Review*, May–June: 162–80.

Taylor, F. W. (1903) *Shop Management*, republished in *Scientific Management* (1947), New York: Harper & Row.

Taylor, F. W. (1911) *The Principles of Scientific Management*, New York: Harper.

Thackray, J. (1986) 'The Great American Robot Fiasco', *Management Today*, November, pp. 86–8 and 92.

Thackray, J. (1987) 'America's Corporate Hype', *Management Today*, March, pp. 69–70, 72 and 75.

Thomas, A. B. (1980) 'Management and Education: Rationalization and Reproduction in British Business', *International Studies of Management and Organization*, vol. 10, pp. 71–109.

Thomas, A. B. (1989) '*The One Minute Manager*: A Sign of the Times', *Management Education and Development*, vol. 20, part 1, Spring, pp. 23–38.

Thomas, K. (1978) *Religion and the Decline of Magic*, Harmondsworth: Peregrine.

Thurley, K. and Wirdenuis, H. (1973) *Supervision: A Re-Appraisal*, London: Heinemann.

Thurley, K. and Wirdenuis, H. (1989) *Towards European Management*, London: Pitman.

Thynne, J. (1991) 'TV Staff Think Pink to Win New Contract', *Daily Telegraph*, 30 March, p. 14.

Tichy, N. M. and Devanna, M. A. (1986) *The Transformational Leader*, New York: Wiley.

Tichy, N., Fombrun, C. and Devanna, M. A. (1982) 'Strategic Human Resource Management', *Sloan Management Review*, vol. 23, no. 2, pp. 47–61.

Tosi, H. L. (1984) *Theories of Organizations*, 2nd edn, New York: Wiley.

Townsend, P. (1971) *Up the Organization*, London: Coronet.

Trump, D. (1987)*Trump: The Art of the Deal*, London: Arrow.

Tversky, A. and Kahneman, D. (1974) 'Judgement under Uncertainty: Heuristics and Biases', *Science*, 27 September, no. 105, p. 1124.

Tyson, S. and Fell, A. (1986) *Evaluating the Personnel Function*, London: Hutchinson.

Urwick, L. (1937) 'Organization as a Technical Problem', a paper of 1933 reprinted in L. Gulick and L. Urwick (eds) *Papers on the Science of Administration*, New York: Columbia University Press.

Urwick, L. (1958) *Times Review of Industry*, London: Times.

Urwick, L. F. and Brech, E. F. L. (1948) *The Making of Scientific Management*, London: Pitman.

de Vries, M. F. R. Kets (1988) 'Prisoners of Leadership', *Human Relations*, vol. 41, no. 3, pp. 261–80.

Vroom, V. (1964) *Work and Motivation*, Harmondsworth: Penguin.

Wahba, M. A. and Bridwell, L. G. (1975) 'Maslow Reconsidered: A Review of Research on the Need Hierarchy Theory', in Wexley, K. N. and Yukl, G. A. (eds) *Organizational Behaviour and Industrial Psychology*, London: Oxford University Press.

Wall, T. (1982) 'Perspectives on Job Design', in Kelly, J. E. and Clegg, C. W. (eds) *Autonomy and Control at the Workplace*, London: Croom Helm.

Warner, M. (1984) *Organizational Experiments: Designing New Ways of Managing Work*, Chichester: Wiley.

Warner, R. (1970) *Julius Caeser*, London: Collins.

Warnes, B. C. (1985) *The Ghengis Khan Guide to Business*, Osmosis Publications.

Waters, L. K. and Roach, D. (1973) 'A Factor Analysis of Need Fulfilment Items Designed to Measure Maslow Need Categories', *Personnel Psychology*, vol. 26, pp. 185–90.

Watson, T. J. (1977) *The Personnel Managers*, London: Routledge.

Watson, T. J. (1980) *Sociology, Work and Industry*, London: Routledge.

Watson, T. J. (1983) 'Towards a General Theory of Personnel Management and Industrial Relations Management', Occasional Paper, *Trent Business School*, Nottingham.

Watson, T. J. (1986) *Management, Organization and Employment Strategy*, London: Routledge.

Watson, T. J. (1987) *Sociology, Work and Industry*, 2nd edn, London: Routledge.

Weber, M. (1947) *The Theory of Social and Economic Organizations*, London: William Hodge.

Weber, M. (1948) 'Bureaucracy', in *From Max Weber: Essays in Sociology*, translated, edited and introduced by H. H. Gerth and C. Wright Mills, London: Routledge.

Weiss, C. H. and Bucuvalas, M. (1980) 'Truth Tests and Utility Tests: Decision Makers' Frames of Reference for Social Research', *American Sociological Review*, vol. 45, pp. 302–13.

Wesley, J. (1909–16) *The Journal of John Wesley*, standard edition, edited by N. Curnock, London: Charles H. Kelly.

Wheeler, H. N. (1984) 'Determinants of Strikes', *Industrial and Labour Relations Review*, vol. 37, no. 2, January, pp. 263–9.

Whitehead, T. N. (1938) *The Industrial Worker*, London: Oxford University Press.

Whitsett, D. A. and Winslow, E. K. (1967) 'An Analysis of Studies Critical to the Motivator-Hygiene Theory', *Personnel Psychology*, vol. 20, Winter, pp. 391–415.

Whyte, W. H. (1957) *Organization Man*, New York: Doubleday Anchor.

Wiener, M. J. (1985) *English Culture and the Decline of the Industrial Spirit, 1850–1980*, Harmondsworth: Penguin.

Wight, O. (1981) *MRP III: Unlocking America's Productivity Potential*, Williston, VT: Oliver Wight Ltd, Publishers.

Wilensky, J. L. and Wilensky, H. L. (1952) 'Personnel Counselling: The Hawthorne Case', *American Journal of Sociology*, vol. 57, pp. 265–80.

Williamson, J. (1978) *Decoding Advertisements: Ideology and Meaning in Advertising*, London: Marion Boyars.

Willmott, H. C. (1984) 'Images and Ideals of Managerial Work: A Critical Examination of Conceptual and Empirical Accounts', *Journal of Management Studies*, vol. 21, no. 3, pp. 349–68.

Willmott, H. C. (1987) 'Studying Managerial Work: A Critique and a Proposal', *Journal of Management Studies*, vol. 24, no. 3, pp. 249–70.

Wilson, N. A. B. (1973) *On the Quality of Working Life*, Department of Employment Manpower Papers no. 7, London: HMSO.

Witt, M. A. and Ireland, R. D. (1987) 'Peters and Waterman Revisited: The Unending Quest for Excellence', *Academy of Management Executive*, vol. 1, no. 2, pp. 91–8.

Woodward, J. (1958) *Management and Technology*, Department of Scientific and Industrial Research Series, Problems of Progress in Industry, no. 3, London: HMSO.

Woodward, J. (1965) *Industrial Organization: Theory and Practice*, Oxford University Press.

Wren, D. (1973) *The Evolution of Management Thought*, 2nd edn, New York: Wiley.

Wyatt, S., Fraser, J. A. and Stocks, F. G. (1928) *The Comparative Effects of Variety and Uniformity in Work*, Medical Research Council Industrial Fatigue Research Board, Report no. 52, London: HMSO.

Yorks, L. and Whitsett, D. A. (1985) 'Hawthorne, Topeka and the Issue of Science Versus Advocacy in Organizational Behaviour', *Academy of Management Review*, vol. 10, no. 1, January, pp. 21–30.

Zaleznik, A. (1989) *The Management Mystique: Restoring Leadership in Business*, New York: Harper & Row.

Zeitlin, M. (1974) 'Corporate Ownership and Control: The Large Corporations and the Capitalist Class', *American Journal of Sociology*, vol. 79, pp. 1073–119.

Zimbalist, A. (1975) 'The Limits of Work Humanization', *Review of Radical Political Economics*, vol. 7, no. 2, pp. 50–9.

Zimbardo, P., Haney, C., Barks, W. and Jaffe, P. (1974) 'A Pirandellian Prison: The Mind is a Formidable Jailor', *New York Times Magazine*, 8 April, pp. 38–60.

Zusman, J. (1976) 'Can Programme Evaluation be Saved from its Enthusiasts?', *American Journal of Psychiatry*, no. 133, pp. 1303–7.

Index